Cambridge Technicals

Level ③

IT

HODDER
EDUCATION
AN HACHETTE UK COMPANY

Although every effort has been made to ensure that website addresses are correct at time of going to press, Hodder Education cannot be held responsible for the content of any website mentioned in this book. It is sometimes possible to find a relocated web page by typing in the address of the home page for a website in the URL window of your browser.

Hachette UK's policy is to use papers that are natural, renewable and recyclable products and made from wood grown in well-managed forests and other controlled sources. The logging and manufacturing processes are expected to conform to the environmental regulations of the country of origin.

Orders: please contact Hachette UK Distribution, Hely Hutchinson Centre, Milton Road, Didcot, Oxfordshire, OX11 7HH. Telephone: +44 (0)1235 827827. Email education@hachette.co.uk Lines are open from 9 a.m. to 5 p.m., Monday to Friday. You can also order through our website: www.hoddereducation.co.uk

ISBN: 978 1 4718 7491 8

© Mo Everett, Saundra Middleton, Victoria Ellis and Graham Manson 2016

First published in 2016 by
Hodder Education,
An Hachette UK Company
Carmelite House
50 Victoria Embankment
London EC4Y 0DZ

www.hoddereducation.co.uk

Impression number 10 9 8 7
Year   2024 2023 2022 2021

Cover photo © Akova/Fotolia
Illustrations by Aptara, Inc. and Barking Dog Art
Typeset in India
Printed in India

A catalogue record for this title is available from the British Library.

MIX
Paper from
responsible sources
FSC™ C104740

Schools have a *Licence to Copy* one chapter or 5% for teaching ✓

CLA Copyright Licensing Agency

Contents

About this book

This book helps you to master the skills and knowledge you need for the OCR Cambridge Technicals Level 3 IT qualification.

This resource is endorsed by OCR for use with the Cambridge Technicals Level 3 IT specification. In order to gain OCR endorsement, this resource has undergone an independent quality check. Any references to assessment and/or assessment preparation are the publisher's interpretation of the specification requirements and are not endorsed by OCR. OCR recommends that a range of teaching and learning resources are used in preparing learners for assessment. For more information about the endorsement process, please visit the OCR website, www.ocr.org.uk.

For any amendments or updates to this book, see www.hoddereducation. co.uk/Product?Product=9781471874918

Key features of this book

ABOUT THIS UNIT

This unit explains how information is held and used by different types of users. You will learn about how organisations use internal and external sources of data and the types of information that may be found.

Know what to expect when you are studying the unit.

LEARNING OUTCOMES

The topics and activities in this unit will help you to:

1 Understand computer hardware.
2 Understand computer software.
3 Understand business IT systems.
4 Understand employability and communication skills used in an IT environment.
5 Understand ethical and operational issues and threats to computer systems.

Prepare for what you are going to cover in the unit.

How will I be assessed?

You will be assessed through an external assessment set and marked by OCR.

Find out how you can expect to be assessed after studying the unit.

How will I be graded?

You will be graded using the following criteria:

Find out the criteria for achieving Pass, Merit and Distinction grades in internally assessed units.

LO4 Be able to present application solutions to meet client and user requirements *P4 P5 P6 M3 D2*

4.1 Pitch content

Understand all the requirements of the qualification, with clearly stated learning outcomes and assessment criteria fully mapped to the specification.

INDEPENDENT ACTIVITY ....

GETTING STARTED ....

(10 minutes)

List the information you believe you need to give a client to ensure that they decide to use your plan for a new network.

Try activities to start you off with a new learning outcome.

PAIRS ACTIVITY ....

GROUP ACTIVITY ....

Carry out tasks that help you to think about a topic in detail and enhance your understanding.

CLASSROOM DISCUSSION

(30 minutes)

Research and discuss standards, such as GSM (Global System for Mobile Communications), and associated technologies such as 3G and 4G. Use your research as a basis to discuss current developments and possible new technologies.

Take the opportunity to share your ideas with your group.

KEY TERM

Asset – anything of value owned by an individual or organisation.

Understand important terms.

KNOW IT

1 List three types of software.
2 Name three types of utility software.
3 Name three voice based communication methods.
4 Describe five popular protocols.

Answer quick questions to test your knowledge about the learning outcome you have just covered.

Assessment practice questions

Below are practice questions for you to try.

Try the types of questions you may see in your externally assessed exam.

● ●

LO1 Assessment activity

> **TOP TIPS**
> ✔ Make sure you use a range of examples, at least three, in your descriptions.

Start preparing for your internally assessed assignments by carrying out activities that are directly linked to Pass, Merit and Distinction criteria. Top Tips give you additional advice.

Read about it

Suggests books and websites for further reading and research.

Acknowledgements

Every effort has been made to trace and acknowledge ownership of copyright. The publishers will be glad to make suitable arrangements with any copyright holders whom it has not been possible to contact. The authors and publishers would like to thank the following for permission to reproduce copyright illustrative material:

Page 2 © Audrius Merfeldas/123RF; **Page 7** © Zoonar GmbH/Alamy Stock Photo; **Page 48** © Oleksiy Mark/Fotolia; **Page 104** © GP Kidd/Blend Images/ Getty Images; **Page 139** © shutterbas/123rf; **Page 145** © Ambrozinio/Alamy Stock Photo; **Page 182** (top) © Denys Semenchenko/123RF; **Page 182** (bottom) © Pensiri Saekoung/123RF; **Page 202** © Aurelio Scetta/123RF; **Page 303** © Photochicken/123RF; **Page 331** © Angela Hampton Picture Library/Alamy Stock Photo; **Page 342** © Goodluz/123RF; **Page 353** © Beecham Research; **Page 354** © www.libelium.com; **Page 356** © Advantech B+B SmartWorx; **Page 361** © Ingram Publishing/Thinkstock

Unit 01

Fundamentals of IT

LEARNING OUTCOMES

The topics and activities in this unit will help you to:

1 Understand computer hardware.
2 Understand computer software.
3 Understand business IT systems.
4 Understand employability and communication skills used in an IT environment.
5 Understand ethical and operational issues and threats to computer systems.

How will I be assessed?

You will be assessed through an external assessment set and marked by OCR.

LO1 Understand computer hardware

(10 minutes)

In pairs, produce a list of computer items which you consider to be hardware and display it for everyone to consider.

1.1 Computer hardware

How do you recognise hardware? It is anything in a computer or information system which you can touch – but remember it is unwise to touch any components that are live (carrying an electric current). Another way of remembering how to identify hardware is that if you drop it, it will be damaged or broken.

The range of computer hardware increases all the time, as **computer components** become smaller and more powerful. Some examples are listed below; take the opportunity to investigate others, especially their uses, benefits and limitations.

Input devices

A computer is only useful if it can communicate with its external environment. **Input devices** enable the user to communicate with the computer and **output devices** allow the computer to communicate with the user.

Keyboard

The keyboard is still one of the most common methods of inputting data or instructions to a computer. The keys allow access to a range of alphanumeric characters, special characters such as '/' or '£' and a number of commands by using the function keys. It also provides shortcuts to specific tasks, for example by pressing the keys Ctrl/Alt/Delete together, the task manager box appears on the screen.

It is not always possible or appropriate to enter data using a keyboard and so other devices are available.

Mouse

A point and click device, the mouse allows the user to communicate with the computer by placing a cursor at a particular point on the screen. The computer screen tracks the movement of the mouse and normally displays its location on the screen as a cursor.

▲ **Figure 1.1** The inside of an optical mouse

🔑 **KEY TERMS**

Computer components – items which together form a computer system.

Input devices – devices that allow the user, which may be another computer or a measuring device, to give instruction or provide data to the computer system.

Output devices – devices that enable the computer system to provide information, data or instructions to another user, which may be computer or human.

Scanner

This input device converts a document or photograph into a digital file that a computer can read or display. Scanners have been developed for other uses such as biometrics. Examples include iris and fingerprint scanning, where the iris or fingerprint is illuminated and photographed.

Sensors

Sensors are physical devices such as thermometers, motion sensors and microphones that send signals to the computer. These signals enable the computer to decide whether an action must be triggered. For example, if a burglar alarm is set, any signal received from the motion sensor suggests that someone is in the building and the computer triggers the alarm.

Microphone

These record instructions from the user, or other sounds that the user wishes to collect. For those who cannot use a traditional keyboard or mouse, this is a very useful device for inputting data.

Graphics tablet

This can be used in a similar way to the keyboard by tapping on **icons**. It is also useful for entering data, such as handwriting or drawings of objects which cannot be captured easily in other ways. It can be hard to control if the sensitivity is set too high or too low, although this can often be adjusted via the software.

Visual display unit (VDU) or screen

This is predominantly an output device, because it displays requests or information from the computer. It does, however, aid the user who is inputting data or instructions because it allows the user to check their work visually, allowing them time to correct errors before confirming their decision.

Barcode reader

This device may be handheld or static, and is used to capture information from a barcode by using a light source, scanner and decoder. They reduce the errors often introduced by manual input. In your coursework, this is recoverable as it can be pointed out and corrected but if, for example, you were dispensing powerful drugs, a wrong letter or digit could have serious consequences.

KEY TERM

Icon – a symbol or image on a computer screen of a program, option or selection.

GROUP ACTIVITY

(30 minutes)

In small groups, research three input devices and produce a brief presentation for others in the wider group explaining the technology of each one, their advantages and disadvantages.

Input and output devices

The touch screen is an example of a single device that can both receive and display data and information. The technologies used to enable the position of a finger or pointer on the screen include: infrared (IR), capacitive and resistive touch.

Table 1.1 Touch screen technologies

Type of touch screen	Explanation
Infrared (IR)	Uses IR emitters that send out infrared light which travels through the glass of the screen. On the other side of the screen is an IR receiver that collects the IR light. If the screen is touched, some of the light is scattered and the receiver records the less intense light. Complex mathematical equations calculate the location of the touch.
Resistive	Uses a glass panel covered by a thin flexible film. Both are covered in a thin metallic coating that has a small electric charge. There is a narrow gap between the glass and the film. When the screen is touched the two metallic coatings make contact, resulting in a change in the electrical charge. This change identifies the touch point.
Capacitive	Uses a glass panel with a clear electrode layer on top covered by a protective layer. When a finger touches the screen, some of the screen's electrical charge transfers from the screen to the finger as it reacts to the body's capacity to store electrical charge. This reduction is detected by sensors at the four corners of the screen, which enable the touch point to be identified.

Output devices

These allow the computer to communicate with the user.

Visual display unit (VDU) or screen

See previous page.

 **GROUP ACTIVITY**

(60 minutes)

In small groups, research the different types of computer screens available and produce a short report on the following features:

- method of display
- resolution
- picture quality
- screen size
- the effect of price on quality.

Printers

There are different types and sizes of printer but the purpose of each is basically the same – to produce hard copy of documents, data, information, images and photographs. Types of printer include inkjet, laser, photo printers, LCD and LED, line printers, thermal printers and 3D printers.

 **GROUP ACTIVITY**

(30 minutes)

Research different types of printer. Each group should explain how each printer works and compare: quality of type speed, impact or non-impact printers, font and graphics and main function.

As a whole group, discuss how these characteristics are influenced by price, and how they affect the usefulness of the product, together with benefits and limitations.

Plotters

These are machines used in areas such as computer-aided design (CAD) for large and accurate drawings from architectural designs to the latest space probe. Originally plotters used a pen to draw lines on paper, and later multiple pens brought colour into the process. While pens have been almost completely replaced by inkjet and laser print systems, it does help us to understand the process to remember that plotters are based on pens. The two main types are the flatbed and drum plotters.

Imagine that your arm is the pen holder, you have a pen in your hand and there is a large piece of paper on the table in front of you the size of a flipchart page. Follow these commands:

1 Raise your pen off the paper.
2 Move it to the bottom left-hand corner.
3 Move vertically 10 cm.
4 Move horizontally 15 cm to the right (point a).
5 Place pen nib on the paper.
6 Move pen 20 cm to the right (point b).
7 Move the pen 30 cm vertically (point c).
8 Move the pen to point a.
9 Raise pen off the paper.

Well done – you have just drawn a right-angled triangle using a flatbed plotter named 'You'!

Developments in technology mean that most pen plotters have been replaced by inkjet and laser heads which move across the paper faster and provide better quality prints.

Speakers and headphones

These provide the user with audio output. The speakers convert the electronic signals in the sound card to sound waves that can be heard by the user. Speakers broadcast to everyone within earshot, which can be a problem if confidential matters are being discussed. Headphones ensure that privacy is maintained; however, the volume of the output can result in temporary or permanent hearing loss if it set too high for any period of time.

Braille terminal

This is a specialist reader for visually impaired users. It displays text through individual cells on the terminal, each of which has rounded metal or plastic pins that protrude above the surface of the cell. The user reads the text or instructions by interpreting the pattern of the pins, just as they would if reading a book written in braille. As the user moves through the text so the braille cells update to form each word. The number of cells can vary between 12 and 84, but for non-portable terminals it is usually 40 cells.

Communication devices

These devices allow one computer device to communicate with another. Some examples are briefly explained in Table 1.1 and more technical detail is given in LO1.5.

When designing apps, consider the needs of visually impaired users. The app should allow for the ability to increase font size and change text and background colours to enable those with some sight to read the app. Ensure that the content is compatible with screen readers so that the content can be heard rather than read.

Table 1.2 Types of communication device

Device	Purpose
Modem (MOdulator-DEModulator)	Although now outdated, modems were one of the first technologies to enable computers to communicate via a telephone line. The modem converts digital signals produced by the computer into an analogue signal, which is required by the telephone line, and another modem converts the signal back to digital format at the other end so that the receiving computer can understand the message. A modem can convert both an outgoing signal and an incoming signal.
Network interface card (NIC)	A card that enables computers to communicate with other computers in a network. It is the hardware connection between the computer and the network cable.
Terminal adapter	Allows the computer to link into an Integrated Services Digital Network (ISDN).
Wireless router	Converts an internet signal into a wireless signal, which the computers and other devices in the network can use to communicate with each other and the router.
Wireless network cards	The means by which the computer and other devices are able to receive and send wireless communication.
Hub	Allows multiple computers to communicate over a network. A USB hub allows multiple peripherals to connect through a single USB port.

GROUP ACTIVITY

(20 minutes)

Identify three uses, three benefits and three limitations for each of the devices identified above or during group discussions. These should be considered by the whole group to reach an agreed view.

1.2 Computer components

Processors (central processing unit (CPU))

The **CPU** (also called processor or microchip) manages all the hardware activities required to receive instructions and data, actions them using the input data and outputs the results. It also manages the various storage devices, both internal and external to the computer, and records where all programs and instructions are located for future retrieval.

The first CPUs had a single core, so they could only carry out one instruction at a time. The next stage was the ability to begin a second instruction before the first was completed, taking advantage of the time that the CPU was waiting for a request or instruction to be completed by the hardware under its control or the human user. Now multicore processors have two or more independent cores integrated on a single chip multiprocessor or linked together in a package. These developments have resulted in a computer being able to run multiple packages.

KEY TERM

Central processing unit (CPU) – the unit that controls the actions of the computer system and manipulates the data required for particular tasks.

UNIT 1 FUNDAMENTALS OF IT

Table 1.3 The components of the CPU

Component	Purpose
Control unit	Ensures that the instructions required to operate the computer are retrieved and interpreted in the correct sequence. This means that instructions and data are transferred from the input or storage devices and placed in the temporary storage of registers in the CPU until the necessary data is ready to be processed in the arithmetic logic unit (ALU) and results stored in the right place.
ALU	Here the computer undertakes the mathematical or logical operations required to complete the instruction. The data is placed in a special register called the accumulator and arithmetic (additions and subtractions) and logical operations such as 'and', 'or' and 'not' are carried out.

Each motherboard is designed for a specific CPU and, as CPU types are not interchangeable, you must ensure that, when purchasing your new motherboard, it is designed for your CPU.

Motherboard

This is the main printed circuit of a personal computer. Components such as the CPU are directly connected to it via sockets; others such as hard drives or network cards use expansion slots or ports. Its printed circuits form the data or communications highway for the computer, ensuring that data and instructions can be transferred or stored where they are needed and located when required.

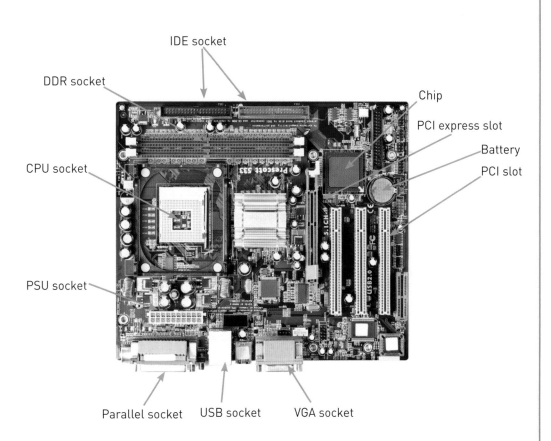

IDE socket

DDR socket

Chip

PCI express slot

Battery

PCI slot

CPU socket

PSU socket

Parallel socket   USB socket   VGA socket

▲ **Figure 1.2** Typical features of a motherboard. Note that actual components vary according to the age of the motherboard

Computer storage

A simple way of thinking of how data and instructions are stored in a computer is to split them into two different categories: primary storage and secondary storage.

Table 1.4 Primary storage

Primary storage device	Purpose
Registers	This is small, fast and is used chiefly by the CPU to store: • data which is to be processed within the ALU • the instructions that inform the CPU as to what is to happen to the data • a third type of information which is that of the operating system which oversees the basic tasks required by a particular computer. (Operating systems are further discussed in Section 2.4.)
Random Access Memory (RAM)	Fast, but slower than those within the CPU and larger in size. It holds almost all other data and instructions that the computer may need for any programs open on the computer. As the programs' requirements change or programs are replaced by others, so the memory is overwritten with the new data and instructions.
Read Only Memory (ROM)	This contains permanent instructions such as the Basic Input/Output (BIOS) program, which, when you switch on the computer, checks that all the expected devices are in place, checks that they are working and loads the operating system into the computer. The BIOS is an integral part of the computer when it is built, unlike operating systems, which can be added later.

Types of primary and secondary storage can be described based upon their location or the protocols they use. One of the most widely used is the Serial Attached SCSI (SAS) protocol that follows the same protocol as SCSI but transmits data serially, one bit at a time along a single wire. These devices can handle up to 3.3 gigabits of data per second and up to 128 devices.

Storage can be internal (held within the machine) or external (where a separate device is attached to the computer through a port). These external devices can be portable – they can be moved from computer to computer and place to place.

GROUP ACTIVITY

(30 minutes)

In small groups, research the following types of external storage devices, with their strengths and weaknesses, and record your findings in Table 1.5. Copy the table onto a piece of paper if you need more space to write. Discuss your findings with the other groups.

Table 1.5 Types of storage

Storage device	What is it?	Strengths	Weaknesses
Flash drives			
Cloud storage			
Solid state discs			
Optical hard drives			

Discuss the disadvantages of each storage device identified in the table and explain what can be done to reduce their effect.

Computer ports

A port identifies the location where a communication channel enters or leaves the computer system, for example on your computer you may see the USB, firewire, mouse and keyboard ports. It is the point at which a device is plugged into the computer and normally has an interface which converts data into the correct format. Each port has a number that allows the computer to identify and select a particular peripheral easily. The different types of port can be identified by their external shape.

Table 1.6 shows some different ports available on a computer.

Table 1.6 Types of port

Device	Explanation
Universal Serial Bus (USB) port	USB ports enable the computer to connect with standalone devices such as printers, cameras, camcorders, broadband modems and mobile devices. The term Universal Serial Bus refers to the standard for digital data communications over short distances covering the cables, connectors and communications protocol used by these devices.
Firewire	Similar to USB in architecture, but conforms to the IEEE 1394 standard so allows different elements to communicate without being linked through a computer network (peer-to-peer). This type of port often links devices which need high speed transfer of large amounts of data (such as camcorders and DVD players) to computers using special cables but, as long as the devices conform to the standard, any computer or peripheral can be linked together.
Serial Advanced Technology Attachment (SATA)	This allows devices such as optical and other hard drives to link to a computer. The port is linked to another port on the motherboard with a 7-pin ribbon cable.
Network ports	The physical ports are those which connect computers to modems, routers or local area networks.
Ethernet port	Used for cable-based networks. Most computers have at least one such port which is linked directly to the computer's network card.

The connection between devices on a network is called a channel, of which there are several types.

A channel can be optical fibre, coaxial copper or twisted pair cable carrying data between storage devices or between a computer and a storage device at high speeds of up to 10 Gbps.

Expansion cards are printed circuit boards, much smaller than the motherboard, which have a connector which allows them to be inserted into an expansion slot on a motherboard.

GROUP ACTIVITY

(30 minutes)

In small groups, investigate the following expansion card types and produce notes on the examples you find, including how each supports the computer in carrying out particular activities. Share your findings with the wider group.

1 sound cards
2 graphics cards
3 storage controllers.

BEWARE! Power supply units should only be opened by an experienced technician when the mains power has been disconnected. Some power supply units can hold a potentially lethal charge for weeks.

Power supply units (PSU)

The power supply unit receives electricity from the mains (alternating current or AC) and converts this into a form which the computer can use (direct current or DC). All units need a cooling system, which in PCs and servers is usually a fan system. Very large computers may use water coolant systems.

1.3 Types of computer system

There are various different types of computer system and we consider a small range here. You should research these and other examples you may discover, considering where they are used, their benefits and limitations and also justify the suitability of each system in a given context.

Desktop systems/servers

The computer can be either made up of:

● individual components, such as screen, keyboard and mouse, with a case which contains the motherboard, CPU, power supply, hard drives, optical drives and connectors and expansion cards
● a single screen and case which incorporates the motherboard and everything else. These all-in-one PCs reduce the space required to house the computer and the need for so many cables. They are also more easily moved. However, the ability to upgrade or repair the hardware is limited compared with the traditional desktop: they are also costlier than traditional desktops.

Desktops allow the user to carry out a range of activities, including document creation, data manipulation, game playing, design and communication facilities for personal or business purposes.

Tablet/hybrid

A laptop or tablet can be used in a variety of locations. The components found in an all-in-one PC are found in a laptop or tablet, but in the case of the laptop the mouse function is replaced by a touch pad and keyboard combined. Many modern laptops can fold back, effectively turning them into a tablet with a screen-based virtual keyboard. They can perform many of the functions of the traditional PC, but the screen size can be restrictive, especially if several documents need to be open at the same time. Loss or theft is also easier.

Smartphones

Smartphones can run applications, send and receive emails, take photographs and videos, record sound, act as a GPS system and run apps to provide entertainment via your music library, your e-book library and your latest game. You can create documents, manipulate data or set your alarm. However, they can hinder human interaction, and reduce spatial awareness when being used.

Security is another issue, as an unlocked phone left in public allows anyone who finds it access to your private life, username and password for your cloud storage if you don't log out of apps properly. The malware and security software available for smartphones is not yet as strong as that for PCs and so care should be taken with sensitive data held on smartphones.

Embedded system/Internet of Things

Embedded computer systems are everywhere. For example, cars have computers which monitor emissions from the engine and adjust the engine settings as required. Other computers check for problems with the car systems and, if so, inform the driver.

The concept of the internet of things describes a global network of connected objects, not just traditional computer networks or even robotic system but anything which could have **RFID** (radio frequency identification) chips embedded within them. With smaller and cheaper chips becoming available all the time, **connectivity** now includes animals with microchips that identify their owners and GPS location, the internal workings of the human body, movement of goods, to name but a few.

See also Unit 17 (page 352).

KEY TERMS

RFID (radio frequency identification) – tiny computer chips which hold information that is transmitted when it passes close to a scanning antenna.

Connectivity – the ability to connect with another computer or information system.

RESEARCH ACTIVITY

Identify three examples of embedded computer systems within the home and explain the advantages and disadvantages of each one.

Mainframe and quantum computers

Mainframes are huge machines designed to solve scientific and engineering problems that require complex calculations or the manipulation, collection and storage of large amounts of data.

Mainframes are reliable and secure because they have rigorous backup capabilities and component redundancy, which means if one component fails, others take its place without stopping the processing or input/output activities. Mainframes are very expensive and require teams of experts to oversee them, and so are used only by organisations that need to process very large amounts of data quickly, such as banks, credit card companies and airlines. They use traditional bit technology, CPUs and storage which use only '1' or '0' to carry out instructions or manipulated data.

Quantum computers are still experimental. They work with quantum bits (qubits) which are not limited to two states as mainframes and PCs are. Qubits represent atomic particles, such as electrons or photons, which can be in several different states at the same time. A fully working quantum computer will be able to carry out data manipulations many million times more quickly than current computers.

GROUP ACTIVITY •••

(30 minutes)

In small groups investigate types of computer systems which would meet the needs of a self-employed photographer who is going to expand his business to include another photographer and a part-time administrator, and list the benefits and limitations of each. Identify the system that you believe to be most appropriate and justify your choice.

1.4 Connectivity

Copper wire connections

Twisted pair (TP) is a common cable, often used in telephone systems. A pair of insulated wires are twisted together. Several twisted pairs can be brought together to form a twisted cable. There are two types: unshielded twisted pairs (UTP) and shielded twisted pairs (STP).

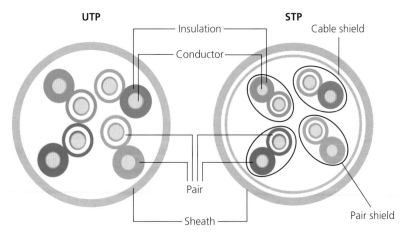

▲ **Figure 1.3** Unshielded and shielded twisted pair

The shielded twisted pair combines shielding and cancellation and wire twisting. Each twisted pair is encased in metallic jacket and four pairs of wires are wrapped in another metallic braid jacket.

GROUP ACTIVITY

(20 minutes)

Another copper wire-based connector is coaxial cable, which you may have seen at the back of your television set, linking it to the aerial socket. Investigate the structure of the cable, as we did for the twisted wire, and identify the similarities and differences between the two types of coaxial cables: thick and thin.

Fibre cables

Optical fibres provide the fastest data delivery by cable. Each fibre is no thicker than a human hair: the thinner the fibre, the better the signal. The signal is sent down a glass rod, or core, as a beam of light, in the same way as you see in an optical fibre lamp. Optical fibre transmission is uni-directional (can only go in one direction), so at least two fibres are placed in a cable to allow bidirectional (going in two directions) transmission.

INDEPENDENT ACTIVITY

(15 minutes)

Describe at least two strengths and two weaknesses of each cable type.

- UTP
- STP
- coaxial
- optical fibre.

Wireless technologies do not use cables but instead use radio frequency (RF) signals to transmit data or instructions between devices, including computers, printers and certain credit or debit cards and payment terminals using electromagnetic radiation. The differences tend to be the wavelengths of the RF waves.

Table 1.7 Types of wireless technologies

	Used for	Range
Bluetooth	Short-range communication between two devices without the need for a wireless network hub.	Within 10 metres.
Wi-fi	Connecting devices via a network hub.	Up to 92 metres depending upon frequency, but can be compromised by obstructions (e.g. metal or brickwork), so more than one network access point may be required.
Laser networks	Sending large quantities of data using a light beam to devices in line of sight. Also satellite to satellite communication.	Up to 10 km, but can be blocked by fog or haze as the droplets refract the light and disrupt the signal.
Infrared technology	Uses infrared LED-emitting light received by a photodiode in the receiving device, e.g. TV remote control. Cheap compared to other wireless technology and works well over short distances.	Devices must be in line of sight and only a few metres apart.
Microwave communication	Uses short radio waves to send signals via microwave towers. Can provide analogue or digital formats.	Devices must be in line of sight with no obstructions between the microwave antennae.

1.5 Communication hardware

These devices transmit analogue or digital signals over wired or wireless channels. We have already discussed the modem, which uses telephone wires to allow computers to communicate. Other examples are:

- Network hub: the central connection point for all devices in the network. All devices have equal call on the resources and receive copies of all transmissions.
- Switch: a device that receives packets (transmissions), processes them and forwards them onto the specific device.
- Router: forwards packets between networks. It needs to be linked to at least two networks, e.g. wide area networks (WANs) or local area networks (LANs), or a LAN and the network of an internet service provider (ISP).
- Hybrid network hub: includes internet access, wireless and wired LANs. They have a fixed number of ethernet ports for wired devices and also broadcast a wi-fi signal.

1.6 Hardware troubleshooting

Identifying hardware faults

Faults arise for a number of reasons, such as power surges, poor maintenance, accidental damage, malware or intentional damage. The one thing you can be sure of is that faults will occur and often they have happened before. IT technicians and help desk staff must log the issue (e.g. battery will not charge, hard drive failure) on a fault log sheet identifying the:

- machine
- owner or users
- fault
- date
- symptoms
- problem history: has this happened before? Is it an intermittent fault? Has it happened to similar machines?
- Back up documentation: what has been backed up? To which location?

KEY TERM

Troubleshoot – the ability to analyse and solve issues with information systems.

When investigating faults:

- Always look for the simplest explanation first; for example, if the computer does not power up, check it is plugged into the mains or, if it is a laptop, plug it into the mains to see if the battery needs charging.
- Record the steps you are taking to identify the fault and confirm that you have completed a test before you start the next one. This confirms that different tests have not interfered with each other and given a false result.
- State the tools you have used to identify the fault.
- Record the actions you have taken to resolve the issue; for example, replaced hard disc, updated drivers, reinstalled software, replaced the motherboard.
- Note the product specification of any new software or hardware.
- Record the time taken and the costs arising from the fault finding and repair of the hardware.

This compiles a history of the issues with the hardware, which can be analysed to identify:

- Maintenance requirements.
- The robustness of particular hardware.
- Trends or patterns that identify which particular sets of actions result in failures, and their timescales.
- 'What if' scenarios.

Troubleshooting tools

Event viewer
When an error occurs on a computer, the event viewer is updated with information about it, including:

- what the problem is
- when it occurred, i.e. date and time
- the seriousness of the problem
- what caused the problem
- an event ID number
- who was logged into the machine at the time.

Self-test programs
These may be provided by the hardware manufacturer such as:

- Power on Self-Test (POST): a function of the BIOS for a particular computer. It checks memory, power supply, hardware, CPU, BIOS and heat/cooling. Two types of BIOS-related diagnostic information are provided:
  - Beep codes: One beep means that all is well from a motherboard perspective, as the CPU is functioning. More than one beep means that an error has been detected. Each BIOS has its own set of beep codes which can be downloaded from the manufacturer's website to identify the particular error.
  - POST codes are a visual, two-character read out of the stage that the POST is at.
- Ping tests the connectivity between the requesting host and the destination host. It uses the Internet Control Message Protocol (ICMP) to send an echo request message to the destination host and listen for a response called the echo reply message. A response shows that the host can be reached. This procedure can be repeated with different hosts until the source of the problem is identified.

- Ipconfig/Ifconfig identifies the specific **IP** configuration of the hosts affected by the problem. It is especially useful where dynamic addressing is used and the **IP address** of each host can change.
- Nslookup aids the diagnosis of issues with dynamic name systems (DNS) addresses. This utility looks up the IP addresses associated with a particular domain name such as ocr.org.uk or bbc.co.uk. If the utility cannot determine this information, there is a DNS issue. This utility can also query DNS servers to find out if there are issues with the default DNS servers.

Diagnostic software

This is available from third parties. Some are free and others require payment. They include memory testers.

1.7 Units of measurements

Computers are powered by electricity which is either 'on' or 'off'. This is represented as '1' and '0' even on home equipment such as kettles. Each one (1) or zero (0) is called a bit, which is short for 'binary digit'. However, to carry out instructions or manipulate data, these patterns of 1s and 0s need to be understandable to both the computer and the human user. Coding computer programs and data in binary is time consuming and likely to result in errors so computer scientists assigned a fixed pattern of bits to decimal numbers and characters. Binary coded decimals (BCD) were formed from a group of only four bits of an eight-bit or one-byte register. The second four bits were used for the sign of the number (plus or minus). These four-bit segments became known as a nibble.

As computers were used for many more purposes than mathematical and scientific equations, the range of numbers and characters to be encoded grew and the four bits could not provide enough unique patterns to cover upper and lower case characters, numbers and special symbols such as comma, full stop and exclamation marks. As a result, eight bits became the new version of binary coded decimal called EBCDIC. This in its turn was superseded by ASCII code (American Standard Code for Information Interchange) and now Unicode, which incorporates non-English language characters such as Chinese and Arabic.

Marketing information about computers refers to terabytes (TB), gigabytes (GB) and kilobytes (kB) of data storage. However, a new computer with its 1TB store only has about 976 GB of available storage space. This is because of the difference between a decimal thousand (1000) and the binary equivalent of 2^{10} (1024).

When computer memory was only a few thousand kilobytes, computer scientists and engineers noticed that there was only 24 bytes of difference from the decimal thousand, so they started to use the decimal unit 'kilo' as shorthand for 1024 bytes.

Unfortunately, as memory size has grown, so has the difference between the two values, resulting in a difference of about 10% when talking about tera values (which is 10^{12} and the binary equivalent of 2^{40} – see Table 1.8). It matters because the speed of transfer of the smaller decimal gigabyte of data is very different from that of a binary equivalent.

Some organisations calculate their data sizes in binary but use the decimal naming conventions. For others, sizes are calculated and named as decimals. Therefore, it is useful to know that there are different units of measurements and understand their relative sizes. For example, giga is bigger than mega but smaller than tera.

In Table 1.8, the term SI (Système International d'Unités) refers to the globally agreed system of base units of measurement. The IEC (International Electrotechnical Commission) is the body responsible for international standards of the electronic and electrical and other related technologies.

Table 1.8 Comparative units of measurement

Decimal values		Binary values	
SI	Bytes	IEC	Bytes
kB (Kilobyte)	$10^3 = 1000$	KiB (Kibibyte)	$2^{10} = 1,024$
MB (Megabyte)	$10^6 = 1,000,000$	MiB (Mebibyte)	$2^{20} = 1,048,576$
GB (Gigabyte)	$10^9 = 1,000,000,000$	GiB (Gibibyte)	$2^{30} = 1,073,741,824$
TB (Terabyte)	$10^{12} = 1,000,000,000,000$	TiB (Tibibyte)	$2^{40} = 1,099,511,627,776$
PB (Petabyte)	$10^{15} = 1,000,000,000,000,000$	PiB (Pebibyte)	$2^{50} = 1,125,899,906,842,624$

Powers of numbers mean the number of times it is multiplied by itself. Let us look at some of the powers of 10.

You can represent the word "power" in a number of ways so 10 to the power of 2 is the same as 10^2 or 10^2 or 10 x 10 = 100. Similarly, powers of 2 are the number of times 2 is multiplied by itself so $2^2=2\text{^}2=2x2=4$.

Note: A number to the power 0 (for example 10^0) is always 1!

As you can see, the difference between a petabyte and a pebibyte is very large. You do not need to remember these numbers, but you do need to recognise the names and the number of bytes in powers of 10 and powers of 2, respectively.

1.8 Number systems

Most programming at user level is carried out using languages such as Python, C++ or Java, which are related to human language. However, for a computer to understand the instructions and manipulate the data, it has to be changed to lines of 1s and 0s. When designing new components or problem solving new programs, it may be necessary to read and interpret some of these instructions and understand how to convert one number system to another.

These are decimal, which humans work with, binary which the computer uses, and hexadecimal, which is used to express groups of binary digits (hexadecimal means sixteen bits or two bytes) as program instructions strings of text characters. These allow the human programmer to more quickly and accurately read the information provided.

For base 10 (decimal), the units are 0 to 9.

For base 2 (binary) the units are 0 to 1.

For base 16 (hexadecimal) we can only use a single character. Numbers of 10 and over are changed to letters and so, for base 16, the units are 0 to 9 and A to F, up to 16.

The position of a decimal number in a line of digits denotes its value. The further to the left, the higher the value.

Table 1.9 The value of 2,174 in decimal units

Thousands	Hundreds	Tens	Units
10^3	10^2	10^1	10^0
10×10×10	10×10	10×1	1
2	1	7	4

The value in words is two thousand, one hundred and seventy-four.

Each location tells us how many units, tens, hundreds and thousands. Number 10 is never in a column because that would move to the next column to the left. For example, adding 1 to 999 results in no units, no hundreds and one thousand.

We can take a similar approach to binary and hexadecimal. In Table 1.10, the number 238 is shown in binary notation.

Table 1.10 The value of 238 in binary notation

Decimal	128	64	32	16	8	4	2	1
Power of 2	2^7	2^6	2^5	2^4	2^3	2^2	2^1	2^0
Meaning	2×2×2×2×2×2×2	2×2×2×2×2×2	2×2×2×2×2	2×2×2×2	2×2×2	2×2	2×1	1
Binary number	1	1	1	0	1	1	1	0

Clue: if the 2^0 is a 1, this means that the decimal equivalent is an odd number, if it is a 0 it is an even number.

1.9 Number conversions

To convert a decimal number to binary, we keep dividing it by 2 and make a note of the remainder. This remainder tells us where the 1s and 0s appear in the particular location. So to convert 215_{10} to binary (the small 10 reminds us that this is a decimal number):

215 ÷ 2 = 107   Remainder (R)1

107 ÷ 2 = 53   R1

53 ÷ 2 = 26   R1

26 ÷ 2 = 13   R0

13 ÷ 2 = 6   R1

6 ÷ 2 = 3   R0

3 ÷ 2 = 1   R1

1 ÷ 2 = 0   R1

Reading the remainders from the bottom, we have 11010111_2.

To convert this number to decimal, we can label each 1 and 0, 0 to 7 from right to left as shown in Table 1.11.

Table 1.11 Example of binary number placement

Binary unit	1	1	0	1	0	1	1	1
Place number	7	6	5	4	3	2	1	0

This tells us the power of 2 by which we must multiply each 1 or 0. So we have:

$1\times2^7+1\times2^6+0\times2^5+1\times2^4+0\times2^3+1\times2^2+1\times2^1+1\times2^0=1\times128+1\times64+0\times32+1\times16+0\times8+1\times4+1\times2+1\times1 = 215$.

If we look at 215, we note that the decimal value requires only 3 digits but the binary number needed eight digits. As the size of the number increases, so does the length of the binary number. For example, 1000_{10} is represented as 11111101000_2.

Computers do not use an alphabet or grammar and so all letter and special characters such as exclamation marks, questions marks and full stops require their own group of bits. Trying to pick out issues from long lines of 1s and 0s is difficult for those involved in computer engineering and computer graphics. So step forward hexadecimal!

Remember the byte, which is eight bits, and nibble, which is half a byte? Consider the range of values which can be identified using just four bits.

$1111_2 = 8+4+2+1 = 15$

Therefore, if we count in 16s we can use these fifteen values to represent 1 to 15.

To convert the number 396_{10} to hexadecimal we divide it by 16, remembering the remainder.

$396 \div 16 \quad = 24 \quad$ R12 (C) – remember, letters are used for numbers over 10.

$\quad 24 \div 16 \quad = 1 \quad$ R8

$\quad\quad 1\div16 \quad = 0 \quad$ R1

Reading from the bottom we have $18C_{16}$.

To convert the hexadecimal number into decimal we carry out a similar approach to that used for the conversion from binary to decimal.

Table 1.12 Example of hexadecimal number placement

Hexadecimal unit	1	8	C
Place number	2	1	0
Power of 16	16^2	16^1	16^0
Meaning	16×16	16×1	16×0

Thus: $18C_{16} = 1\times256+ 8\times16+ 12(C)\times1= 256+128+12=396$.

KNOW IT

1 Convert the decimal number 407 to:
   a binary
   b hexadecimal.
2 Convert hexadecimal number 23F to:
   a binary
   b decimal.
3 Convert binary number 1110011 to:
   a hexadecimal
   b decimal.

LO2 Understand computer software

GETTING STARTED

(10 minutes)

In pairs, produce a list of the software which you use on your computer.

2.1 Types of software

There are many ways in which computer software can be classified. One way is by considering how it was developed:

- Is it copyright protected or available to all?
- Can the user make changes to the **source code**?
- Is it developed for a particular organisation or for general use by many individuals and organisations?

These differences are considered below.

Open source software

This means that the source code, produced by the programmer, is made available to anyone who wishes to debug, improve or modify it. Some producers of the original source code may restrict access and modification for all or some of the **code** but the principle is access for all.

Closed source software

This is closely guarded and can by protected by intellectual property rights and copyright, with the full force of the law being brought down upon those who flout the restrictions. When purchasing such software, you are purchasing a right to use it but you do not own it.

GROUP ACTIVITY

(20 minutes)

In small groups, describe at least two advantages and two disadvantages of open source and closed source software.

Off the shelf and bespoke software

A business wanting to replace or introduce applications such as financial planning or inventory systems may ask: 'Should we buy a general package and then use the parts we need, or is the way we work so different that we should have a package written especially for us?'

The first option is often referred to as 'off the shelf', as the package is pre-designed, and (when the term was invented) came in a box that you literally took off the shelf (these days, it is likely to be downloaded but the principle is the same). You may be able to make small adjustments, such as to colour or layout, or design forms and reports, but, overall, you may have to change some of your systems and work practices to fit the software.

> **KEY TERMS**
>
> **Source code** – code, written by programmers in a high or low level programming language, which is converted into a list of instructions for the computer to provide various functions and actions.
>
> **Code** – groups of symbols, characters, words, letters or figures used to represent messages or instructions.

Bespoke software, like a bespoke suit or shirt, it is made to your exact measurements. It is expensive and takes time for the designer to identify your needs and convert them into a specification to turn into the program. The time it takes to provide a working program also needs to be considered. There may also be a discussion over who owns the intellectual property rights.

Shareware

If you are not sure what you need, you can try shareware for a period of time, often 30–60 days, before you have to purchase the product. At the end of the trial period you either pay the purchase price or the software locks you out. All intellectual property rights and copyright remain the property of the shareware author.

Freeware

Freeware is distributed free of charge, although there may be restrictions on upgrades or no warranty. All rights remain with the writer or publisher. The range of freeware products run from small, special utility programs to well-known programs such as Acrobat Reader, iTunes and MSN messenger which are available to all.

Embedded software

This is a piece of software which may be embedded in a traditional PC or devices we do not consider to be computers, such as microwave ovens, GPS systems, smartwatches and guided missile technology.

 **GROUP ACTIVITY**

(45 minutes)

Investigate the types of software that could be used by a new small business, a clothes shop which buys stock from wholesalers and sells to the public online.

Investigate possible software options from each of the software types identified in 2.1 and explain what type of software each is and at least one strength and weakness for each example.

From this, make a final set of recommendations.

2.2 Applications software

Applications software is designed to carry out tasks such as accounts management, text creation and editing, presentation preparation and design drawing, which would be required whether or not a computer was available. They can be split into different types to aid the user in recognising the right software for a particular purpose.

Productivity software

This is designed to enable you to carry out your task or role accurately, effectively and efficiently. You have no errors (or at least can edit them out), it produces the correct outcome, in line with your instructions, and you do not waste time or resources. Examples of such software include word processors, databases, email, webinars and webcasts.

Development tools

These are software tools which help those who are creating new software for other purposes. This software could be a programming tool used to create, debug, enhance and maintain programs during their lifecycle. Examples are compilers, assemblers, disassemblers and debuggers. It could also be an application development tool which assists software developers to develop websites and mobile application tools.

Business software

This refers to software which supports one or more business activities. Business here should be considered in its widest sense, as it includes not only project management tools, CAD/CAM design packages and management information systems (MIS) but also specialist software, such as expert systems which gather specialist information for a particular area and apply it to new problems, for example medical diagnosis.

2.3 Utility software

Computers can suffer from viruses, loss of memory or slowness at some point. Utility programs are small pieces of software that can help the computer perform more efficiently or effectively. Examples include backup facilities, which remind you to back up your data in case of hardware failure, loss or theft of the computer. The antivirus utility regularly scans the computer for evidence of malware activity or presence; it also checks for new threats and removes them to a 'quarantine location' where they are held until the user confirms that they are to be deleted.

GROUP ACTIVITY

(30 minutes)

Investigate the advantages and disadvantages of three different types of software utility and produce a presentation.

2.4 Operating systems

The operating system is the most important software in any computer system. It is a group of systems software which manages the resources of the computer, for example by:

- controlling the time each task is allowed in the processor
- interrupting when a more urgent task takes priority
- ensuring data is stored properly and the location recorded
- retrieving data from storage
- monitoring input and output.

It is normally supplied with the computer and may only run on that hardware (for example, iOS is only installed on Apple products). However, other operating systems such as Windows can be installed on a range of devices, including Apple products.

Operating systems differ with the role expected of them. For example, a single user operating system is found on PCs and tablets, where only one user can operate the device at a time, whereas a multiuser operating system has facilities which enable two or more users to have access at the same time.

Extra facilities are required by a multiuser operating system; for example, it must be able to prevent several users accessing the computer processor at the same time and overwriting each other's software or data. Users should not be able to 'see' each other on the system and should be unaware that anyone else is using the system.

GROUP ACTIVITY

(60 minutes)

Rashid and Anita are setting up a company to develop handheld infra-red security camera systems. They plan to monitor these systems on behalf of their clients, which will include military and defence contractors. They want to review application, utility and operating systems software to identify the most appropriate software.

Both Rashid and Anita have used computers for many years and so have heard terms such as 'off the shelf', bespoke and open source but do not fully understand what is meant by each term or indeed their strengths and weakness for a given situation.

They have asked you to report back on the pros and cons of each type of software.

1 In groups, work together to provide a short presentation on the types of software they could use and the relative advantages for the business.
2 Produce a report on the range of different software needed to run the business. Ensure you provide a justification for your choices.
3 The company is going to use a mixture of single and multiple processor systems. Rashid and Anita have asked for a brief presentation on the similarities and differences between the operating systems for each one. Produce a presentation covering their requirements.

2.5 Communication methods

Email, instant messaging, text messaging and Short Message Service (SMS)

These are written communications, although the introduction of emoticons recognises that some pictorial information is also communication. Email and instant messaging require internet access, whereas text messages and SMS are sent to mobile telephones via the mobile network. Many mobile devices, including tablets and smartphones, offer both internet and mobile network access and so all of these services can be accessed simultaneously through one or more service provider.

Table 1.13 Types of written communication methods

Communication method	What does it do?	How does it work?
Email	The most flexible of these methods, it enables both short messages and detailed discussions and allows the attachment of large files such as reports, presentations and images.	Sent via a mail server. Client software connects the user's computer to the mail server. Permits hyperlinks, which can take the reader directly to a particular web page. Email software can be provided with the computer, downloaded from the internet or provided by internet service providers (ISPs) that host email on remote servers.
Instant messaging	The user communicates directly with their contacts as they are both online. Messages are typed in a small window which appears on both screens.	Sent via a mail server. The software is a utility of the client software which uses a proprietary protocol (a communications protocol which has one owner) and which is not understood by other instant-messaging services so users can only talk to those on the same service (although some utilities now allow contact to one or two other services).
Texting and Short Message Service (SMS)	Both work in the same way but SMS restricts the characters in a message to about 180.	The software uses the control channel or pathway between the mobile phone and the mobile phone tower. A text message is sent as a packet of data, which includes the message and the addresses of the receiver and the short message server centre (SMSC). It is held until the receiving phone is available.

Voiceover Internet Protocol (VoIP)

This method can apply to digital telephone systems, video-conferencing and teleconferencing as well as to users with a computer, microphone and speaker system. Each has a codec (coder and decoder), which can be hardware or software. This device converts analogue sound or vision to a digital signal and carries out a reverse process by decoding the signals. To send this information, extra information is required, such as the IP address of the recipient.

The range of hardware and software is wide and a protocol (an agreed method of communication behaviours) allows them to communicate. The International Telecommunications Union (ITU) has a suite of protocols (H.323) which apply to both audio and video transmission. Other protocols, such as SIP (Session Initiation Protocol) enable mobile devices and computers to communicate over the internet using a SIP address. It requires a SIP client to be installed on the device and a SIP address, which is available from various sources. SIP and H.323 are not compatible.

Personal assistants

Personal assistants, such as Siri or Cortana, are software applications that recognise and act on voice commands. They can adapt to the user's speech, including accents, as the interaction continues. If the software cannot understand an instruction, it asks for it to be repeated or provide a pre-programmed list of commands to aid understanding.

2.6 Software troubleshooting

PAIRS ACTIVITY

(30 minutes)

Discuss the advantages and disadvantages of each type of communication and produce a table of your findings.

Troubleshooting should be a logical step by step approach to monitoring, identifying, diagnosing and correcting errors that arise. This should complement the careful recording of each step of a log of the events, which may be useful for future faults or to identify what may have caused an unexpected issue or outcome.

Common faults

Common software faults include:

- A system freeze, where the whole system locks and no key or click can release it, which may be as the result of a virus or software bugs.
- The frozen blue screen of a Windows-based system, which can be caused by issues with driver software.
- Software error or 'bug' due to poor coding or coding typing errors.
- Updates – ironically these can occur because an upgrade has not been applied and so the software malfunctions, or causes a malfunction because it has interfered with existing software.
- Unusual behaviour, such as only half a document appearing in a word-processing program.
- Software failing to load.

Troubleshooting tools to investigate a problem

Tools and techniques which assist with software fault diagnosis include:

- Network monitors examine the traffic between computers – for example, the types of **data packets** – for errors. The system not only identifies current issues but also provides a set of benchmarks once the system is set up and stable. These can regularly be compared with the actual state of the network at a particular time.
- Virus scanners check whether malware is being run in the background and slowing down the system.

Fault finding documentation

See LO1, page 14.

2.7 Protocols

Computers communicate with other devices using protocols – common rules and standards. You may already be familiar with names such as IP, TCP, POP3 SMTP and HTTP – the final 'P' usually stands for protocol.

> **KEY TERM**
>
> **Data packet** – data is not sent as a single stream across the internet but instead it is parcelled into one or more packets, each of which has a header with additional information such as the IP address of the sender and the receiver.

When troubleshooting, use the process of elimination: always start with the most straightforward explanations and see if they solve the problem. For example, if the mouse cursor is working erratically, disappears or does not follow the mouse movement, it may have run out of battery power or not been plugged in. If not, move on to check if the driver is installed properly and so on.

KNOW IT

1 List three types of software.
2 Name three types of utility software.
3 Name three voice-based communication methods.
4 Describe five popular protocols.

These protocols can be grouped in various roles, as shown in Table 1.14.

Table 1.14 Types of protocol

Reason for protocol	Examples
Linking computers across the internet required an agreement on how data was to be broken down and what exactly an internet address is. These are the oldest internet protocols and enable all types of device, brands, software and operating systems are able to communicate.	• The Transmission Control Protocol (TCP). • Internet Protocol (IP). • UDP (User Datagram Protocol): an alternative to TCP mostly used with connections which tolerate loss and disordering of the packets sent.
Ensuring the appropriate transfer of information between devices attached to the internet, including the control signals and how the data is to be structured.	• Simple Mail Transfer Protocol (SMTP). • Post Office Protocol 3 (POP3).
Dealing with how different data types should be structured.	File Transfer Protocol (FTP) and HTTP (HyperText Transfer Protocol).
Managing the network.	• Internet Control Message Protocol (ICMP): sends messages about the condition of the network rather than the data traffic. • Simple Network Management Protocol (SNMP) obtains a range of statistics such as those for status of the CPU, memory, buffers, interface traffic and errors which it is also able to verify.

LO3 Understand business IT systems

GETTING STARTED

(10 minutes)

In pairs, list the types of networks that you use or have used – at home, at school or college and in the workplace.

3.1 Types of servers

A server is normally considered to be a powerful computer or device which serves a particular need for a network. It can also be a piece of software that operates on a network device. While almost any computer can act as a server, it requires extra memory and computing power to run both the computer and the needs of the rest of the network. Specialist servers carry out one particular service for the network.

The most common servers are the following.

File

A file server is useful for businesses or individuals who need to hold and manage large numbers of files. It stores files, indexes them, remembers where they are to retrieve them and takes responsibility for security of the files, ensuring that only those who are entitled to read them can do so and only those who have the rights can edit or delete them. A further role for the file server is to ensure that backups are made at an agreed time, so that data can be restored if there is an accident or disaster.

Print

Print servers manage the printing of documents. They control printers on the network, allowing a group or groups of employees to send print requests to specific printers. It can also reroute print requests, if there is a fault or incident, to the nearest appropriate and available printer. It can manage the electronic print queue by sharing the load across the available printers.

Application

Application servers are designed to install, operate and monitor the applications shared by other devices on the network. Although all users share some applications, such as word processors and email, the server also manages security of restricted access applications such as financial and human resource software.

Database

Some application servers may have a specialised role as database servers, which manage databases with multiple users. These servers are database-architecture independent – the server will manage all activities, whether it is a relational database, flat file or object-oriented.

Web

A web server can also refer to hardware or the web server software. It is an internet server that reacts to HTTP requests to deliver content and services from a client.

Mail

A mail server or a mail transfer agent (MTA) is software or a device which acts as an electronic post office. It receives emails from users on the network, both in the same domain and from external senders, and forwards it to the recipients, who may be local users or external senders. For external senders, the mail server passes it to the mail server of the recipients' domain. Normally, mail servers use SMTP to send the mail and POP3 or IMAP to receive it.

Hypervisor

This is software written for a particular processor which manages different operating systems or copies of the same operating system on a single computer or computer system. It manages resources such as the processor, memory and devices so that each operating system not only receives the resources it needs but also prevents it clashing with the other operating systems. See also LO3.2.

3.2 Virtualisation

Virtualisation is to create a simulated or virtual network, computer or server using software.

Server virtualisation is not new; it has been used in mainframes since 1970s. Normally the operating system and hardware are closely linked so that

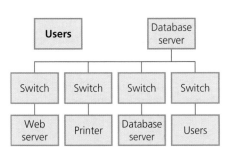

▲ **Figure 1.4** An example of a print network with different servers attached

only some applications can run simultaneously to prevent problems such as registry conflicts. To operate additional applications, additional physical servers need to be installed, possibly running only a single application. Server virtualisation enables a single physical server to run several applications, each appearing to have its own server.

Storage virtualisation works in a similar way by separating the physical storage server from the logical storage server. It can take two forms:

- Block-level, which allows a storage area network or SAN to use numerous storage arrays across the network as if they were a single array.
- File-level, which allows network attached storage (NAS) and removes the link between the data items and their physical locations on a particular file server.

Cloud computing is not virtualisation. The cloud uses existing technology to deliver services, such as security, storage and data manipulation, to users over a network. It is used like a utility – you can increase the size or range of your usage through payment.

Hybrid cloud computing is a mixture of private cloud, public cloud and locally owned services. As its activities and data requirements change, so the organisation can adjust its usage more effectively and efficiently.

GROUP ACTIVITY

(45 minutes)

In small groups, investigate the advantages and disadvantages of virtualisation and give a presentation on your findings.

3.3 Networking characteristics

Types of local area networks include the following.

Peer-to-peer

Each computer is linked to one or more computers directly rather than going through a server. There are several forms of peer-to-peer networks.

The star network

Each node (a workstation or device) connects to a central network device such as a computer, hub or switch. If the central device is a hub, it will send all packets of data to all devices, whereas if it is a switch, it will only send packets to the destination device. A star network has the advantage that if one cable or device fails, the remaining cables and devices will continue to function. A disadvantage is that if the central computer, hub or switch fails, the entire network goes down.

Bus network

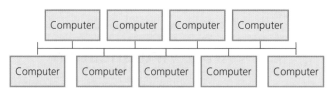

▲ **Figure 1.6** A bus network

Here, the peripherals are attached to a single cable with terminators at each end.

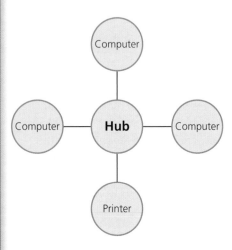

▲ **Figure 1.5** A star network

The advantages include:

- attaching a new device is easy, so if one peripheral fails the others are not affected
- it is cheaper in cabling terms than a star network
- transmissions are in both directions
- transmission is more likely to be read as it is received by all devices relating to the recipient.

The disadvantages include:

- the difficulty of identifying a faulty peripheral
- if the main cable should fail, then the entire network will go down
- adding additional devices can slow the network down significantly
- the possibility of the transmissions crashing into each other.

Ring network

Ring networks have one directional communication through a cable. The message is received by each computer in the ring between the sender and receiver. Each computer in the chain sends the data packet to the next computer until the receiving device receives it. Often the message is boosted or regenerated to maintain signal strength.

Rings use a method known as token passing to prevent problems of multiple messages on the network colliding. A small data packet known as the token is continuously transmitted around the ring. When a device has data to transmit, it has to wait until the token arrives. At that point, the computer checks to see if the token is already being used by another device. If not, it adds its own data and control information such as the address of the receiving device and sends the token on its way. When the notice of safe delivery is received the token is released back to the ring.

Mesh network

There are two types of mesh network:

- Total mesh topology where every **node** (connection) in the network is connected directly to all other nodes. If a connection stops working all the traffic on the network can be rerouted around the problem.
- Partial mesh topology has some nodes connected to only a small number of nodes whereas others are connected to all the other nodes. This reduces the rerouting options if a connection fails, but it is cheaper than the total mesh because there is less cabling, for example.

Cabled mesh networks are very costly because of their complex cabling requirements but wireless mesh networks are cheaper because they do not need cabling.

Client server

In the networks identified above, all the devices are independent in that they carry out their own tasks with their own software. They may share data but not applications. Client server networks are different. One device, which may be a computer or a specialist server, provides services such as applications, storage or internet connections to its clients (the other computers in the

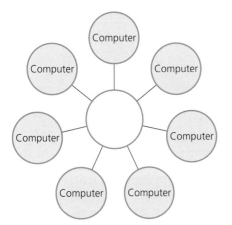

▲ **Figure 1.7** A ring network

▲ **Figure 1.8** A mesh network

🔑 KEY TERM

Node – a connection, redistribution or end point on a network; anything with an IP address.

network). Larger networks may have several servers, as shown in Figure 1.4, providing different services.

It is possible to link networks through switches, gateways and routers, to allow for greater flexibility.

The choice of topology will depend upon a number of factors:

● The number of computers to be networked.
● The spread of the network, e.g. room, building, city, country or continent.
● The cost of the topology, e.g. a bus topology is cost-effective in a single room with only a few devices. A star topology with a central hub running an ethernet system is a reasonable approach for several devices and servers, as long as they are within a single building or in buildings on a single site.
● The amount of money available.

3.4 Connectivity methods

LAN

Token ring local area networks (LANs) were discussed in LO3.3.

An alternative is to use an ethernet network LAN. The cabling allows messages to travel in either direction, unlike token ring networks which only communicate in one direction. Half duplex ethernet LANs allow communication in both directions but only in one direction at a time. However, if two messages are simultaneously placed on the network and crash into each other, this may bring the network down.

To enable the network to recover from this problem, a media access control (MAC) method called Carrier Sense Multiple Access with Collision Detection (CSMA/CD) is used. It works as shown in Figure 1.9. Back off is the randomly calculated time that a device will wait to try to resend the message (the time it will back off from transmitting). Each device carries out its own calculation and so, in theory, only one will be ready to transmit once the collision is cleared.

WAN and MAN

A wide area network (WAN) can be transglobal, or cover whole countries or continents. Networks operating over smaller distances such as a town, city or cluster of close cities are called metropolitan area networks (MANs). Each type of network has its own rules or protocols to ensure that generic devices can communicate.

Examples include ASDL (asymmetric digital subscriber), which supports faster transmission of data over the copper wire telephone lines than the traditional voice modem. ISDN (integrated services digital network) is a set of standards for digital transmission of data, video and voice over traditional telephone copper wire. Leased lines, rather than operating through national and international telephone wires, provide a fixed-bandwidth data connection. This means that the bandwidth is only available to the leasee, avoiding a slowdown in transmission when the network is busy.

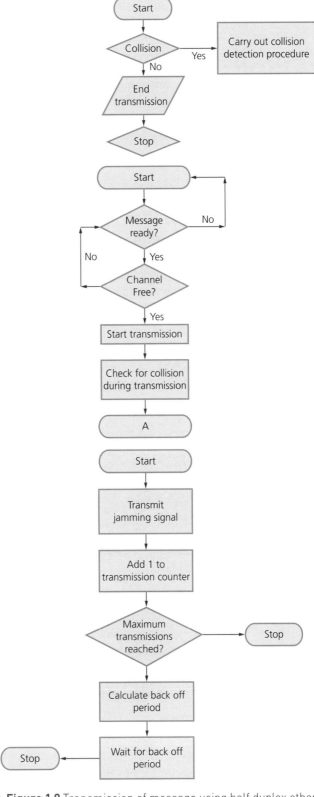

▲ **Figure 1.9** Transmission of message using half duplex ethernet

Voice

Data and voice communication can be sent over telephone wires or by cellular or satellite technology. The clearest and most reliable method is over fixed cables between the sender and receiver. If it is not possible to be linked to a handset or computer which is plugged into a public switched telephone network (PSTN) (e.g. while travelling or in remote parts of the world), cellular (mobile phone) and satellite communication is appropriate.

However, cellular technology requires the towers which carry transmitter/receivers to be in line of sight to the user's communication device. Disappearing into tunnels on a train, standing in a remote field or being shielded by large buildings can disrupt this point-to-point communication. Also, providers do not like to share their communication systems with other providers as they risk losing revenue from new customers.

Satellites

Satellites in geostatic orbit (those that appear to stay in a single location over Earth) are point-to-multipoint communication systems as they receive transmissions and rebroadcast them to receivers. If required, the satellite can be moved to another location relatively quickly. However, the distance between the satellite and the ground, normally about 75,000 km (46,603 miles), means there is a delay between the transmission of the signal and its receipt, which can be seen on television news reports from remote locations. Data transmission is also compromised by this issue, especially when trying to transfer large files.

3.5 Business systems

Businesses have developed many systems to manage and manipulate data and aid business practices.

MIS

Management information systems (MIS) refers to the software and hardware used by managers to obtain the necessary information for accurate decision-making and monitoring the effectiveness of decisions. The system continuously gathers internal and external data, and refines and organises it in one or more databases where it can be interrogated by those with access rights. The data can be downloaded, for example for:

- reports and other documents
- spreadsheets and strategic decision support systems
- functional systems such as those for marketing, sales or production.

Used wisely, an MIS can provide evidence of:

- the status of the organisation
- areas of improvement, e.g. rising sales
- areas of risk, e.g. falling sales, loss of market share
- personal or group responsibility for success or failure.

Limitations of MIS systems are:

- cost of creating and installing the system
- poor or inflexible design which does not meet current or future needs of the organisation
- data that is out of date, incomplete or incorrect because of poor error checking facilities

- end users who do not use the system properly; this is often caused by lack of training
- it does not make judgements; it only provides the information needed for decisions.

CRM

To ensure that customer needs are met, data must be gathered, analysed and shared. Customer relations management (CRM) is a process that tracks how the business interacts with current and potential customers. A computer-based CRM system supports such activities by holding records of client communications, meetings and documents. This information is available to those with access rights.

A CRM system allows a business to centrally hold customer information such as:

- contact details
- customer histories
- leads for new customers
- leads for new services.

Although CRM is primarily aimed at sales and customer support functions, marketers also use CRM to aid their understanding of current sales, prospective sales and forecasting future trends.

Limitations to CRMs include:

- Software issues, such as limits on data storage size or emails.
- Integration difficulties with other organisational systems.
- Lack of training leading to poor data entry and incorrect data.
- Resistance by sales staff who believe that using digital information rather than face to face meetings with clients reduces their ability to understand subtle communication behaviours.

SOP

Standard operating procedures (SOPs) are detailed step-by-step guides to how functions should be carried out within an organisation to ensure that they are carried out accurately and in the same way each time. The outcomes from each activity should always be the same, leaving an audit trail in case of disputes or external investigations by regulatory bodies. SOPs should also be created for business systems such as those outlined above, to ensure that the data and resulting information remains accurate and useful. Software can aid the production of SOPs.

Limitations of SOPs include:

- Imposing restrictions and details which result in inflexible practice and a lack of innovation.
- Too much time being spent on the admin rather than doing the job.
- The necessity of updating the SOP to reflect new statutory or regulatory requirements.
- Lack of version control. If updates to the SOP are not recorded with a date and a brief statement about the changes, individuals could be working to different versions, which can cause serious problems.

Help desk

When a user of a large, complex or widely spread system has a technical problem, it is useful to have a knowledgeable person ready to solve it. For straightforward problems, instructions can be given to the user and the issue resolved immediately, but complex problems can be actioned by a technician visiting the location and resolving the problem or providing a temporary fix. This is normally managed through agreed levels of support for departments or customers.

Limitations include:

● Cost of setting up an in-house help desk with hardware, software and staffing.
● Cost of buying help desk services from an external source (third party).
● Issues with availability of the help desk, for example, the need for 24-hour call out; availability during bank holidays.
● Loss of service through breakdown of communication systems.

> **KNOW IT**
>
> 1 Identify three types of server, one of which must be virtual.
> 2 Identify three network topologies that could be used in a small business.
> 3 For each of the purposes below identify the most appropriate business system.
>   a Support for an end user whose computer has crashed.
>   b A system to improve sales to your clients.
>   c An audit trail of actions taken by staff while carrying out risk assessment on a computer system.
> 4 Define virtualisation.

LO4 Understand employability and communication skills used in an IT environment

4.1 Communication skills

Working in the IT industry requires communication skills because individuals need to work independently and in teams, and provide support to, or acquire information from, those without any technical knowledge.

Interpersonal skills

Face-to-face communication involves more than just talking. You must also provide a positive image of yourself, your colleagues and your organisation. Think about what makes you take an instant like or dislike to someone when you first meet them. Signals may be through eye contact (e.g. looking directly at the person to whom you are talking, not allowing your eyes to wander) and body language. Depending on the circumstances, folding your arms and slouching rather than sitting up on your chair can give the

GETTING STARTED

(20 minutes)

Imagine you work as a software developer. Identify what communication skills you think you need and explain why they are important.

impression that you have no interest in what is being said or done. Some body language can be considered insulting, such as yawning when someone is talking to you.

Verbal communication

This needs to be effective and appropriate for the situation. You must know when to use technical or specialist terms and when to provide simple explanations in easily understood English. Some communications are formal, such as in meetings, while others may be more informal, such as working with close colleagues. Therefore, the language needs to be adjusted, for example, 'Hiya mate!' may be acceptable when speaking to a peer but not to senior colleagues or customers.

Questioning techniques

When trying to help those with IT problems or find out what is required, e.g. for a new system, careful questioning should help to acquire the information needed. Types of questioning techniques include:

- Closed questions, where the answer will be one word or a very short factual answer, e.g. 'Do you want a drink?' or 'How many days are there in November?'
- Open questions, where there is no obvious answer or where opinions are required, such as 'How did she react?', 'Why did you select that laptop?'

Avoid leading questions, e.g. 'Is the computer always this slow to start up?'

Written communication

It is important to distinguish between formal or informal written communication. Formal communication might be a letter of application for a job, while informal written communication is usually more casual and spontaneous, e.g. text message or email to a friend. Whether something is formal or informal will depend upon:

- The organisation's policies on documentation layout.
- Whether the communication is between colleagues or external bodies.
- Whether the communications have legal status.

You should become familiar with the business's policies and procedures for written communication, such as the format of reports, letters, emails and social networking.

Barriers to communication

Some circumstances prevent the message being given or received. They can include:

- Noise: both physical noise, which makes listening difficult, or noise in your own head generated by worries or concerns, which results in loss of concentration on the conversation.
- Language: this can be due to the inappropriate use of complex or technical terminology.
- Physical barriers such as deafness, where sign language or clear enunciation for lip reading is required to ensure successful communication.

4.2 Communication technology

Communication is aided by a range of technology – some forms are written and others are verbal.

- Presentation software can include text, graphics, video and audio images and is used to tell a story or used to support someone presenting information.
- Word processing – used for the production, editing, printing and storing of text on a computer, e.g. writing letters, reports, books, leaflets and posters.
- Email – the distribution of electronic messages from one computer user to another via a network.
- Web – a system of internet servers that support specially formatted documents often connected via hyperlinks.
- Blog – a regularly updated web page run by an individual or small group taking the form of a personal journal which is accessible to the public.
- Vlog or video log – a form of blog which includes video clips.
- Instant messaging – a communication service which enables a person to communicate privately with another individual in real time over the internet.

GROUP ACTIVITY

(20 minutes)

What communication technology would you use if you worked as a computer support technician for a small PC repair company? Justify your answers.

4.3 Personal attributes

These are the qualities individuals have which enhance their technical skills and make them useful employees.

Table 1.15 Personal attributes in the workplace

Attribute	Meaning	Possible role type
Decisiveness	Understands that difficult decisions have to be made in a timely manner, to protect the organisation or individual.	Leader
Punctuality	Demonstrates responsibility, dedication and a willingness to take personal responsibility.	All job roles
Self-motivation		
Leadership		
Respect		
Dependability		
Problem solving		
Determination		
Independence		
Time management		
Punctuality		
Team working		
Written numerical and verbal skills		
Planning and organisation skills		

PAIRS ACTIVITY

(30 minutes)

Complete the table, briefly explaining why each attribute is useful and any particular roles to which the attribute would apply. The first two have been completed for you. Copy it onto a piece of paper if you need more space for writing.

4.4 Ready for work

Present an image that says that you are prepared for work, which includes being ready to represent the organisation to any visitors and to show the importance of personal presentation. Examples include the following.

- Dress code – some organisations have dress codes that require a uniform or a dark suit, while others may be happy if everyone arrives in t-shirts and jeans. Whatever the code, employees must dress appropriately for the situation.
- Presentation – clean clothes and good personal hygiene help to give a professional impression, as others need to feel comfortable when working closely with you. Good grooming shows respect for the organisation and colleagues.
- Attitude – someone with a 'can do attitude' is positive about their ability to achieve success, even if things are not going well. Someone who has a responsive attitude readily accepts change and is open to suggestions made by others.

4.5 Job roles

From chief information officer to trainee help desk operator, all roles require certain attributes and skills.

> **CLASSROOM DISCUSSION**
>
> Find examples of job descriptions, attributes and skills for the following IT job roles:
>
> - network manager
> - IT technician
> - programmer
> - web designer
> - animator.
>
> Discuss why particular attributes and skills would be appropriate for each role.

4.6 Professional bodies and 4.7 Industry certification

Anyone can claim to be an IT specialist; unlike the medical or teaching profession there is no requirement to be registered or to undertake particular qualifications. However, professional bodies such as the British Computer Society (BCS), which is also the Chartered Institute for IT, seek to raise the status of the IT professional. It sets standards of behaviour and supports IT professionals in achieving recognition of their qualifications as well as skills developed through working in the industry. Professional bodies provide a number of benefits such as:

- building a network with like-minded professionals
- identifying career opportunities as many advertise job opportunities
- continuous professional development opportunities through seminars, special interest groups, journals and qualifications.

Disadvantages include:

- cost – fees can be several hundred pounds
- time – attending meetings and events for general or specialist group or local branch meetings
- does not guarantee that you will have a better job or earn more money.

Training includes certificated courses which provide the individual with national and/or international recognition of the level of knowledge, understanding and experience in certain areas of IT. They also provide the opportunity to achieve new skills and knowledge for future roles.

 CLASSROOM DISCUSSION

Look at a range of industry awards and the bodies who offer them, such as CISCO®, and consider:

- What is the purpose of each award?
- How does achieving the award benefit the individual?
- How does employing staff who hold the award or providing opportunities to study for them support an organisation?

KNOW IT

1 What interpersonal skills would you use when communicating with a client on how to set up their email account?
2 Suggest two methods of communication technology that could be used to create a user guide on how to install a wireless printer.
3 What personal attributes would you need for this role?
4 You are working as part of a team developing bespoke information systems for businesses. Some of your colleagues are working on a project and need help as they have very short deadlines and are concerned that they will not meet them. What attitude would you show to your colleagues?
5 Give two advantages and two disadvantages of being a member of a professional body.

LO5 Understand ethical and operational issues and threats to computer systems

GETTING STARTED

(15 minutes)

Computer systems are open to a number of threats. In pairs, discuss and identify as many threats as you can to computer systems. These can be for standalone computer systems for a single user as well as computer systems which are part of a network.

KEY TERM

Whistle blowing – making a disclosure that is of public interest.

KEY TERMS

Code of practice – a set of rules which explains how people working in certain professions are required to behave.

Ethics – the accepted behaviours and beliefs of society or groups within it which influence how people react to situations.

5.1 Ethical issues

Whistle blowing

Whistle blowing is usually when an employee discloses that some form of serious unlawful practice is taking place within their place of work. The activity could include miscarriages of justice, illegal activity, threats to individuals and/or damage to the environment. Whistle blowers are protected by UK law against any form of 'punishment' by their organisation, for example, unfair dismissal or not being promoted.

Disability/gender/sexuality discrimination

Behaving ethically can be underwritten by law; for example, the Equality Act (2010) ensures equality of treatment for all people, irrespective of colour, race, disability or gender. These and other characteristics are classified as protected. Examples of discrimination could be people not receiving equal pay for the doing the same job because of their gender, disability and/or sexuality.

Use of information

The Data Protection Act (1998) ensures that personal data is used responsibly. When designing, developing and/or using information systems, ethical considerations should be made with respect to how the information is collected, processed, stored, used and distributed.

Codes of practice

There are many codes of practice within the workplace to provide ethical guidance. An organisation may have a **code of practice** for confidentiality in relation to its clients, for example, so if you saw confidential information while developing an information system you would be bound by your organisation's code of practice not to share any of the information you have seen. There are codes of practice for **ethics** (how you behave), quality assurance (how the organisation ensures that quality is maintained with respect to the products and/or services it provides), equality and discrimination (being fair and objective with advice and actions provided to employees and clients).

Staying safe online

There are guides on staying safe online to avoid problems with individuals who do not behave ethically or perhaps have a different ethical code from those of society as a whole. See Unit 3 for more details.

5.2 Operational issues

These cover a wide range of circumstances that could jeopardise individual departments or the entire organisation. Some examples are as follows.

Security of information

Failure to protect information from loss, corruption, illegal duplication, or being stolen, manipulated or hacked can provoke poor publicity, which can result in loss of business, bankruptcy or even fines and court cases. Loss of production information and sales data can leave a business unable to meet its requirements.

Health and safety

Failure to protect employees and clients or visitors can reflect badly on the organisation if reported in the press. It can also result in large compensation claims, court cases, fines or even imprisonment in the most serious instances, such as loss of life. There is also an ethical or moral issue, as risking the lives and health of employees through a careless attitude to their safety is not acceptable behaviour.

Disaster and recovery planning

Organisations take note of all the issues that could risk their assets, employees and existence. They will produce a plan to either reduce the risk to the lowest possible level or provide alternative facilities or locations. For example, backing up computer data as often as necessary will ensure that minimal data is lost if there is a computer failure. Placing copies of the backup data in different physical locations in case of fire, flood or earthquake is also a possible disaster plan.

Organisational policies

Organisations have policies to establish the rules for acceptable behaviour and guidelines for best practice in certain work-related situations. An acceptable use policy stipulates what a person can and cannot do when using the network and/ or internet while at work. Schools and colleges usually require their learners to sign an acceptable use policy before they will issue them with a network ID. A code of conduct policy sets out the standards of behaviour expected from employees while working on the premises or the premises of their clients.

All organisations need to change over time because of different factors which include the following.

Scale of change

This reflects the needs of the business, such as replacing a slow network with a faster optical fibre system, introducing an extranet or allowing customers to log into some systems externally. It also provides remote access for employees so that they can access work from home.

Change drivers

These are things which must change, such as new legislation, new entrants into the market, an increase in the number of platforms that can share, distribute, license or sell music, or new business practices.

5.3 Threats

Security covers the identification of threats like:

- Phishing: misleading individuals or organisations into parting with their confidential and personal data to commit fraud.
- Hacking: not all hacking is external, as employees also hack their own company systems. This includes looking at files or locations to which they do not have right of access; creating, modifying or deleting files without permission; or defacing web pages.
- Trojan (horse): introducing a piece of code which, when certain conditions are met, will carry out an action which will be detrimental to the system, e.g. wiping data.
- Interception: when the data packets on the internet are intercepted by a third party and copied, edited or transferred to a new location.
- Eavesdropping: can refer to interception, but is particularly listening to communication traffic not intended for the reader or listener such as email, instant messaging, faxing or video-conferencing.

> **KEY TERM**
>
> **Change management** – the application of standardised methods and procedures, allowing for the efficient, effective and prompt handling of any identified changes that are required to control the IT infrastructure. This is to minimise the potential number, and impact, of risks upon the service provided.

- Data theft: illegally removing copies of personal or company data from information systems.
- Social engineering: the manipulation of individuals to trick them into giving sensitive information, for example, claiming to be from the IT department and asking for a password and username to check whether the PC has a virus.

To protect against these and other attacks a range of security measures is available. Normally, these are broken down into physical security and digital security.

5.4 Physical security

Examples include:

- Locks and keypads for preventing access to computer rooms or storage facilities or to prevent access to hard drives.
- Biometric readers are electronic devices to determine a person's identity. They can do this by detecting fingerprints or eyes and matching them to records in a database.
- Radio frequency identification (RFID) uses radio waves or electromagnetic waves to identify and track individuals, animals and items of importance.
- Tokens, small hardware devices, such as a keyfob or a smart card, which allow a person access to a network (for example, the tokens sent to customers by some banks to access online banking services).
- Privacy screens to prevent the content being seen or read by anyone not sitting in front of the screen.
- Shredding or cutting up documents and optical discs into sufficiently small pieces that it is impossible to reconstruct them. This is one of the most effective methods of protecting physical data no longer required from falling into the wrong hands.

5.5 Digital security

Examples include:

- Anti-virus and anti-spyware are both programs that protect the computer system from other programs which are maliciously downloaded. Anti-virus means that the software identifies and quarantines or destroys computer viruses. Anti-spyware carries out a similar role with spyware.
- Usernames and passwords provide protection at two levels. The username is linked to a group or groups. These groups allow access or give permission for the user to access particular software such as financial systems or HR. The password can allow the user access to the information system and software such as internet access, word processor, spreadsheet and email. Further passwords may be required for particularly sensitive data.
- Firewalls are used to prevent unauthorised access to or from a network. They can be implemented via hardware, software or both. Firewalls filter the traffic that flows into a PC and/or network through an internet connection and block anything that it deems harmful to the computer system or network. There are three types of filtering mechanisms:
  - Packet filtering – the firewall analyses the 'packets of information' (i.e. data) and blocks any unwanted or offensive packets.
  - Proxy – the firewall takes on the role of a recipient and sends the data received to the node that had requested the information.

- Inspection – the firewall marks key features of any outgoing requests for information and checks for the same key features of the data coming into the computer system/network, deciding whether it is relevant.
- Permissions – rules that determine who can access an object and what they can do with it. An example would be the permissions granted to people to access a shared file on a network system; so some people may only have read-only rights, while others will be able to edit the file as well.
- Encryption is when data is encoded (converted into a coded format), so that it cannot be understood by people who are not authorised to see it. The only way that someone can read encrypted data is with a secret code or key.

5.6 Safe disposal of data and computer equipment

Legislation

A range of legislation covers the disposal of data and computer equipment. These include the Waste Electronic and Electrical Equipment (WEEE) directive, which makes clear that the computer equipment needs specialist knowledge and tools to ensure safe dismantling. The UK's Waste Acceptance Criteria (WAC) deals with the disposal of monitors, for example. The Hazardous Waste (England and Wales) Regulations 2005 also applies as mercury, hexavalent chromium and other toxic chemicals found in computer systems.

The Freedom of Information Act (2000) and the Data Protection Act (1998) contain clear legal requirements for the safe destruction of data.

Overwriting data and electromagnetic wipe

These are ways of removing data from hard discs. Overwriting is when data is sent to the disc and this overwrites the '1's and '0's already on the disc. Unfortunately, once is normally insufficient to remove all evidence of the existence of the data. The process must be repeated several times and even then very sophisticated forensic techniques can often retrieve some of the data.

Electromagnetic wiping involves the use of a degausser which has a very strong permanent magnetic or an electromagnetic coil. This method can also destroy the disc itself if great care is not taken, but it does remove the data.

Physical destruction

As seen in LO5.4, physically destroying hardware containing data by shredding can be effective. Some businesses provide secure bins for confidential information, the contents of which are destroyed.

> **KNOW IT**
> 1 What is a whistle blower?
> 2 An organisation is concerned that if the server was to break down, they may lose their data. What operational issue would they need to consider?
> 3 What does RFID stand for?
> 4 Give two examples of how permissions could be used as a digital security method on a network.
> 5 Identify two ways in which data can be securely removed from a hard disc.

Assessment practice questions

Below are practice questions for you to try.

Section A

For each question, put a tick in the right hand column of the table to show the correct answer.

1 Which of these items is ordered correctly, from the smallest to the largest? (1)
a gibi, tebi, kibi, mebi, pebi
b gibi, kibi, mebi, pebi, tebi
c kilo, mebi, gibi, tebi, pebi
d kilo, gibi, mebi, tebi, pebi

2 Which of the following is **not** a computer component? (1)
a RAM
b keyboard
c power supply
d sound card

3 Which of these is a business system? (1)
a SOP
b MOP
c DOP
d LOP

4 Which of these is an ethical issue? (1)
a biometrics
b encryption
c use of information
d security of information

5 Which of these is **not** a threat to computer systems? (1)
a bias
b interception
c eavesdropping
d social engineering

6 Which of these is a disadvantage of using the cloud for storage? (1)
a usability
b cost savings
c accessibility
d disaster recovery

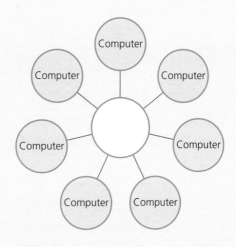

7 Which topology is shown in the diagram? (1)
a client server
b ring
c mesh
d star

8 Which type of network is often connected through public networks, leased lines or satellites? (1)
a WLAN
b WAN
c MAN
d PAN

9 Which protocol is used to automatically provide IP addresses to network computers? (1)
a IGMP
b ARP
c DNS
d DHCP

10 Is the following statement **TRUE** or **FALSE**? (1)
Freeware is computer software that is available free of charge and has no restrictions on redistribution for which source code is not available.

11 Which of the following shows the conversation of 124 in decimal to binary? (1)
a 00111010
b 01010110
c 11111000
d 01111100

12 Which of the following shows the conversion 11100010 to decimal? (1)
   a 220
   b 226
   c 210
   d 216

13 Which of the following shows the conversion of 250 to hexadecimal? (1)
   a FB
   b FH
   c FA
   d FE

14 Which of the following is an example of digital security? (1)
   a biometrics
   b interception
   c RFID
   d encryption

15 Which type of virtualisation is the sharing of computer resources, software or data through the internet? (1)
   a network virtualisation
   b server virtualisation
   c storage virtualisation
   d cloud virtualisation

Section B

Grab and Go is a fast food outlet with six branches across the Northwest of England. This growth has taken place over the past three years and each branch has its own computer network which links via email to the others. All sales and financial records are sent weekly via email to the head office, which is the site of the original outlet.

The owner has decided that the organisation needs a network that will link the shops electronically and enable all data relating to the business to be stored centrally on a server at head office. You have been asked to work with a local IT consultant to design the new system.

1 Explain two advantages and two disadvantages of using a multiple processor system to run the system. (1)

2 The IT specialist has suggested that, rather than a server at head office, the data should be held in the cloud. The owner asks you to compare the two options so that he can make a decision. Compare the use of a server to store company data compared to using a cloud service. (6)

3 Draw a possible topology for a network to join the individual computers into a single wide area network. You should label all of the hardware technologies involved. (8)

4 Outline three ways in which the wide area network could be connected. (6)

5 Evaluate the use of a barcode reader system in reducing errors and updating the stock levels across the outlets. (6)

6 The IT consultant has recommended that Grab and Go purchases bespoke software to run its stock control system. You believe that shareware programs could be used instead. Explain the difference between the two types of software. (5)

7 With the introduction of a new computer network, the IT consultant has suggested that a network manager should be appointed. As an IT technician, you feel that this is an opportunity for you to obtain a promotion.
   a Explain the personal attributes that are required for both roles and what evidence you could provide of current attributes. (3)
   b Outline the additional personal attributes required by the new network manager. (3)

8 Explain why Grab and Go should undertake a disaster planning and recovery event to protect its data. (4)

9 Describe three threats against which Grab and Go should protect itself. (6)

10 Explain three physical security methods which should be implemented by Grab and Go to protect its computer systems. (6)

11 Explain how Grab and Go should dispose of its old computer systems and the data held on hard discs safely and why this is important. (8)

Unit 02

Global information

ABOUT THIS UNIT

This unit explains how information is held and used by different types of users. You will learn about how organisations use internal and external sources of data and the types of information that may be found.

You will study the importance of good management of data and information and the impact that this can have on the ability of organisations to compete with one another.

This is a mandatory unit for this qualification.

LEARNING OUTCOMES

The topics and activities in this unit will help you to:

1 Understand where information is held globally and how it is transmitted.
2 Understand the styles, classification and the management of global information.
3 Understand the use of global information and the benefits to individuals and organisations.
4 Understand the legal and regulatory framework governing the storage and use of global information.
5 Understand the process flow of information.
6 Understand the principles of information security.

How will I be assessed?

You will be assessed through an external assessment set and marked by OCR.

LO1 Understand where information is held globally and how it is transmitted

(10 minutes)

Individually, think about the number of organisations that hold information about you and the type of information they hold (e.g. name, medical records etc).

As a group, create a list of these organisations and the type of information that they hold. Are there any surprises? Is there one organisation, other than your school or college, that appears on everyone's list?

1.1 Holders of information

Categories of holders

There are many different categories of holders of information.

Individual citizens hold information about themselves, including personal data, such as their date and place of birth. They may also hold similar information about others, such as phone numbers and email addresses of their family or friends. They may hold information about organisations, even those with which they have no direct contact. This information may have been passed by third parties, read on the internet or in books, or even have been stolen.

Business organisations hold some of the same information as individuals. For example, they will hold the dates of birth and places of birth of their employees. They may also hold commercial information about competitors, financial information about their own business and general information about relevant markets.

Government and healthcare services hold a great deal of information about us. Every year, employers pass on information about how much we have earned and the tax we have paid. The electoral roll holds information about where people live and healthcare services hold medical records such as when we have visited doctors and the treatment we received. The government is also likely to hold some information about individuals of which that individual is not aware. As an example, healthcare services may hold medical information, or the government, or one of its agencies, may hold information that has been gathered through investigations which have yet to be published. These could, for example, be investigations into tax affairs.

The government holds information about other countries and will, when necessary, share some of this with the public. For example, the Foreign Office may offer travel advice based on intelligence gathered from abroad.

Charities and community organisations also hold information. For example, charities may hold information about the bank accounts of donors, whilst community organisations may hold contact details for members of the community.

PAIRS ACTIVITY

(40 minutes)

As a pair, create a table listing the types of holders of information.

For each type of holder, describe what information each will hold.

Present your findings to others in the group.

KEY TERM

Digital divide – the difference in access to digital resources in different areas of the world.

PAIRS ACTIVITY

(30 minutes)

Research the availability of broadband and other access issues in each of the following countries.

Present your findings as a table.

- Afghanistan
- Saudi Arabia
- Australia
- Belgium
- Canada
- Denmark
- South Africa
- China.

Location

Data is held in different locations. Examples include the following.

Developing and developed countries

Developing countries tend to have a less-developed industrial base than developed countries. Their human development index (a measure of life expectancy, education and income per head of population) is also lower than that for developed countries.

Alongside the less-developed industrial base, these nations tend to have less access to computers and the internet. This therefore means that information dispersal and gathering is harder than for developed countries.

Urban and rural

An urban location is in a city or other built-up area. Rural locations are in the countryside. Rural areas tend to have poorer internet access (for example, slower broadband speeds) making accessing online information harder.

Comparison of technologies available and access issues across the global divide

Access to the internet is not spread evenly throughout the world and this inequality is the focus of the global divide. It impacts on a range of areas, including education, tourism and democracy.

1.2 Types of information storage media

Information can be held in many different ways.

Paper

Paper is a traditional form of information storage and includes forms, handwritten notes, maps and telephone directories. However, it is easily damaged when handled, costs a lot to transport and can be hard to keep secure.

Optical media

Better known as music and film storage formats, CDs and DVDs are methods of digital information and data storage that can hold information of many types. One of the key uses is for software distribution. These are called optical media because they are written and read by laser.

Magnetic media

Magnetic media uses magnetic patterns to store data. The most common example is the magnetic hard drives inside most computers. Data can be stored on external hard drives. Data can also be stored on tapes. This media is most frequently used for backup or archiving.

Solid state media

Solid state media stores data and information in circuitry rather than a magnetised disc or tape. An example is an SSD (solid state drive), these are increasingly popular because of their speed. SSDs can also be used within computers in place of hard drives, where they have the advantage of not requiring air cooling, as their lack of moving parts means that they do not overheat.

▲ **Figure 2.1** An SSD card

Characteristics

Different forms of storage media have different characteristics. For example:

- Mutability (the ability to change the content of a storage medium): some devices, especially CDs and DVDs, are in read-only format and cannot be edited. Other devices (and media like paper) are in read/write format, which allows repeated reuse.
- Robustness: solid state media, because it has no moving parts, is less likely to be damaged if dropped and so is often used in portable devices, while hard drives, which rely on an internal spinning disc as the storage medium, are frequently damaged if dropped. If magnetic media is placed near magnets, the information held on them can become inaccessible.
- Access to data: for example, tape storage has to be searched from beginning to end to find a particular file and is best used for storage that does not require quick access to particular files.
- Cost: paper is relatively cheap but the costs of sending large amounts of paper-based information (such as books) by post or courier are high because of their weight. Hard drives remain cheaper but slower than SSD cards, although hybrid storage options are available.
- Storage capacity: this is the amount of data that can be stored on each device. As miniaturisation has progressed, so more data can be held on most forms of storage.

Purpose

The fundamental purpose of storage media is to store information. Once this purpose has been accepted, then issues such as how easily the information needs to be accessed for the given purpose become important. For example, the relative difficulty of accessing information held on a data tape means that it is an unsuitable format for general day-to-day storage.

Advantages and disadvantages

Different storage media can have different advantages and disadvantages, which will impact on the choice of media. As mentioned above, the robustness of solid state devices means that they are extremely useful in devices that are likely to be dropped. As desktop and laptop devices are less likely to be dropped, magnetic hard discs are more likely to be used, and the advantage of the relative cheapness of these storage devices reflected in the price.

The relative cheapness of CDs means that these are fast becoming a throw away storage device. For example, many people will choose to make a CD copy of a music CD to keep in their car. This copy may not be looked after as well as the original CD, but if damaged, the low cost represents a small financial implication and a second copy can be easily made.

1.3 Types of information access and storage devices

Handheld device

These are smaller portable devices that can either be held in the hand or worn. Examples include smartphones (mobile phones which include aspects of computer functionality, including internet access), smartwatches (e.g. iWatch; FitBit), eBook readers (used to read digital versions of books, e.g. Kindles) and small tablets (smaller versions of tablet computers, e.g. iPads).

Portable devices

Portable devices can be easily transported. Laptops are computers that only differ from desktop machines because of their portability, while tablet devices are as portable as laptops, but typically have less processing power.

Fixed devices

Fixed devices are not designed to be portable. They include desktop computers, which may be considered the traditional form of computer, smart TVs, which are televisions that include aspects of computer functionality, and games consoles, which are specialised computers designed primarily for playing games.

Shared devices

Shared devices may be accessed by more than one user at a time. For example, a database server is a computer that runs and provides database services for other computers. Data centres are usually commercial operations that provide access to the internet and a non-stop internet presence for clients who would otherwise not be able to afford it, while cloud storage devices (e.g. Dropbox) allow users to store data and information remotely on the internet.

Characteristics and purpose

Many of the characteristics of information storage and access devices are the same as those described in LO1.2.

Other characteristics include the following.

- Processing power (the amount of calculations that can be completed in a fixed period of time).
- Versatility (the ability of a device to complete different tasks). Games consoles, for example, used to focus simply on games playing, but recently have become more versatile by offering services that may be associated with desktop computers.
- Storage capacity (the amount of data that can be stored on the device).

Information access and storage devices can have different purposes. The main focus of games consoles is clearly on playing video games. Desktop and laptop computers, for which the main difference is their portability, are powerful devices with a high processing power and so may be used as media devices, to support office operations, or as personal computers, where they combine office-type tasks with internet access and games playing. These devices also usually benefit from a large storage capacity.

Handheld devices and tablets tend to be used for tasks that do not require high processing power. They are therefore excellent for accessing the internet and some games playing, but are not suitable for complex processing tasks, such as running databases.

Advantages and disadvantages

Advantages and disadvantages relate to the functionality and characteristics of each device. For example, a portable device may be used anywhere but may not offer sufficient processing power, while a high-powered desktop machine is limited to one location and so would be unsuitable for someone who regularly worked away from the office.

GROUP ACTIVITY

(30 minutes)

In groups, research the advantages and disadvantages of each of the storage devices described in LO1.3.

Explain the information as a presentation.

1.4 The internet

Originally based on text and a few images, the internet now also conveys information via videos and sound and many other forms of information.

A network of interconnected networks, spanning the world

Networks are made when computers and other devices are connected. Most organisations organise their computers together to form a network and have one point of access from that network to the internet. Therefore, the internet may be considered to be a number of networks, each joined to other networks. Due to the global spread of computer technology, this may therefore be considered a worldwide network of computers.

Internet connections

Type of connection

Connections to the internet can be made in different ways. For example, copper-cable is based on the electrical conductivity of copper and is still the most popular form of connectivity due to its low cost. Optical-fibre uses strands of glass or plastic instead of copper and data is transferred as pulses of light, rather than electrical charges.

GROUP ACTIVITY

(30 minutes)

Research into four of these types of internet access:

- dial-up
- broadband
- fixed broadband
- fixed wireless
- satellite
- wireless hotspots
- mobile phones.

Describe each method and say how it would be used and by whom.

Present your findings to the rest of the group.

Characteristics

Different types of internet connections have different characteristics. For example:

- The speed of data transfer can differ for different internet connections. Copper-cable, for example, has a lower bandwidth than fibre-optic and is, therefore, a slower means of connection.
- Range is the distance over which a signal can be sent on each type of connection. Satellites are able to send signals from the boundaries of space, while microwave can only send to devices that are in direct line-of-sight.
- Data differences: because of the high frequency used, microwaves, for example, can carry a large amount of data (approximately 30 times the capacity of other forms of radio transmission).

1.5 World wide web (www) technologies

Types of www technology networks

Although they are closely linked, the internet and world wide web (www or web) are not the same thing. The internet is a global network of connected computers. The www is formed by the web pages on the internet – the internet is used to access the web. When it was developed, the web used three main technologies to ensure that it could be used and accessed by all computers connected to the internet – the hypertext transfer protocol (HTTP), URL and HTML. They create www technologies like intranets and extranets. Table 2.1 describes these technologies.

Table 2.1 Types of www technology

www technology	Description	Characteristics	Example of purpose
Internet	Worldwide network of interconnected networks	**Public** **Open access**	A web page on the internet provides customers with access to information they need and so can be seen as supporting the marketing process.
Intranet	A network that is not connected to the internet and is only available to those within an organisation (e.g. a business or school). Intranets hold information needed by those who are inside the organisation, but which is not intended for wider distribution.	**Private** **Closed access**	Can be used to provide resources that are only needed by employees or should not be shared with the general public, such as sales information
Extranet	A website that provides restricted access to resources for an authorised set of users from outside the organisation	**Private** **Shared access**	Can be used to provide access to a supplier for online ordering.

INDEPENDENT ACTIVITY

(30 minutes)

One of the founding principles of the world wide web was Tim Berners-Lee's insistence that the www should be based on cross-platform, open source, software.

You have been asked to write a short article explaining how the growth and success of the www was affected by the use of cross-platform and open source software.

Research the terms 'cross-platform' and 'open source'.

Write a short magazine article explaining the impact of these decisions.

1.6 Information formats

Information on the internet comes in many different formats.

Web pages

These are the fundamental information format on the internet. Web pages may be static, which means that they remain constant unless edited by an author, or dynamic, which means that the web page is built afresh whenever loaded, based on criteria set by the web server. This means that, theoretically, the web page could appear differently to a user or different users every time it is opened.

Blogs

Blogs or 'weblogs' were originally personal web pages on which the owner comments about aspects of their own lives. To some extent, these were originally online diaries. More recently there has been a rise in themed blogs where individuals report on areas of interest such as fashion, literature and politics.

Blogs are now also being used by organisations to demonstrate their expertise by passing on content and information to followers.

Podcasts

A podcast can be a sound file or sound and video file that can either be downloaded to a device or played online. It comes in chunks or episodes. True podcasts are usually created as stand-alone presentations in their own right, and are not based on material that may already have been presented in other formats, and are often made as part of a series. However, some radio programmes are also converted into a 'best bits' podcast, or made available as a whole programme after it has been broadcast.

As well as being convenient, the ability to access such resources at any time creates a bank of searchable materials that can support academic research.

Streamed audio and video

Streamed audio and video is a relatively new feature on the internet and, due to the high bandwidth required to stream such features as they would appear on more traditional formats, have come about as networking and processing technologies have improved.

Formats can include streamed real-time radio and television, as well as catch up shows, where content may be accessed after it appeared 'live' on its original format. YouTube is a great video source that you have probably used. Spotify is an example of a music streaming (audio) service.

Social media channels

Social media channels are those sites such as Twitter, Facebook, LinkedIn and forums and discussion boards that allow users to interact, share comments and views and generally 'be social'.

As stores of information, they offer huge potential. The fact that they hold the comments and views of many users means that they represent a huge source of data that can be used for marketing purposes.

Document stores

Online document stores are also a relatively new feature on the internet. These sites are what is also called 'cloud storage' and include sites such as Google Docs, Dropbox and OneDrive.

Files can be uploaded to and downloaded from such sites, or updated locally on a personal computer and then automatically synced to the cloud.

RSS feeds

An RSS (rich site summary) feed is a small amount of information that may only be relevant for a few moments (such as the announcement of a flash sale), or may be an announcement or advert for an upcoming event. The format enables many small messages to be sent easily and so any one who receives RSS feeds may receive many during the course of a day.

Purpose

The purpose of each format should be obvious. RSS feeds, for example, can be used to inform recipients of bigger events which may then be supported by information on websites or blogs.

Blogs could hold similar information to that found on a website, but are presented in a more personalised manner, while the information held on either could also be on a file held in a document store

Accessibility

Each type of information format offers different degrees of accessibility. A file on a document site may be a synopsis of a streamed TV episode and so presents the information in a shortened form that is quicker to read than watching the whole episode. Alternatively, the visual nature of the original TV source could make the information more accessible. Many people like blogs because they are informal and this builds up almost a personal relationship with the reader, while the short and sharp nature of an RSS feed allows a message to be sent that is, by definition, short and to the point.

1.7 Advantages

For individuals

The internet has many advantages for individuals. Communications have been revolutionised and the chatty letter that 30 years ago was sent by surface mail has now been replaced by the email, for example. This has led to a huge increase in the speed that information may be sent between individuals.

Social media has led to an increased likelihood that friends stay in contact. Working relationships can be made more efficient, as social media lends itself to online conversations which are almost in real time. One impact of this is that remote workers are able to develop close working relationships with others with whom, traditionally, they would have had little contact.

The availability of data and information online has also had a huge impact on the knowledge available to us. While sites such as Wikipedia are not regarded as reliable for academic research, they are nevertheless great starting points for more in-depth research, or places where interesting facts can be researched for fun.

Finally, the convenience of the internet should not be overlooked; for example, being able to pay bills and check bank accounts from any device and at any time of the day.

For organisations

Taken as a whole, the internet is one huge store and source of information. It offers organisations the opportunity to transfer information across the world at a speed that was previously totally impossible (e.g. via websites or financial transactions). Not only can this information be transferred quickly, but this can also be achieved at a relatively low cost.

1.8 Disadvantages

For individuals

Alongside the advantages, there are also disadvantages. The amount of personal information shared daily on social media sites, for example, means that identity theft is increasing. To many people, the cost of accessing the internet can be a problem, as can be the poor quality of the connection and the impact it has on their ability to access information that requires a high bandwidth.

For some, the internet can be a source of distraction. In schools, students working on the internet may be distracted away from their work by games, video streaming sites or social media. Having too much information available can also be stressful, as it may be difficult to distinguish the most useful information.

The internet has also introduced cyber-bullying, when it can be harder to avoid bullies than in person, with sometimes devastating results.

For organisations

High-quality websites need to be created and maintained. This is not only time consuming but also costly. Online data stores, just like any other file storage system, need maintaining. Again, this is costly and also could result in the wrong information being deleted.

The internet also offers some people more of an opportunity to take action against an organisation. Websites can get hacked and data can get stolen. As well as having a cost impact, such attacks can influence the reputation of the organisation. Even when an attack has not taken place, the protection that must be put in place can be costly, as well as requiring specialist staff.

> **KNOW IT**
> 1 Compare the characteristics of digital and optical media.
> 2 What is meant by the term 'mutability'?
> 3 Identify one similarity and one difference between an intranet and an extranet.
> 4 'The internet is everyone connected to everyone else.' Explain this statement.
> 5 Describe two advantages and one disadvantage to an organisation of using the internet to distribute data.

LO2 Understand the styles, classification and the management of global information

(10 minutes)

How many different types of data do you receive during a day? Create a mind map of the sources from which you receive information on a typical school or college day and the sources from which you receive information on a day over the weekend.

Try to explain any differences in the type of data you receive at school or college and the data you receive out of school or college.

2.1 Information styles and their uses

Text

Text (written format) is the simplest format in which to keep information. However, different character sets are used in different parts of the world. This text, for example, is written in western character set. Other character sets include Cyrillic, which is used in Eastern Europe and parts of Asia, and Arabic, which is used in areas where Arabic is spoken.

Graphic

Diagrams are probably the most obvious examples of graphics, as they are usually intended to provide instructions or convey knowledge. Logos represent an organisation and also convey information. For example, some logos contain the organisation's name (e.g. Kellogg's or Google) while others are represented without words (e.g. the Olympic rings, Twitter or Firefox). Either way, they are designed to visually convey certain information about the brand (e.g. the Firefox wraps around the world, suggesting global coverage and passion), which may be received subconsciously.

Video

Information is conveyed as a visual and audio presentation. Seeing others performing tasks, for example, or showing examples of what they are talking about, is usually more engaging than just listening to a person talk about their work. A video of how a petrol engine works is likely to be far more interesting and informative than a verbal description.

Animated graphic

An animated graphic is an image where elements move and change. They offer an advantage over a video, as they can include step-by-step instructions, as well as text. Individual scenes can be shown for longer on the animated graphic than they would on video, so that the full process can be seen. Scenes can zoom in, or give exploded views, so that what is happening can be seen in greater detail.

Audio

Audio refers to any recorded sound and can therefore include the spoken word, as well as music. The tradition of using songs to tell a story is not a modern phenomenon and there are many examples, from folk through to opera, of important political or social stories being told through music. Music can also be used to help check what (for example) guitar exam pieces should sound like, or as a medium to remember facts like the order of the planets in the solar system.

One clear benefit of presenting information as audio is that it becomes accessible to those who are visually impaired.

Numerical

Numerical information is presented as numbers. This includes financial information, such as profit and loss accounts, or statistical information, such as the average age of a class of students.

However, other information may be shown as numbers. Dates and times are also presented as numbers and so are included within this area of information.

Braille text

Braille is a tactile form of writing that uses dots on a page and is read by touch. Because set patterns of dots are used to represent individual letters, braille may be considered another form of text or language. Braille is capable of holding the same information as any other form of written text. It can't be replicated electronically, but braille printers can replicate written text for braille readers.

Tactile images

As well as braille, information may be presented in other tactile ways. For example, a viewer can feel certain images and experience their shapes through touch, rather than just by sight. Tactile imagery can portray any of the features of visual images except colour.

NASA's project to create tactile images from images captured by the Hubble Space Telescope is a good example of how images that would not otherwise be accessible have been made available to people who cannot explore them by sight.

Subtitles

Subtitles allow deaf viewers to access audio information. Films, interviews and other news items can also be translated via subtitles.

Boolean

Boolean information is any information that can only be in one of two forms. Therefore, the answer to the question 'is the dog alive' can only be 'yes' or 'no' and so is Boolean.

Tables and spreadsheets

Numerical data may be held in many forms. Using a database or a spreadsheet means that the data can be analysed by inputting queries, for example, and patterns identified.

Charts and graphs

Charts and graphs present data in a more visual manner than lists of text by using lines or boxes. Many people find charts and graphs easier to use when identifying trends or comparisons.

2.2 Information classification

More than one of the following descriptions of information can be applied to one piece of information.

Sensitive

Sensitive information should not be generally available, usually if it could cause harm if it was released. This definition works for business information as well as it does for personal information. An example of sensitive personal information would be medical records. This information is clearly personal and so should not be generally available.

Non-sensitive

An example of non-sensitive information business information would be the addresses of shops in the chain, or of the head office.

Private

This is information about individuals or organisations. This information includes addresses, phone numbers, nationality, gender and marital status. It is covered by the Data Protection Act and so would need to be held in a manner that was legal. Any other information that was not personal would not be covered by this Act.

Public

This is information about government and other publicly owned organisations.

Personal

Personal information is private information about individuals. e.g. an individual's phone number.

Business

Business information is information about businesses, e.g. the annual sales figures of an organisation.

Confidential

This is private information that should be kept private. This is a higher degree of restriction than sensitive information, e.g. a report about the needs of an individual student in a school. This information would be needed for some staff, but not for all and definitely not for the other students.

Classified

This is public information that should be kept private. e.g. the NHS patient database.

Partially and completely anonymised

Information that is completely anonymised has had any information that could link the record to the source, or the person or organisation it's about, removed; while partially anonymised information has had some information removed.

Impacts on different stakeholders

Stakeholders are those who have an interest in or are impacted by, the actions of an organisation. Stakeholders can be internal (those who are inside the organisation) or external (those who are not inside the organisation).

Different holders of information have to take account of these classifications. For example, confidential personal information needs to be held more securely than non-confidential information.

2.3 Quality of information

Characteristics

Information can have many characteristics, for example:

- Valid information is useful, generally because it fits the need to which it is being put. There are many reasons why information can be considered valid. For example, information should be on time and accurate.
- Biased information presents a one-sided view. It may be correct, but ignores any other information that could present an alternative view, e.g. information about a house that is for sale may focus on the positive features – such as the new kitchen – but ignores the fact that the house lies below the flight path to an airport.
- Comparable information can be compared with similar information, e.g. comparing the annual sales of two organisations of a similar size but in different countries.

Importance of good quality information to stakeholders

The more reliable the information, the better the quality of the decision as it provides a clear focus for objectives. For example, research information could be the basis for innovation, while sales information could be used to inform strategic decisions. If this information is not accurate, or biased, then the decisions made are based on false or biased information which would then undermine the effectiveness of any decisions made.

Consequences of poor quality information on stakeholders

Poor quality information can lead to bad decisions. The impact could be a failed project, or a missed opportunity, but the longer term impact could be that the information being given by the organisation may be wrong, or that the organisation's reputation may be damaged. For example, if a research project interviewed a small number of people, the conclusions that are drawn may not be applicable to the general public and so a new product, for example, may not sell as well as intended.

2.4 Information management

Information management is the process of controlling information so it is used effectively.

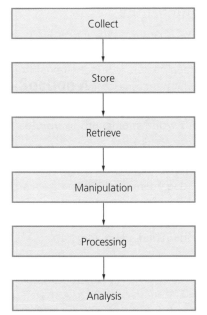

▲ Figure 2.2 The information management process

Collecting, storing and retrieving

Information needs to be collected, stored and, if it is going to be easily used, available for retrieval. A database store allows information to be collected via a form, stored as records and then retrieved and sorted using queries. For example, if you wanted to join a swimming club, you could fill in a form on its website. This information would be stored on its members' database and a search to find all members who have joined in the last seven days would bring up the email address you supplied.

Manipulating and processing

This is the stage where information is processed for analysis. The swimming club could produce a graph showing how many members joined for each of the preceding 12 months.

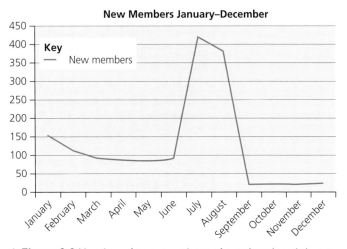

▲ Figure 2.3 Number of new members of a swimming club over the past 12 months

Analysing

At this stage, the information is looked at so that patterns can be identified. In Figure 2.3, there was a large increase in members in July, with virtually no members joining in September. This information is useful on its own, but if these dates linked with other events, such as a June campaign to get new members, this information would suggest the campaign was successful.

Securing

Information needs to be kept securely in order to protect it. Sensitive or confidential information could be protected from access by others by encryption. Information needed to run the business could be backed up so that it cannot be lost. For example, the swimming club would need to keep members' direct debit information securely, possibly on an encrypted hard drive.

Transmitting

Once information has been processed, it may need to be transmitted within or outside of an organisation. For example, a student's school report is created by collecting information from tutors, then analysed by one tutor who looks for patterns such as high achievement or poor behaviour, and then sent home to parents. The swimming club newsletter may have monthly articles that need to be collated before newsletters are emailed or printed and posted to members.

Impact on individuals and organisations

Processing information places responsibilities on individuals and organisations. Extra security has costs, such as extra servers, anti-virus software and back up locations. However, these costs are offset against the benefits gained by processing information, which includes the impact of the knowledge gained.

LO3 Understand the use of global information and the benefits to individuals and organisations

3.1 Data versus information

Information is in context, data is not

The difference between data and information is context. The numbers 7, 11, 6 and 5 on their own are meaningless. They could refer to anything. However, if one is told that they are shoe sizes within a family, this context gives them meaning.

Data is information that has been coded and structured in some way, ready for processing, storage or transmission

During research, when an interviewer asks an interviewee a question, the answer is provided in the context of the question. This information from the answer is combined with information from other interviewees and is no longer the information about each of a series of individuals. Instead, it is information about the group of interviewees as a whole.

In this way, this information becomes data again. For example, the question may have asked people for their favourite fruit. Each individual answer was information, but 140 'apples', 160 'bananas', 75 'pears' and 3 'kumquats' is data, especially when 'apples' was option 1 (and so '1' was recorded), bananas were option 2 and so on.

In this way, information becomes data ready for processing into 'the bigger picture'. Once it is processed, and a new context applied, it becomes new information.

3.2 Categories of information used by individuals

Communication

A simple email home while on holiday, saying how your day has gone, includes information. What you have sent is clearly information, but other information may range from comments about the weather to the fact that the email was sent at 4 a.m. local time.

Education and training

Education and training generates a lot of information. We have already mentioned school reports, but could also talk about lists of grades provided to a student by their tutors. This could be paper based, but could also be stored online in an intranet, for example.

Entertainment

There are some superb films, but some are terrible. Websites such as Imdb and Rotten Tomatoes provide a synopsis of each film they list, as well as overall scores based on the views of people who have seen the film. These can be used to plan which films to watch.

It is worth noting that the score given to a film is based on the people who have seen it and so can change as more people report back. When a new film comes out, the first people to watch it are those who are most keen to do so; their reviews are likely to be more positive than those without a special interest. This is a good example of bias.

Planning

Many people use shared electronic diaries to help them plan their lives. In a work context, these enable colleagues to arrange meetings on days when others are available, while members of a family can see what commitments individuals have and plan accordingly.

PAIRS ACTIVITY

(40 minutes)

Create a database to store information about the gigs you been to. Use this database to record the data about the last five gigs each of you attended.

Financial

Banks and other organisations are able to provide us all with a lot of information. Not only can they simply tell us how much money we have in our accounts, so that we can plan our expenditure or savings, but they can also group our expenditure so that we can see the sort of goods and services we are buying. This can be a very useful way of managing our budget.

Research

Information can be stored and, if searchable, used again. Other people's experiences of holiday locations, disasters when cooking or advice on why your car may not be working are all available through research and can be extremely useful.

Location dependent

One benefit of storing information in a searchable format is that parameters, such as location, can be applied. This could be as simple as searching online for 'Chiropractors near here', which would bring up a list of local practitioners. This does not mean that chiropractors do not exist anywhere else, but merely limits those that you are shown so that you do not have to sift through everyone on the data store.

Benefits and limitations

Most information is presented for a clear and beneficial purpose. This benefit may only be felt when the information is accessed and used.

For example, a student is given an idea of their likely grades to show them in which subjects they are making good progress. If the student uses this information to choose subjects to continue studying, this is a benefit. However, information can also have limitations. The raw list of grades may hide the amount of effort that has gone into improving one area, even if that is not reflected by showing a top grade.

3.3 Categories of information used by organisations

Knowledge management and creation

As organisations grow, they need to employ staff to carry out specific tasks, which includes access to and use of information.

Knowledge management is the process of bringing together all of the information held by an organisation to gain a better insight. For example, one branch of the organisation may be based in a key market and hold specific information that could be used by other branches. If this information is not shared, mistakes could be made or opportunities missed. By managing the information so that it is available to all, it is hoped that such mistakes may be avoided and opportunities exploited.

Management information systems (MIS)

A management information system is designed to provide key information needed to aid the management process in making strategic decisions. These systems therefore present an overview of information, rather than every detail.

The clarity that can be achieved by presenting key information, or information that has been gathered by analysing many sources, leads to decisions that are based on the 'big picture' rather than focusing on small items of information.

An example would be the level of sickness over the previous 30 days that might be held in the individual personnel record of each member of staff. The nature of the illness, or the names of each individual involved, may become important at some stage, but an initial decision about the need to use agency staff, for example, can be based simply on the overall figures.

Marketing, promotion and sales

Organisations use information as part of the process of selling. For example, sales figures may identify an increase in sales of a product in a specific region. This could be exploited via the use of targeted marketing, so that sales in this region could grow even further. Information gathered from customer loyalty cards can provide information about purchasing patterns of key groups, such as those aged under 26. The use of these customer loyalty cards can also be linked to shops in which they were used and so organisations can also analyse by geographical areas. Such information is clearly valuable in planning marketing campaigns, for example.

Financial analysis and modelling

Sales can be measured by units sold or by the revenue raised. Measurements based on the value of sales is termed financial analysis and can be used to show information such as the top selling brands or periods during the year when sales are high. This information can be used to create models of expected customer behaviour. For example, if sales figures for a region show that 10 million tins of beans were sold, if the population of the region grew by 25%, modelling would suggest that sales of beans would also grow by 25%. However, if other factors were important, such as that people may buy fewer beans and switch their demand to more expensive products as their income grew, this could also be included in the model.

Contact management

This is the management of all contact between a business and other people. As an example, software could be used to hold bookings for a children's entertainer. The information held would be the actual date and time of the booking, as well as other information, such as the name of the client and their telephone number.

Decision making

Information is researched so that a decision may be made; sales figures are gathered so that future plans may be generated and contacts are managed so that the correct equipment is available for a specific event. Decision making is therefore the fundamental rationale for information use. These decisions could range from whether or not to turn the sprinklers on to water the grass at the Head Office to whether or not to start selling in Bulgaria. Each decision will be based on separate sets of information.

Internal and external communication

In some cases, the information presented is the same. So, for example, Christmas opening hours could be shared with colleagues (internal communication) and customers (external communication).

However, other information, such as the location of a secret testing station, may only be intended for internal communications, while information about the launch of a new product may be intended for customers.

Big data

Big data is large volumes of data – both structured and unstructured – that inundates a business on a day-to-day basis. Big data can be analysed for insights that lead to better decisions and strategic business moves.

Benefits and limitations

Effective management and use of information can be key to the success of a business. Contact management can ensure that an organisation keeps its appointments and provides the service that has been booked. Sales data can be used to plan future campaigns and to identify specific markets into which the organisation should move, while a well-organised MIS can present management with clear and concise information allowing decisions to be made based on an analysis of all of the information available.

The limitations of these information systems come from the choice of information that is taken into account when they are created, the quality of the analysis that is applied and the extent to which the information is presented at the time it is required. If either of the first two factors are not met, the information presented will be incorrect, while if the information is not available when it is needed, the decisions made will be based largely on guess work.

3.4 Stages of data analysis

See also Unit 7 LO1 (page 197).

1. Identify the need

This is where the objectives of any data analysis program will be set. By the end of this stage, it should be clear what is hoped to be learnt from the project. This would include the information that is required from the completed project.

2. Define scope

This stage defines the restrictions on the project. For example, the overall budget may be set, or times by which the information must be available identified.

3. Identify potential sources

The planners of a project should be able to identify a wide range of sources and ensure that the information gathered is suitable, provides enough information to cover the objectives and is unbiased.

The actual source of data depends on the project. For example, customer surveys can be a good source of opinion about how well the organisation is meeting their needs.

4. Source and select information

This is the stage where the information is gathered and the best is selected. The gathering process use existing information; for example, sales figures or population growth projections.

The selection process is intended to exclude any information that may not be suitable. For example, an interviewer's poor interpersonal skills could have a negative effect on the answers given by some interviewees, making the results unreliable or inaccurate. This information would skew the conclusions based on that **data set**. In such a case, it would be better if this information was ignored.

KEY TERM

Data set – a group of related data.

5. Select the most appropriate tools

See also Unit 7 LO1.2 (page 197).

As we have seen, information may be presented in many different ways. Charts and graphs present information visually, so that patterns may be identified. Regression analysis considers how changing only one of many different variables affects an outcome. For example, when we talked about the possible impact of an increased population on sales of tins of beans (LO3.3), we mentioned that income may also have an effect. Regression analysis would try to model the impact of a change in population, while holding other possible factors as they were before. This information is generally presented graphically.

An example of regression analysis could be to measure the impact of an increase in price on the sales of a product, while at the same time holding all other variables that could impact on sales, such as advertising, customer income and price of competitors' products, constant. This results in a clear relationship between the one factor that has changed and a measurable outcome, such as sales figures.

Trend analysis can be presented in many ways, but it attempts to present findings over time, so that behaviour patterns over time, rather than at one precise moment, are identified.

6. Process and analyse data

This is the stage at which the data that has been collected is entered into software and analysed. For example, data could be entered into a spreadsheet and a graph produced to show the information visually.

7. Record and store information

This is the stage at which any report into the findings is written. This includes all of the results that have been processed.

8. Share results

This final stage of the process is where the results are published so that stakeholders may inspect them. This may be in the form of a written, printed report, or could be pages on a website, for example.

3.5 Data analysis tools

See also Unit 7 LO1.2 (page 197).

Appointments 5 February		
Date of App ▾	Time ▾	Reason ▾
05/02/2016	09:20:00	Follow up
05/02/2016	09:40:00	Referal
05/02/2016	10:00:00	Referal
05/02/2016	10:20:00	Patient request
05/02/2016	10:40:00	Patient request
05/02/2016	11:00:00	Patient request

Data tables

A well-structured database uses separate data tables for different types of information. For example, a database of patients would have one table that just held information about patients, and a separate table that held information about doctors, while a third would hold a table of which patients have seen which doctors and on which date.

A data table can show patterns in information. For example, Figure 2.4 shows the results of a query linking appointments for one day at a doctor's surgery and the reason for the appointment.

A number of different patterns can be observed. First, most of the patients have booked their appointment in advance. Second, the majority of patients have reported 'flu' as their reason for the visit.

Visualisation of data

This is a tool used to help people understand the significance of the data by putting it into a visual context. Patterns, trends and correlations are much easier to recognise when data visualisation is used.

Trend and pattern identification

This is similar to the visualisation of data where you would use a comparison line graph to analysis sales over a month period for, say, the last five years.

Data cleaning

An important part of data management is making sure that the data that is held is relevant and up-to-date. Data cleaning is the process of removing or improving out-of-date data. For example, if you deliver milk and someone has not ordered from you for the past two years, they may not do so in the future so you could remove their details from the database.

Similarly, periodic checks to ensure that the correct address is held for each customer is also good practice. In some cases, the same customer could be recorded with two separate addresses, so contacting the customer on both should identify which to delete.

Geographic information system/location mapping

The ability to track the geographical location of staff or items that are being shipped around the world can be a real benefit for organisations. Staff can be tracked so that delivery times can be confirmed with customers, while individual items can be tracked so that they may be found if lost. Customers can track the path of a courier in real time and thus know when they may expect a delivery and so plan their day.

INDEPENDENT ACTIVITY 👤

(40 minutes)

Use data analysis tools to analyse the data held in your database of gigs.

Present your results to the group.

3.6 Information system structure

Open and closed systems, characteristics, benefits and limitations

An open system can interact with other systems to exchange information even if they have different platforms. A closed system cannot. One of the disadvantages of having an open system is that it is a wonderful playground for hackers. A closed system is more secure.

> **KNOW IT**
>
> 1 Describe the difference between data and information.
> 2 Identify one benefit of each of the following uses of information to an organisation that sells fruit:
>   a) Planning what fruit will be sold on particular days.
>   b) Education of staff about types of fruit.
>   c) Research new varieties of fruit.
> 3 Identify the information that would be required by an organisation wishing to model potential sales growth rates for the next 12 months.
> 4 Describe how creating a future sales growth model benefits the organisation.
> 5 Explain the term 'regression analysis' and describe how it can be used as an analytical tool.
> 6 Produce a table describing the benefits and limitations of open and closed systems.

LO4 Understand the legal and regulatory framework governing the storage and use of global information

4.1 UK legislation and regulation relating to the storage and use of information

> **GETTING STARTED**
>
> **(10 minutes)**
>
> How aware are you of legislation and other restrictions on the use of information?
>
> Your digital footprint is the trail you leave when you use the internet and other digital services, and which others can follow.
>
> As a group, discuss steps you have taken to reduce your digital footprint. How has legislation affected how your digital footprint?

Current UK legislation and regulation

A number of UK Acts of Parliament impact on the storage and use of global information.

Data Protection Act (DPA) 1998

The Data Protection Act governs the way in which organisations collect, process and store private data. There are eight key principles:

- Data should be processed fairly and lawfully.
- Personal data can only be obtained for clearly stated purposes.
- The amount of data collected and stored should not be more than required.
- Personal data should be accurate.
- Personal data should only be used for the purpose for which it was collected.
- Personal data should only be processed within the rights of the data subject.
- Personal data should be protected from theft or unlawful access.
- Personal data cannot be transferred to anywhere outside of the EU unless the country to which it is being transferred has the same level of legal protection for data as set by the DPA.

Regulation of Investigatory Powers Act (RIPA) 2000

This Act covers the power of public bodies to carry out investigations and surveillance. This includes surveillance of communications.

Table 2.2 Types of surveillance

Type of power	Typical use
Interception of communication	Reading post, email or phone tapping
Use of communications data	Investigate the type of communication used but not its content
Directed surveillance	Following people
Covert human intelligence sources	Undercover agents, informers
Intrusive surveillance	Bugging houses, tracking devices on cars

Protection of Freedoms Act 2012

This is a wide reaching Act that ranges from strengthening the Freedom of Information Act through to how DNA, fingerprints and footprints should be stored, handled and destroyed.

Privacy and Electronic Communications Regulations 2003 (amended 2011)

This Act governs the ways organisations can use electronic communications to contact customers. The core theme is privacy, including the right to be able to relax without interruption at home, so for example, not being bothered by unsolicited emails or phone calls.

Freedom of Information Act 2000

This Act provides the public with the 'right to access' information about the activities carried out by public authorities. As a general rule, the Act defines public authorities as organisations that are funded by the state. However, charities, for example, are exempt.

Computer Misuse Act 1990

This Act basically covers hacking, specifically:

- unauthorised access to computer material
- unauthorised access to computer systems with intent to commit another offence
- unauthorised modification of computer material.

Information Commissioner's Office (ICO) codes of practice

These codes of practice interpret the Data Protection Act and apply them to specific practices. For example, there is a code of practice for the use of CCTV, including when it is acceptable to use automatic number plate recognition software.

Copyright, Designs and Patents Act 1988

This Act provides the person who created a piece of art or music, or who designed or invented a particular technology, with control over what they have created as well as restricting the rights of others to use it.

Equality Act (EQA) 2011

The Equality Act of 2011 combined a number of previous Acts into one overall Act intended to protect UK citizens from being discriminated against. As well as bringing other Acts into one overall Act, it also strengthened some protections that had already existed.

Impact and consequences of UK legislation and regulation on organisations operating in the UK and the way they handle information and individuals' personal data

The impacts of UK legislation on holders of information have been huge. Individually, for example, the Data Protection Act has meant that organisations have had to review and improve their data security. The Privacy and Electronic Communications Act has meant that organisations have had to change their working practice and, in the case of cookies, warn visitors when their websites use cookies.

Actions that can be taken by organisations to comply with legislation and regulatory requirements

See also Unit 3, LO3, page 97.

At its most simple, information holders need to do what the Act requires. Therefore, many organisations have decided to keep all personal data they hold within the EU, for example. However, many call centres based in other parts of the world, like India, need access to personal data about EU citizens. Therefore, to comply with the Act, India has data protection laws that match those applied within the EU.

GROUP ACTIVITY

(40 minutes)

Research each of the Acts mentioned above. Describe the impact of each Act on information holders.

Create a presentation of your information.

4.2 Global information protection legislation and regulation

Regulation relating to data protection outside the UK

The eighth principle of the Data Protection Act governs whether data can be transferred between countries. As we have seen, the data protection laws in India are sufficient for data and information covered by the UK Data Protection Act and so data may be stored and processed there. However, other countries in the world do not have the same level of data security and so data may not be transferred to the country.

Data may be transferred anywhere within the EU, as each country's level of data protection is equivalent to that of the UK.

The United States Department of Commerce has set up a 'Safe Harbour Scheme' that, if complied with, gives sufficient protection for UK data to be stored and processed in the United States. However, if the intended receiving organisation has not signed up to the scheme, data cannot be transferred unless it forms part of a passenger name record, for example on a plane. This covers the transfer of data between EU airlines and the US Department of Homeland Security.

If data needs to be transferred outside the EU and the receiving country does not have the same level of data cover, the sender has to assess whether adequate safeguards can be applied to the data to bring the data protection level up to an acceptable standard.

Comparison between data protection legislation and regulation in different countries

GROUP ACTIVITY

(40 minutes)

Table 2.3 shows a list of countries. For each country, compare the data protection legislation in that country with the data protection available in the United Kingdom. You might find it useful to copy the table so that you can make more space for writing.

Table 2.3 Comparing data laws in other countries

Country	Name of applicable laws	Comparison of these data protection laws in this country with those in the UK
USA		
France		
Indonesia		
Australia		
Canada		
South Africa		
Pakistan		

UN Convention on the Rights of Persons with Disabilities (UNCRPD)

The UN Convention on the Rights of Persons with Disabilities includes a specific recognition of the right of access to information systems (article 9) as well as the right to use digital means to express opinions (article 21).

For example, websites have to be planned so that they can be used by those with disabilities. The use of Alt tags on images, so that website reading software can say what an image is, has allowed people with visual impairments to access sites more easily.

4.3 Green IT

Global requirements on organisations and individuals

Green IT is an attempt to make computing more eco-friendly. This can influence the materials that make computers, the manner in which they are manufactured, the way in which they are manufactured, how they are transported and how they are eventually disposed of.

Many local initiatives recycle computers for use by others. This is an example of organisations taking a global awareness viewpoint in an attempt to extend the working life of computers beyond the relatively short one that business may dictate.

United Nations Climate Change Summits

These annual meetings discuss climate change and ways in which the threat can be reduced and managed. Their focus has been on the reduction of carbon footprints across the world and in doing so they have considered the use and disposal of computers and computing equipment.

UK Government policy

In 2011, the Greening Government ICT strategy made a commitment to adopt more green policies across government departments. The use of cloud storage and shared services were identified as areas in which the government could reduce its carbon footprint.

By adopting the use of cloud storage, for example, it was hoped that computers would be used more efficiently, because the need for each section of government to have its own data storage facilities would be replaced by the use of online storage which would, because of the reduction in number of individual computers and storage required, be a cheaper and more efficient use of resources.

PAIRS ACTIVITY

(30 minutes)

Research and create a presentation showing how one named event and one named organisation have taken action to reduce their carbon footprint..

Reducing carbon footprint

Many organisations, events and individuals now accept the importance of reducing their **carbon footprint**.

Purpose

If Green IT is successful, then the negative impact of IT is reduced and the climate benefits. The reduction in emissions that lead to climate change should reduce the pressure on the ecosystem, while any reduction in pollution or non-degradable waste allows us to create a more sustainable society in which future generations may prosper.

Benefits

If the working life of computers can be extended, or the **digital footprint** of individuals, events and organisations reduced, the production of greenhouse gases and the rate of climate change are reduced.

There is also a positive impact on the reputation of organisations, many of whom have made their commitment to reducing their carbon footprint a central part of their marketing strategy. As organisations achieve their green targets, so customers tend to think more positively about their products, are more likely to buy them and increase sales.

Finally, any successful project to reduce carbon footprint reduces costs. More efficient use of energy reduces energy costs, while recycling reduces the costs of disposing of waste.

KNOW IT

1 Identify and describe four principles of the UK Data Protection Act.
2 Compare the impact of the Protection of Freedoms Act (2012) and the Freedom of Information Act (2000) on an organisation.
3 Describe three actions that an organisation can take to be considered a Green IT organisation.
4 Describe two advantages to an organisation if they adopt a Green IT policy.

GETTING STARTED

(10 minutes)

Your school or college uses data and information collected about you to write reports and references. Think about your most recent report or reference.

What information was included, what was its source and who was the intended audience?

LO5 Understand the process flow of information

5.1 Information sources and data types

Internal source

This is information that comes from within an organisation. Examples include internal financial reports, such as the level of sales being made in different markets or the cost of running the transport fleet of lorries; or market analysis, which is an internally produced report into how international and national markets are faring.

External source

This is information that comes from outside the organisation. Examples include supplier price lists, which are lists of products and the price charged for them, and financial reports from a third party, which would have the same focus as internally produced financial reports, but would be produced by someone outside the organisation.

Primary data

This is data that you collect, rather than buy from a third party. Examples include reports that have been created by employees, such as the result of a period of observation outside a cinema, counting how many males and females went in.

Secondary data

This is data that has been collected by others outside the organisation. Examples include survey results that have been collected for a different organisation (and usually for a different purpose) or factual information provided by third party, such as the prices charged by an organisation.

Qualitative data and quantitative data

The fundamental difference between these is that quantitative data is data that has been gathered by measurement, while qualitative data is data that describes (see Unit 7, 1.1, page 196. An example of quantitative data would be the number of staff working in an organisation, whereas qualitative data would be their opinion about a new initiative.

INDEPENDENT ACTIVITY

(10 minutes)

Complete Table 2.4 to show whether the data is qualitative or quantitative.

Table 2.4 Examples of qualitative and quantitative data

Data	Qualitative	Quantitative
The colour of a car		
The number of blue cars sold last year		
Results of a questionnaire gathering data about age of students attending a college		
Results of a questionnaire gathering suggestions for a new design of eco-home		
The height of a building		
Do people like chocolate?		
How many people like chocolate?		

Purpose

Different data sources provide different types of data that suit different needs. For example, secondary data can be a relatively cheap way of gathering non-specific information. If you needed to know how many people lived in a certain city, primary research would involve many hours of research so you could simply use the results of somebody else's research.

However, secondary data is probably of limited use for really focused research. Imagine a shampoo manufacturer wants to gather information on how many people would buy its new apple-scented shampoo. Secondary data may exist about sales figures for a rival's apple scented shampoo, but would that be accurate enough as a gauge for the success of the new product? It may be a good starting point, but it would not be a wholly reliable source of data on which to base a marketing and production policy.

5.2 Data flow diagrams (DFDs)

Data flow diagrams model how data flows through a system (see also Unit 7, LO4.1, page 214). An example system could be used to create termly student reports.

External entities

External entities are sources of the data that is input into the system and those to whom data that is output is sent and who are also external to the system itself. In the example we are considering, the external entities would include teaching staff (inputs) and parents (outputs). A database that held the collated reports for an individual student would be an internal entity as it is within the system.

Processes

These are ways in which the data in the system is collated. In the example, there would be one central process which would collate the scores and comments made by individual tutors into one overall report for each student.

Data stores

Data stores represent any real world store of data held in the system. This could be a computerised database, but could also be an inbox on someone's desk.

Data flows

These are the flows of data between the entities and the processes.

Standard symbols used

It is probably best to say that there is some dispute over the standard symbols used. However, the ones that are used most often are shown in the table below.

Table 2.5 Standard symbols

Symbol	Purpose
	External entity
	Process
→	Data flow
	Data store

LEVEL 0 DFD

These are sometimes called 'context diagrams' and show a data system in little detail, but allow the user to get an idea of how data flows through a system as a whole.

LEVEL 1 DFD

These are DFDs that focus on one system and are therefore in more detail than a level 0 DFD.

A common mistake with data flow diagrams is to indicate the action on data flows, not the data that is being moved. For example, someone could write 'tutors submit their comments'. This would be wrong as it is an action. The correct label would be 'comments about students', as the comments are data.

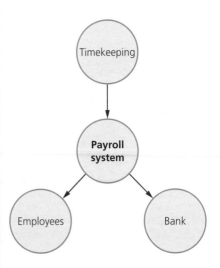

▲ **Figure 2.5** DFD with entities and flows (hi level)

Connectivity rules for drawing Level 1 DFDs

Drawing data flow diagrams can be a complicated task. However, there are some rules that make the process a little easier.

At least one input or output for each external entity

This may seem obvious, but each entity is either submitting or receiving data. If not, why are they on the DFD?

Data flows only in one direction

This causes some confusion. In this case, the confirmation is a separate form of data and the arrow has a different label.

Every data flow is labelled

Each data flow must have an arrow showing the direction of flow of the data, as well as a label identifying the data that is being transferred.

Every data flow connects to at least one process

This is another possible source of confusion. However, logically, each data flow is either going to a data store, after the data has been processed, or is coming from a data store, ready to be processed.

At least one input data flow and/or at least one output data flow for each process

In order for a system to work, data must come from somewhere at the start of the process and go somewhere at the end. However, the source of the data could be another system, so that this system is processing data created elsewhere, and the output could be to another system, which does further processing.

In the example of the student reporting system, the reports could output to an 'analysis and action' system that makes decisions about individual students based on the reports they have been given. This analysis and action system would be a separate system to the report gathering system.

Impacts affecting the flow of information in information systems

Data flow systems rarely completely fail to transfer data. Far more likely is that the flow of data is delayed. If the system is computerised, even partial system failure could result in a delay while the technology is improved.

Human error could result in data being lost or misfiled, so that it would need to be found, or simply result in data being processed in the wrong order of importance (such as where someone works on their favourite project, rather than the one that actually needs doing).

Breakdowns in working relationships can result in delays, especially where the means of transfer of data involves two people meeting. However, there could be a delay because someone put off doing a task because they do not like the person waiting for the outcome.

LO6 Understand the principles of information security

GETTING STARTED

(10 minutes)

How would you be affected if all the data held about you was stolen and used by someone else?

As a group, consider how your life would be affected if all the data held about you was:

- Stolen so that you could not get to it.
- Stolen, so that someone else could **also** use it.

6.1 Principles of information security

See also Unit 3 LO1.3 (page 89).

Confidentiality – information can only be accessed by individuals, groups or processes authorised to do so

Not only is this a key aspect of the concept of information security, but it is also a legal requirement under the Data Protection Act. It is the responsibility of the organisation to ensure that data is safe and to take measures to protect that data. These measures could be physical, such as ensuring that data is kept in a lockable cupboard, or electronic, such as restricting access to a computer network that holds data.

Integrity – information is maintained, so that it is up to date, accurate, complete and fit for purpose

This is another practical as well as legal consideration. Inaccurate data can lead to conclusions based on false information or time being wasted on phone calls to numbers that no longer exist or are no longer relevant. The requirement to maintain data is also part of the Data Protection Act.

Organisations should have a planned pattern of data maintenance. This could simply be a process of checking the data periodically, possibly by sending contacts a list of the data that is currently held about them and asking them to confirm that it is correct. Organisations should also have a culture of checking and reporting when data is inaccurate. As an example, a tutor may try to phone a parent to pass on information. If they were to find that the student's home telephone number is not correct on the school's system, that tutor should be able to pass the information on so that records may be updated.

Availability – information is always available to and usable by the individuals, groups or processes that need to use it

The challenge here is making sure that the data is available to those who need it (and in a format that they can use) and making sure that it is kept safe from unauthorised access.

One of the challenges is that if data is not easily accessible, users may decide to make their own copies. This is a security risk, as the more copies of data there are, the harder the data is to protect. Therefore, organisations need to ensure that their information systems and associated hardware and software work as intended and that staff do not feel the need to make extra copies.

6.2 Risks

Unauthorised or unintended access to data

Unauthorised access to data is any time that data is seen or used by those who should not see or use it. The reason for someone seeking to access the data could be espionage, which is for the purpose of gaining an advantage over the original data holder (such as stealing sensitive information), or as a result of having poor information management. This would include accidental access, when a member of the public finds a discarded print out, or is able to see data while a member of staff is working in a public area.

There are two possible impacts here. First, if the data is sensitive, a competitor may gain an advantage from seeing it. The second impact would be caused by a possible infringement of the Data Protection Act if the lost data included personal data.

Accidental loss of data

Accidental loss of data refers to a loss of the data itself, rather than a loss of a copy or version of the data. Therefore, in the previous example, the loss of a printout would not result in the loss of the source of the data.

First, human error can be at fault. This could be someone deleting the file or throwing away the paperwork. The second cause is a technical error or equipment fault. For example, the computer on which a database is stored could fail. This would result in loss of data if there was no backup.

A final impact would also be that the organisation will have breached the Data Protection Act if the lost data included personal information and so would be liable to prosecution.

Intentional destruction of data

This is generally seen as being motivated by a desire to harm the organisation that holds the data. Examples include computer viruses that delete or encrypt data that is held or targeted attack that involves a third party accessing the data and deleting it.

There are two options when data is lost. Either the data needs to be replaced, which could result in a loss of reputation and trust, as well as costing money, or the loss is ignored. If the loss is ignored, then any positive future impact of having the data is lost. The impact therefore depends on the relevance of the data that is lost.

As with accidental loss of data, there is also a potential impact caused by the failure to comply with the Data Protection Act.

Intentional tampering with data

Tampering with data means that the data is changed in some way, but is still available. There are a number of reasons for this. For example, a student may wish to change their exam scores and so access a teacher's laptop, or an organisation may wish to change the figures in a rival company's research.

In each case, the impact on the data-holding organisation would be that any decisions based on that data would be flawed. A secondary impact may be a negative effect on the reputation of that organisation, as they are seen as having poor data security.

6.3 Impacts

Loss of intellectual property

Intellectual property is anything that has been created by an individual. Therefore, a written report, a design for a new machine or a piece of artwork would be considered intellectual property.

The impact of its loss depends on the nature of the item taken, copied or accessed. If a hacker removed the plans for a prototype of a new product, this would have a huge negative effect.

Loss of service and access

A hacker who accesses vital log-on information could use services that you have purchased. This may result in a worsening or total loss of your own service. For example, a hacker accessing wi-fi log-on passwords could reduce bandwidth. If the hacker accessed the password and changed it to something else, the wi-fi would be inaccessible.

While at home a lost wi-fi password would be easily fixed by resetting related devices, where the service is controlled by a third party, they may have to be contacted before any passwords are reset. This would mean that the system was unusable until that organisation had been contacted and the change made.

However, if the passwords stolen were for systems that were set up internally, loss of passwords could result in a total loss of that system.

Failure in security of confidential information

If data is not kept securely, it is accessible to others. Where that data includes confidential data, the loss means that confidential data is, potentially, available to all. The impact of this depends on why the data was confidential in the first place.

Loss of information belonging to a third party

An attack on a business's servers not only impacts on the business, but also on any business or individual it holds data for. Data in the cloud is held on servers owned by other businesses so, if the organisation that loses data provides **cloud storage**, the data lost will belong to third parties.

Loss of reputation

If an organisation fails to keep data safe, they have failed to meet their legal and moral obligations and so they will be viewed negatively by many customers and potential customers, leading to lost sales and a drop in income.

Threat to national security

National security may be defined as a direct physical threat to a country. However, it could also be a threat to the financial security of the state.

Therefore, any data or information that is stolen could be a threat to national security. Clearly, the theft of the address of a random individual will be less of a threat than the theft of the design of a prototype being developed by a large UK business with international links and a multimillion-pound annual turnover, or the location of a military testing station.

Recent cases of failures of information security

Failures of information security are often huge news. These could be failures by the state, or by businesses operating within the state.

KEY TERM

Cloud storage – online storage capacity.

GROUP ACTIVITY

(10 minutes)

You have been asked to research recent failures of information security for a newspaper article. You need to provide information about **three** different failures.

Your research needs to focus on:

- The cause of the failure
- The impact of the failure on the business or organisation involved
- The impact of the failure on members of the public
- Any action taken by the organisation to reduce the chance of the failure happening again.

Present your research as a table, showing the key data required.

EXTENSION ACTIVITY

Individually, use your group's research to write the newspaper article.

6.4 Protection measures

Policies

Organisations need to have policies in place that allow for data to be protected. Staff access rights place limits on which members of staff have access to files. Therefore, the more sensitive the document, the fewer members of staff should have access to it. Individual staff can be made responsible for the security of data in their area. This allows for a more focused security than having one person responsible for all data. Because it appears in the job description of individual members of staff, there is a greater incentive for staff to take the responsibility. Included with this policy could be staff training on how data of any type should be handled. This may focus on sensitive data, but could also include general training on data protection and other key areas.

A data recovery policy covers how data should be backed up to protect against deletion or corruption, and is part of a disaster recovery policy.

6.5 Physical protection

Locks, keypads and biometrics

Physical protection may also be used to protect data. Access to individual workstations or server rooms can be physically stopped by locking doors, locking screens via the keypad or putting padlocks on machines.

Although **biometrics** uses digital means to gather information, the protection it provides is still physical. For example, biometrics can scan physical characteristics, such as fingerprints, and use these to control access to resources.

Placing computers above known flood levels

One form of information loss that is often ignored is loss through natural causes, such as from flooding. Placing machines on a second floor, to where flood levels are unlikely to rise, is a simple form of protection.

Backup systems in other locations

Backup does not protect data from loss or theft, but mitigates the effect if data is lost or stolen, as it provides a copy. However, backups only provide the data from the time when backup occurred. This means that any data created since the backup is lost.

All organisations should have a backup policy based on the need to protect vital information and at a time when most vital data is captured. For example an overnight backup would be appropriate for an organisation that adds data between 9 a.m. and 6 p.m., but adds no more until the next morning.

Security staff

Security staff are sometimes considered to be a form of physical security, as they are a physical restriction on access to data simply because they reduce the risk of an unauthorised intruder accessing the data storage system.

> **KEY TERM**
>
> **Biometrics** – the measurement and statistical analysis of people's physical and behavioural characteristics. As each biometric is unique, this is a highly effective method of identifying individuals.

Shredding old paper based records

This form of protection is effective in protecting data falling into the wrong hands. If paper based records are not shredded, then there is a risk that confidential or sensitive data may be found and used by others.

6.6 Logical protection

This final level of protection uses digital, or logical, methods to protect data.

Tiered levels of access to data

This form of protection is the application of the staff access rights policy and is the process of making certain information only accessible to certain staff. Depending on the access relevant to a person's job role they may not have any access to certain information stored on the system. They may have 'read only' rights – they can 'look but not touch'. They may have full access, which means that they can amend the data as well.

Firewalls

Because **firewalls** monitor the traffic in and out of a network, any traffic that does not meet the rules for the firewall will be refused passage in or out of that network. Therefore, data is protected from unauthorised access from outside an organisation, as well as being protected from being sent out of a network.

Anti-malware applications

Any software that protects a computer from malware would fit into this category. Anti-virus protection is the most common generic type but other types of software, such as popup blockers or spyware, would also be included.

Obfuscation

Obfuscation is purposely making something unintelligible so that it cannot be understood. For example, code may be obfuscated to prevent it from being stolen and modified. A human cannot read obfuscated code but, as the meaning remains the same, computers can still understand it. Obfuscation can be carried out by individuals or, more commonly, by specialist software.

Encryption of data at rest

Data at rest refers to data that is stored on digital media while it is not being transferred between devices. It is becoming common practice to encrypt data while it is stored, as one can never be sure when a hacker may attempt to get into a device, or if a device may be lost or stolen.

Encryption of data in transit

Data in transit refers to data that is being sent between two users. Generally, this could be via email, but from the work in LO1, you should be aware that there are many ways in which data could be transferred.

As with data at rest, it is good practice to protect data while it is in transit. This protects against data interception (such as interception of emails) as well as against theft of the device being used to transport the data.

KEY TERM

Firewall – a form of network security that monitors data traffic into and out of a network. The traffic is assessed against set rules and only allowed through the firewall if it fits those rules.

Password protection

A password could be applied to the file, folder or storage device on which the file is held. This method of protection is effective if the password is strong, and, in most cases, dissuades the casual hacker who simply wants to take a look at your data. However, unless you are using a really complicated password, determined hackers will eventually get into a file.

This does not mean that you should not password protect your data, just that you should be aware that a password does not guarantee that the file will not be accessed.

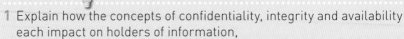

KNOW IT

1 Explain how the concepts of confidentiality, integrity and availability each impact on holders of information,
2 Explain two ways in which unauthorised access to information may impact on the holders of information.
3 What is meant by the term intellectual property?
4 Explain two different methods of disaster recovery that could be used by an organisation.
5 Describe two physical methods of data protection.

Assessment practice questions

Below are practice questions for you to try.

Section A

International Phone Sales (IPS) buys previously owned smartphones in developed countries and sells them to customers in developing countries. Sellers contact the business via telephone, email or web forms.

IPS has a chain of shops in developing countries and these are its main form of contact with customers. However, sales operatives also travel to meet potential customers and attend trade shows.

IPS wants to increase sales of new smartphones to their markets in developing countries and is using content on their website to support this project.

1 a Describe how the access to communications technology differs between developed and developing countries. (2)

  b Explain **one** possible impact of the different levels of technology in developed and developing countries. (2)

  c When a customer contacts a sales operative, initial details are recorded as handwritten notes. Identify **one** characteristic of handwritten notes. (1)

  d Identify and justify **two** additional types of paper-based storage that could be used by sales operatives working for IPS. (4)

2 IPS operates an intranet, an extranet and a website.

  a Compare and contrast how IPS could use its extranet and intranet. (4)

  b IPS wants to increase sales of new phones to customers in developing countries. Explain the benefits of streamed video on the website for this purpose. (2)

  c Identify **one** further information format that would be suitable for inclusion on the website. Justify your recommendation. (3)

3 IPS uses a database to store data about smartphones sold and to whom. An extract from the table holding data about items sold is shown below.

Extract

Table 2.6 Extract from IPS sales database

Date_of_sale	Buyer_reference	Country_of_sale	Purchase_price	Sales_price	Profit	Condition_of_phone
17/02/2016	17A56	Namibia	£17.00	£36.00	£19.00	Good
18/02/2016	17C78	Namibia	£9.00	£42.00	£33.00	Good
18/02/2016	11P50	Namibia	£24.00	£70.00	£46.00	Excellent
			£0.00	£0.00	£0.00	

a Identify a field in the table that holds the **numerical** information style. (1)

b List **two** other information styles used in the table. (2)

c Suggest and justify **one** further information style that could be used in the table. (3)

d State **one** field in the table that could hold personal information. (1)

e Identify **one** field in the table that could hold information that was subject to bias. (1)

f The Sales Manager of IPS needs to know if there are any patterns in the monthly sales of smartphones. She has chosen to use graphs and charts to analyse the monthly sales data. Evaluate the use of this data analysis tool for this purpose. (4)

g Every two years, IPS reviews the data held in its database of items sold and to whom and carries out a process of data cleaning.

  i Describe what the term data cleaning means in this context. (1)

  ii Justify the use of regular data cleaning by IPS using examples. (4)

4 The Marketing Executive of IPS is investigating potential markets for previously owned smartphones in China and has asked for a report on the sales of competitors' products in this market.

a Describe **two** possible constraints that could affect how information is collected for this report. (4)

b Justify the use of **one** possible internal source of information that could be used for this report. (2)

c Once the information has been sourced, it will need to be analysed. Explain **two** factors which need to be taken into account when choosing the most appropriate tool to analyse this data. (4)

d The data collected will be used to create a model of projected sales for the first year of trading in China. Assess the benefits to IPS of creating a model of potential sales. (5)

Section A total [48]

Section B

You do not need the case study to answer these questions.

1 Data and information are used globally. Explain the difference between data and information. (2)

2 An interviewer working for a Market Research organisation asks interviewees a series of questions. The information that is given by the interviewees is then coded for use in a database.
   a Explain, with an example, how coding the responses from interviewees converts the information that has been provided into data. (3)
   b Explain **one** moral reason why information gathered from interviewees should be anonymised. (2)
   c One principle of the Data Protection Act states that personal information should be protected from unauthorised or unlawful processing. Identify **one** other principle of the Data Protection Act and explain the impact that it may have on an organisation that carries out market research. (3)
   d Explain, **with examples**, possible impacts for an organisation if the interviewer influences the interviewees' answers. (4)

3 Organisations can choose to follow a Green IT policy:
   a Identify two items that could be included in a Green IT policy. (2)
   b Explain one possible benefit to an organisation of following a Green IT policy. (2)

4 Describe **two** possible impacts, on the organisation as a whole, of the payroll function failing to meet the principles of data security. (4)

5 Compare the differences in access to data between individual citizens and educational institutions. (4)

6 AGGCE uses an MIS to manage data about personnel. Explain the benefits to AGGCE of using an MIS to manage this data. (4)

Section B total [30]

Unit 03

Cyber security

LEARNING OUTCOMES

The topics and activities in this unit will help you to:

1 Understand what is meant by cyber security.
2 Understand the issues surrounding cyber security
3 Understand measures used to protect against cyber security incidents.
4 Understand how to manage cyber security incidents.

How will I be assessed?

You will be assessed through an external assessment set and marked by OCR.

LO1 Understand what is meant by cyber security

(10 minutes)

List the types of information, personal and business, you would NOT want to share with strangers, on a flip chart for the wider group to consider during the unit.

⋯⋯⋯⋯⋯⋯⋯⋯⋯⋯⋯⋯⋯⋯⋯⋯⋯⋯

🔑 KEY TERM

Malware – short for 'malicious software', it includes viruses, worms, Trojan horses, ransomware, adware, spyware and any other piece of software which can harm the system, the computer or the individual who uses it.

1.1 Cyber security aims to protect information

Cyber security is how organisations and individuals protect their information assets, data, software and hardware. One model for managing cyber security is called the CIA triad, standing for Confidentiality, Integrity and Availability.

Confidentiality

From your Getting started task you should be aware that everyone has data and information which they do not want to share with everyone – things you want to keep confidential. In some cases, this right to confidentiality is a legal right through the Computer Misuse Act (1990) and the Data Protection Act (1998) and these will be discussed in LO 2.6.

Table 3.1 describes why cyber security is important.

Table 3.1 Confidentiality, Integrity and Availability (the CIA Triad)

Cyber security protects:	Why?	From whom?
Confidentiality: rules which restrict access only to those who need to know.	Personal data such as: • Your financial position. • Embarrassing information, such as a photograph which seemed funny at the time but which you would not want a possible employer to see. • Information which would enable someone take money from you. Organisational data: • Sales or marketing information. • Customer details. • Financial data. • Personnel records. Government data: • National security. • Defence plans. • International negotiations.	Individuals: • Use it against you by publishing it widely or bullying you. • Steal your identity. • Steal money from your bank account. • Use your credit card. Organisations: • Obtain confidential financial information. • Publish sensitive documents or data. • Steal intellectual property. Governments: • Leaked security plans, agent details, security activities. • Leaked defence plans, troop movements, weapon specifications. • Financial plans.
Integrity: the level of assurance which can be given as to the accuracy and trustworthiness of the data.	Your data is the equivalent of a virtual you. Change the data and this virtual person changes too and not always for the better.	Any action which can: • Enter incorrect data accidentally or intentionally. • Make errors when updating data. • Adding incomplete records to data files or databases. • Transfer errors between devices. • Enable hacking activities. • Enable viruses or Trojans which may compromise the data.
Availability: the level of assurance that the data will be available to those who need it when they want it.	Personal: • Unable to access bank account. • Unable to pay bills. • Unable to access diary information. Organisational: Unable to fulfil: • Customer orders. • Employee salary payments. • Instructions for carrying processes.	• Hardware malfunctions. • Software malfunctions. • Natural disasters, e.g. earthquakes, fire, flood. • Problems caused by humans such as loss of power, **malware**, hacking, spillages, loss of data.

1.2 Types of cyber security incidents

A wide range of cyber security events can befall individuals and organisations, some of which we identified above. In this section we will look more closely at a range of activities and their effects.

Unauthorised access

Unauthorised access refers just to gaining access to computer systems, networks, data and programs without permission – it does not include carrying out any other activities. Examples include:

- Hacking is carried out by hackers and involves gaining access to the system through any means other than being given a legitimate username and password. This can be achieved through the carelessness of the user leaving these items in plain sight so that they can easily be seen, or by generating thousands of different passwords to find the correct one.
- Escalation of privileges gives an individual rights of access and editing which normal users do not have. There are two types of escalation:
  - Vertical: the invader obtains or may have legally received permission for low level access. By finding flaws in the security systems or operating system, they increase their access level to allow access to username creation, access levels, networks or data files. This method has been used to gain access to Android and iOS smartphones.
  - Horizontal: the invader does not add higher levels of access but gains access to other, normal users', areas. They might have stolen the username and password or seen another's data because of a program fault.

Information disclosure

Organisations and individuals maintain large amounts of information, some of it personal and confidential to the employee or employer, such as salary scale, court judgements, disciplinary activity, state of health, national insurance number, tax codes and bank details.

For many organisations, information is one of their most valuable assets. These can include ideas and research into new products, business plans for expansion, takeovers or cut backs as well as stock levels, purchasing agreements, customer contracts and discount arrangements, all of which could be useful to another organisation. Additionally, there may be evidence of events which could prove damaging to the organisation if they were reported in the media, such as large payoffs or the employment of family members in jobs with significant salaries.

Governments handle and retain huge amounts of information, ranging in the United Kingdom from handwritten documents to recent digital data. Most will be of limited interest or value, but some information can be valuable, such as how many soldiers are available for deployment; how many aircraft can take to the air at one time; feedback from ambassadors on their opinions of new heads of states or senior politicians; agents working in other countries; and the monitoring of other countries' leaders or communications.

Insiders who are unhappy or have carried out activities which make them susceptible to blackmail can be preyed upon by people with no right to the information, to obtain copies. Hackers can use their knowledge of human

Unauthorised access is activity intended to gain access to data, networks, computer system hardware or software without the permission of the owner or other responsible individuals or organisation.

Unauthorised inspection is reviewing or reading data, information or systems documentation without permission of the appropriate owner or manager.

Unauthorised modification is changing data, information, programs or documentation without permission.

Unauthorised disclosure is allowing information to pass to any person or organisation without permission.

behaviour (e.g. use of simple passwords or using the same password for everything), or computing to obtain access to the information system and obtain electronic copies of information which can be used against the organisation, individual or country.

Modification of data

Data is entered, amended, stored and deleted by those with authorisation. Sometimes this may be accidental, when the security or access levels are lax and someone with poor knowledge or understanding of the system manages to alter or delete information. On other occasions, individuals or groups seek access to the system using a range of tools to steal, destroy or alter the data or the software which operates or manages the information system. When data is illegally modified, it is to blackmail and/or to cause disruption or harm to an organisation or individual.

Inaccessible data

There are ways in which users can be denied access to services or data to which they require and have the necessary permissions. These attacks are normally linked to malicious software. Most username and password systems have an automatic account lockout (you will have noticed this if you have mistyped your password, usually at least three times) to reduce the likelihood of a hacker trying to guess your password.

Alternatively, you may receive an email claiming that you have been locked out of your account and asking you to download an attachment and go through a process to reinstate your account. The attachment is a piece of malicious code which will damage your computer system, preventing you from accessing the data you need.

Another way in which access can be prevented is through a denial of service (DoS) attack. This involves sending so much traffic to a particular computer system or website that it cannot cope, denying access to legitimate users. This approach is usually used to bring down corporate systems, such those used by banks, news networks and other financial systems.

Destruction

All systems store data, as we have noted already. It is created, edited, manipulated and, when no longer required, deleted. However, it can also be destroyed intentionally through the introduction of malware such as viruses or Trojan horse software. Some software can randomly destroy data whereas others, such as Trojans, may target specific data, such as falsified personal records or payments.

Theft

As with stealing property or money, stealing data or information can be very profitable. Hackers will obtain access to specific information about individuals, who may be living or dead, use this material to create a new identity and set up new bank accounts for criminal transactions or sell properties owned by someone else, for example. Spying is an old profession and theft of information such as military plans, research findings or economic data is much faster using computer systems.

1.3 The importance of cyber security

From the discussions in LO1.1 and 1.2, you can see that organisations, individuals and computer systems must be kept safe from attack.

The need to protect personal data

Losing your personal data can result in your identify being stolen. Table 3.2 below identifies types of personal information and the ways in which it can be used.

Table 3.2 Examples of misuse of personal data

Data type	Consequences of theft and possible misuse
Health records	• Refusal of personal insurance. • Loss of job opportunities. • Altering records to give a false impression. • Using the record to obtain benefits illegally.
Name and address	• Interception of mail allowing access to further detailed information. • Ordering of goods to be sent to your address and intercepting their delivery or selecting the option of sending the goods to another address.
Bank details	• Creation of mortgages, bank accounts and loans without your knowledge. • Withdrawal of funds. • Closure of legitimate accounts.

The need to protect an organisation's data

Organisations are required to take all necessary steps to protect financial and personal information held about employees, for example, and failure to do so can result in fines and appearances in court. Additionally, the publicity resulting from such failures could cause a loss of trust and respect from customers.

Intellectual property is also an important source of income for companies, but if the results of research were to be stolen or made public, then the ownership of any innovation could be disputed, resulting in expensive court cases.

Publication of development plans could result in rises in the price of land or buildings or competitors could adjust their own plans to take advantage of this knowledge. Again, this could prove costly to the organisation. Taken together these types of issues could result in the organisation closing down.

The need to protect a state's data

This was discussed in LO1.2 above.

KNOW IT

1 What do the letters CIA stand for in CIA triad?
2 List two examples of unauthorised access.
3 List three types of information which an organisation might not want to be disclosed.
4 List two reasons why personal data should be protected.
5 Identify three types of data which might be stolen.

LO2 Understand the issues surrounding cyber security

(10 minutes)

List all the electronic devices which may be subject to cyber security incidents.

2.1 Threats to cyber security

It is often assumed that cyber threats are always the result of criminal activity, but this is not always the case. Threats can have accidental and natural causes as well.

Vulnerabilities

Vulnerabilities are flaws or issues that results in weaknesses in the security of a system. They can be intentional, accidental or a natural phenomenon. A range of vulnerabilities are outlined in Table 3.3.

Table 3.3 Examples of threats to cyber security

Type of threat	Examples
System attacks	• Denial of service (see LO1.2, page 88). • Botnet: attackers place a piece of malware on a group of computers to form a network under their control. This enables them to access sensitive data on the individual machines, launch denial of service attacks, install more malware or send spam emails. They can also sell the botnet software they have created. • Social engineering: gaining the trust of individuals and using that trust to influence them to give confidential information. For example, a teenager, posing as a Verizon employee, tricked a legitimate employee into giving the director of the CIA's (the USA's secret service) personal information including his four-digit bank card code. He also accessed the director's personal email account which contained sensitive government documents and personal information about government employees.
Physical	Any threat to the system or computer through physical access. These include loss or theft of equipment e.g. tablet or laptop, portable memory.
Environmental	Any threat which is a result of a natural event such as: • floods • fire • earthquake • very high winds.

Accidental

Accidental threats are those that can happen without any intention on the part of the individual to cause harm. These include:

● dropping an item, such as a tablet, or spilling liquid on a computer or other item of equipment and breaking it, resulting in the loss or damage of information

- responding to a hoax email without realising what it is
- accidentally uploading malware on a piece of software or data file which has come from a respected source
- accidental deletion of data or software.

Intentional

These are normally criminal activities because the intention is to cause harm to the computer or system. We have met these already such as hacking, social engineering and theft.

Organised crime

Organised cyber crime includes **cyber enabled crime** and **cyber dependent crime**. According to the British Bankers Association, using 2015 figures, it is impossible to measure the full cost of financial crime but **money laundering** in the UK is estimated to cost the country £24 billion a year. Hackers can use **data mining** to identify individuals and businesses and collect comprehensive data which allows them to carry out a range of crimes such as:

- stealing identities,
- stealing intellectual property,
- emptying bank accounts
- blackmailing individuals and organisations.

State sponsored

Countries have always spied on each other and the internet is just another way of doing it. Spies hack into the information networks of foreign powers and their major organisations to identify vulnerabilities, business strategies, government policies and plans for nuclear facilities, power plants and military campaigns. The country that is spying can use the information to undermine its enemies through a range of activities, such as making and selling cheaper copies of equipment to reduce the profitability of the home manufacturers and sending malware attached to apparently legitimate emails to senior personnel.

PAIRS ACTIVITY

(30 minutes)

For each of the types of cyber threat identified above, investigate an example of each that has been carried out or occurred in real life. Present your examples to the wider group.

KEY TERMS

Money laundering – the process by which criminals hide the origin of the proceeds of their crime by transferring the money through different bank accounts and countries to make it look as if it comes from a legal source.

Data mining – the use of sophisticated tools, such as artificial intelligence techniques, neural networks and statistical tools to identify trends and patterns in large data stores.

Cyber enabled crime – committing crimes such as fraud, theft and bullying via IT.

Cyber dependent crime – crimes that can only be carried out using computer networks or systems. These include: spreading malware, hacking and denial of service attacks.

2.2 Types of attackers

Table 3.4 Types of cyber attackers

Hacktivist	Individuals and groups which use computers and computer systems to promote their own views on a particular issue such as human rights, animal rights or ethics. They hack into computer systems and cause disruptions such as denial of service attacks, steal or destroy information and put individuals, organisations and countries at risk. What is the difference between a hacker and a hacktivist? It depends upon your point of view; if you agree with the views of the hacktivists then they are honourable individuals or groups who seek to right a wrong or demonstrate the evils of a particular government, individual or group. If you do not, then they break laws, regulations and ethical considerations for their own gain.
Cyber criminal	Anyone who commits a cyber crime by breaking national or international law. They may use the computer in different ways to carry out the crime: • As a tool to aid the crime; for example, to commit fraud, send spam. • To aim the crime at a particular computer or computer system; for example, looking up information they are not entitled to read, installing a Trojan horse, spreading malware, stealing data, altering data. • To store illegally collected data.
Insider	Computers are not always attacked from outside the organisation; in many instances, it is individuals within organisations who cause the damage. The types of insider attacker are: • Disgruntled employees who feel they have been passed over for promotion, been made redundant or have suffered some other real or perceived injury. • Employees with severe personal problems, for example, being in debt due to gambling, large credit card debts, alcoholism or drug abuse, may sell their companies data to try and repay the debts or steal money directly from the organisation by, for example, fraudulently adding increments or changing pay scales or claiming expenses for non-existent expenditure.
Script kiddie	Also known as a skid or skiddie, it refers to the skill level of the individual and not their physical age. So anyone without the technical expertise to create their own software or means of hacking into a computer system, but who does use software or scripts created by others to carry out hacking, is called a script kiddie.
Vulnerability broker	Several companies make money by either finding program bugs themselves or buying them from researchers or hackers to sell the information on – but not to the company who created the program. So, for example, if the latest version of your widely used operating system has a flaw which you have not found but is discovered by Bugs Ltd, a vulnerability broker, the only way you will find out that the bug exists will be if the problem is made public. As those who pay for this kind of information are organisations or countries who wish to use this flaw to their advantage, it may stay hidden for a long time. This compromises the security of your customers.
Scammers	Scammers try to cheat you by offering goods or opportunities to make some quick money. Scams often come via emails and are only activated if you click on them. An example is the holiday scam, when you are offered the holiday of a lifetime, all expenses paid, if you pay a few hundred pounds to claim it. When you forward the money electronically to the account given, you hear no more: there is no holiday and no refund of your money.
Phishers	Phishers want to gain your personal data (such as your name, your password, bank account and credit card details) to allow them to steal your identify and personal information. You receive an email claiming that your email or bank account has been compromised and you must log in through the link in the email to change your password and protect yourself against fraud. The site is a fake, although it may look real and, if you enter the details asked, the data will be sent to another location where it will be used and/or sold on to others who can use the information.
Cyber terrorists	There is no single definition for cyber terrorism but generally it is the use of computer systems, including communication systems, to cause fear or intimidation in society through destruction of or damage to people, property and systems. The individuals who carry out these activities are called cyber terrorists.

Characteristics

Many articles and definitions state that hackers, for example, are normally young, male, highly intelligent, curious and possess an ability to think in the abstract. They are also claimed to be introverted.

However, while some of these characteristics, such as being curious and the ability to think in the abstract, are likely to be true, the others are not so easily assigned. For example, an internal attacker may be older, male or female and driven by a need to obtain funds or right a perceived wrong and have learned how to circumvent or corrupt a system through experience.

2.3 Motivation for attackers

All attackers have a reason for their activities, many of which we have discussed in the preceding sections.

> The first hackers were very good programmers who hacked through machine code to correct errors or improve the program. However, this term now refers to anyone who breaks into a computer or system to steal or damage information or disrupt the system.

PAIRS ACTIVITY

(15 minutes)

Complete Table 3.5 by entering the type of attackers from Table 3.4 who could be motivated by each of the reasons given.

Table 3.5 Motivations for attackers

Motive	Type(s) of attacker
Espionage (spying)	
Righting perceived wrongs	
Publicity	
Fraud	
Public good	
Thrill	
Income generation	

As a group, discuss the completed tables, which could be displayed on flip charts or on a screen, and agree a range of attackers for each motive.

2.4 Targets for cyber security threats

People

We have looked at instances of cyber security threats to individuals, such as spam, phishing and malware attacks, as well as how they can be recognised. Other areas that need to be considered are:

KEY TERM

Cookie – a small text file sent from a web server that is stored on the user's computer to track and store information about the user's activities.

● Internet shopping: fake websites, which look similar to the genuine site, can result in your name, credit card number and password or bank details being stolen and the goods you have paid for never arriving. Unauthorised **cookies** can track the types of sites you visit and use this information to enable others to send you unwanted emails and popups.
● Social media can be particularly challenging as employers may find information about you which you would prefer to remain private. Photographs and videos of silly behaviour may seem funny at the time, but when viewed weeks, months or years later by firms looking for reliable, trustworthy staff, they may suggest that you lack the attributes they want.

Organisations

All organisations, whether private, public, governmental or not for profit, can find themselves subject to cyber threats. These threats include internal and external hacking, denial of service, theft of data, theft of equipment, data misuse including editing, deleting or adding records, blackmail and loss of reputation.

Equipment

Mobile devices are the biggest cyber security threat to businesses and individuals. The concept of 'Bring Your Own Devices' (BYOD) enables mobile devices to be used in unsecure locations so data can be copied or diverted by other devices on the same network. They can also pick up malware, through downloading apps, software and email, and pass that on to the organisation's systems once reconnected with the secure network. Mobile devices are also easy to leave unattended in public, leave behind on transport or be stolen from bags and jackets. The users are using their equipment for legitimate purposes but their lack of security results in potential or actual harm to their own or their organisation's systems.

 **PAIRS ACTIVITY**

(30 minutes)

Identify three different mobile devices and research the types of threat which each device is susceptible to. Record your findings.

Information

Information is valuable not only to individuals and business, but also to those who can acquire power, money or their chosen objectives by stealing, publishing, altering or destroying it. Whether as an individual or part of an organisation, care must be taken to protect it.

2.5 Impacts of cyber security incidents

These have been discussed at appropriate points within this unit.

GROUP AND INDEPENDENT ACTIVITY

(50 minutes)

Independently, research a particular cyber security incident and summarise:

- Type of threat.
- Type of attacker(s).
- Motivation for the attack.
- The target of the attack.
- The impact of the incident.

Come together as a group to review the summaries and agree a common view.

2.6 Other considerations of cyber security

So far we have looked at the cyber threats or crimes themselves, in terms of what they are, why they occur, who is harmed by them and how they are avoided.

This section describes aids to protect individuals, organisations and data from such attacks.

Ethical behaviour

Ethics and ethical behaviour are complex and can vary between cultures, countries and individuals. The cyber world is no different. Malicious hacking is frowned upon but ethical hacking is not. Ethical hackers are IT specialists employed or contracted by system owners to methodically attempt to penetrate a computer system or network to identify vulnerabilities that could threaten the system and/or its data and produce a fix. As the hacker is trying to protect the system by breaking into it, this is considered to be ethical.

An organisation monitoring its employees' emails, for example, to ensure that they are not carrying out private or social business at work on company systems, can be considered appropriate by some organisations and managers but unethical by others.

> Professional bodies such as the British Computer Society (The Chartered Institute for IT Professionals or BCS) and the Association of Computing Machinery (ACM) have codes of ethics or codes of conduct which IT professionals agree to abide by when they join.

Legal

There are a range of UK laws that govern computing. These include:

- Regulation of Investigatory Powers Act 2000: makes it an offence to intentionally and without lawful authority to incept any communication which is transmitted on a public or private communication system.
- Communications Act 2003: makes it a criminal offence to transmit text messages or emails via a public communications network which are:
  - grossly offensive
  - indecent
  - obscene
  - menacing.
- The Computer Misuse Act (2000): makes the following an offence:
  - unauthorised access to computer materials
  - unauthorised access with intent to commit a further offence
  - unauthorised modification of material.

  Two important points about the Computer Misuse Act:

  - the individual must know that they are not authorised to access or modify the system
  - it is not necessary to actually carry out a further offence, merely to intend to do so is the offence.
- The Data Protection Act 1998 is discussed in Unit 2, LO2.2 (page 57) and in Unit 13, LO2.5 (page 336).

Operational

Ways in which the systems can be protected from cyber security threats include the use of encryption – turning data and information into a format which can only be read by someone with the key. There are two main types of encryption:

- Symmetric key, where the encryption and decryption codes are the same.
- Asymmetric or public key, where the encryption key is available to anyone to use and encrypt data but only the person who receives the message receives the decryption key.

Surveillance of the network or computer system is another way in which cyber security threats can be identified or prevented. Here the traffic on the network is monitored to identify what messages and instructions are moving through it, who is sending and who is receiving them. Similarly, data, which is normally sent in packets rather than one large file, can be viewed by software in a process called 'packet sniffing'. Packets are intercepted, inspected, analysed and returned to the network, without the sender or receiver being aware of what is happening.

GROUP ACTIVITY

(10 minutes)

Identify two ways that network managers could protect their systems using operational procedures.

Implications for stakeholders

All users, technical staff and managers involved in computer systems have responsibility for the proper use of their systems. Codes of practice and codes of ethics enable organisations to provide their employees with clear guidance on what is acceptable practice and what is not.

Laws are useful but are only effective as a deterrent. If the law is broken then the system has already been damaged, although fines and imprisonment may deter others. The wording of the law also needs to be carefully considered. For example, the Computer Misuse Act (2000) refers to 'unauthorised' access or modification. This means that the individual must know that they are not authorised – otherwise they could claim that they believed they were allowed to access the information system or modify it. Therefore the organisation needs to make clear, in contracts of employment or similar documents, where the limits of authorisation are drawn.

The Data Protection Act (1998) requires organisations to take steps to ensure that the data they hold meets the requirements of the eight principles. Failure to comply can result in fines or imprisonment.

Therefore, everyone who uses a computer or network system must be informed of their rights and responsibilities in ensuring that only legal and ethical activities are undertaken.

KNOW IT

1 Give three examples of system vulnerabilities.
2 What is the difference between a hacker and a hacktivist?
3 Identify four reasons why computer systems are attacked.
4 Give three examples of threats to mobile devices.
5 Name three pieces of legislation which are relevant to computers and networks.

LO3 Understand measures used to protect against cyber security incidents

It is obvious that it would be better not to have any cyber security incidents and to prevent any threats rather than deal with the results. In this section, you will learn about the steps which can be taken to reduce the risk of a cyber attack and its consequences.

3.1 Cyber security risk management

Risk management does not mean removing all risk as that would be impossible without closing down all systems and leaving them switched off. Instead, we:

- identify the risks
- measure the risk, i.e. how likely it is and how serious would the effect be
- monitor and report on the risks
- control the risks
- audit and adjust the risk management process.

Identify assets and analyse risks

In computer systems and networks there are a range of assets. These can be grouped as:

- Hardware resources, e.g. servers, computers (desktop, laptop and tablet), printers, scanners, plotters.
- Software resources, e.g. word processors, databases, spreadsheets, utilities, bespoke software, financial packages, specialist production packages, drawing packages, CRM.
- Communications equipment, e.g. hubs, routers, bridges, gateways, modems, cabling, telephone systems.
- Information and data, e.g. customer data, employee records, contract data, financial reports, production figures, production costs, sales figures, marketing information.

The value of each asset must be calculated because risk management costs money and organisations cannot afford to put in place protection that is going to cost more than the value of the asset. Assets may also be dependent upon other assets. For example, an old server may be worth less than the data stored on it, but its loss will result in the loss of the data too, so protecting the server is a worthwhile investment.

For risk management purposes, each asset is considered in terms of the types threats it may face.

Risks can be measured in other ways than merely cost, such as the types of incidents which may occur or how likely it is that these incidents will occur.

Risk management involves taking steps to monitor the system or network to identify its weaknesses or vulnerabilities and put in place sufficient and appropriate security measures to reduce or eliminate the risk.

Mitigate risks and testing for vulnerabilities

Testing helps to mitigate risks in a system and vulnerability testing is discussed in LO3.2.

Monitoring and controlling systems record what is going on within the network or system including when the actions occurred. Control systems maintain a log of the activities identified during monitoring but also control access to data, hardware or software. These measures ensure that, after an incident, the culprits can be identified, whether the damage is accidental or intentional. Log files contain information such as transactions, updates to records or files, who has logged on and when, what they accessed, read, edited, created or deleted. Other logs include system boot, system shutdown, network activity and disc space. These logs can also document problems and provide evidence to enable the correction of system and security issues. Risk management policies should include the retention and archiving policies for these valuable data.

Each asset is assessed for its vulnerabilities; for example, lack of physical controls on access doors, PCs and servers being susceptible to power surges and poor password management for the finance system. Vulnerability tools or scanners can identify issues such as software defects, incorrect configuration, back doors and unsecure accounts.

The cost to the organisation if the vulnerability was exploited by an attacker is calculated and the effect of such an event identified. This can take a number of forms, such the impact or probability of such an event.

GROUP ACTIVITY

(10 minutes)

Complete Table 3.6 by selecting an asset from each group in the bullet points on the previous page and identifying a possible, realistic vulnerability.

Table 3.6 Asset vulnerabilities

Asset group	Asset	Vulnerability
Hardware		
Software		
Communications equipment		
Information/data		

Protecting vulnerabilities

After identifying the vulnerabilities within the system or network, they should be prioritised or organised into those which are critical and those which will cause little or no real damage.

The way in which the vulnerabilities are dealt with is known as remediation, and this has a number of forms.

A back door or trap door is a method by which a programmer or network manager bypasses the normal security procedures. A piece of software or code within a program is used as a short cut by the author to access a particular area, possibly to speed up troubleshooting or to correct programming errors. Unfortunately, hackers also create or identify back doors to install malware, access and manipulate data.

- Patch deployment. Software issues are identified and reported to the software designer who provides patches or hot fixes which will remove the vulnerability.
- Manual. For small networks, rather than use automated tools, the technician or network manager will take the steps required to remove or reduce the vulnerability.
- Automated tools. These tools can identify and repair vulnerabilities without the intervention of the manager or technician. They normally include administrative tools that enable the manager to decide which vulnerabilities should be repaired and when, so as to reduce the costs and disruption to users.

This is not a one-time process. New vulnerabilities are appearing all the time so scanning should be repeated regularly. The precise timescales will vary with the size, complexity and value of the assets, but would normally be at least annually. Figure 3.1 is a useful aid to understanding how vulnerabilities are managed. Note that it is a cycle – as soon as you finish one step you move to the next one and continue until vulnerabilities no longer exist – which is very unlikely!

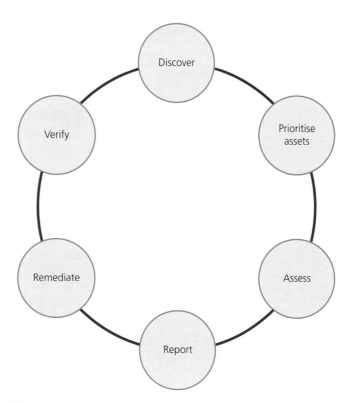

Figure 3.1 Vulnerability management lifecycle

 **GROUP ACTIVITY**

(30 minutes)

Identify and describe at least one vulnerability scanner and one automated remedial tool and share this information with everyone else.

Cost/benefits

This is the cost of implementing security against the benefits that it would bring. This will vary with the value of the asset, which could include replacement costs and the cost of recreating the data – which may include the cost of collecting and manipulating the primary data.

3.2 Testing and monitoring measures

Intrusion detection systems (IDS) are designed to expose any attempts by attackers to overcome security controls to compromise data or other resources. There are different types of such systems including network based (NIDS), which monitors traffic on the network by intercepting data packets, processing the data and identifying suspicious traffic, and host based (HIDS), which detects unusual, unauthorised or illegal activities on a specific device. All of these systems collect and log suspected intrusions and alert the appropriate manager.

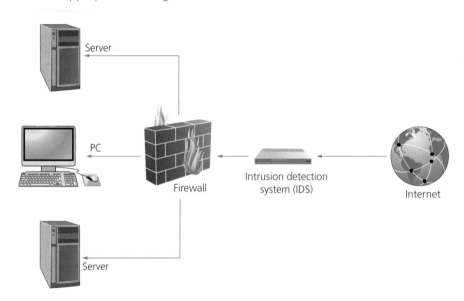

▲ **Figure 3.2** Intrusion detection system diagram

Intrusion prevention systems (IPS) are devices or programs that detect attempts at intrusion and take action to prevent them. These systems can be hardware devices or software running on servers or virtual environments. Unlike intrusion detection systems, the IPS is connected just like any other part of the system and all traffic flows through it. It creates alerts and logs events but, most importantly, it can block attacks. As with an IDS, an IPS can be network based or host based.

Vulnerability testing can be active (where the tester interacts directly with the component being tested, such as using network scanners), automated or passive (such as traffic monitoring, where data is captured on the network and analysed offline). Testing is not monitoring – its purpose is to see how the system copes when subjected to conditions which would cause the vulnerabilities to become apparent. For example:

● network services tests look for internal and/or external openings to identify how the vulnerabilities could be exploited by internal or external attackers

- social engineering tests try to convince employees to part with passwords, usernames and other sensitive data to evaluate the success or failure of the policies, procedures and processes designed to protect against such attacks
- physical security tests are when testers attempt to gain access to rooms or buildings and/or remove computers, hard drives or recycling bins to assess the effectiveness of the current security.

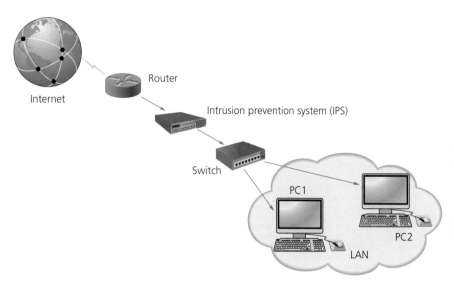

▲ **Figure 3.3** Intrusion prevention system diagram

3.3 Cyber security controls
Characteristics of security controls
We will now look at ways in which we can minimise risks to our computer systems. This includes potential threats to physical resources, computer systems, data and any other useful assets. Controls are intended to reduce the risk by deterring, delaying or stopping an attack.

Physical
These devices control physical access to the system or network. They can include security guards, biometric readers that can identify individuals by analysing their unique physical features, swipe cards, number pads or alarm systems. They all prevent individuals or groups accessing the physical locations of the system or network.

Hardware
Sometimes removal of items can simply be prevented by the addition of hardware such as:

- safes for storing copies of important or confidential data
- cable locks, which enable laptops, computers, etc. to be firmly attached to a large and immovable object, such as a heavy desk or piping, using steel cables and a strong lock.

> Biometrics, for our purposes, means the identification of individuals by using their biological characteristics. These include fingerprints, retinal or iris scans or facial recognition.

Software

Software methods of security have been discussed throughout the unit but, to recap, they include:

● anti-malware software, which locates and destroys or quarantines malware
● operating system updates, which correct or remove vulnerabilities that have come to light
● firewalls, which protect networks by controlling and monitoring traffic entering or leaving the network
● patch management, which means planning what patches are to be applied to software and at what time. Patches are small pieces of software that update a computer program to remove vulnerabilities, bugs in the coding or improve the performance of the software.

Data, encryption and cryptography devices

Data is held in storage, in the CPU registers during use, in data streams or portable storage devices during transit, in the cloud or in central servers.

The value of the data must be balanced with the cost of protection. Some of the ways in which data can be protected include:

● Hard drive encryption for mobile devices and other systems that hold confidential data.
● Regular assessments of the data to ensure that confidential data has been identified and encryption has been put in place.
● Private and public key cryptology to protect confidential data in transit.
● Evaluating the security policies, procedures and processes of your cloud storage provider to ensure that they are appropriate and applied correctly.
● Only moving data between networks using reliable, validated and encrypted means.
● Blocking support for DVD, external hard drive or USB storage facilities unless absolutely necessary to the organisation.

Procedures

Unless there are agreed policies and procedures governing how the system or network must be protected then failures are possible, not through any intention to cause a problem but through ignorance or forgetfulness.

The range of policies and procedures will vary with the size and purpose of the organisation, but the most frequently used are shown in Figure 3.4.

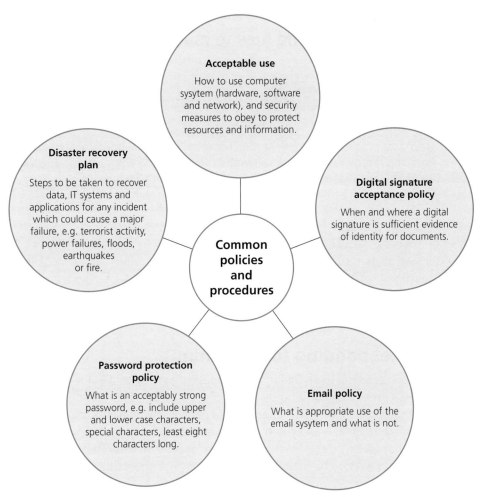

▲ **Figure 3.4** Examples of IT policies and procedures in organisations

GROUP ACTIVITY

(30 minutes)

Review your school or college's policies and procedures on acceptable use and email. (Note that the names of the policies may be slightly different from those in Figure 3.4.)

Which users need to know about the policies and procedures? Select one type of user, one policy or procedure and produce a presentation that explains:

● What the policy/procedure is for.
● What it means for the actions of the user.
● Why it is important to the school/college that the policy or procedure is followed correctly.

KNOW IT

1 List three assets of a computer system and one cyber security risk for each.
2 Explain the difference between monitoring and controlling systems.
3 What do the initials IDS, HIDS, NIDS and IPS stand for?
4 Give four examples of ways in which physical access to a computer system or network can be controlled.
5 Briefly describe three different types of control procedures.

LO4 Understand how to manage cyber security incidents

(10 minutes)

Have you ever experienced a cyber security incident, either as a user or as part of a team that needed to manage the situation? What happened? If you were a user, what information did you get about it? If you were on a team, what plans were in place to deal with it? Do you think it will happen again?

Everyone should be prepared for an incident, as far as possible. We shall look at how you should respond and how you record what has happened using a logging system so that lessons can be learned for the future. All staff must be aware of what has to be done, their role in ensuring that everything is completed accurately and in line with the procedure and how to respond to unforeseen outcomes.

4.1 Responding to an incident

How you respond to an incident is difficult to anticipate. People faced with adversity may react differently from how you expect; for example, someone you thought would be strong and make necessary decisions may lose their nerve, while others who you thought would panic may step forward and take charge. Try to ensure that everyone focuses on what they have to do and what needs to be done. The following points should be addressed.

Know responsibilities, know who to contact, know procedures

Everyone needs to know their own responsibilities during or after an incident. Some responsibilities could include:

- Shutting down the system to prevent damage due to natural events, such as flood or fire, or because that is the only way to stop an intrusion.
- Ensuring team members know what they have to do and when, and that they carry out their responsibilities correctly.
- Informing appropriate personnel, e.g. supervisors, managers, senior managers within the company as well as emergency services or specialist companies employed to deal with incidents on behalf of the organisation and certain customers.
- Knowing the responsibilities of others within the organisation for dealing with incidents. As well as the personnel above, colleagues in the same team and other teams may need to become involved. If relevant people are unavailable and you know what their responsibilities are, you need to find out who is next in line to take over the role or, if necessary, take over the additional responsibilities yourself.
- Knowing what procedures are in place that need to be used and in what order they need to be followed. For example, if someone has tried to enter a secure computer room then contacting security and following the procedure for dealing with human intruders (such as contacting

▲ **Figure 3.5** Flooded offices are one type of incident that needs to be anticipated

security staff, monitoring CCTV and calling the police) is more useful than implementing the procedure for checking whether the correct patches have been installed.

Know the extent of the incident and contain the incident

It is important to know what type of incident it is (e.g. a denial of service attack) and how much damage it has caused. For example, is it an attack at network level affecting the routers or IP switches? Is it at application level to use up resources? Are huge amounts of data being sent to the network, using up the processing power or bandwidths?

The incident may need to be contained before it can be stopped. If a virus has infected a computer, firstly check to see if the antivirus software is working. Has it identified the virus, detected it and removed it? If not, can you identify any important data that the virus is trying to access or external sites which it is trying to contact? If so, remove the data from the network until the virus is contained and block the sites that the virus is trying to contact for all traffic in either direction. Other ways in which incidents can be contained include:

- isolating whole systems
- changing the passwords of systems administrators if they have been compromised
- closing particular email servers and ports
- blocking unauthorised access.

Eradicate and reduce the impact of the incident

Eradication means removing the elements of the incident from the system or network. This may include disabling user accounts that have been penetrated, identifying a vulnerability which may have enabled the attack and lessen or remove its possible consequences. Find all hosts within the organisation that have been damaged so that remedial activity can take place. It is important to know what does not work, so as not to waste time when trying to contain and eradicate a threat.

Recover from the incident and confirm the system is functioning normally

The aim of every disaster recovery plan or business continuity plan is to never be implemented. Avoiding cyber security incidents is always the best policy, but things do go wrong. Organisations should have a disaster recovery plan that provides a pathway to methodically and quickly recovering from the effects of an attack. Some people argue that business continuity plans and disaster recovery plans are different names for the same thing. Others say that disaster recovery is only for major issues, such as terrorist attacks and natural disasters like floods, earthquakes and fires, whereas business continuity planning includes smaller events such as a single attempt to enter a computer suite.

Some specialists argue that disaster recovery planning is only for technology recovery whereas business continuity planning includes getting the business up and running. Both plans will include time lines with recovery objectives.

Government agencies, such as the UK's cyber security 'fusion cell', bring industries, information security specialists and government together to exchange information on cyber incidents and threats and the techniques for combating them.

It also aims to enable the monitoring of security incidents in real time.

The purpose of this body and other international organisations such as ISF (Information Security Forum) and ISACA (Information Systems Audit and Control Association) is to reduce the impact of cyber security attacks by sharing knowledge and expertise.

For example, if a major earthquake prevents entry to the building, then the policy could state that the backup system held in a facility 100 miles away must be running within five hours and the backup data from the previous four backups must be recovered within six hours.

After the recovery has been completed and all systems working, the normal risk assessments and testing must be carried out to ensure that the system is functioning as expected.

GROUP ACTIVITY

(30 minutes)

Research an example of a disaster recovery plan and a business continuity plan and compare and contrast their structure.

4.2 Cyber security incident report

The actions taken to resolve a security incident should be logged to provide evidence for future approaches to similar instances.

Most organisations have their own cyber security incident report that provides important information and identifies key players and key decisions to be taken as the event unfolds. While individual organisations will have their own layouts and some specific ways of recording information, the following elements will normally be included:

- The title and date of the incident. The precise incident and when it occurred. The date is relevant because it can be cross-referenced to other events such as updating of patches, or anti-malware software.
- The target of the incident. Was it the organisation? Was it a particular department?
- Incident category. What was the severity of the incident? Normally these will be categorised as:
  - critical: lives could have been lost or critical system safety, such as the management of a petrochemical refinery, could have been compromised
  - significant: the incidents could include severe loss of reputation, disruption to services or financial loss
  - minor: inconvenient, such as loss of access to the system for a few hours
  - negligible: it had little impact on most of the system and system users, with limited disruptions for about an hour, loss of some data but nothing which could not be recreated easily.
- A description of the incident: what exactly was the problem? How was it identified? What was the nature of the incident?
- Type of attacker(s): was the attack internal, external, a single hacker, or an attack by a group or government?
- Purpose of the incident: what was the attack trying to achieve? Was it for financial gain? Political advantage? Destruction of reputation?
- Techniques used by the attacker(s): phishing, theft of passwords, denial of service, unauthorised access to buildings and facilities, etc.
- Impact of the incident: what impact did it have on sensitive data, business reputation, access to information?

- Cost of the incident: what has it cost to recover from the incident? Was it significant in terms of reputation, financial loss and/or lost working time?
- Response needed: was the incident reported, or did it need to be reported to the authorities, e.g. police, cybercrime units, software owners, specialist companies that have been employed to deal with incidents on behalf of the organisation and certain customers?
- Future management: this may be a separate document, but will consider the following:
  - A review of the incident, considering the reality of dealing with the incident against the plans of action in place. What worked and what did not?
  - Evaluate the findings to identify trends, omissions and failures resulting from the incident.
  - Update of documentation, key information, procedures, policies and controls to accommodate the review and evaluation findings to improve the plans.
  - Recommendations for changes that may be necessary beyond the current plans.

KNOW IT

1 Summarise why you should know your responsibilities for dealing with an incident.
2 Outline why it is important to contain the incident.
3 What plans may be used to aid recovery from a cyber security incident?
4 Identify four incident categories.
5 Identify six areas which should be covered in a cyber security incident report.

Unit 3 Assessment practice questions

Below are practice questions for you to try.

Section A

Your local clothes shop, 'Dress for the Occasion', has decided to expand to include menswear. The shop has used a single computer-based system, set up several years ago by the owner's son. He has now added a second computer for the menswear system and linked them together via a wireless network. The network hub also provides access to the internet.

The whole system was recently shut down after a virus was introduced on to the system through an email. Knowing that you are studying cyber security, the owner has asked you to identify potential threats to the system and provide him with advice and guidance on how the system should be protected. He would also like you to provide him with a handbook of common cyber security terminology, for future reference.

The opening of the new department has caused some friction as the shop assistant who has worked with the firm for 10 years has been passed over for the manager's role in favour of a younger, new member of staff with more experience of menswear.

While you are talking to the owner, the book keeper comes in to say that he has lost his laptop with all the financial data on it but that there is a fully backed up copy on the PC in the office.

1 a Describe what is mean by *unauthorised access*, in terms of a computer system. (2)
  b Describe one way in which unauthorised access could affect Dress for the Occasion. (2)

2 a Identify two types of organisational data that could be compromised as a result of the unauthorised access described in answer b. (2)
  b Identify two cyber threats which could arise as a result of the new manager's appointment in menswear. (2)
  c Explain the possible motivation for one of the two threats identified. (3)
  d Identify two vulnerabilities that could be exploited at Dress for the Occasion. (2)
  e Discuss possible outcomes for Dress for the Occasion if its network security is not improved. (10)

3 a Recommend two software and two hardware controls which would be beneficial to Dress for the Occasion. Write your answers in Table 3.7.

Table 3.7 Software and hardware controls

Software controls	Hardware controls
1.	1.
2.	2.

  b Explain why Dress for the Occasion should implement an email policy. (3)
  c What type of incident is the lost laptop, identified in the scenario? Select one from the list below by putting a cross in the box next to it. (1)

Table 3.8 Types of incident

Level of significance	Tick/cross
Negligible	
Minor	
Significant	
Critical	

  d Justify your choice of category in 3(c). (7)

Section B

The case study is not required to answer these questions.

1 a Give the full names for the terms identified by their initials in the box below. (4)

Initials	Name
IDS	
HIDS	
NIDS	
IPS	

  b Summarise the purpose of each of the items identified in 1a. (8)

2 Following a recent denial of service attack, you have been asked to create a cyber security incident report template. Explain the purpose of such a report. (2)

3 Summarise six sections that should be contained in a cyber security incident report other than the title and date. (6)

Unit 04

Computer networks

ABOUT THIS UNIT

Today, networks are not limited to allowing computers and their peripherals to communicate with other computers. Mobile telephones, household devices such as central heating systems and smart locks can also be networked, allowing you to monitor your work and home from any location. In business, many organisations could not function without the world wide web – think of Amazon, eBay and banks. The demand for network engineers, technicians and administrators provides a range of job opportunities and options for career progression.

This unit will provide you with the knowledge and practical experience to plan, implement and maintain computer networks. We will start with the hardware and then build the components into working networks. The protocols described are limited to those most commonly found in network systems, but they will provide you with sufficient underpinning experience to work with other protocols when the opportunity arises.

Some content in this unit is described in other units, especially Unit 1. You should re-read the sections identified alongside the new information in this unit, so that you can more fully understand networks.

LEARNING OUTCOMES

The topics and activities in this unit will help you to:

1 Understand the concept of networks.
2 Be able to plan computer networks to meet client requirements.
3 Be able to present network solutions to clients.
4 Be able to plan maintenance activities for computer networks.

How will I be assessed?

You will be assessed by producing evidence from set scenarios or from work that you carry out as part of a work placement or employment. The evidence will demonstrate your ability to plan, build and maintain computer networks, in line with IT and business requirements and standards. The evidence will be assessed by your tutor.

How will I be graded?

You will be graded using the following criteria:

Learning outcome	Pass assessment criteria	Merit assessment criteria	Distinction assessment criteria
You will:	To achieve a pass you must demonstrate that you have met all the pass assessment criteria	To achieve a merit you must demonstrate that you have met all the pass and merit assessment criteria	To achieve a distinction you must demonstrate that you have met all the pass, merit and distinction assessment criteria
1 Understand the concept of networks	**P1** Explain how network addressing is used	**M1** Compare and contrast the OSI and TCP/IP networking models	**D1** Discuss the role of TCP/IP in networks
	P2 Explain security considerations for computer networks		
2 Be able to plan computer networks to meet client requirements	**P3** Create a network specification to meet an identified client requirement	**M2** Justify security measures for inclusion in an identified network solution	
	P4 Produce planning documentation for the implementation of an identified network solution		
3 Be able to present network solutions to clients	**P5** Communicate the network solution to the identified client	**M3** Recommend performance tools to benchmark network solution	
4 Be able to plan maintenance activities for computer networks	**P6** Create a maintenance plan for the network solution		**D2** Evaluate the selection of maintenance activities for the network solution

LO1 Understand the concept of networks *P1 M1 D1*

GETTING STARTED 👤

(10 minutes)

List the types of networks you have used or know about, and identify their hardware components.

1.1 Network interfaces

Network interface devices (NIUs) allow connections in local area networks (LANs) and wide area networks (WANs). Whichever device is used, it carries out the same purpose by allowing different devices and networks to communicate by providing a single, common transmission **protocol**. Examples of network interface hardware include wireless access points, hubs and routers (see Unit 1, LO1.5, page 14) and software network interfaces (e.g. iproute2).

🔑 **KEY TERMS**

Network interface – the hardware or software which connects two or more devices to each other.

Protocol – a set of rules, standards and principles which allow network devices to exchange data.

1.2 Network types

LANs and WANs are discussed in Unit 1, LO3.4 (page 30). A wireless local area network (WLAN) uses high-frequency radio waves to communicate between devices and to share data. This means that networks can be set up more quickly than ethernet LANs, which need cables to carry communications and data.

1.3 Network components

Servers are described in Unit 1 (LO3.1, page 26) but there are also proxy servers which have a specific role in networking. The proxy sits on the network between a server which supports a particular application (e.g. email) and the network devices. When a device needs to contact the email server, it sends a request to the proxy server, which carries out checks to ensure the validity of the request and forwards it to the email server.

Hosts are described in LO3.2 and wireless access points, hubs and routers are described in Unit 1, LO1.5.

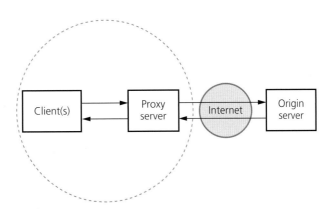

▲ **Figure 4.1** Example of a network with a proxy server

Workstation is the term used for any computer connected to a local area network. They are usually personal computers or laptops but can also be designed for a specific role, usually technical or scientific, and are more powerful than personal computers and only run software designed for that purpose.

A host can be:

1 A device or program which provides services to smaller or less capable devices or programs on a network.
2 A computer system or server which holds data and/or programs which can be accessed by a remote device or computer system.
3 Any computer or other device, including printers, scanners and instrumentation, connected to TCP/IP networks and which has its own IP address.

(10 minutes)

1 Identify four different network topologies.
2 Produce a diagram to represent each of the identified topologies.

The following protocols are explained in Unit 1 LO2.9:

● Internet Protocol (IP)
● Transmission Control Protocol (TCP)
● User Datagram Protocol (UDP)
● File Transfer Protocol (FTP)
● Simple Mail Transfer Protocol (SMTP).

KEY TERM

Network ID – the part of the TCIP/IP address which identifies devices on a LAN or internet. It is vital to the tracking and management of hardware, data and devices required by users and also helps to maintain security of the network.

KEY TERM

Datagram – a discrete independent message, sent over a network, which has its source and destination information attached to enable accurate routing.

1.4 Network topologies

These are described in Unit 1 LO3.3 (page 28) and 3.4 (page 30).

1.5 Network protocols

A network protocol provides a set of rules and conventions (standards) which govern how devices on a network:

● identify themselves and each other
● communicate with each other
● bundle the messages they send or receive into packets of an agreed size and layout.

Some network protocols go further and provide additional services such as:

● a receiving device that sends a message to the sending device to say that a packet has arrived (an acknowledgement)
● data compression, which compresses the number of bits used to store data.

When packaging messages, the protocol provides a set of rules which identifies how the package should be structured; for example, with a header describing:

● what is being sent
● which **network ID** it is being sent to
● how many parts the communication has.

The communication has a maximum number of bits and ends with a trailer which states that the communication is complete or whether another package will follow.

The ethernet protocol relates to the most popular of the LAN networks. It has a number of elements such as frames, physical layer and MAC operation, which will be looked at in more detail in the following sections.

802.3-2015 is the latest IEEE approved draft standard for ethernet.

1.6 Networking models

Also known as a reference model, the purpose of a network model is to help the designers and developers of network hardware and software to picture how their product will work with others (interoperability). We shall look at two of the most widely used models: OSI 7-layer and TCP/IP.

OSI 7-layer model

Open Systems Interconnection (OSI) 7-layer is a standard independent of any protocol which describes how network devices communicate. It is a theoretical model which provides a generic guide to the development of network protocols and interfaces. Each of its seven layers represents a group of linked functions. Each layer has a particular purpose, so design and debugging on one layer can take place without causing issues with the remaining layers.

The layers are stacked on top of one another in a particular order and this is often referred to as the OSI model stack. The stack is also split into two parts:

● the upper or host layer
● lower or media layers.

Table 4.1 The OSI 7-layer model

Layer no.	Layer title	Purpose	Location
7	**Application** Supports the applications and end user processes IT IS NOT AN APPLICATION ITSELF	**Messages and packets** • Identification of communicators (Is there anybody out there?) • Assessment of network capacity (Will the network let me contact them now?) • Data syntax (Can we understand the message?) • User authentication and privacy (How do you know it is me?)	Upper/host Application-specific functions: • Formatting • Encryption • Connection management
6	**Presentation** Usually part of the operating system	Packets Converts data into a suitable format so it can be understood by the application. It also: • supports data compression and encryption • decides data structure • communicates through gateways and application interfaces.	
5	**Session** Allows applications running on different computers to communicate with each other	Packets • Sets up the communication link between applications. • Manages the link, e.g. if using half duplex, this layer determines whose turn it is to transmit data. • Terminates the link. • Authenticates and reconnects link after an interruption.	
4	**Transport** The postal service, ensuring that data packets arrive error free and without loss	**Datagrams**, segments and packets • Puts the data into the correct packet format. • Delivers the packet. • Checks the packet has arrived. • Retransmits the packet if not received. • If data packet is damaged, arranges for resubmission.	**Lower/media** Provides: • routing • addressing • flow control.
3	**Network** Transfers data around between the internet	Datagrams and packets • Examines the logical network address. • Converts it into physical machine addresses on the receiving computer and reverses it when a message is sent back. • Routes packet using routers. • Detects transmissions errors (error control). • Retransmits correct data. • Regulates the speed of data transfer (flow control). • If the packet is too large for a network on the route to handle, it is fragmented and reassembled by the receiving device (fragmenting packets).	
2	**Datalink** Responsible for transferring data between devices. It responds to requests from the network layer above and the issues requests to the physical layer below	Bits and packets • Encodes bits into packets prior to submission. • Decodes packets back into bits. Divided into two sublayers: • Media access control (MAC) layer which controls how computers on the network gain access to the data and obtain permission to transmit it. • Logical link control (LLC) layer controls packet synchronisation, flow control and error checking.	
1	**Physical** Includes: • network medium • physical network topologies • network card • process of transmitting and receiving signals from the network medium.	Four general functions: • Definition of the hardware specification, e.g. maximum length of cable, width of cable, physical connectors, voltages. • Data transmission and reception, e.g. amplifiers and repeaters. • Encoding and signalling. • Topology and physical network design, physical layout and structure of network.	

Remember the order of the layers by memorising this sentence:

All **P**eople **S**eem **T**o **N**eed **D**ata **P**rocessing

INDEPENDENT ACTIVITY

(20 minutes)

Complete the table below by providing the full name of the protocols relevant to each of the OSI levels and a brief description of their role. The first one is part completed for you as an example.

Table 4.2 OSI 7-layer and associated protocols

OSI layer	Protocol	Full protocol name	Description
Application	FTP	File Transfer Protocol	The simplest method for sending and receiving files over the internet, FTP splits the files into a number of segments and gives each one a reference number so that the ...
	TELNET		
	WWW		
	HTTP		
	TCP		
	NFS		
	SMTP		
Presentation	JPEG		
	MIDI		
	MPEG		
	Music, image, movie formats		
Session	NFS		
	SQL		
	RPC		
Transport	TCP		
	UPD		
	SPX		
	NetBEUI		
Network	IP		
	IPX		
	RIP		
	ARP		
	ICMP		
	RARP		
	EGP		
	NetBEUI		
	DLC		
Datalink	HDLC		
	LLC		
	SLIP		
	PPP		
Physical			

The layers of OSI 7 can only communicate with the layer above and the layer below. Figure 4.2 shows how this works.

LOGICAL NETWORK ADDRESS

Every device connected to a network communicates with other devices. To do this, it needs an address, much as business and homes have addresses to be able to receive post. Every device which communicates across the internet needs a unique address.

TRANSMIT	USER 1		USER 2	RECEIVE
Data	8	User	8	Data
Data	7	Application layer	7	Data
Data	6	Presentation layer	6	Data
Data	5	Session layer	5	Data
Segment	4	Transport layer	4	Segment
Packet, datagram	3	Network layer	3	Packet, datagram
Frame, cell	2	Data link layer	2	Frame, cell
Frame, bit	1	Physical layer	1	Frame, bit
Physical link (layer 0)				

▲ **Figure 4.2** How data is transferred between network devices using the OSI model

1 The user transmits data from the computer to the application level.
2 The data is passed down through the layers to physical layer, which is the only layer able to communicate with other devices and networks.
3 The data is sent along the physical link to the receiving computer.
4 It moves up through the layers and arrives with the user.

TCP/IP model

TCP/IP (Transmission Control Protocol and Internet Protocol) is a four-layer protocol-based standard used in all internet communications. It is a standard communication protocol in some networks but is aimed particularly at the internet. The IP maps how devices move data from one to another and TCP identifies how the communication across the link arrives accurately and without any missing elements.

Both TCP/IP and the OSI 7-layer model have layers and a similar design; however, TCP/IP has only four layers.

Table 4.3 TCP/IP layers

Layer no.	Layer title	Purpose
1	Application	Provides applications with the means to access the services of the other layers and defines the protocols used by the applications to exchange data.
2	Host–host transport	Provides the application layer with session and datagram communication services.
3	Internet	Provides addressing, packaging and routing functions.
4	Network interface	Places TCP/IP packages on the network medium and receiving them on the network medium.

Each layer is directly related to one or more protocols used to carry out the tasks or tasks for which it is responsible.

Table 4.4 TCP/IP layers and associated protocols

Layer	Protocol suite					
Application	Telnet	FTP	SMTP	DNS	RIP	NMP
Host–host transport	TCP			UPD		
Internet	IP				IGMP	ICMP
	ARP					
Network interface	Ethernet	Token ring		Frame relay	ATM	

INDEPENDENT ACTIVITY 👤 ······························

(20 minutes)

Complete Table 4.5 by providing the full name of the protocols provided for the specified TCP/IP layers, with a brief description of each protocol.

Table 4.5 Common protocols

TCP/IP layer	Protocol	Full protocol name	Description
Application	DNS		
	NMP		
Internet	IGMP		
	ICMP		
Network interface	Ethernet		
	Token ring		
	Frame relay		
	ATM		

1.7 IP Versions

The internet protocol (IP) is a set of rules or standards to make sure that data is accurately transferred between devices on a single network, multiple networks or the internet. It ensures that the datagrams or packets have address information or tags at a known location. This process is known as encapsulation.

It works in a similar way to the Royal Mail postal system, as shown in Figure 4.3.

Walk to the post box (communication channel)

Postal route (network and internet route) unknown

The letter (message)

Letterbox (source host)

Old friends (the destination host)

▲ **Figure 4.3** Sending a message via the mail

You, the sender, place the letter in the envelope and write the address on the envelope (datagram and address). You put the letter in the post box (the source host). After that you have no part in how it is delivered to the recipient. It may go by road, rail, air or sea, depending on which methods are available to the postal services along the route.

Similarly, the datagram is encapsulated (addressed) and put into the system by the sender, in this case the source host (the computer sending the message). Again, the sender has no part in how it reaches the destination host (receiving computer). The routing of the datagram depends upon the intermediate networks. Unlike letters, datagrams may be split into two or more instalments and each part is individually addressed. Each part can take different routes and times to complete the journey.

IP is a connectionless protocol – when the host dispatches the datagram, the route it will take to reach the required address is unknown.

The IP protocol assigns an address to each device on the network. For IPv4, this is a 32-bit length address and for IPv6, the most recent version of the internet protocol, a 128-bit length address. This is important because, in some countries, the 32-bit address system has run out of numbers.

Differences between IPv4 and IPv6 are shown in Table 4.6.

Table 4.6 The differences between IPv4 and IPv6

Difference	IPv4	IPv6
Addresses	32-bit length	128-bit length
Address representation	Binary numbers represented in decimal notation	Binary numbers represented in hexadecimal
Fragmentation	Carried out by the source and the forwarding routers	Carried out only by centre
Internet Protocol Security (IPSec)	Optional	Built in
Configuring addresses	Static (manual) configuration if ipv4 addresses or dynamic configuration (DHCP) required	Auto-configuration is available.
Address Resolution Protocol (ARP)	Available for mapping mac addresses to ipv4 addresses.	Replaced by Neighbour Discovery Protocol (NDP)
Packet flow	Not identified	Available via the flow label field in the IPv6 header
Checksum field	Available	None
Internet Group Management Protocol (IGMP)	Manages membership of multicast groups	Replaced by Multicast Listener Discovery (MLD)
Broadcast message	Available	Via an IPv6 multicast address which always starts ff00::/8

GROUP ACTIVITY

(30 minutes)

Produce a guide for new network technicians explaining what network addressing is, its purpose and how it works.

Extend the guide to explain the OSI and TCP/IP models to include their similarities and differences and where networking addressing sits within these models.

1.8 Network addressing

In LO1.7, we saw that all devices on a network have a unique address assigned to them so that they can send and receive information. We shall now consider the different elements of network addressing.

Table 4.7 Types of network addressing

Addressing method	Description
DHCP (Dynamic Host Configuration Protocol)	Used to allocate IP addresses and supply configuration information to any device, including servers, mobile devices and desktop computers, allowing them to communicate on a network using the Internet Protocol (IP).
MAC (Media Access Control)	A physical address, unique to a particular network device. For example, if your computer has a network interface card (NIC), its MAC address is hard-coded (read only so cannot be changed) or hard-wired (electronic circuits wired during the building of the NIC).
APIPA (Automatic Private IP Addressing)	A Microsoft Windows facility which takes over if the DHCP server fails. It allocates an IP address in the private range 169.254.0.1 to 169.254.255.254 to a client machine, which in turn checks that the address is unique using ARP. When DHCP is available again, clients automatically update their IP addresses.
Class (routing)	The classes were assigned by IEEE to meet the needs of different types of networks. There are five classes (see Table 4.8) but only the first three are available to identify workstations, switches routers, etc. The first eight bits of the IP address refer to the class (e.g. A, B). If we know the class we can work out how many of the remaining bits refer to the network ID and which to the node ID.
Classless	Removes class boundaries to release 'wasted' addresses from the class/network/node convention. Instead, there are just two groups of bits, each of variable length. The first is the network prefix, which identifies one or more network gateways, and the second is the host. The organisation is assigned sufficient address blocks for its number of hosts.
Private	A private internet address is assigned by the Network Information Centre (InterNIC) to organisations so that they can create their own private network. The devices on your home network such as tablets, computers, printers, mobile phones will have private IP addresses. No device outside of your network can directly access any of your devices without a Network Address Translator. Computers on private networks within organisations will normally have a private IP address.
Loopback	A special range of IP addresses 127.0.0.0 to 127.255.255.255, used for testing communication or transportation. A data packet is sent using a loopback address and is immediately returned to sender, unchanged. If it is not received, there is an issue, possibly with the network card.
TCP ports	A number given to user sessions and server applications in an IP network. The number is allocated by the Internet Assigned Numbers Authority (IANA) and is located in the packet header. It allows the type of packet to be identified, e.g. email, voice over internet (VOIP) etc.
Default gateway	A gateway is an access point or IP router that a networked device uses to send data or messages to another device on a different network or the internet. Default means that the particular gateway is used by the device automatically, unless an application states an alternative gateway.

Class addressing

The list of IEEE IP classes is shown in Table 4.8. Note that D and E are restricted.

Table 4.8 IEEE IP classes

Class	Start address	End address	Available to hosts?	Purpose
A	1.0.0.0	127.255.255.255	Yes	Large network
B	128.0.0.0	191.255.255.255	Yes	Medium network
C	192.0.0.0	223.255.255.255	Yes	Small network
D	234.0.0.0	239.255.255.255	No	Reserved for multicast
E	240.0.0.0	255.255.255.255	No	Reserved for research purposes

The number of bits available for network ID and host ID vary depending upon the size of the network; for example, in Class A, the first eight bits give you the Network ID (the network the device is attached to). Bit 8, the first bit, is always 0 and so we can have 2^7 addresses – that is 128 possible networks. The remaining 24 bits are available for the use of the devices or hosts which are attached to the individual networks 2^{24} or 16,777,216 in total.

If you move to the small network address or Class C, the first 24 bits are available for the network address; however, in fact, there are only 21 as bits 8 to 6 – the first 3 bits are always set to 110. So we have 2^{21} or 2,097,152 networks but only 8 bits for the number of devices or hosts. This means there can be up to 2^8 or 256 devices per network.

PAIRS ACTIVITY

(30 minutes)

In pairs, research class and classless addressing and prepare a presentation on your findings. Present your findings to the rest of the group for further discussion.

1.9 Network data units

By now you should recognise that data are not just placed on a route between computers or networks in the hope that they will arrive safely and in the right order. We have already mentioned headers and packets, for example. We shall now look at three ways in which data is transmitted.

The ethernet frame is one of the ways in which data is organised for transmission over a network. Each data packet has three types of data:

1 Address fields holding the address of the sending device and the receiving device, to prevent data ending up in the wrong hands.
2 The data being transmitted, which will be somewhere between 64 and 1500 bytes. More than one packet will probably be needed to send files or images.
3 Error-checking field. The sender creates a code number which depends upon the type of data and its length. This field holds that code. The receiving device carries out the same calculation and compares the version of the code it has created with the one in this field. If they are the same, the data has arrived safely; if not, something is lost or damaged and a request will be sent for another copy (this is why the sender's address is important).

When sending data across the internet (a datagram), it is still necessary to break the data down into packets. These IP packets contain the header data, which includes information such as:

- IP version
- IP header length in 32-bit words
- level of importance
- total length of the packet in 6 bits
- packet identifier
- whether it can be fragmented into smaller packets
- packet number
- time to live (countdown to destruction from the moment of creation so that it does not keep looping around the network)
- protocol (i.e. TCP or UDP)
- header checksum which also identifies errors.

The packet also contains the sending address, receiving address, security and the data itself.

TCP performs a number of roles and one of them is to take the stream of data sent by an application, cut it up into TCP packets (or segments) and send them to the IP layer so that the IP packet information can be added.

The segment has a header section and can carry control information and data at the same time as well as the data. The format is:

- Source port (a 16-bit port number for the process which created the TCP packet on the source device).
- Destination port (a 16-bit port number for the intended final destination of the data on the destination device).
- Sequence number (the order of the first byte of data in this segment).
- Acknowledge number (if the ACK bit is set, the segment is sending an acknowledgement of receipt and also sending the sequence number of the next segment the device expects to receive).
- Data offset (the number of 32-bit words in the header). This tells the receiving device how far down the segment the data content starts.
- Reserved for future use (must be zero).
- Control bits (further instructions/information for the receiving device, e.g. URG if set means this segment is a priority, PSH if set requests that the data is immediately pushed to the receiving application, Fin fi set requests that the connect is closed).

Network security

This is covered in Unit 3 LO 3 AC 3.1, 3.2 in particular, but also generally across this unit on cyber security and Unit 1 LO5, AC 5.2 to 5.6.

Virtualisation

This is covered in Unit 1 LO3.2 (page 27).

 RESEARCH ACTIVITY

(30 minutes)

Research a particular example of network virtualisation from the following categories of software and create a presentation explaining the function and facilities offered.

- Platform virtualisation.
- Emulation.
- Hardware virtualisation.
- Virtual machines.
- VMware.

KNOW IT

1 What is the purpose of a network interface?
2 What is a proxy server?
3 List three network protocols.
4 List the layers of the OSI 7-layer model.
5 Give the bit length of IPv4 and IPv6 addresses.

LO1 Assessment activities

Below are three suggested activities that have been directly linked to the pass, merit and distinction criteria for LO1 to help with assignment preparation; they include Top tips on how to achieve the best results.

Activity 1 – pass criteria *P1*

You have been asked to produce a guide for new learners to explain the purpose of network addressing. Research the protocols and approaches used to address devices and messages on networks, providing examples to support your ideas.

Activity 2 – pass criteria *P2*

Your network manager is appalled at the number of viruses which have been introduced to the network through users uploading their own software and data, even though they are not supposed to. You have carried out a brief survey and discovered that users have little understanding of how or why networks should be protected. Your manager, impressed with your initiative, has asked you to produce a simple guide to network security, explaining the dangers of poor network security, the types of security issues and how they may be avoided.

Activity 3 – merit criteria *M1* and distinction criteria *D1*

Several colleagues have been arguing about the similarities and differences between OSI7 and TCP/IP networking models and how important or relevant these are. You decide to carry out a comparison of the two models, so that everyone can have an agreed view. Research OSI 7 and TC/IP and present your findings to the group.

Build on this presentation by discussing the specific role of TCP/IP in network communications.

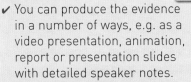

TOP TIPS

✔ You can produce the evidence in a number of ways, e.g. as a video presentation, animation, report or presentation slides with detailed speaker notes.
✔ You could provide the evidence as a set of guides for junior technicians starting their careers in networks.
✔ For activity 3, look at the role of TCP/IP in networks for different topologies.

LO2 Be able to plan computer networks to meet client requirements *P3 P4 M2*

GETTING STARTED

(10 minutes)

Select a computer network you are familiar with and list the hardware and software which makes up the network.

Without good planning, it is likely that the network will:

- be unable to meet client requirements
- not run efficiently or effectively
- require expensive reworking if any potential difficulties are not identified at the planning stage.

It may even not work at all. To help you avoid any or all of these issues we will now discuss what planning is required to aid the successful design and implementation of a computer network to meet the client requirements within budget, in time and recognising all technical constraints.

First, find out whether the client requires a new network or wishes to update their current system. The reasons for the client having the network need to be clearly identified and recorded. You also need to find out the size of the organisation or department requiring the network and its location. Whether it is on one site or several sites is also important as it will affect the type of network or networks needed to meet the requirements.

Planning and developing a network could provide evidence for Unit 8 Project management.

2.1 Network configuration

Network components

All networks, except for virtual ones, must have hardware and so it is important to obtain a list of network components which the network will require. The precise range will vary with the type and purpose of the network but it could include the following.

For a wired network

Ask:

- How many devices need to be linked by cable?
- Where will the cabling run?
- How much cable will be required?

This may not be clear at an early stage, but a rough estimate should be possible by considering that at least one switch and one router will be required, as well an expected number of devices, all of which will need cabling. Also consider the location of the network (e.g. within a single room, building or site). All of this information should allow you to estimate the requirements.

For a wireless network

There is still a need for some cabling as the wireless router will need to be wired to the internet access device, and there may be a need to plug wired devices into the router. Other considerations include:

- A wireless router.
- Wireless NICs, one for each device.
- An internet access device, which could be DSL or a cable modem.

For all networks

Consider:

- Routers to enable communication between networks, switches to communicate between devices. Ensure the capacity of these devices is greater than that required by the proposed network because bottlenecks may slow down the communications, reducing productivity and probably requiring an expensive upgrade soon after the network is installed.
- Servers managing a range of software or services, such as email, need to be identified.

Network operating systems

Network operating systems (NOSs) distribute the functions of the network across networked computers and allow simultaneous access to shared resources. If the network is a client server system, specialist software enables client requests for shared resources from the servers. A NOS is able to support multiple user accounts simultaneously and allows them to share resources via multitasking and multiuser environments.

Some NOS features are listed below, and the plan should identify the network requirements that will meet client needs, in terms of:

● performance: e.g. accuracy, efficiency, response times, device CPU utilisation
● scalability: the ability to maintain or enhance the performance of the network when additional processors are added to the system
● robustness/fault tolerance
● security: can the NOS identify a sufficient range of issues
● management and monitoring tools available within the operating system (e.g. a network analyser) which allow the network administrator to check whether the system is coping with the traffic and that there are no holdups.

Using this information, the type of NOS (e.g. Unix, Linux, Windows etc.) can be chosen.

2.2 Network services

DHCP

All devices on a network require an IP address, so the first decision is whether to use a static IP address for all or any of the devices. It is either set up manually by the network administrator or manager or DHCP automatically sets a dynamic IP address for each device when it connects to the network. Some devices require a static IP address, such as a local web server.

Routing

Choose the correct routing protocol to ensure that your IP addressing plan will work effectively and efficiently. All routing protocols decide the most suitable path for data to be transmitted between the sender and receiver. They also state the way in which routers in a network share information and report changes to the network which may affect the choice of route. The choice of router protocol depends upon a range of criteria, the most common ones being the following.

● Convergence speed: how quickly a set of routers agree on the state of the topology of their network.
● Scalability: how large a network can grow using a specific routing protocol.
● Resource usage: how much CPU time, memory and link bandwidth the protocol uses.
● Class or classless: (see LO1.8, page 118). Class routing does not have the subnet mask facility and cannot provide variable-length subnet mask capability. Classless routing includes the subnet mask. So, if for a Class C address for your printer, for example, the IP address is 192.168.08.1, the first

PAIRS ACTIVITY

(40 minutes)

Research two different NOSs and present your findings to the rest of the group for discussion.

three groups of 8 bits represent the network part or network ID and the last 8 bits represent the host address. To identify the subnet mask, setting all the network address bits to 1 and all the host digits to 0 gives us a fixed subset mask of 255.255.255.0. Classless routing allows the network part to be any length. For example, we can move 1 bit from the host part to the network part so the subnet is now 255.255.255.128. So we can have two subnets – one which contains all addresses between 192.168.08.0 to 192.168.08.126 and one which contains all addresses between 192.168.08.128 and 192.168.08.254. So how does the router know that an address includes a submask? The number of 1s available in the subset mask when converted to binary is counted and the number gives the size of the subnet. So, for 255.255.255.0, the number of 1s is 8×4=24 and so it is written as 255.255.255.0.

- Ease of implementation and maintenance: this determines the level of expertise and knowledge required of the network administrator who has to implement and maintain the network in line with the routing protocol requirements.

A range of routing protocols are available including:

- RIPv1 (Routing Information Protocol) version 1
- RIPv2 (Routing Information Protocol) version 2
- OSPF (Open Shortest Path First)
- IGRP (Interior Gateway Routing Protocol)
- EIGRP (Enhanced Interior Routing Protocol)
- BGP (Border Gateway Protocol).

Internet connection sharing

This allows you to share a single IP address, obtained from your internet service provider, with the other devices on the network. The devices each have a non-routable (private) IP address which is mapped to the external (public) IP address. This will allow devices on the LAN to access websites or cloud storage, for example.

Wi-fi access

A wi-fi access point will enable you to connect wireless devices to your cabled network.

This can be useful when you need to add devices to an existing network or to provide access to a network where extending the cabling would be impossible for reasons of access and/or cost.

Other services

Consider what services, other than sharing files, the user requires of the network, e.g. printing, email services, access to the internet, access to storage servers, etc.

2.3 IP configuration

IP configuration can take the form of a static, permanent IP address which provides a permanent IP address for a device, making it easier to locate. IP addresses are assigned automatically by a DHCP server, for example, to a device which connects to the network. This means that the address may be different each time the device is switched on and connects to the network.

Routing and masking were discussed in LO2.2.

RESEARCH ACTIVITY

(30 minutes)

A small legal firm want to implement a new network. They want personnel to be able to access the network to use email as well as to create, edit and read documents, spreadsheets and a database of their clients. The administration staff will require full access permissions and the solicitors only require read-only access. All staff will require Internet access and support for remote working. In addition, the business has a website where potential customers can submit an online form to ask for a member of the team to contact them. Identify the network services that will be required and justify your decisions.

2.4 Testing tools

Ping and Ipconfig were discussed in Unit 1 (LO1.6, page 15) and help to test connectivity between the sender and receiver hosts.

- Pathping is used to check for packet loss – whether any packet or packets fail to arrive at their final destination. This is often a warning of network congestion, where there are more data arriving at a router or network segment than it can handle, so the network drops the packets.
- Tracert is a utility which traces the exact route taken by packets between the sender and receiver and the time taken for them to reach the final destination, allowing bottlenecks and other issues to be identified.
- Route (e.g. Traceroute) is a computer network diagnostic tool which wil display the route (path) and measure any delays in the transit of data across an Internet Protocol network.

2.5 Network specification

A network specification sets out the elements shown in Table 4.9 below. Its purpose is to clarify for the client and the development team just what they are required to achieve.

Table 4.9 Network specification

Section	Outline content
Stakeholder requirements	What they want the network to achieve, e.g.: • reduce costs • improve productivity • improve communications between employees and/or clients, irrespective of location.
Applications	What applications are required, e.g.: • finance systems • HR systems • facilities management • office systems, e.g. word processing, spreadsheets • webinars • video-conferencing.
Services	• user management, e.g. username and password creation, allocation of access rights • email, e.g. email software, maximum storage capacity (mail box limit) • printing • system administration, e.g. arranging for new software applications, updating software, version control.
Constraints	What restrictions are there, e.g. costs, time.
Security	See Unit 3 and Unit 1 LO5.2 to 5.6. The appropriate range and level of security will depend upon a risk assessment carried out to identify: • the physical access controls required • what wi-fi security is appropriate; for example, security protocols such as WEP, WPA and WPA2 and network passwords • network security will include the type of firewall, hardware, software or hybrid. Beware of using MAC filtering as your only means of security. Every device has a unique MAC address. Your router will normally allow any device to connect to the network, but if you set it up to accept only devices with a known MAC address to join, then in theory, only those devices you recognise will be allowed to access the network. Unfortunately, MAC filtering is easily bypassed software which allows hackers to read the traffic and identify the MAC addresses which enable access.
Purpose	For example: • better internet access • network printing to reduce hardware capital and maintenance costs, shared data storage • file sharing.

2.6 Network plan

The plan should provide the developer with a clear understanding of what is required. It may be a single document, possibly with appendices or a set of different linked documents. Whichever approach is taken it should have the following elements.

User requirements

These may include the following.

- Tasks that need automating.
- Tasks that need to be carried out more efficiently.
- Whether there is an existing network which needs to be upgraded or connected to the new network.
- What business applications are required, e.g. word processing, financial management, email.
- Whether multiuser applications will be required, e.g. databases or project management systems.
- Whether email, internet access or a web server are required.
- The estimated number of users who will use the network, now and in five years' time.
- Whether strong network security is essential.
- Costs and budgetary constraints.

Components

These will vary with the actual design, but will include items such as:

- cables
- wireless access points
- routers
- gateways
- computers
- servers
- printers and other devices.

Services

See Table 4.9.

Software

This includes all software including operating systems, firewalls, anti-virus and other security software, performance monitoring software and applications.

Configuration requirements

A computer network includes hardware such as:

- clients' computers which access shared network resources through one or more servers.
- servers
- media – the cabling or fibres which connect the devices
- peripherals – shared printers and other devices provided by the servers
- routers
- switches.

Software components include:

- operating systems
- protocols
- applications.

Each component has settings which can be changed by the network manager to tailor its behaviour. All settings which are modified and those that do not need changing together make up the network configuration.

Security plan

This identifies the individual responsible for particular elements of the plan, a list of minimum security controls, training requirements for staff, audit and risk assessment plans and contingency planning.

Test plans

The created network must be tested and so a range of plans have to be designed. The main two are as follows.

Configuration test plan

The configuration requirements for each device or piece of software need to be tested to ensure that the configuration has been successful and that it achieves the expected outcomes in terms of a working network. The plan should include:

- The type of component being configured, e.g. server, router, operating system, application.
- If appropriate, the individual identifier for the component, e.g. client 1, email server.
- The test or tests to be carried out, e.g. ping, loopback, router interface.
- Opportunity to record the results of the test and any retests that have to be carried out if issues are identified.

This list of results can be used in future as the benchmark or baseline to check how well the network is working and also for comparison when changes are made as a result of upgrades or network expansion.

User acceptance test (UAT) plan

After all our hard work creating the new network, it is important that is accepted by the client, otherwise we may not get paid! So, a user acceptance test plan should be put in place which will ensure that, on completion, the user or users will be happy with the results. The plan could include:

- A description of all possible system functions.
- Input data for all tests.
- Acceptance criteria for agreeing that acceptance testing is successfully completed.
- All user constraints which must be considered as part of the testing.
- Definition of testing procedures.
- Test cases designed to identify any contradictions between the software products and the requirements.
- Test cases designed to identify any contradictions between hardware devices and the requirements.
- Test cases designed to identify whether timing constraints are met by the network.

RESEARCH ACTIVITY

(30 minutes)

In pairs, research two examples of a security plan. Identify ten security controls and outline their purpose.

Post-test evaluation:

- Were test run activities and outcomes documented?
- Was the UAT carried out in line with the test plan?
- Have users reviewed the outcomes of the tests?
- Were all defects accurately documented?
- Were all defects resolved?
- Does the network meet all user requirements?
- Have the users made their judgement based on the agreed acceptance criteria?
- Did each user sign off the output?

KNOW IT

1 What is the function of DHCP?
2 Name three routing protocols.
3 What is the difference between Pathping and Tracert testing tools?
4 Name five elements that could be included in a user acceptance test plan.

LO2 Assessment activities

Below are three suggested activities that have been directly linked to the pass and merit criteria for LO2 to help with assignment preparation; they include Top tips on how to achieve the best results.

You have been asked to create a network for a small department store with two sites, one in Southwich and one in Overwich, 20 miles apart. Currently, both sites have their own LAN but are not connected to each other. The only external facility is email, through a third-party email provider. The daughter of the founder has taken over and is a business graduate who appreciates the value of IT and the internet as business tools. She has asked you to plan a new network for the firm. You have a meeting to discuss her precise requirements, the funding available for the new system, the maintenance costs and security.

Activity 1 – pass criteria *P3*

Conduct an interview with the owner and create a network specification that will meet the requirements of the business.

Activity 2 – merit criteria *M2*

The client is particularly concerned that the network and data are protected from theft, denial of service and malware attacks. Make a presentation justifying your ideas for security measures.

Activity 3 – pass criteria *P4*

Create the planning documentation for the network, where necessary providing options such as types of router, applications, topology, etc.

TOP TIPS ✓
- Take your time to make sure that you fully understand the purpose of the network and the client requirements.
- Once you have read the initial brief from the client, make a note of any questions you need to ask.

GETTING STARTED

(10 minutes)

List the information you believe you need to give a client to ensure that they decide to use your plan for a new network.

LO3 Be able to present network solutions to clients *P5 M6*

3.1 Solution proposal

It is likely that you will, having considered the client requirements and constraints for the network, have two or even three possible solutions and recommendations to present to the client. This may take the form of a presentation with a question and answer session alongside a written report or just a written document; the approach you take will be led by the client. Whichever method is used, it will require the following sections and content.

Client requirements

It is likely that, as you prepare your plan, you may have informal meetings and discussions as well as more formal, well-documented meetings with the client that will change the original requirements. You should therefore start by stating the current client requirements.

Physical network design(s)

The different options for the physical network are described, together with the reason for the options being presented. This will include the strengths and weakness of the following areas:

● devices to be linked to the network
● technologies to be used.

Logical design

This concentrates on the way that data passes through the network between devices without considering the physical layout. The content of the design will include the following.

● Logical topologies and protocols: refer to how network devices communicate fixed by the network protocols, which control the way in which data moves across the network. Topologies include ethernet, a logical bus topology protocol and token ring, which is a logical ring topology protocol.
● Protocols have been discussed in LO1.6 and 1.8 and will vary with the type of network being offered.
● Addressing: the plan of the logical network will also identify the IP addresses for each device on the network. These may be private or public. Remember: a public IP address is issued by the ISP, while the router will issue private IP addresses to each device inside the network.
● Security is important and the logical network will also include security measures. You must convince the client that the organisation's data and employees will be protected as well as the network itself.
● Configuration: this should follow the content of the network plan, ensuring that the client understands how the configuration will affect the way in which the network operates.

Network design test plan

How will you and your client know that your network works? By thoroughly testing the design. The test plan should cover:

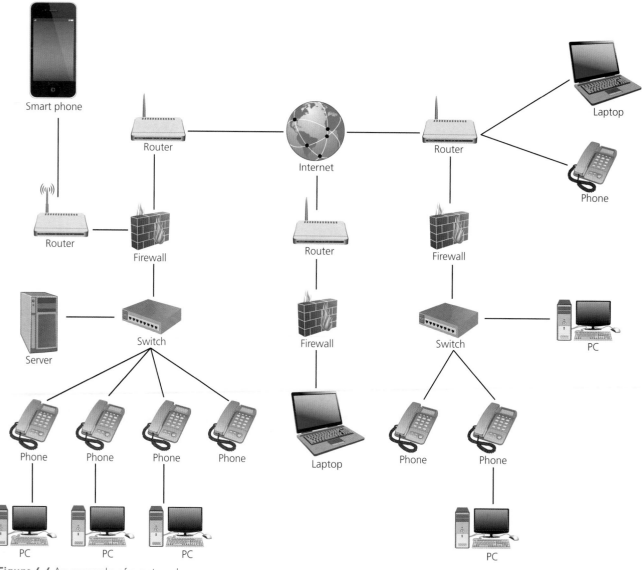

KEY TERMS

Throughput – the speed with which a given amount of data can be processed or passed between nodes.

Network map – a graphical representation of the computers and devices on the network that shows how they are connected.

● The test objectives (what do we want to know?)
● The acceptance criteria (how will we know that the objective has been met?)
● The types of tests to be carried out may include:
  • **throughput** tests
  • availability tests: running an application for an agreed timescale, collecting data on failures and repair times and comparing this with the service level agreement percentage availability originally agreed
  • network equipment and resource testing
  • checking that the shared devices, e.g. printers are available to all users
  • scripts testing.

The purpose of the network test design plan is to enable the client to understand the network solutions that would meet their needs. **Network maps** showing the physical layout of each solution help them to visualise your solutions. The map will show how each computer and device on the network is connected. An example is given in Figure 4.4.

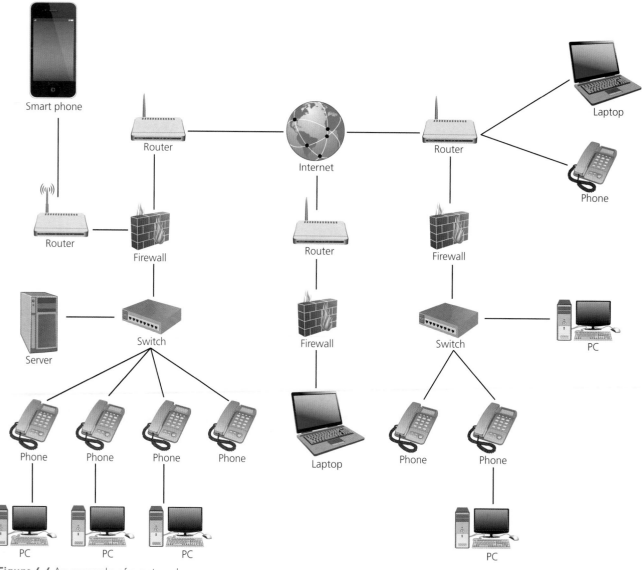

▲ **Figure 4.4** An example of a network map

GROUP ACTIVITY

(40 minutes)

Research two different network design test plan templates and identify the similarities and differences. Present your findings to the group and develop a template for future use.

Apps and software are available to help you map networks. Some are free to download and can be synced with other common software.

Installation schedule

The actual schedule will vary depending on the size and complexity of the network. However, any schedule should include the following elements.

● Identification of the activities that need to be undertaken to install the network, such as installing cable in the equipment room or configuring the computers on the network causing possible disruption to employees.
● The sequence in which the activities must be carried out – can some activities run in parallel, and do others have to be sequential?
● Estimate of the time required for each activity to be completed. This is not an exact science as it is based upon experience (whether you have carried out a similar activity before), and scaling up. For example, if it takes 15 minutes to install the operating system on one machine then to install it on 12 machines will take about three hours.
● Estimate of the resources needed to install the network. These can include:
  ● financial resources: what is the budget for installation?
  ● equipment resources, such as drill for enabling cables to be passed through walls, electronic circuit testers
  ● personnel resources, e.g. builders, electricians, and network team development members.
● Monitoring and control of the schedule: how you will ensure that timings and costs are met.
  ● recording the actual use of resources and the timeliness of activities starting and finishing
  ● taking steps to correct issues with the schedule.

Component configurations

The configuration plan is the required configuration details for each component and the order in which components should be configured, making sure that the network configuration is completed quickly and accurately.

Configuration test plan

This was described in LO2.6 (page 127).

User acceptance test (UAT) plan

This was described in LO2.6 (page 127).

3.2 Performance benchmarking tools

Although every effort is made to make sure that the new network will meet current requirements and has the capacity for future growth, issues can arise. The network performance must be regularly monitored against its benchmark. Fortunately, a range of tools can be used to carry out this role for the network manager. These can include:

● Testing data transfer rates between computers.
● Stability testing: is the internet connection performing to the required standard at all times? Is it sometimes slower than expected?
● Reliability testing: is the hardware or software component consistently carrying out its function in line with its specification?
● TCP/IP protocol testing.

Your recommendations should form part of the presentation.

KEY TERM

Network benchmarking tools – software which carries out one or more tests to compare current performance against an agreed standard.

(20 minutes)

A range of benchmarking tools are available, some of which are free. In pairs, investigate two different benchmarking tools for two different types of benchmark identified above. Present your findings to the rest of the class.

1 What is the difference between a logical and a physical network design?
2 What is the purpose of a User Acceptance Test?
3 List four types of test which could be carried out by performance monitoring tools.
4. What is the difference between a public and private IP address?

LO3 Assessment activities

Below are two suggested assessment activities that have been directly linked to the pass and merit criteria in LO3 to help with assignment preparation; they include Top tips on how to achieve best results.

✔ Remember to communicate with your client in language that they can understand, avoiding jargon and explaining technical concepts where necessary.
✔ Show that you have researched benchmark tools by ensuring you give reasons for your recommendations.

Activity 1 – pass criteria *P5*

Using the plan you devised for the activities in LO2, create a presentation about your suggested network solution for your client, ensuring that you can justify each of the areas identified in LO3.1.

Activity 2 – merit criteria *M3*

At the end of your presentation for activity 1, you must recommend, with reasons, your choice of performance benchmark tools for this solution and why they are appropriate.

LO4 Be able to plan maintenance activities for computer networks *P6 D2*

(10 minutes)

List the maintenance tasks that you carry out on your own computer, network or other devices.

Everything wears out, breaks down, is overtaken by a new version or becomes obsolete. Networks are no different, in spite of doing everything possible during the design and development phases to ensure that it will meet specified needs for at least five years. A maintenance plan will help us to:

● prevent some issues, such as loss of protection against malware
● identify issues and problems at an early stage and reduce their effect by correcting them at the earliest opportunity
● create a plan to cope if major problems do occur (contingency planning).

4.1 Maintenance plan

Maintenance considerations will vary with the complexity and type of network, but most will include the following.

- The network configuration map for devices, together with any reconfigurations which have taken place.
- The network configuration map for the software, including memory requirements or driver settings.
- Organisational policies covering:
  - user access controls
  - adoption of new devices and software
  - network security.
- Schedule of event reviews, e.g. every three days.
- Checklist for hardware devices:
  - hardware removed from the network
  - hardware added to network
  - any hardware faults on clients, printers, servers, etc.
  - functionality of peripherals, are they performing as expected?
  - cabling and connections for cracks, breaks, disconnection or incorrect connection
  - error indicators, e.g. red or flashing lights.
- Checklist for software:
  - updates available
  - updates installed
  - appropriate anti-malware update schedule
  - updated drivers, e.g. for printers
  - product licences validity and currency.
- Event logs:
  - check DNS, security, application and system logs
  - check for service failure on start-up
  - ensure necessary services are available on start-up and disable those which are not required
  - troubleshoot any warnings or error events
  - archive old event to files with correct dates; the definition of 'old' is set by organisational procedure.

4.2 Maintenance issues

Maintenance is mainly carrying out activities that ensure that the network remains up and running as effectively and efficiently as the original design and plan intended. Experience has taught network managers that some issues are more likely to occur than others. Table 4.10 describes some of the most common issues.

Table 4.10 Common maintenance issues

Issue	Possible source	Possible treatment
Introduction of a virus	• Infected emails • Infected software installation • Hacking	• Anti-virus software • Firewall installation or reconfiguration • Software updates
Hardware malfunction or breakdown	• Worn parts • Foreign bodies • Drivers not updated • Power surge	• Regularly clean and check components • Remove small objects which may have fallen into the device • Power surge protectors
New hardware not working properly, e.g. running very slowly or erratically	• Drivers are not updated • Connectors or cables damaged	• Check for updated drivers • Check connectors and cables for breaks or damage and replace if necessary
Replacement hardware not working	• Systems requirement of new hardware not compatible • Installer is corrupt • Firewall blocking connections	• Check the system requirements and update if necessary • Obtain new installer • Configure firewall to enable access
Operating system updates not loading or causing other malfunctions	• System requirements are not compatible • Missing patches or updates • Reboot of system required	• Update system • Check for patches or updates and install if available • Reboot system, following agreed procedures, e.g. warning of shut down, saving of all data, etc.
New software not loading or malfunctioning	As above	As for software updates
Network activity is slow	• Poor configuration management • Security vulnerabilities • IOS version proliferation • Outdated hardware • Diagnostic and performance tools • Unauthorised software	• Review configuration for errors, security issues, authentication issues • Check all security measures are up to date and monitored • Review and reduced IOS versions by updating devices or replacing them • Plan removal and replacement of outdated hardware over time • Review range of tools and identify alternatives which have lower resource requirements • Remove all unauthorised software and put in place policies and procedures to prevent further installations
Security	• Failure to update security software • Loss or theft of portable devices' electronic media • Insecure transmission or storage of sensitive data • Password compromised • Malware infection • Insecure disposal of storage devices • Security settings	• Ensure all security software updates are installed and monitor status regularly • Secure devices and files when unattended • Do not leave devices on show in rooms or cars • Shred sensitive data before disposal • Encrypt data on portable devices including hard drives • Do not access sensitive data over public networks • Transmit sensitive data only if encrypted • Instigate a policy of regular changing of passwords and password strengths • Update anti-malware software and remind users not to open unknown links or attachments • Securely delete all sensitive data prior to disposal of equipment

4.3 Troubleshooting

Troubleshooting has been discussed in Unit 1 LO1.6 (page 14) and 2.8 (page 25). Diagnosing faults and rectifying them quickly is an important part of maintenance planning.

GROUP ACTIVITY ···

(10 minutes)

Research at least two examples of diagnostic tools for each of the network components identified in the bulleted list:

- hardware
- software
- IP utilities
- hardware
- software
- data transmission.

EXTENSION ACTIVITY ···

Create a small network for four people and carry out relevant tests to test functionality and stability. Develop a network test plan and document the results. Provide evidence of your analysis of the results, as well as how you have addressed any issues and re-tested to confirm that any issues have been resolved.

4.4 Disaster recovery

This was discussed in Unit 1, LO5.2 (page 40) and Unit 3, LO4.1 (page 104).

The network is designed to store and transport the orgnisation's data and information, so the disaster recovery plan for the network must include the backup procedures; for example, how often data should be backed up and where the backup should be stored. This may be in a fireproof safe on site, copies securely stored in another town, country or continent. The setup of ghost or potential host sites in another building, which could be located in the same place as the backup, whereever that is. Backup generators in case of power loss may also be put in place. These elements will normally form part of an overall disaster recovery plan which has been discussed in Units 1 and 3.

4.5 Software/hardware updates

This was discussed in Unit 3, LO3, AC 3.1 (page 97) and Table 4.10 above.

It should be clear that software and hardware updates can do more than provide extra functionality or remove that annoying and pointless extra click before you reach the command you want. Software updates, even for applications, can improve security by removing weaknesses in the program. Hardware or software firewalls are essential for security purposes and need to be updated as hackers find new ways of avoiding the current firewall security. Specialist anti-malware software clearly need to be updated in response to new threats. Performance updates for networks are the upgrading of the hardware such as switches and cabling. These changes should be recorded in a configuration file that records and tracks all changes made to the network.

GROUP ACTIVITY ···

(20 minutes)

A range of benchmarking tools are available, some of which are free. In pairs, investigate two different benchmarking tools for two different types of benchmark identified above. Present your findings to the rest of the group.

4.6 Performance management

Performance monitoring was discussed in LO3.2.

Testing the performance when the new network is set up sets the baseline or starting point against which to measure future performance. These measurements form the benchmarks for all future tests when the network is changed, for example the introduction of new devices or the introduction or updating of software. If performance is enhanced, then a new benchmark is set. If performances are reduced, then action must be taken to restore it to the benchmark.

The performance measures will vary with the type of network, but normally include the following.

- Bandwidth: the maximum rate of data transmission measured in bits per second.
- Response time: this is the time between the end of query or command being entered on the network by the host and the start of the response from the receiving device.
- Workload: the amount of information or data that a network can transport in a given time.
- Error rates: the number of bit errors – the number of bits in a data stream which have been changed during transmission. This may be due to signal distortion, noise or interference.

KNOW IT

1 Name four types of information which should be present in a maintenance plan.
2 Outline four types of maintenance issues.
3 Explain one method that could be used to diagnostically test IP addresses.
4 What is performance management?

LO4 Assessment activities

Below are two suggested assessment activities that have been directly linked to the pass and distinction criteria in LO4 to help with assignment preparation; they include Top tips on how to achieve best results.

Activity 1 – pass criteria *P6*

Using the network you planned for LO2 and LO3, create a maintenance plan for the new network.

Activity 2 – distinction criteria *D2*

Evaluate your choice of maintenance activities for ensuring that the network will have little down time due to maintenance issues.

TOP TIPS

✔ Ensure your maintenance plan is realistic given the resources available.
✔ Remember that when you evaluate, you make a qualitative judgement taking into account different factors and using available knowledge, experience and evidence.

Virtual and augmented reality

This unit deals with two different types of computer-affected reality. Virtual reality is a simulated environment intended to place the viewer within a real or imagined space, which the user is free to explore and experience visually and sometimes physically. Augmented reality uses technology to deliver a view of the world which is different from that seen by the naked eye, through the use of overlaid layers.

In this unit, you will learn about both forms of technology and will then plan and design – having been given a brief – both a virtual reality and an augmented reality product. You will then create one of the products you have designed. Your final task will be to use the knowledge and understanding you have developed to suggest future applications and uses of these technologies.

This unit is mandatory to the emerging digital technology practitioner specialist pathway due to its relevance to emerging digital technologies. The unit supports the development of skills, knowledge and understanding relevant to a job role in the areas of 3D modelling, digital transformation and the film and games industry.

LEARNING OUTCOMES

The topics and activities in this unit will help you to:

1 Understand virtual and augmented reality and how they may be used.
2 Be able to design virtual and augmented reality resources.
3 Be able to create a virtual or augmented reality resource.
4 Be able to predict future applications for virtual and augmented reality.

How will I be assessed?

You will be assessed by producing evidence from set scenarios or from work that you carry out as part of a work placement or employment. This evidence will be assessed by your tutor.

You will be graded using the following criteria:

Learning outcome	Pass assessment criteria	Merit assessment criteria	Distinction assessment criteria
You will:	To achieve a pass you must demonstrate that you have met all the pass assessment criteria	To achieve a merit you must demonstrate that you have met all the pass and merit assessment criteria	To achieve a distinction you must demonstrate that you have met all the pass, merit and distinction assessment criteria
1 Understand virtual and augmented reality and how they may be used	**P1** Describe the uses of virtual and augmented reality by organisations	**M1** Explain the impact that an identified virtual reality resource has had on society	**D1** Assess the impact that an identified augmented reality resource has had on society
2 Be able to design virtual and augmented reality resources	**P2** Produce a design specification for a virtual reality resource for an identified purpose		
	P3 Produce a design specification for an augmented reality resource for an identified purpose		
3 Be able to create a virtual or augmented reality resource	**P4** Develop a virtual reality or an augmented reality resource for an identified purpose		
	P5 Test the product during creation and once complete	**M2** Make adjustments to the design based on outcomes of testing	**D2** Evaluate the development stages during the creation of the resource
4 Be able to predict future applications for virtual and augmented reality	**P6** Suggest possible future roles of virtual and augmented reality in future applications	**M3** Evaluate the specific benefits to be gained by repurposing current examples of virtual and augmented reality into identified roles	

LO1 Understand virtual and augmented reality and how they may be used *P1 M1 D1*

GETTING STARTED 👤

(10 minutes)

Individually, think about **virtual** and **augmented** reality and how it affects you.

As a group, discuss how virtual and augmented reality impact on your day-to-day lives.

Are you aware of virtual and augmented reality or is it something that occurs almost without you noticing?

🔍 KEY TERMS

Virtual reality – the process of creating a virtual world into which the user or experiencer is thrown.

Augmented reality – the process of manipulating reality as seen by a user.

1.1 Virtual reality as a concept

Pioneers of virtual and augmented reality

Many people can claim to be pioneers in the field of augmented and virtual reality. The unit specification includes examples you can research, but you can also find out about the impact made by others not on this list.

Douglas Engelbart

Engelbart founded the Augmentation Research Centre in Menlo Park, California, where he led research into human–computer interaction.

His motivation was to make the world a better place by using computers. He believed that computers could be used to collect information towards a common good, and so developed them from being devices that sat in the background number-crunching to being devices with which people could easily interact.

Engelbart's legacy included the invention of the mouse, contributing to the work on hypertext and working on the development of GUIs as part of his drive to make computers accessible to all.

Ivan Sutherland

Sutherland created the first augmented reality system. This system was limited by the technology available at the time and only showed simple two-dimensional wire-framed images.

Tom Caudell and David Mizell

Caudell and Mizell were the first to coin the term 'augmented reality'. Their work showed that augmented reality required less processing power than virtual reality, as augmented reality causes fewer pixels to be changed when applying an augmented reality layer to an already existing layer.

PAIRS ACTIVITY

(40 minutes)

As a pair, research the work of the three virtual and augmented reality pioneers mentioned above. Create a short presentation about the motivation, impact and legacy to the field of virtual and augmented reality of each of the pioneers.

Present your findings to others in the group.

Uses of virtual and augmented reality

US Military Nuclear Defence system

Virtual reality provides a risk-free training programme in what would otherwise be an extremely dangerous environment. In systems such as VIEWPro (Virtual, Interactive Environment for Weapons Procedures), trainees can practise dismantling nuclear weapons.

Pilot training

This is another area where virtual reality can be used to avoid risk. Trainee pilots sit in a realistic cockpit space which moves to simulate a plane and which can also have outside influences, such as weather, applied.

Figure 5.1 Learning to pilot a plane is a complex skill that is made safer by virtual reality

The Mattel 'data glove'

A data glove is an interactive haptic device that simulates control of devices and provides touch feedback.

The Mattel data glove (Mattel Power Glove), released in 1989, was an early example of augmented reality device, being a controller for Nintendo gaming devices. The glove was a combination of traditional Nintendo controls, program buttons and numbered buttons, as well as ultrasonic transmitters that were used to calculate the movement of the glove.

Personal guidance system for visually impaired

Visually impaired people may have difficulty moving through an environment without knowing if objects block their progress. Augmented reality can scan objects and provide information to the user about what is being scanned. Not only can this help with the identification of routes and potential hazards, but it can also help visually impaired people to identify objects around their home.

Chameleon

You should be familiar with video-conferencing and how it allows participants to both hear and see the others taking part in a meeting. Chameleon is an improvement on that system and allows all participants to meet in a virtual reality world, where each participant is represented by an avatar, which copies the movements of the participant.

This system combines the advantages of video-conferencing (primarily the removal of the need to travel) and adds the impact of the subtle gestures and body language by which people communicate alongside speech. Hopefully, the fact that everybody can see these gestures means that the meeting will have better outcomes than if it were carried out by video-conferencing.

1.2 Areas of use

Here are some examples of case studies you could explore further.

Architecture

The process of designing buildings – architecture – needs to present designs in such a way that viewers can imagine the final outcome. It is possible to create a virtual building through which the viewer can move, allowing a more realistic and accessible experience than simply looking at the designs on paper. This allows the architect to create a model of the completed building, so that the layout can be checked for design faults. The advantages to the original architect of being able to see their design in 3D are clear.

Business

Virtual tours can be used to explore a business environment, prototypes of products can be presented so that they can be explored from different angles (like the use of virtual reality in architecture) and the cost of training new staff can be reduced by virtual reality training packages because they can be completed repeatedly without the need for a specialist to deliver each session.

Education

Websites such as BBC History use virtual reality to recreate historic events and locations. The virtual tour of a First World War trench (www.bbc.co.uk/

history/worldwars/wwone/launch_vt_wwone_trench.shtml), for example, allows the viewer to explore a trench system in a way that is practically impossible for most people in real life.

Some schools use virtual reality apps to allow students to access extra levels of information behind **trigger images**, thereby allowing those who are interested to access more information than is included in a poster, for example. This information may be included in further documents, websites or videos, which appear on the user's device when the trigger image is viewed.

Entertainment, leisure and the media

Some games can integrate images taken by the player into the game itself. For example, Star Wars Arcade: Falcon Gunner (THQ Wireless) allows the player to play in real time scenes that are available from their camera, while ARBasketball (Augmented Pixels) allows the player to play basketball by using the device to track hand movements and throw the ball into a net projected onto a flat surface.

The media uses both augmented and virtual reality extensively. Virtual reality tours and walk-throughs are a frequent element of news broadcasts, while on-screen projections are commonly used in sports and other programmes.

Healthcare and surgery

The benefits to be gained of seeing and exploring virtual bodies for training purposes are clear. Concepts and procedures may be explained, and indeed practised, via virtual reality, without the trainee leaving their seat; while augmented reality could be used to provide real-time statistics (such as blood pressure or heart rate) to a surgeon during a procedure.

In the near future, the combined use of virtual reality and robotics within surgery could bring huge benefits as the combination of the practical skills held by surgeons with the extreme accuracy of robots could result in more successful outcomes from surgery.

Military

The ARC4 system provides the wearer with an overlay that gives them more information than is available to the naked eye. Battlefield sensitive information, such as showing locations where road side bombs or other forms of attack have occurred or the location of friendly forces, will have a clear impact on the effectiveness of fighting forces.

The system can also be linked to a weapons guidance system, with the viewer potentially able to model the impact of any action so that the extent of any collateral damage can also be gauged.

Sport

The current use of these technologies in sport is limited to visualisation of traditional sports. The uses of virtual reality as part of the training processes for different sports are clear, while the use of augmented reality to enhance the audience's experience is an area of growth. It is planned that Google Glasses will provide the viewer with a constant stream of information that will enhance the live view, providing detailed, expert, information that would previously only have been available to a viewer watching sport on television or online.

1.3 Possible impacts

Many of the possible impacts have already been considered in section 1.2 on areas of use. However, the range of possible impacts needs to be considered in its own right, as this could be important when you complete LO4 (page 160), and also the possible impacts may be felt in more than one of the areas of use mentioned above.

Visualisations of designs

This impact is the transformation of a design from 2D to 3D, especially in manufacturing. The size of the product does not influence the benefits of visualisation. Indeed, the ability to create a scaled-up virtual version of some very small products would provide the designer and other users with the opportunity to investigate the product in more detail than would be possible if it were normal size.

Simulations

This area of impact overlaps slightly with training. However, simulations give a virtual version of an event or procedure and do not necessarily provide any training. For example, a simulation could be used to explore the impact of an event. Any risks to life or negative impact on the environment would be reduced or removed. The fire brigade uses simulation when training firefighters on what to do in burning and smoked-filled buildings.

Training

Training provides an opportunity to learn, practise and develop skills. Providing training in the real world can be expensive and requires the trainees and the trainer to be present. They also incur travel and accommodation costs. It can be cheaper overall to incur the one-off cost of creating a virtual reality training programme, and it's also cheaper for the trainee or employer as the training can be completed at a convenient time and location.

The internet is full of self-training programmes for skills such as driving, which can be then practised via a virtual reality programme.

Demonstrations of concepts

As we saw in the sections on education and medicine, there are many ways that virtual and augmented reality can be used to provide clear instructions about a concept to the trainee. This use of virtual reality also allows for the demonstration to be paused and repeated until the viewer is confident that they understand the concepts being demonstrated.

Virtual tours

In tourism, virtual tours are intended to give a flavour of what may be experienced in real life by the visitor and so, hopefully, increase the number of people wishing to visit the attraction. However, virtual tours are also becoming part of other areas, including education, to provide a visualisation of the location being studied and so remove the need for time-consuming and expensive trips.

Virtual tours can also give viewers a chance to explore an area before it is visited in person. Google Streetview for example, shows a drive-through presentation of areas, so that the viewer can check out where they are thinking of buying a house, for example.

TOP TIPS ✔

- ✔ Think about different types of organisation, for example businesses, colleges, charities and special interest groups.
- ✔ To assess is to offer a reasoned judgement of something using relevant facts.
- ✔ When assessing the impact of your chosen resource on society, consider both sections of society (for example, people of a certain age, particular communities or those with disabilities) and, if appropriate, society as a whole.

LO1 Assessment activity

Below is a suggested assessment activity that has been directly linked to the pass, merit and distinction criteria in LO1 to help with assignment preparation; it includes Top tips on how to achieve best results.

Activity 1 – pass criteria *P1* merit criteria *M1* and distinction criteria *D1*

You work for a small publishing company and have been asked to write a report into the benefits and impacts of virtual and augmented reality.

You decide to start by describing how these technologies are used by organisations. You will then focus on specific uses of virtual and augmented reality. Then you will assess the impact of an identified virtual reality resource and an identified augmented reality resource on society.

LO2 Be able to design virtual and augmented reality resources *P2 P3*

GETTING STARTED

(10 minutes)

Individually, think about a design project you have completed, not necessarily for this qualification.

Divide a sheet of paper into two columns. At the top of the left hand column write 'Pros' and at the top of the right hand column write 'Cons'.

In the left-hand column, write down as many benefits of planning as you can. In the right-hand column, write down as many drawbacks of planning as you can.

Share your list with a partner. Working together, try to answer the question 'why is it important to plan a project?'

You will now design a virtual and an augmented reality product. In LO3, you will create one of your two designs. You should be provided with one scenario, from which you should be able to design a virtual reality and an augmented reality resource.

Your designs should include the standard design tools you will have used for other design projects (such as a mood board and a story board) and all of the elements that you wish to include in the final product. Because of the difference between virtual reality and augmented reality, it is likely that you will need to create different designs for each product.

2.1 Technologies

Before you create your designs, you will need to think about the technologies you will be using. The device or devices you use don't matter, as long as they deliver both virtual and augmented reality. It is as possible to create a successful resource using your smartphone as it is using more expensive equipment.

Hardware

As a starting point, you need to think about the devices for which you will be designing. There are many to choose from, and a wide range in price. Take account of the hardware available to you. Make sure that you take account of any restrictions at the planning stage, rather than having to amend your plans later.

Processor

In computing, the processor takes the inputs, interprets them and then provides an output. With virtual reality, the inputs include head and possibly hand movements, while the output will be visual and possibly sound. With augmented reality, the input will be a visual trigger, and the output will be whatever form the augmentation takes.

The processor will need to do a lot of work, so the quality of the user's experience will be affected by the capabilities of the processor. When planning your product, you need to be aware of the specification of the processor and plan to use its full capacity, but not more than is available.

Display

AR and VR can use a variety of devices, which may be handheld, head-mounted, head-up or even shown via eyeglasses. The most appropriate display depends on the resource. It could be a 3D image that you explore on your own computer. Alternatively, it can be a fully immersive experience that makes use of headsets or glasses that give the wearer the impression that they are in a different room. This experience can be further enhanced by **haptic devices** that allow the user to feel their virtual world.

Possibly the most famous device for virtual reality is the Oculus Rift device. This combines 3D vision and 3D spatial sound to create a total immersive experience. Also included is a set of Oculus Touch controllers with sensors that allow the user to have a fully 360 degree experience.

KEY TERM

Haptic devices – devices that simulate touch.

Other headsets at the more expensive end of the market include the HTC Vive and the Sony PlayStation VR, which aim to provide a similar virtual reality experience to that provided by the Oculus Rift; while the Microsoft HoloLens combines both virtual reality and augmented reality in one device. The HoloLens can be used to play games such as Minecraft when it is projected onto a suitable surface.

At the other end of the scale, Google Cardboard combines a cardboard headset and your smartphone to create 360 degree experiences that follow your head movement. Not only can you create your own virtual reality apps for it, but you can also download and try those created by others. This is a cheap and easy introduction to virtual reality.

A head-up display can also be used as part of an augmented reality experience. This is a transparent display that shows data so that the user does not have to look away in order to get the information.

Figure 5.2 A head-up display can be used to show information to car drivers

Any of these devices could be used to show a virtual reality product, while your own smartphone or iPad could be used to run an augmented reality presentation. When planning your product, make it clear what device you are planning to use with the product you are creating.

Sound

You will need to consider the specific sound devices you have available. The main difference here is between headphones, which make the experience more private, and speakers, which make the experience more public. As it is possible to buy speakers and headphones relatively cheaply, you are not as limited in your choice as you would be when planning the display devices and so can decide to buy speakers or headphones to suit your plan.

Sensors

Sensors are key parts of any virtual reality system. They sense how the person who is using the system is standing and any movements they make. The system you are using will have built-in sensors and you will, of course, be restricted by the range of sensors available. Your planning should show how you intend to use the range of sensors available.

- GPS and a compass can be used to sense where someone is and the direction they are travelling.
- Optical sensors use cameras and LEDs to measure the position and way in which a person is standing. This can be a very effective method of interacting with the surroundings, but like any other system that uses light, there can be a problem with line of sight.
- Accelerometers are the sensors that measure whether or not a device is moving and, if so, the direction it is moving. Smartphone games where the player's character is controlled by tilting the device use the accelerometer.

Input devices

Cameras capture images and microphones capture sound. Most devices have both, but they do not always work together.

You also need to take account of the input devices included with the device. For example, you can expect a smartphone to have a camera that can be used to input a trigger image for an augmented reality presentation. However, can you also use the microphone with the same device at the same time?

Software

Range of products available

Different software will allow you to create different outcomes and it is vital that you explore the software you already have, as well as any software you can get hold of easily.

When planning, make sure that your initial **design specification** includes what software you are going to use and that you justify your choice. Once you have decided on the software, identify the key features you will use to create your product.

Many products are available for free download. While these may not have all of the features of their more expensive competitors, it is a good idea to be sure that what you need to create is not possible with the free version before you decide to buy it.

Features of the software

Different software will have different features. For example, when the user looks at an augmented reality app trigger, the app should react to the angle at which the user is looking at the trigger so that the overlaid image or feature is similarly angled. Without this, the overlay will look awkward compared to the view that the user has of the trigger image.

This is difficult to achieve, but some software includes features that make this process easier. For example, ARToolKit is software that makes augmented reality apps. It is open source (which means that you can use it without needing to buy a licence) and uses computer vision technology to easily align the overlay with the orientation of the original trigger image.

While creating augmented reality may simply be a case of laying layers over a trigger image, virtual reality can be more complicated. Some software requires the user to program quite complex procedures. However, others offer a simpler process, sometimes using relatively straightforward

KEY TERM

WYSIWYG (What you see is what you get) – a visual method of creating a product by adding elements so that the position of the elements and how they react is determined visually and not by direct coding.

WYSIWYG interfaces to create the virtual reality experience. For example, SixenseVR SDK allows the user to work on a WYSIWYG interface and also provides a library of pre-existing assets that the programmer can use in their virtual reality application.

INDEPENDENT ACTIVITY

(60 minutes)

Research the range of software available to you.

Create a presentation that describes:

- the software itself
- where it may be found (e.g. available on your centre's network, freely downloadable etc.)
- the main features of the software
- ease of use.

Image registration

This is mainly to do with augmented reality and is the process of converting images into set co-ordinates so that the computer can work with the image. It is part of the computer vision technology mentioned above.

Image registration will take key co-ordinates from an image and use these to align the image and the overlay so that they take account of the original orientation and position of the trigger image.

Augmented Reality Mark-up Language (ARML)

Like all new technologies, different versions of augmented reality and the code behind it have been developed by different software manufacturers. Augmented Reality Mark-up Language is an attempt to create a standard so that, eventually, all augmented reality viewers can access all augmented reality apps, rather like all web browsers can access all web pages.

The language has three main concepts:

- Features are the actual physical image that is going to have the augmentation layer added to it.
- Visual assets form the augmentation layer.
- Anchors are the points that link the physical image and the augmented layer. As the view of the physical image changes when the viewer moves, so the image of the augmented layer changes as the anchor points move relative to the viewer's view.

2.2 Design

If you adopt a superficial approach to planning and try to do the minimum, it is likely that you will come up with problems later, especially as the ability to decide on what will not be included is a key part of the planning process.

The design process you follow will not really differ from other design processes and should therefore include some tasks with which you have already had experience.

Remember that you have to design a virtual reality and an augmented reality resource at this stage.

Aims of the product

The aims of the product will be dictated by the brief that you are given and can be broken down into four main areas as follows.

Intended outcome

You need to design both a virtual reality and an augmented reality product, but you must differentiate between them. Each design must clearly be focused on the technology to which it applies.

The intended outcome should also be linked to other factors, including the intended target audience and the style and feel of the product. For example, if you are asked to design a very technical academic product, your design should reflect this. The colours you use, the text, the images and even the message itself will be tailored towards this particular outcome. Clearly, if you are asked to create a product that is aimed at young children, the focus and content will be very different.

Success criteria

For example, if you are asked to create an augmented reality product that is triggered by an image of an animal and which, once triggered, brings up a video of that animal, then your immediate **success criteria** would be:

1 Animal as a trigger.
2 Video of the animal as the augmented layer.

However, there may be other success criteria that are not immediately clear. This is where your knowledge of target audiences would be useful. If, for example, you know that the augmented reality product is going to be used in a children's ward at a hospital then your success criteria could include items that would make the product interesting to children – so the trigger image would need to appeal to children. Typically, for younger children, this would be a non-scary colourful image, like a cartoon.

RESEARCH ACTIVITY

(60 minutes)

You have been given the design brief below.

> We would like you to create an interactive, virtual reality Escape the Room product that will be used as revision materials for the theme of input and output devices. The game will be targeted at students completing their Computing GCSE.
>
> The product should appeal to both genders and allow students to practise questions where they have to identify suitable answers, and describe and explain the use of different devices.
>
> The product should be colourful and include voice and visual output.

Identify the success criteria from this design brief.

Information to be delivered

This design aim is not just about 'what' but also 'how'. Whether you are working with a virtual reality or an augmented reality product, you are going to need to create all elements; so, for augmented reality for example, do not expect to be given the trigger image or the overlay. The 'how' aspect will be the manner in which the information is to be delivered.

Don't assume that you will only be delivering information if you create an augmented reality product. Consider some of the virtual reality products that we discussed at the start of this unit. As the user explores a virtual reality First World War trench, they are experiencing a visualisation of a real event. That visualisation can include as many or as few elements as the designer wishes. To a large degree, the only restriction is reality, and even that can be changed for the sake of impact. Every item in that visualisation is an experience of what it was like to be in a First World War trench. Therefore, every item included in the visualisation is information.

When you are planning your products, think about how you could include the required information. Could you include artefacts that tell a story? Could you use signposts to give a message? A virtual reality product based in a school could make use of white boards and posters, while an augmented reality product could have, as its overlay, a poster, an image or even a video, providing different ways in which your message could be delivered.

Where the product is to be used

You will need to design for the location in which your product is to be used. This could be the general location – such as the children's ward discussed above – or a specific location, such as a position in a room. For general locations, your design should match the nature of the room and the product. With the example of the children's ward, your design can clearly show that you are aware of the specific needs of a very particular product.

The augmented reality trigger image could be a whole painting or a section of a painting. Your choice of trigger images is important, as the wrong choice could result in some of your message not being accessed.

Imagine that you have been asked to create an augmented reality product for a large painting hung on a wall so that many people can see it. You have been asked to explain the importance of different parts of the painting. If you choose as your trigger images parts at the top of the canvas, you risk making those trigger images inaccessible to shorter or younger people. It would be better to have the same message triggered by a range of different images, in different locations on the canvas.

Financial plan

Plan how you intend to spend any money available for the project in order to achieve success. Each item you plan to spend money on should contribute towards the success of the project, even if only in a small way. The major headings of a financial plan include:

● An assessment of the environment in which the project is to take place: not the room in which you will be coding, or where the product is to be used, but the business environment. You will need to state the nature of the product and its competitors, or any similar products of which you will need to take note.

For the purposes of this project, you will probably not be allocated any real spending money. However, you could still be given a theoretical budget for the project – if so, you will be required to show how you plan to spend it.

- A restatement of the objectives of the project: its intended outcomes.
- A list of the resources that will be needed to achieve the objectives (labour, equipment and materials), including how many **person hours** the task will take
- The amount of each resource you will require, e.g. the hours needed for one person to complete the task, or a combination of hours from different people.
- The costs of each resource: e.g. who will be doing which task, and how many hours it will take, especially if each person is to be paid a different hourly rate.
- The total costs.
- A list of the risks and issues with the budget as it has been set: mention if the budget and the amount you need to spend are very close, as your estimate could be inaccurate. Also note if any of the equipment and materials that you intend to use are likely to fluctuate in price, especially if this fluctuation is likely to result in a price rise for that item.

Quality plan

A quality plan explains how you intend to make this product to match the quality policy of your organisation, in terms of how the quality of the project outcome will be measured.

Target audience

The intended audience will impact on the design as these will be the people who will, if all goes well, use the product. For your design to appeal to this target audience, you will need to have a clear understanding of what generally appeals to them. 'Generally appeals' is a key term here, as you will need to target your product at the average preferences of the target audience, rather than the interests of a small minority. For example, an augmented reality product targeted at young people should use, as its trigger image, something that will appeal to them, or should present, as the augmented layer, something that will be of interest to this group. It would be unlikely that an image of a stately home, for example, would be suitable, as the majority of this target group would not find this interesting, even if some might.

There are many ways you can describe your target audience. Typically, it is broken down into three key areas. You may find that not all of these factors are relevant when you complete your design but you should at least be aware of them, as you may be surprised at how important each is.

- *Age* is usually expressed as an age range rather than an exact age.
- *Gender* should also be clear. If you are in doubt, take your lead from the brief or ask for clarification from the client.
- *Income* usually influences the target audience because, as an individual person's income increases, so their demand for certain products diminishes. Also consider the hardware for which you are designing the product. Some output devices that can be used with virtual reality are, to some extent, appealing because they are expensive. If you are asked to design a product that could be more effective if it was accessed on one of the more expensive products, then income is definitely a factor you should consider.

Target audience can be a useful way of helping you design a product and it will help if you have a clear direction from the brief. If, for example, the product needs to be aimed at men aged between 21 and 30, and you know that this age group really likes fluffy bunnies, then you can include that in your design. However, the target audience for a product may be so wide that it is impossible to define. This is usually because the product itself is extremely general. In marketing terms, if you were asked to design a virtual reality product about life in the twenty-first century, you are far more likely to have a general audience than if you have been asked to design a similar product about life in the fifteenth century.

INDEPENDENT ACTIVITY

(30 minutes)

Below is a list of products. For each product, describe the likely age, gender and income of the target audience.

- organic cheese and rosemary bread
- a printed TV guide
- a Hollister t-shirt
- a Starbucks latte
- a heating system that can be controlled remotely via a smartphone.

Nature of the product

You will need to consider whether the product is to be used by one person or many users, continuously or at a specific time. If the product is truly aimed at one person, then that person should be absolutely central to your design. However, if the product will be used by many different people, then this needs to be stated.

Content including resource plan

You are clearly going to have to plan the content of your virtual reality and your augmented reality products. This should start with a discussion of the resources you will need (in general terms) and then move on to the layout and content.

If you have completed an in-depth financial plan, then you will have already created a resource plan. If not, then you will need to create the plan now, covering the amount of labour, equipment and materials you plan to use.

Design tools

Your plan should convert the ideas in your head into a design that could, if necessary, be followed by others. This process of creating physical designs for products is called visualisation and there are a number of tools that you could use.

Storyboarding

A storyboard is used to detail the content of a presentation or visual experience by showing its key points. The storyboard will show details of what is happening at each point. This could be any of the following:

- a reference to characters who would be on the screen at that point and what they are doing
- details of any music or sound effect that should be heard
- other relevant information, such as the mood of the shot at that point.

An example storyboard for one section of a virtual reality product is shown in Figure 5.3. In this example, the viewer starts with a straight on view of a room. The room has two doors, one to the left and one to the right. This section of the storyboard follows the movement into the right hand room.

1. Shot of room with two doors leading off. Doors are at extreme left and right.

2. Close up of right-hand door from viewer's perspective.

3. Internal shot of right-hand room. Window open.

4. Close up of window from viewer's perspective. Sunny outside is visible.

Figure 5.3 Part of a possible storyboard for a virtual reality product

Your storyboard should have sufficient detail for a third party to follow.

When creating a storyboard, you should first identify the key points of your virtual reality product. If your product does not involve user interaction, this could be key events along a linear storyline. If, however, your virtual reality product involves user interaction, then you will need to include the key points at which the user interaction can make a difference, including options available to the user at that point. Possibly the easiest way to plan these key points is to create a timeline.

A sample timeline for a virtual reality product is shown in Figure 5.4. This timeline is for a walk through of a virtual reality product modelling the planned structure of a simple, single-storey building.

The timeline shows the user moving from one room (or virtual reality scene) into another. This is a key point, as the view must change as the user moves from one room to the other.

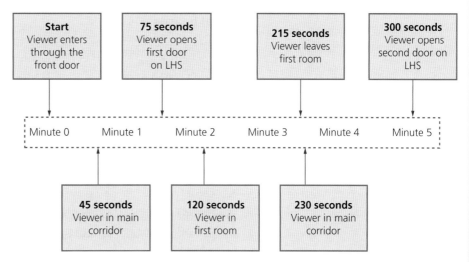

Figure 5.4 A possible timeline for a virtual reality product

Once you have identified your key points, you can then create a section of the storyboard for that point.

This technique could be applied to an augmented reality product by using the point at which the trigger image(s) are accessed as a key point in the overall story, and then use the stages or layers that appear after that point as the other key events. We will discuss how to use trigger images later in this section.

Mind mapping

Mind mapping can be an excellent way to organise your thoughts into plans, especially if you are a visual learner. A mind map is an organised representation of your thoughts, with spurs leading off into differing trains of thought, each spur representing a particular theme or group of ideas.

In Figure 5.5, the mind map shows how a student could organise their thoughts before beginning an essay on 'The importance of chocolate'. The mind map deals with it as a food stuff, a product that can be sold and a means by which one can gain favour with others by using it as a gift. The plan has each of these key themes as spurs from the central question and uses different colours to group and organise each theme.

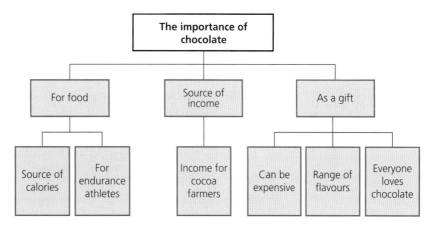

Figure 5.5 A mind map plan for an essay on 'The importance of chocolate'

Mood boards

A mood board is an important part of the design process, yet is often overlooked. It is a collection of anything that can help to describe the intended mood or feel of a product and is used both as part of the design process itself, but also as part of the process of trying to pitch an idea.

A mood board can include images, text and samples of materials. Each item should contribute to the overall message. For example, a photograph could express an emotion or a style of photography that the designer wishes to feature in their work. A cartoon image may express a feeling of fun, or may be a statement of the style of images that the designer wishes to use.

Whichever items you include, the completed mood board should clearly give an idea of the style of product you intend to create.

PAIRS ACTIVITY

(60 minutes)

You have been asked to design a virtual reality product called 'A trip back in time'. The product is a visualisation of a late 1960s pop and rock festival.

- As a pair, decide on the success criteria and style for your product.
- Individually, use the success criteria to create a mind map for the app.
- As a pair, decide on a final version of the mind map.
- As a pair, create a mood board for the product.

Trigger image(s) and the stage(s) that follow on from the trigger being accessed

When planning an augmented reality product, you will appreciate that the stages that follow on from the trigger image being accessed are the augmentation layers that we have talked about throughout this unit. An augmented reality product may include one or many different trigger–layer relationships.

The best way to plan each of these relationships is to create a flow diagram. A sample flow diagram for an augmented reality product is shown in Figure 5.6. In this example, the layer which appears after the trigger image is accessed is a video, but the layer can take many different formats.

Hardware and software requirements

Think about the hardware and software requirements of the products being designed. For further advice on the range of hardware and software available, refer to the Technologies section of LO2.1.

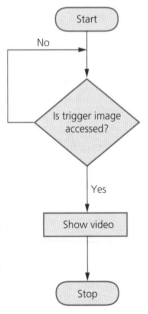

Figure 5.6 A flow diagram for part of an augmented reality product

KNOW IT

1 What is a haptic device?
2 Describe how image registration is used in augmented reality. Why would an image with few identifying features not be a suitable image to use as a trigger image?
3 What is meant by the term 'accelerometer'?
4 Identify *two* features of a mood board.

LO2 Assessment activity

Below is a suggested assessment activity that has been directly linked to the pass criteria in LO2 to help with assignment preparation; it includes Top tips on how to achieve best results.

Activity 1 – pass criteria *P2 P3*

Your design studio has been asked to design:

- a virtual reality product that will introduce viewers to health and safety issues to take into account when installing IT equipment
- an augmented reality product to give advice on how to install a double-glazed window.

Produce a design specification for both.

TOP TIPS ☑

✔ Remember to include all the elements of a design brief that are described in LO2.
✔ Include diagrams and other visuals as appropriate.

LO3 Be able to create a virtual OR augmented reality resource *P4 P5 M2 D2*

GETTING STARTED 👤

(10 minutes)

Identify three areas of your school or college that could be improved by the introduction of a virtual or an augmented reality resource.

How would you know if others agreed with you that these would be good projects?

How would you know if the completed projects

- Worked as intended?
- Appealed to the target audience?

You will now be creating one of your two designs. Because of the wealth of different software available, this section will not focus on any one piece of software, but will discuss how you could complete and evidence each stage.

3.1 Develop

In this section, you will need to develop your product.

Create the trigger point of interest

For augmented reality, this would be the creation of the image that will trigger the appearance of the augmented reality layer. If you are asked to create a wholly new image as a trigger, make sure that the image is suitable. Some images, for example, do not include enough detail to act as triggers. For example, a very faint image, or one with very few points on it, would not provide enough points for the software to use to differentiate between different trigger images.

You may also be asked to create an augmented reality product that uses an existing image or location as the trigger. In this case, you are defining the area of that already existing image, or particular view of that location, which will be the particular trigger.

Finally, do not forget that you may need to create a number of different trigger images.

Create the layer(s)/overlay(s)

This is the layer which will appear once the trigger image has been allowed to activate the augmented reality product. This layer could be an image, a video or even a website, depending on what you have planned and what your software allows.

If you are going to create a virtual reality product, you will not be basing your creation on trigger images and overlays, but interacting scenes and rooms.

3.2 Testing

Testing is the process of making sure that the product you have created does what it is meant to do. There are three main ways that you should test your product. We will discuss each of these below.

Create and use a test plan

A test plan is developed before the product is created and should test every aspect that has been planned. We plan the testing at this stage, so we can check to make sure that what we wanted to do has been done when we have a completed product.

There is a range of techniques you can use to test a product. The two types that you are most likely to use are the following.

- Visual test – you are simply looking, e.g. if you needed to check that a coded element has appeared as intended.
- Event test – you are checking that something that you have coded actually happens.

So, for an augmented reality product, you could test to make sure that the trigger image works as you have planned. This is not simply a case of pointing a device at the trigger and hoping, but is making sure that the trigger works for different devices and in different settings. For example, you could check that the trigger image works in different light settings.

The test plan is shown with three columns. Later, once testing has begun, two further columns are added to show the results of the test.

Part of a test plan is shown in Table 5.1. The title for each column should be clear.

Table 5.1 Part of a test plan for an augmented reality product

Function being tested	How it is tested	Expected result
Trigger image	Point smartphone at the trigger image	Augmented layer appears.
Trigger image	Point iPad at the trigger image	Augmented layer appears.

The first step is to list everything that needs to be tested. This may seem obvious, but this step is one that many people do not complete properly. Once you have this list, plan how you will test each item. Think of all the ways in which the item could not work. For example, if you have an object in a virtual reality product with which the user is meant to interact, there are a number of things that could go wrong. Imagine that you have placed a button into a virtual reality product.

● The button may not appear.
● The button may appear in the wrong place.
● The button may not behave as intended.
● The outcome of the user touching the button may not be as intended.

The first two items on this list can be tested by looking: does the button appear? Is the button in the correct place? The third and fourth items are both tested by interacting with the button by pressing it. For the fourth test, you would check that once the button has been pressed, the event that you want to happen does happen.

Once you have decided *how* you will test your product, the final stage is to describe what should happen. This is important, because testing is sometimes carried out by someone who does not know the program (this is called black box testing). If you do not tell the black box tester what to expect, how can they report whether the test has failed or been successful?

Although you must plan your test plan before you create the product, you should not use it until the work is completed.

Test during development

Testing during development is different to testing on completion and is something that we do, whatever we are making. If we are cooking, we will taste the food; if we are coding, we will check that the module we have just written works. Unfortunately, because it is done informally as part of our work, we often forget to record that we have done it. However, it is vital that this testing is recorded, as it then forms part of the 'story' of what you have done and can be used to inform future coding.

There are many ways that you could record the testing you have done during development of a product. It's simplest to complete a record or diary of what you complete each day, along with an indication of what testing you have done that day.

End user testing

The final stage of any project is when you pass the work over to the client for testing. The client themselves may then test it or, more usually for software, get an end user to test it. The end user may differ from the client, because the client will be the person who commissioned the product, while the end user is someone at whom the software is aimed.

While end user testing is usually organised by the client, you will need to organise it as part of this project. When you organise end user testing, you are asking the testers to check that the product you have created meets the original project criteria. So, for example, if the original brief said that the virtual reality product had to appeal to a target audience aged between 10 and 16, then you should use end users from that age range, and check, for example, whether they find the product interesting and engaging.

Review against original success criteria

This is the stage where you draw all of your information together to check that what you have made fits your success criteria. You should remember that your success criteria may have changed as you have worked with the client, so make sure that you are comparing your work to the final criteria.

You should check each of the criteria and show how well it has been met in a discussion document where you argue your case. If you think that your product meets particular success criteria, and you have the evidence to back that up (such as the end user feedback), then say that you have been successful. However, you also need to state if you think that the product has not met the success criteria.

3.3 Evaluation

Once you have completed the testing and reviewing, you can start evaluating your work. This is the process of giving your work a sense of value as a project, being honest with yourself and others. The work here is organised around a set of questions.

Design stage

This is where you go right back to the very start of the project and reflect on the design process. There is only one question to answer here.

Has the product identified success criteria?

Every project should be targeted at clear outcomes. Your evaluation of the design process should focus on the success criteria which you created, reflecting the results in more detail. Are these criteria clear and were they sufficient? If you decide that your original criteria were totally sufficient, then you should say so – with evidence. If you felt that the original criteria were insufficient, you should comment on this too.

Project management stage

In this section, you will answer two questions in order to reflect on how well you managed the project as you progressed from the original design through to the completion of your project.

Has the project deviated from the original scope?

You will need to compare the final product to the original scope of the project. There are two focuses for this task. The first is whether you have met the original scope, and the second is whether you have achieved what you set out to do and more. Of course, it is also possible that you got so carried away while making your product that you have ended up with something that bears little resemblance to your original brief!

The starting point for this question is to reflect on what you originally intended to do. If your original plans have changed and the scope has expanded, build this into your assessment. Once you have decided on the scope against which you are checking your completed project, you simply need to compare them.

Has the project deviated from the budget as defined in the financial plan?

Even if you are only dealing with a theoretical budget, rather than a real one, you should still be tracking how you have used resources, including time. If, for example, you have overrun, then you are likely to have spent more on staffing than you had planned, even if you are treating staffing as a theoretical cost.

Creation stage

This stage focuses on the process of making the actual product and includes four questions.

Has the project delivered business benefits identified in the business case?

Your original plan identified the business benefits for the project. Now you need to compare the benefits of the product you created with the benefits that you planned to achieve.

Has the project achieved the objectives in the terms of reference?

This question follows on from the previous one, in that you need to check what you have achieved, compared to what you intended to achieve, as defined in the terms of reference – the statement of the project's purpose, objectives and how it will be achieved.

Has the project deviated from forecast resource levels as per the resource plan?

The resource plan will have set out the raw materials that you intended to use. As you have worked through your project, you will have tracked your usage of raw materials. You should now compare your planned and actual use.

Has the project conformed to the management process as per the execution phase?

The final question is to do with how well you managed the project during the whole of this stage. To some extent, the questions you have already answered in this section will provide you with some sources of information, but you should also consider other aspects of the management process, including communications within any team with which you are working, as well as client acceptance of the completed product.

Identify potential improvements for similar future projects

This is the final stage of your evaluation and is where you bring together all of your previous evaluations. By identifying future improvements, you are showing that you can reflect on the evaluations and apply them to a future project.

Having completed the evaluation tasks, you may have a long list of issues. These should then be the areas on which you concentrate. However, you could also reflect on the areas where you have been successful. For example, despite having completed a particular section successfully, you may decide that you could have completed it more efficiently or more effectively.

LO3 Assessment activities

Below are three suggested assessment activities that have been directly linked to the pass, merit and distinction criteria in LO3 to help with assignment preparation; they include Top tips on how to achieve best results.

Activity 1 – pass criteria *P4*

Both of your designs from the previous exercise have been accepted. You have been given the opportunity to develop one of your designs.

Choose ONE of your designs and create a working prototype.

Activity 2 – pass criteria *P5* and merit criteria *M2*

As part of your work, you must test your prototype and then make any improvements so that the prototype works as intended.

Activity 3 – distinction criteria *D2*

Your employers have asked that you evaluate your work as part of your annual review. Evaluate each development stage to show how and why the prototype was developed.

LO4 Be able to predict future applications for virtual and augmented reality *P6 M3*

GETTING STARTED 👤

(10 minutes)

As a group, discuss the changes in technology in general over the past seven years.

How many of these have been wholly new ideas and how many of these have been developments of older ideas?

You may consider completing this part as a journalistic piece, where you present a report to camera.

For this final section, you need to take all of the learning, research and practical experience you have accumulated while working through this unit and put it together to identify future applications for these technologies.

You need to identify wholly new applications as well as identifying how you can **repurpose** existing products so that they can impact in areas other than that in which they are currently used. You should use your imagination as well as your practical understanding when completing this task.

4.1 Future uses

Consider future uses to which these virtual and augmented reality technologies may be put. You won't know every virtual and augmented reality project that is currently in development, so you may suggest a product that already exists, and also think creatively about suitable applications. You should also identify how your suggestions could impact on society. These impacts should be positive!

Possible developments of virtual and augmented reality and how these may impact on society

There are five areas you could consider in your answer for this question. They are as follows.

Advances in treating injuries or disease

Consider impacts such as training, remote operations or areas where there is a high chance of diseases being transferred.

Leisure activities

Consider computer, card or board games and general entertainment – games that do not exist, or games that could be improved by virtual or augmented reality.

Environment

Many ideas could fit this general heading and you should not, for example, forget that any product that reduces the use of fossil fuels would have a positive impact on the environment. For example, a pre-visit tourist resource would reduce the use of petrol, or an augmented reality app could show how a house could be made more energy efficient.

Home

As well as entertainment applications, virtual and augmented reality could be used to improve decorating (both to deliver training and visualise the outcome). Augmented reality could have huge impacts on home purchasing and home furnishings.

Education

There are many areas you could consider, for example:

- Improving the content of lessons. Augmented reality could be used to provide differentiated materials as part of a presentation. This could be really beneficial for language lessons.
- Assessment. Augmented reality could be used to set questions during a presentation, or trigger images could be used to access themed questions.

(60 minutes)

Review the five suggested areas where virtual or augmented reality could impact.

Each member of your group should take one of the suggested areas and research the use of virtual and augmented reality within this area at present.

Suggest one way in which virtual or augmented could impact on these areas.

Present your suggestion to the group as a presentation.

4.2 Repurposing

How existing products may be repurposed and used in wholly new ways

Just because a certain application has already been created, it does not mean that with a slight tweak or a bit of thought these products cannot be used differently. For example, a tourist guide product that was created to show visitors how to explore an Elizabethan manor house could also be used to introduce users to Elizabethan architecture.

Benefits of repurposing using current examples of resources in new ways

The benefits you identify will be based on your own opinion of the impact and possibly benefits across many areas, including the quality of the impact, the efficiency of the impact and cost implications.

Already existing products that are beneficial in medicine could be used in animal welfare. Historically, products such as x-rays, which were originally developed to treat humans, have been used to treat animals, as the physiology is fundamentally the same. Similarly, virtual or augmented reality products could be repurposed.

The costs of developing medical products are huge and so one of the clear benefits of repurposing a product is that the costs of developing the product can be spread across many different markets.

Similarly, many products that were originally developed for use in business can be reused within education. The benefits would not only be improvements in the quality of the lessons that are delivered, but also the cost savings that could be made. For example:

- a virtual or augmented reality product created for a specific business activity could be used to support this unit
- a virtual reality product created for use in medicine could be used to study human biology
- a virtual reality product created to show how to build a car engine could be used within a science lesson to explain how an internal combustion engine works.

Heads-up display used to augment learning in schools

There are a number of benefits for this technology in education; for example, the ability to overlay instructions or assessment criteria on a written sheet, giving in-depth instructions so that students are always aware of what they need to do. The user could click on the image if they are stuck, or all users could be given the image as a general overlay.

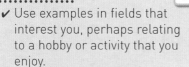

KNOW IT

1 What is meant by the term 'repurposing'?
2 A virtual reality product that has been used for many years within the Aeronautical industry to help in teaching aerodynamics has recently been bought by a group who build model aircraft. Explain ONE benefit that the group of model aircraft enthusiasts will get from using the virtual reality product
3 Explain ONE further reason why the group may have chosen to purchase this virtual reality product.

LO4 Assessment activity

Below is a suggested assessment activity that has been directly linked to the pass and merit criteria in LO4 to help with assignment preparation; it includes Top tips on how to achieve best results.

Activity 1 – pass criteria *P6* and merit criteria *M3*

Research uses of virtual and augmented reality. Identify ONE use of virtual reality and ONE use of augmented reality that could be repurposed. Describe and evaluate the advantages and benefits of doing so.

Present your suggestions to the group as a presentation.

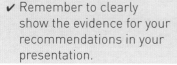

TOP TIPS
✔ Use examples in fields that interest you, perhaps relating to a hobby or activity that you enjoy.
✔ Remember to clearly show the evidence for your recommendations in your presentation.

Unit 06

Application design

How will I be assessed?

You will be assessed by producing evidence from set scenarios or from work that you carry out as part of a work placement or employment. This evidence will be assessed by your tutor.

LEARNING OUTCOMES

The topics and activities in this unit will help you to:

1 Understand how applications are designed.
2 Be able to investigate potential solutions for application developments.
3 Be able to generate designs for application solutions.
4 Be able to present application solutions to meet client and user requirements.

How will I be graded?

You will be graded using the following criteria:

Learning outcome	Pass assessment criteria	Merit assessment criteria	Distinction assessment criteria
You will:	**To achieve a pass you must demonstrate that you have met all the pass assessment criteria**	**To achieve a merit you must demonstrate that you have met all the pass and merit assessment criteria**	**To achieve a distinction you must demonstrate that you have met all the pass, merit and distinction assessment criteria**
1 Understand how applications are designed	**P1** Describe the key stages in application development	**M1** Compare and contrast different application development models	
2 Be able to investigate potential solutions for application developments	**P2** Gather client requirements for an application solution	**M2** Conduct a feasibility study of different solutions for the client requirements	
3 Be able to generate designs for application solutions	**P3** Illustrate the requirements, functioning, and designs of an application solution, using diagrams		**D1** Justify design choices identifying the advantages and disadvantages of each
4 Be able to present application solutions to meet client and user requirements	**P4** Present a proposed design solution to the identified client	**M3** Negotiate adaptations with the identified client to refine the design solution	
	P5 Create a prototype based on the design solution		
	P6 Gather client and/ or user feedback on the prototype		**D2** Implement improvements based on the analysed client and/ or user feedback

LO1 Understand how applications are designed
P1 M1

GETTING STARTED 👤

(5 minutes)

Why is it important that a product is developed following rules, guidelines, or the phases of an application development model? Discuss why there should be a structure and rules for a developer to follow when producing a product.

1.1 Stages of application development models

There are a number of different **application development models**, and these are often split into distinct phases. The names of these phases can differ depending on the application development model you are following, and some may split one of these phases into several smaller phases, or combine two into one.

Requirements analysis

In this phase you are gathering information about the application that the client wants, or needs. You are investigating what is currently in place and

> **🔑 KEY TERM**
>
> **Application development model** – a method of producing an application that divides the process of development into distinct phases.

developing an idea of what your client wants. There are a number of ways of gathering information, and these are described in more detail in LO2 (see LO2, page 169). At the end of this phase you will produce a requirements analysis (see Unit 9 LO2, page 252), which is presented to the client, who needs to agree with it before you can move on to the next phase.

Design

The design phase involves outlining potential solutions and developing a plan from the requirements analysis for the creation of the product. Aspects of the design phase are covered in LO3 (page 175) and the design phase is covered as a whole in Unit 9 LO2 (page 251).

Implementation/coding

In this phase the product is actually created and tested throughout the development. This testing allows for errors to be corrected and the product to be refined. See Unit 9 LO3, page 261.

Testing

Testing takes place both throughout the product's implementation, and once it is believed to be complete. When the developer is satisfied with the application, it is given to the client or end user to compare with their original requirements. See Unit 9 LO3, page 261.

Deployment

Once the client has tested the product, they will decide if it is to be accepted, accepted with amendments, or not accepted. If the product is to be accepted, the handover of the product is arranged with the client. See Unit 9 LO4, page 264.

Maintenance

All applications require maintenance, whether it is to correct errors, improve the performance, or adapt the application for new requirements. Maintenance needs planning and agreement with the client. See Unit 9 LO4, page 264.

> **KEY TERM**
>
> **Deployment** – the implementation of a product.

(INDEPENDENT AND GROUP ACTIVITY)..........................

(20 minutes)

Create a mind map for the different stages of application development models. Add each stage as an offshoot from the main, then extend these, for example:

- tasks to be carried out
- documentation produced
- people involved.

Join with another person, or as a group. Compare mind maps and add content to your own from the other students.

1.2 Characteristics and features of application development models

There is a range of application development models. Each one uses the application development phases but in different ways. They vary in the way the developer moves through the stages, and who is involved in the

production and suited to different scenarios or products. These models can also be combined to bring the benefits of each model together.

Waterfall model

The waterfall model lets the developer move through the phases in order, but with the option to return to the previous phase if needed. The developer can continue to move back up the phases, but must move back down in order. See also Unit 9 LO1.1, page 245.

Iterative model

In this model, one part of the product is worked upon first, and this part moves through the phases. On the next **iteration** a further requirement, or function, is added and it moves through the phases. This is repeated until a final, complete product is produced.

KEY TERM

Iteration/iterative – repeating a process or processes.

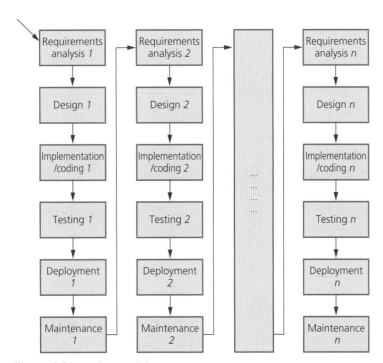

Figure 6.1 Iterative model

Agile development model

Agile development allows a product to be worked on and refined iteratively. The development may begin with a small part of the product that is added to through each cycle. Agile development is a combination of both iterative and incremental development models. See also Unit 9 LO1.1, page 246.

Rapid application development (RAD) model

RAD means less time is spent producing requirements, specifications and designs. Prototypes are not necessarily planned first and are worked on iteratively with a team of developers refining the prototypes into the final product. The prototypes are tested during their development and at the end of the production of each new prototype. This testing can also involve the end user throughout the development, so they can see, assess and evaluate each prototype, as opposed to leaving their input to the later stages of the model.

Spiral model

The spiral model uses prototypes that are worked on and refined as the phases are worked through repeatedly. See also Unit 9 LO1.1, page 245.

Prototype model

Prototypes are developed in the early stages, for example to demonstrate the functional requirements or the design of areas of the product. These are shown to the client who provides feedback for refinement. These prototypes can be refined or thrown away as a new prototype is developed.

These are just a few application development models; there are more that you can research independently.

GROUP ACTIVITY

(30 minutes)

In a small group, research a different application development model, including:

- its key features, or elements, or model structure
- its benefits
- its drawbacks
- example products, or scenarios, where that model is best used.

Present your findings to the other groups.

KNOW IT

1 Identify the six application development phases.
2 Explain the different between the waterfall model and the iterative model.
3 Describe the prototype model.
4 Compare the characteristics of the waterfall model with the agile development model.
5 Identify a scenario where the RAD model would be most appropriate.

LO1 Assessment activities

Below are two suggested assessment activities that have been directly linked to the pass and merit criteria in LO1 to help with assignment preparation; they include Top tips on how to achieve the best results.

Activity 1 – pass criteria *P1*

Create an A5 booklet, or a presentation for the application development phases. Include:

- examples of the processes involved in each phase
- the documentation, or output, that is produced in each phase.

Activity 2 – merit criteria *M1*

Add to your booklet or presentation, describing different application models. Include:

- similarities between the different models
- differences between the different models
- the types of project each model is most appropriate for.

TOP TIPS ✓

✔ Make sure you use a range of examples, at least three, in your descriptions.
✔ Describe each phase or model first, before looking at the differences and similarities.

LO2 Be able to investigate potential solutions for application developments *P2 M2*

(5 minutes)

You need to produce an application for a client and need to investigate their requirements.

Discuss the different ways that you could find out the information you need.

> **KEY TERM**
>
> **Data redundancy** – data that is repeated or excessive, i.e. not required.

2.1 Methods of gathering user requirements

In the requirements analysis phase, the current application (if there is one) should be investigated. You will need to find out what the client and all potential end users require the application to do. You may also need to investigate current methods of carrying out tasks, or performing the functions and actions that the current application (if there is one) performs. This information can be gathered in a number of ways, depending on the situation and the information you need to find.

Methods of gathering requirements are also covered in Unit 11 LO2.

Client and user interviews

An interview usually involves a face-to-face discussion with the client and all potential types of end user (interviewee). There are two types of question: open and closed.

Closed questions limit the response expected, for example a yes or no response, or ask for a specific example. The interviewee is not expected to expand or explain their answers. These questions give you facts and are easy to answer. They also provide data that can be easily assessed and compared; for example, if you are interviewing a large number of people you can quickly compare their answers.

Open questions allow the interviewee to explain, give their opinion or reflect upon something. They provide longer answers but also allow for further discussion and expansion. The answers can provide depth and understanding, but the results are also more likely to be subjective (opinion rather than fact). The results are difficult to compare or produce statistical data from.

Leading questions need to be avoided where possible when planning an interview. The wording of a leading question prompts the interviewee to answer in a specific way, which could be biased or inaccurate. Leading questions can be difficult to avoid, and sometimes impossible, for example you may need to ask what the problems with a current system are.

Funnelling involves a series of questions that are either:

● closed questions, which are expanded on, moving towards open questions; for example:

> When planning an interview, it is important to use a range of open and closed questions.
>
> Example closed question: Do you use an application every day?
>
> Example open question: How do you use the application?

> Example leading question: Why has the current application been so unsuccessful?
>
> Could be changed to: Tell me about your experiences with the current application.

- Do you use the application daily?
- What do you use the application for each day?
- How does this help you do your job?

● open questions, which are expanded on, moving towards closed questions; for example:
  - Tell me about your experiences with the current application.
  - How does that help your job?
  - Which tool do you use most?

Interviews need to be structured and systematic. They require planning to ensure they cover all requirements, do not miss any areas, and do not go off topic. They will usually start with an introduction to explain the purpose of the interview, before moving through the questions in a logical manner, ending with thanking the interviewee for their time.

It is possible to rush interviews, and the interviewee can be left feeling pressurised to give answers quickly. This can lead to inaccurate information. The interviewees need to be given time and encouraged to think about their answers before giving them. They should also be asked for further detail, thought, or clarification in their answers to make sure you have gathered all the information that you need.

Observation of tasks

Observing how the tasks are currently performed lets you see the steps that are taken, the data that is used, the processes that take place, and the outputs produced.

All possible tasks (including those that may not be involved in the actual application but that feed into it or rely upon it) will need to be observed, with all types of end user. Different users will have different requirements and will use the application in different ways. You will need to take notes, videos or photos of the processes to have a record for analysis.

Analysis of existing documents and systems

Existing systems need to be observed and experienced. Any documentation that is to be replaced or integrated in the application needs to be gathered and analysed as to its contents, who uses it and its purpose. This can be carried out in conjunction with observing the tasks, as documents can be gathered ready for analysis.

In the analysis of these documents and systems, the following will need to be identified.

● The purpose.
● Who uses it.
● How it is used.
● What it contains (data).
● Where the data comes from.
● What processes are involved.
● How it is produced (if it is an output).
● Where it fits with other areas of the system.

GROUP ACTIVITY

(45 minutes)

A library requires a new system for recording books and loans, calculating books past their return date, sending letters to customers, etc. The library has three employees who all work as librarians.

Work as a group to design an interview to find out about the application the library needs.

Test your interview on a member of the group and make refinements if needed.

2.2 User requirements

Functional requirements

Functional requirements identify what the new application needs to do. Table 6.1 shows the different requirements.

Table 6.1 Functional requirements

Data and information collected and used in the existing approach.	Identify the data that the current systems make use of, how this is used and where it comes from.
Data and information collected and used in the new application.	The new application may require different data and information from the existing approach, for example some data may be redundant, further data may be needed, or it could come from a different place, person or piece of software.
Functions or processing that the application should perform.	A list of **measurable processes**, stating every function that the application needs to carry out.
Outputs from the application.	Each output needs to be clearly identified, along with where its information comes from (how it is generated), what the output will look like and who or where it will go to.
Core functional requirements.	The functions necessary for the application. They must all be achieved and are fundamental for the application to work, or be acceptable to the client.
Optional functional requirements.	These are functions that are not fundamental to the application, i.e. the application would work (and may be acceptable to the client) without them.
User interface requirements, including accessibility requirements.	The type of interface will need determining and any additional requirements, such as style of input, methods of output, and any requirements for people who require accessibility options (e.g. larger font, option to change the font colour, a different language, voice recognition etc.)

> **KEY TERM**
>
> **Measureable process** – an action (e.g. calculation) that a user (or tester) can identify has happened correctly or not. For example, a measureable process is that a submit button stores data in a database: this either happens, or does not.

Constraints

A constraint is a restriction that limits what the solution can do, or how it has to be built. A range of constraints need to be considered. Several possible constraints are described below, but a range of other constraints may exist that will need consideration.

- Hardware constraints: the hardware that the application will run on or make use of. It may be a constraint as the client may specify the hardware, e.g. the current hardware as new hardware will not be purchased. This may limit what the solution can do, as the hardware may not be powerful enough to perform some actions.
- Software constraints: this is the software that the application has to use, or interact with. The solution may have to interact with other software packages (off-the-shelf or bespoke) and the solution needs to be able to retrieve, or send, data to these packages.
- Platform constraints: the platform is the make of hardware, and/or the operating system. Software that runs on one platform may not work correctly on a second. This may be a constraint as the organisation could be using an old operating system and are not able to upgrade, therefore the application must be compatible with this operating system.
- Development constraints: the developer may be limited to using set software to produce the system, for example if the client is familiar and experienced with a specific piece of software this may need to be used in the new application.

PAIRS ACTIVITY

(15 minutes)

Consider the library scenario. Work in pairs to list the constraints and limitations, then combine as a group to share your ideas. Create a combined list of constraints and limitations.

Limitations

A limitation restricts what is implemented. The scope of the solution is a limitation – it may restrict it to specific functions and confine what it can do. Constraints, such as limited funding or software options, may mean some aspects of the solution cannot be developed because they take too long, or they cannot be made with the software required.

2.3 Possible solutions

There could be several solutions, using different hardware and software, and covering different requirements (e.g. some optional functional requirements may be included or excluded from different solutions). Each solution may include prototypes and need to identify which requirements they include. The solutions will need evaluating for suitability and presented to the client, who will make the final decision on which solution they feel is most appropriate for their needs.

INDEPENDENT AND GROUP ACTIVITY

(10 minutes)

Consider the library scenario. Identify a solution that you feel would meet the client's needs.

Share your solution with the group, considering the similarities and differences between the solutions each person has identified.

2.4 Feasibility study

The feasibility study determines if it is possible (or viable) to develop a product. This is conducted after the investigation as the requirements, constraints and limitations are now known and the developer can decide if they are able to produce the project.

Feasibility studies are also covered in Unit 11 LO1 (see page 270).

Technological requirements

This looks at the technological needs of the product (hardware, software etc.). It needs to determine whether the product can be produced, and if the hardware and software exist to produce it. It will also need to determine if the application can be produced with the technology available.

Economic or financial costs of development and potential benefits

The client will have a budget for the production of the application. Costs need to be estimated and compared with this budget to see if it is financially viable to produce the application. The minimum viable product will need to be identified. Some optional functional requirements may need to be excluded to bring the cost down.

The cost may be greater than just the production of the application and may include maintenance costs and the cost of changes required to the organisation to implement the application, e.g. the cost of additional staff to maintain the application.

Legal issues

The potential products need to be evaluated against relevant legislation; for example, if an application is to store personal data it must comply with the Data Protection Act 1998.

Operational impact

Operational impact refers to the environment within the organisation where the product is to be deployed. This may consider how the organisation's functions will be affected by the product, whether it will fit in with the organisation's culture and work with their existing business practices. The range and scope of changes needs to be identified.

Scheduling and resources

The schedule is the timing, in this case how long it is estimated the product will take to produce. The client may need the product within a set time frame, which the developer may or may not be able to meet.

Resources can be technological or human, and these should be available when they are needed during the development process.

Some restrictions may be negotiable (e.g. cost, timings) and the outline solutions may extend these to show the client what is possible with some flexibility. If the result is that the application is not feasible, a developer may need to decline the job.

(20 minutes)

Create a mind map of the feasibility study. Include each of the sections as an off-shoot from the main and add details and examples of what may be analysed in each section.

KNOW IT

1 Identify five elements that will be included in the functional requirements.
2 Describe what is meant by a constraint.
3 Explain why more than one possible solution is created.
4 Identify the five key areas investigated in a feasibility study.

LO2 Assessment activities

Below are two suggested assessment activities that have been directly linked to the pass and merit criteria in LO2 to help with assignment preparation; they include Top tips on how to achieve the best results

For (at least) one of your units you will be creating a prototype for an application. For both of the activities below, use the product that you are creating as a basis for them.

Activity 1 – pass criteria *P2*

1 Design an interview (or several) for your client and end users, using a range of question styles. Consider the design of the structure of your interview and make sure you cover all aspects of the product.
2 Carry out the interview with your client and end users and summarise the results.
3 Observe your client and end users interacting with the current product, or current methods of carrying out the tasks. Collect any documentation that you may need.
4 Use the results of your investigation to write a set of functional requirements.
5 Write a report that lists your functional requirements, and summarises the constraints and limitations that you have found that will impact on the solution.

Activity 2 – merit criteria *M2*

1 Identify potential solutions (at least two) for the product. Include details such as the requirements they cover and the key features.
2 Create a presentation to show the potential solutions to your client.
3 Carry out a feasibility study based on the potential solutions. Make sure you cover all the relevant headings in this unit.
4 Write a report for each potential solution, detailing the feasibility study you have carried out.

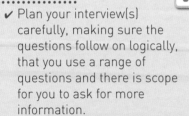

TOP TIPS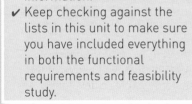

✔ Plan your interview(s) carefully, making sure the questions follow on logically, that you use a range of questions and there is scope for you to ask for more information.
✔ Keep checking against the lists in this unit to make sure you have included everything in both the functional requirements and feasibility study.

GETTING STARTED

(5 minutes)

Discuss the importance of designing a solution before producing it. Discuss what needs to be designed in an application. For example, what needs to be designed for a hotel booking system?

LO3 Be able to generate designs for application solutions *P3 D1*

3.1 The use of diagrams to represent aspects of the design of an application

Diagrams are used to show what the system will look like, how it will work and who is involved with the application. Different diagrams can be produced depending on the application being designed.

Functional requirements

A use case diagram identifies all of the people involved in the application and how they will interact with it. Figure 6.2 shows a use case diagram for a hotel.

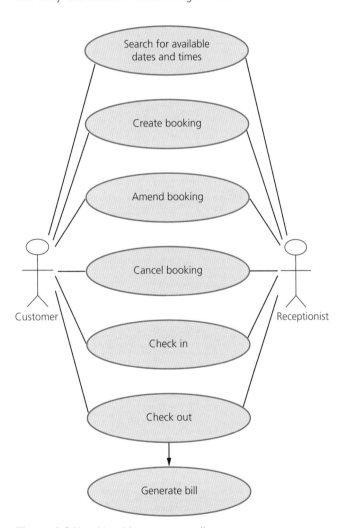

Figure 6.2 Hotel booking use case diagram

The people who interact with the system are shown as stick people, with their 'type' written below. The actions that they, and the system, perform are drawn in rectangles with arrows indicating who is involved in their actions. For example, in Figure 6.2 the customer is the only user involved in searching for available dates and times for a booking, whereas both the customer and the receptionist are able to create a booking.

Processing and data handling

A range of diagrams can be created to show how data will move through the system, and how the processes will work. Below are some examples of the diagrams that may be used in the design of the processes, there are others that you may need to investigate and use in the design of your application.

Flow chart

A flow chart shows the processes involved with the system, including what is input and output. Flow charts are also covered in Unit 11, LO3, page 281.

Figure 6.3 shows the common symbols used in flow charts.

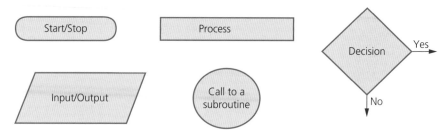

Figure 6.3 Common flow chart symbols

These symbols are combined to illustrate how parts of a system work. The detail can vary, from giving an overview to illustrating exactly how each part of the process works. Figure 6.4 shows an example flow chart for a customer searching for availability in the hotel.

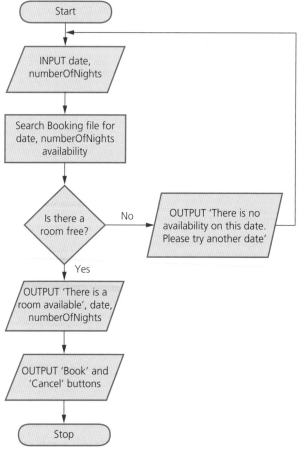

Figure 6.4 Customer booking flow chart

This could be expanded further, for example the search booking file could be expanded to show how the file is opened, searched and data retrieved.

Data flow diagram

A data flow diagram shows how data moves through the system, including the files that are accessed and the people who are involved in the processes. As with flow charts, these can be shown in more or less depth depending on what is required. A data flow diagram shows the external entities that interact with the system, and how they interact as well as the data stores that are used, whereas a flow chart plans the **algorithm** that is to be developed.

Figure 6.5 shows common symbols used in a data flow diagram.

Data flow diagrams are also covered in Unit 2 LO5 (page 74) and Unit 11 LO3 (page 280).

Figure 6.6 gives an example data flow diagram for the hotel booking system. This shows the customer searching for availability and making the booking. The entities involved are the customer and receptionist, the diagram shows what information they input and receive from the system. This could be expanded further to show what happens when a customer has used the system before, for example retrieving their details.

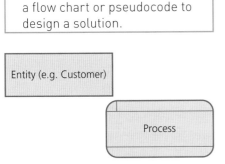

Entity (e.g. Customer)

Process

Data Store

Figure 6.5 Common data flow diagram symbols

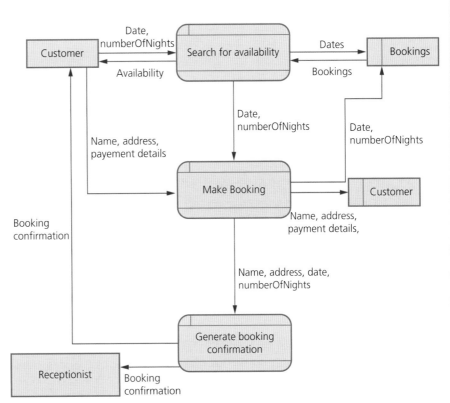

Figure 6.6 Data flow diagram for creating a booking

Class diagrams

A class diagram is used with object-oriented programming. It shows the classes involved in a system and how these inherit attributes and methods from other classes. Each class has its own box, with its name at the top, then its attributes listed, and finally its methods.

Figure 6.7 shows an example class diagram for the hotel booking system. The associations between the objects are shown with arrows and numbers representing one to many associations.

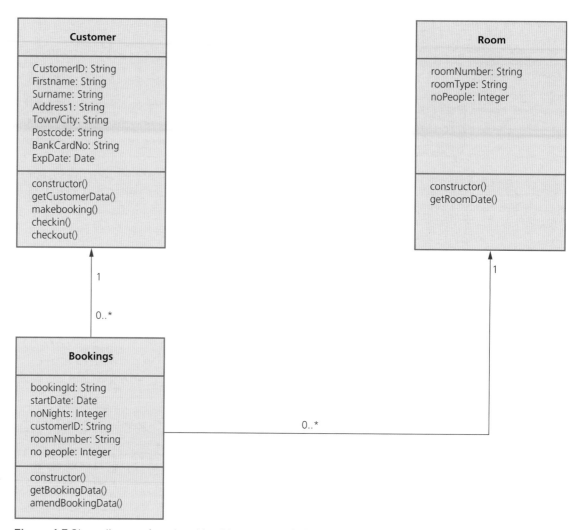

Figure 6.7 Class diagram for a hotel booking system. 0..* means there is a range from zero to many

Different relationships can exist between objects.

- Aggregation means that one class is part of another, e.g. a keyboard is part of a monitor. This relationship is shown with an open diamond.
- Composition is stronger than aggregation, and means that if one class is deleted, the other cannot exist either, e.g. a processor and a computer – if the processor is removed the computer no longer works. This relationship is shown with a shaded diamond.

Classes can also inherit from another class – they take the methods and attributes of another class, but they can edit these and make them function slightly differently; for example, a savings account can inherit from a bank account, but it may apply interest or charges differently.

Object diagrams

An object diagram is also used in object-oriented programming to show the instances of objects and how these relate. Figure 6.8 shows an object diagram for the hotel booking system. It has an instance of each object, showing the data in each instance and how these relate.

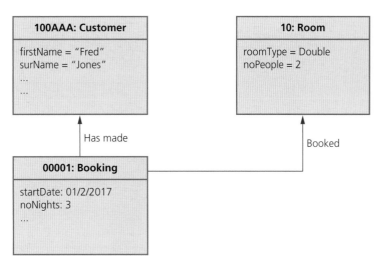

Figure 6.8 Object diagram for hotel booking system

Entity relationship diagram

This shows the relationships between tables in a database. There are three possible relationships: one to one, one to many, many to many. Figure 6.9 shows each of these three types of relationship.

Entity relationship diagrams are also covered in Unit 11 LO3 (page 283).

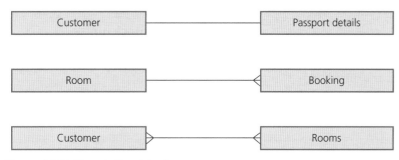

Figure 6.9 Entity relationship diagrams

One customer can only hold one passport. One room can be booked many times. One customer can book many rooms, and one room over a period of time can be booked by many people. The many to many relationship is removed through normalisation of a database, so they are rarely seen in entity relationship diagrams.

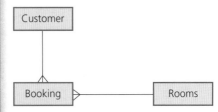

Figure 6.10 Hotel booking entity relationship diagram

GROUP ACTIVITY

(60 minutes)

As a group, discuss the different diagrams available. Which would be suitable for designing the library application? Why would some work and others not work?

In pairs, take one type of diagram that the group agrees is suitable. Produce the diagram for the library application.

Share your diagram with the group, and discuss any problems or improvements that could be added to each.

Tables and relationships are combined to produce one diagram. Figure 6.10 shows a complete entity relationship diagram for the hotel booking system.

User interface designs

User interface designs show what the interface (input and output) will look like to the end user. They are not focused on functionality, but on content, layout and style. Two diagrams that can be used to design a user interface are described below, there are further diagrams that you may need to investigate and use in the design of your application.

Wireframe diagram

This is a blueprint of what the interface will look like. It will show key areas, content and features (e.g. drop down lists, progress bars), but the content will not be included.

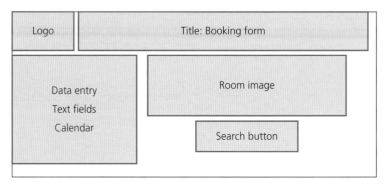

Figure 6.11 A wireframe diagram of a hotel booking form

Figure 6.11 shows an example wireframe diagram of a booking form for the hotel. It gives an indication of the layout of the page and where key elements will go, such as the title, search button, data entry fields. It also gives an idea of how data will be entered, such as through text fields and a calendar to choose options from.

A wireframe diagram provides a basis for the end user to determine if the structure is sufficient, and it can be used as a basis for a graphical mock-up.

Graphical mock-up

This is a prototype of the interface, with the content included, colour schemes added etc. so that the user can see how the content will appear and what it will look like. This may be created using the software, or tools, that the final solution will use, or it may be created with drawing software. This gives the end user a better feel for the system, and they can decide if the content is sufficient, or if something is missing.

3.2 Standardisation of design

A standardised design encourages familiarity, increases success and reduces workload by using algorithms and methods that have already been tried and tested. Several features of a standardised design are described below; you will need to investigate standardisation that is appropriate to your application and this may be wider than those given below.

Standard algorithms or processes

These are common processes across a range of applications. For example, standard searching algorithms include a linear search, binary search etc. These algorithms are used in a variety of situations, and have been written and rewritten many times. Using these algorithms can save you time as you don't need to start from scratch.

Modularisation

A modular design splits a problem into sub-problems (**modules**), which are then split into further sub-problems. This process is repeated until each sub-problem can be solved independently. Through modularisation, an application can be split into sub-routines; each one can be solved and tested independently before being combined into one program. Modularisation allows modules to be reused as they can be taken out of the program and used elsewhere.

To create a modular design, a structure diagram is usually created. This shows the main problem at the top of the diagram, and then it is split beneath.

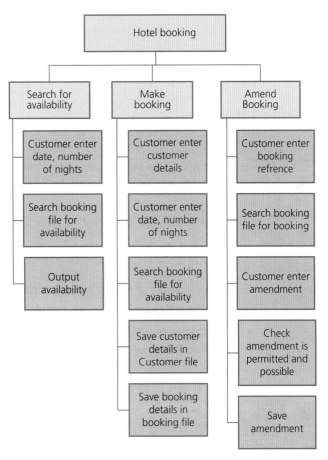

Figure 6.12 Hotel booking structure diagram

Figure 6.12 shows an example partial structure chart for the hotel booking system. The system 'Hotel booking' is at the top of the diagram, and this is split into the three modules below. Even in this small diagram there are repeated actions, such as 'Search booking file for availability'. When this is created, this module can be written once and used in both aspects of the program.

PAIRS ACTIVITY

(15 minutes)

Continue the hotel booking structure diagram, adding sub-modules for checking in, checking out and generating a bill. Expand each of these sub-modules to show their own sub-modules.

Cross-platform standards

Cross-platform refers to an application being used on different operating systems, or on different hardware, for example on both a Windows and Mac computer. It could also refer to the software used to run it, for example a web application will need to be compatible with different web browsers, such as Chrome and Internet Explorer. A cross-platform standard may involve using a programming language that can run on more than one platform.

Java is an example of a multi-platform language. To run a Java program, a Java virtual machine is installed on the computer, whether it is a Windows or Mac computer. The virtual machine will allow for compatibility.

It is not always possible to create a cross-platform compatible application; sometimes a second or third version is needed. Potential platforms should be considered in the design and analysed as to how compatibility can be ensured or aided.

Standard protocols

A protocol is a set of rules that are set out and followed. For example, in communication, a protocol would identify the language of the data being transmitted, the speed of the transmission, etc. When writing an application, the standard protocols to be used need to be investigated. For example, HTTP is a standard protocol for web data communication and the use of hyperlinks.

Standard protocols are often developed by standards organisations (see Unit 9, page 249). They identify standards that they recommend are implemented by developers. When followed, this allows for compatibility across software, as each developer will be using the same protocols.

Standard interface widgets (appearance of buttons, dropdown menus, hyperlinks)

Interfaces are the methods by which data is input, and information (or data) is output from a system. Standard interface widgets are the elements used for this interface; for example, drop down boxes to enter data where there are a number of options. A hyperlink, for example, is usually blue and underlined.

By using these standard interface widgets, the users will already be accustomed to their purpose and will be familiar with how to use them. This will, therefore, decrease the time it will take users to learn how to use the new application.

Common user interface layouts, icons and labels through application

Although rarely noticed, most applications have a similar structure and design to their interfaces. For example, a title is usually at the top of a page, buttons such as 'next' or 'submit' are usually at the bottom right of a screen. A save icon is usually an image of a floppy disc (even though they have not been used for many years) because people are familiar with this icon and know that it means to save.

Figure 6.13 Examples of interface widgets

Figure 6.14 Common icons

Menus also have a similar structure; open most applications and there is a File menu that includes Save, Print, etc.

Using these standard, common user interface layouts, icons and labels increases familiarity for end users; increased familiarity can improve user confidence and reduce the time it takes for end users to learn how to use the software.

INDEPENDENT ACTIVITY

(10 minutes)

Open two applications on your computer, tablet or phone. Identify the common interface layouts, and standard widgets that are in the applications.

3.3 Advantages of proposed solution

When you have developed a proposed solution, you need to justify to the client how it meets their requirements. The justification will be used when comparing different designs, and when presenting the proposed design to the client. Below are a number of ways a proposed solution could benefit an organisation. There may be additional advantages to your particular solution.

Automation

By including, or improving, **automation** in the design of a solution, the need for users to control and operate the system may be minimised; for example, an automated database that links to a website. Identifying these areas can demonstrate reduced running costs or ease of performing tasks.

Operational efficiency

Increasing operational efficiency reduces the time end users spend interacting with the system, performing tasks, or the speed processes are performed. This improves efficiency.

Cost effectiveness

The cost effectiveness of an application will compare the cost of producing it with the outcomes. If cost effectiveness is good, the cost may still be high but the outcomes are significantly greater; for example, the efficiency and improvements that the client will experience will be significant. If an application has a poor cost effectiveness, then the improvements to operations will be weak and the cost may not be justified.

Globalisation

Globalisation refers to how the application will be integrated worldwide. This is only relevant to applications where a global (or at least more than just small) market is appropriate.

Improved communication

Communication can be both internal and external and effective communication is vital to a business. If an application can improve communication methods (internally, externally or both) these benefits can be highlighted.

KEY TERM

Automation – the use of computers and electronic equipment to carry out tasks that were previously done manually.

Customisation and adaptability

A rigid application may be appropriate in some situations; however, if the client can customise it, or if it can be easily adapted in the future, it may be seen more favourably. This will allow the client to adapt the application if their needs change, or customise the application in the future to make it more efficient and effective for the organisation.

Increased markets

The application may allow the client to access further markets; for example, it may allow a shop to sell online or in other countries. By accessing these markets, the client will be able to gain more customers, sales or users.

Ease of access for customers

Standard practices enable a solution that is familiar to customers and allows for ease of use and access. The ease of access for users with accessibility problems can increase the range and number of users.

New marketing opportunities

An application may provide new marketing opportunities by increasing the range of customers or providing a new platform for sales.

Customer or user information

An application may provide the opportunity to store further customer or user information, or record their actions. These could be used to inform future decisions.

Real-time information

This is information that is provided as it is generated. For example, a hotel booking system can provide real-time information by showing all bookings when they are made. This system could be extended to analyse bookings and profits as each booking is added. By providing real-time information, an organisation will be up to date with its figures and be able to respond to any problems as they occur.

New employment

An application may introduce new roles within the client's organisation, for example a web application may require a manager to maintain the data and keep it up to date. This new role can provide expertise to the client and improve jobs and employment rates.

INDEPENDENT ACTIVITY

(10 minutes)

Consider the hotel booking application and one of the designs you created in the previous activities. List the advantages this application brings to the hotel.

3.4 Disadvantages of proposed solution

A proposed solution for an application is unlikely to just have advantages. The developers and client need to know the downsides, especially if there are a number of proposed solutions, so that they can weigh the advantages against the disadvantages, as a compromise may be required. A number of these possible disadvantages are described below. There may be further disadvantages that you need to consider for your application.

Financial cost

The cost may be within the client's budget, but there needs to be a comparison of this cost against what the application provides. A solution may cover the fundamental requirements, but none of the optional requirements, and be at the top of the client's budget. This may not be financially viable.

Changeover costs and risks

The new application may be replacing an existing paper-based or computer-based system. When the application is produced, there will be a change-over period. There will be risks, such as loss of time, loss of data, etc. There is also a cost, both financial and time related; for example, if a new application will take several days to change over from the old system, the amount of work and custom lost will need assessing.

Training needs

End users will need training on a new application. The extent of this training need could be financial (the cost of trainers, cost of paying end users to undergo training) and time based (end users will not be doing their jobs while training). The less training required for a system, which can be reduced through familiarity and the use of standards, the less time and cost incurred.

Lack of job security and job losses

The implementation of new technology may make some jobs redundant. This introduces fear among employees, as the new automation may make their jobs redundant. A solution that creates a significant number of job losses can be seen as having a negative implication.

Security issues

Security relates to the safety of data and systems. Security needs to be built into any application, but potential security risks need to be identified.

Privacy issues

Data needs to be kept private, and organisations must follow the Data Protection Act 1998. Any potential risks to the privacy of information, or issues relating to privacy within the system, need identifying.

Potential customer concerns

In some situations, there may be customer concerns over a new application, how it will work and how it will impact on their experience and activities. These concerns need to be identified and addressed.

Loss of personal contact

By automating systems, a human element can be removed from a process, and this can cause concern and problems. For example, in the hotel booking system, rooms can be booked without any contact with staff in the hotel. This can cause anxiety from both the customers, who may not feel secure about using an automated booking system, and from the staff who are not involved in the bookings.

(10 minutes)

Consider the hotel booking application and the design that you used to consider the advantages of the solution. List the disadvantages that may be associated with this solution.

··

KNOW IT

1 Identify four diagrams that can be used in the design of the processes in an application.
2 Explain the difference between a flow chart and a data flow diagram.
3 Identify two diagrams that can be used to design a user interface.
4 Explain the importance of using standard interface widgets and designs when designing an application.
5 Identify three advantages that need considering when analysing a proposed solution.
6 Identify three disadvantages that need considering when analysing a proposed solution.

LO3 Assessment activities

Below are two suggested assessment activities that have been directly linked to the pass and distinction criteria in LO3 to help with assignment preparation; they include Top tips on how to achieve the best results

For (at least) one of your units you will be creating a prototype for an application. For both of the activities below, use the product that you are creating as a basis for them.

Activity 1 – pass criteria *P3*

Consider the different diagrams that you could use to design the application. Produce at least one diagram for each of the following points:

1 functional requirements
2 processes
3 data handling
4 user interface design.

Activity 2 – distinction criteria *D1*

Revisit the design you produced for P3. Write a report to accompany your design, justifying your design choice. Make sure you identify, and explain, the advantages and disadvantages of your solution.

TOP TIPS

✔ Activity 1 requires a minimum of one diagram for each section; some processes may require several diagrams to cover all processes thoroughly.
✔ Make sure you annotate all of your diagrams, clearly identifying their purpose and where they fit in the proposed solution.
✔ Check the list of advantages and disadvantages that you need to consider. They may not all be relevant to your design, but make sure you have considered each one.

LO4 Be able to present application solutions to meet client and user requirements *P4 P5 P6 M3 D2*

(5 minutes)

Why should your client be involved in the design process? Discuss how and when the client and end users(s) should be involved, and what function they play in the design process.

4.1 Pitch content

When you have completed your design(s) you need to present your proposed design solution to your client. You cannot proceed with the development of the application until your client has approved it and you have signed confirmation of this agreement.

The **pitch** content is the details included in your presentation of the proposed solution. Several elements that could appear in your pitch are described below, but there may be further areas to cover.

KEY TERM

Pitch – the delivery of a business plan, usually performed verbally, e.g. through a presentation.

What is the proposed design solution?

You will need to present your ideas for the solution, including the functional requirements and your diagrammatic designs. This can be in the form of a presentation, and/or a report. You will need to describe the purpose of your solution, and how your solution meets the original criteria.

Who would be interested in it?

You need to identify who the end users of your application will be. This is more than simply stating them. You need to describe their roles and requirements from the application, and how your solution meets their requirements.

Why is it a valuable idea?

You will need to justify your proposed design solution and explain how it meets the original requirements. You should also use the advantages you have identified to explain how it will be used and how it will add value to the client.

What makes it effective?

Linked to your design advantages, you need to explain what features, elements or processes within your system will make it successful, and how these meet the original purpose and requirements you identified.

GROUP ACTIVITY

(20 minutes)

Select and watch an episode of *Dragons Den* where a software application is being pitched (e.g. www.youtube.com/watch?v=s8d5wxGEGc8). Assess the content of the pitch against the criteria listed above. Identify the good content, and how the rest could be improved.

4.2 Effective pitch delivery

The content of a pitch is important, but how it is delivered can make or break the pitch. Here are some key points to consider to ensure your pitch is effective.

Courtesy

You will be presenting to an audience who can approve your designs and allow you to develop your application. Basic manners and being polite to your client(s) will give a good impression and demonstrate your attitude towards your work.

Speak clearly and concisely

You can use a presentation and notes to guide you, but try not to expect the client to read the presentation. You need to speak clearly and concisely, without going off topic or giving detail that the client does not need to know. For example, the client will want to see that the design meets the requirements, but may not be interested in exactly how the data is accessed from the files.

Be aware of body language

Both your body language and that of the client can convey a lot of meaning. By appearing enthusiastic and animated you can enthuse them about your application. If you stand beside the presentation, looking down and not engaging with the client, they are less likely to be enthusiastic.

Accurate spelling, punctuation and grammar

If you are producing a report and/or presentation, ensure all aspects are thoroughly checked. A computer-based spellchecker and grammar checker can be used, but documents should also be checked by people, as computers (and people using computers) can still make mistakes. Read the documents out loud to yourself, or someone else, before finalising them to make sure they make sense.

Engage the audience

Linked with body language and speaking clearly and concisely is the need to engage with the audience. Speaking directly to them and, if appropriate, including them through questioning or asking for feedback can keep them engaged and interested.

Be honest

Be honest throughout the pitch. If there are problems with your design, or it will not meet all the requirements, you need to make this clear. If you exaggerate or are dishonest, when the client receives the final application and this is discovered you could face significant problems.

Be positive

Your pitch should express any problems or disadvantages in a positive way. For example, if there is a significant disadvantage of a proposed solution, explain how you aim to overcome this. For example, if the cost will be high, emphasise the impact the solution will have on long-term cost savings.

GROUP ACTIVITY

(30 minutes)

Re-watch the *Dragons Den* pitch from the previous activity. Assess the effectiveness of the pitch delivery. Identify any points covered in this section that they did not follow.

Watch a second pitch (e.g. www.youtube.com/watch?v=kzcQtXA5Gc8) and compare the two, which one was more effective? Why was it more effective?

4.3 Effective responses to questions

When answering questions, be concise and ensure you are answering fully. Do not rush to respond – make sure you take time to think through your answer. If you cannot answer a question then be honest, but let them know that you will find out and provide a date, or time, when you will answer them. Note down the question.

A number of points to consider when preparing for and responding to questions are described below. There may be further points to consider or that you can use to prepare for your pitch.

Anticipating likely questions

Plan for questions you think may be asked, though not all questions can be foreseen. Any questions that you think may be asked can be incorporated into the pitch where appropriate, or appendices can be added to a report for the audience to refer to.

Giving a positive response

Even if you have to give a negative answer, for example you cannot reduce the cost of the development, emphasise the positive areas, for example how the application is providing value for money.

Seeking clarification where necessary

Ask for clarification on any questions you are not sure of. For example, you may not understand what the person wants to know, or you may have misunderstood the question. It is better to ask for the question to be repeated, or to ask a question to help you understand it, than to give an incorrect answer or not answer the question.

Recognising improvements and responding in a way that suggests how these can be incorporated

It is unlikely that your solution will be perfect in every way. Gain feedback from the client to help you refine your application. If a possible improvement is identified, or suggested, then you need to look at how to incorporate it into your application and discuss this with the client. To do this, you need to have a secure knowledge of how your proposed solution works so you know and understand its capabilities and what can and cannot be done.

(60 minutes)

Consider the hotel booking system. Independently, produce a pitch to deliver the concept of the booking system and how it will work. Plan the presentation and deliver it to the group.

The group should ask questions of the person presenting their application design and provide the presenter with feedback on the effectiveness and quality of their pitch and how effective their responses to questions were.

4.4 Prototyping

Purpose of prototyping

A prototype is a small part of a system that may not be functional or is only partially functional. A prototype is created to demonstrate an element of a system to a client or end user, to obtain feedback that can be used to refine the prototype or design of the application. By using prototypes, the client will see aspects of the application before it is complete. This will usually mean they are happier with the final product because they have been able to suggest refinements throughout the process, instead of waiting until it is complete to see it.

Features and formats of prototypes

A number of different types of prototype can be used, or combined.

- Functional. It performs actions and functions that the final system will perform. It could be used to demonstrate some processes, so the client can experience the stages involved.
- Illustrative. This is usually an interface, such as an input or output screen. The interface does not fulfil any purpose other than showing the client what it will look like and what will be included on it.
- Evolutionary. This is built on during the design and development process. It is refined, and new modules added to it, until it becomes the final application.
- Throw-away. This shows the client features or designs, and is not used again. It may be created in different software to the final application; for example, a drawing program is used to create an illustrative prototype. This needs to be recreated in the software being used for the development.

Interviewing and questioning techniques

An important element of prototypes is the interaction with the client (or end user) who is evaluating the prototype. Information gathering techniques are covered in LO2 (page 169).

(10 minutes)

Consider the different types of prototype. In which situations, or applications, do you feel each one would be most appropriate?

For example, would the hotel booking system benefit from an evolutionary or throwaway prototype, or a combination of both?

4.5 Aspects for user feedback

Once you have delivered your pitch and answered your client's questions, you need to gather their feedback. Record it in a document and have the client agree that it covers everything they have identified.

Meeting core requirements and any optional requirements

You need to gather feedback on the extent to which the design meets the functional requirements. This should be divided into the core requirements and which of the optional requirements are also included. The client may say that some requirements are missing, or there could be a greater or lesser emphasis on some aspects than required.

Effectiveness

The client needs to feed back on how well the proposed design solution, and/or prototype, meets the functional requirements. This should be a direct comparison against each requirement, where the client can state how well it is met and if anything needs changing.

Usability

The client needs to assess how easily they can carry out actions or processes based on what they can see. An interface, for example, can be assessed if the client can understand what its function is and how to perform it.

The client can also assess the readability of the interfaces and whether the outputs, or displays, are clear and contain all necessary information.

The interfaces can finally be assessed against navigability; for example, how well the menu system and buttons allow a user to move through the different pages, screens and menus.

Learnability

The client can evaluate the proposed solution against how easy it will be to learn. If the client is asking many questions about how the design will work, and what will need to be done to make it work, further training may be required.

The clarity of the function of each component can be assessed; for example, is it obvious what each button on an interface does? Are there instructions on the screen to guide the user, or is it clear what needs to be entered, selected or clicked?

 **PAIRS ACTIVITY**

(30 minutes)

Swap the design that you have produced for a product, or prototype, with another member of your group. Assess the other person's design against its usability and learnability. Feed back your assessment and discuss what could be done to improve it further.

4.6 Analysis of client feedback and discussion

Once your client has provided their feedback and you have discussed the findings with them, you need to analyse the feedback.

Identify distinct points in feedback

Your client may have made a large number of comments, and some will be more significant than others. Both the positive and negative points can be identified here.

Identify required changes

Identify whether any of the comments from the end user involve a design change. Some (or all) of these changes may be related to the distinct points you have identified from the feedback. The changes that need to be made can be identified along with these points, if they naturally follow, for example: Feedback point: the client has identified that the user needs to see the booking details before entering payment details. Change: When the client clicks on 'Pay', the booking details need to be displayed at the top of the page, with the space to enter payment details below it.

Identification and implementation of improvements based on feedback

After evaluating the feedback, and identifying changes that are needed, the improvements need to be made. This may involve changing the interface design, to adding or amending processes. The changes may be small or significant, but they all need documenting and linking to the changes you identified.

Once you have made the appropriate changes to your design, you need to present your changes to your client, and gather feedback to ensure that your design meets their requirements prior to developing it. This could be carried out in person, over the phone or through video-conferencing where appropriate. This is beyond the bounds of this unit, but would need completing before development can start.

Refining designs based on feedback is also covered as part of Unit 11 LO4 (page 293).

> ### KNOW IT
> 1 What should be covered in a pitch for a proposed design solution?
> 2 Identify five elements that make a pitch delivery effective.
> 3 Explain the benefits of using prototypes in the design of your solution.
> 4 Explain why it is important that the client provides feedback on your design.
> 5 State what you should do if your client identifies a core requirement that is missing from your design.

LO4 Assessment activities

Below are five suggested assessment activities that have been directly linked to the pass, merit and distinction criteria in LO4 to help with assignment preparation; they include Top tips on how to achieve the best results.

For (at least) one of your units you will be creating a prototype for an application. For the activities below, use the product that you are creating as a basis for them.

Activity 1 – pass criteria *P4*

1 Write a report and/or presentation as a pitch of your design for your client. Consider the method you will use to deliver your presentation, and make sure you have included speaker notes or a script identifying what you will say.
2 Deliver your pitch to your client.

Activity 2 – merit criteria *M3*

1 Discuss the design with your client, and ask them to evaluate your design against the functional requirements, its effectiveness, usability and learnability.
2 Identify the changes or adaptations that the client needs and record the results in a form that the client checks and signs.
3 Implement the changes to your design that the client requested.

Activity 3 – pass criteria *P5*

Create a prototype, or several prototypes, for your agreed design solution. These should cover the interface and at least one aspect of the functionality of your design.

Activity 4 – pass criteria *P6*

1 Present your prototype to your client.
2 Discuss the prototype and compare it to the functional requirements.
3 Ask the client to provide feedback.
4 If appropriate, present your prototype to potential end users and ask for their feedback as actual users of the system.
5 Document the feedback provided and summarise the findings.

Activity 5 – distinction criteria *D2*

1 Analyse the client and end user feedback (where appropriate).
2 Identify any improvements that need to be made to the design and prototype.
3 Get the client's approval of the improvements you have identified.
4 Implement the changes to your design and prototype. You should now have up to three versions of your design documentation, showing the changes made throughout.

TOP TIPS ✓

✔ Proofread your pitch before delivery and ask at least one other person to proofread it as well.
✔ Practise your pitch before delivery, using another person to act as the client.
✔ Design a form for your client to complete when providing feedback, so there is structure to any discussions and they can record their findings and sign any agreements.
✔ Save your designs and prototypes with different version numbers, e.g. V1.0, V1.1, etc. to show how they have changed during the design process.

Unit 07
Data analysis and design

ABOUT THIS UNIT

The collection and analysis of data is fundamental to a range of IT systems and organisational activities. Qualitative and quantitative data need to be gathered and analysed to reach conclusions about what has been found.

In this unit you will learn about the skills and techniques that are used by data analysts to identify the qualitative and quantitative data that needs to be collected, and to cleanse and transform this data into a data model. You will learn about different types of data, and the stages of data analysis that are undertaken to produce a model.

You will be required to investigate the information requirements for a business scenario, and use a range of techniques to collect and analyse the data. From this you will produce a data model and data design documentation to present to the stakeholders in the business, before evaluating the model you have produced.

How will I be assessed?

You will be assessed by producing evidence from set scenarios or from work that you carry out as part of a work placement or employment. This evidence will be assessed by your tutor.

LEARNING OUTCOMES

The topics, activities and suggested reading in this unit will help you to:

1 Understand the purpose and stages of data analysis and design.
2 Be able to investigate client requirements for data analysis.
3 Be able to develop data design solutions to meet business requirements.
4 Be able to present data analysis and design solutions to stakeholders.

How will I be graded?

You will be graded using the following criteria:

Learning outcome	Pass assessment criteria	Merit assessment criteria	Distinction assessment criteria
You will:	To achieve a pass you must demonstrate that you have met all the pass assessment criteria	To achieve a merit you must demonstrate that you have met all the pass and merit assessment criteria	To achieve a distinction you must demonstrate that you have met all the pass, merit and distinction assessment criteria
1 Understand the purpose and stages of data analysis and design	**P1** Explain the types of data that can be analysed **P2** Summarise the stages of data analysis	**M1** Explain the importance of accurately identifying information requirements prior to data collection	
2 Be able to investigate client requirements for data analysis	**P3** Establish the data analysis and design requirements for a specified business requirements		
	P4 Gather data for the specified business requirement using quantitative and qualitative techniques	**M2** Develop the data requirements for the specified business requirements using different qualitative and quantitative data analysis methods	
3 Be able to develop data design solutions to meet business requirements	**P5** Create the outline scope of the data design model for the specified business requirements		**D1** Construct the logical data model for the specified business requirement
4 Be able to present data analysis and design solutions to stakeholders	**P6** Prepare the data design documentation for a presentation to stakeholders	**M3** Present the data design documentation to stakeholders	**D2** Evaluate the logical data model against the original specified business requirement

LO1 Understand the purpose and stages of data analysis and design *P1 P2 M1*

GETTING STARTED

(15 minutes)

What is data? Discuss the difference between the terms 'data' and 'information'.

Data – raw, unorganised facts that need to be processed.

Qualitative – information which includes descriptions, opinions, attitudes and views.

Quantitative – factual, often numerical, information.

Structured data – data that has been organised, e.g. in a table.

Unstructured data – data that is not organised.

1.1 Data types

Data can come in a variety of forms and gained from a variety of methods. A number of these are described below.

Qualitative

Qualitative data is descriptive data that cannot be measured, but can be recorded. For example:

- names and addresses
- people's favourite flower
- the texture of a wall
- people's opinion of their current computer system.

It is not numeric, so it cannot have formulae applied to it.

Quantitative

Quantitative data is measureable and is usually in numeric form because it records a quantity. For example:

- the number of people who work in a company
- the time it takes to complete an activity
- the size of a room
- the number of records a database stores.

The data collected is numeric; therefore, it can have formulae applied to it.

Structured

Structured data is organised in some manner, often using a database and/or spreadsheet format. The data is often organised into tables, with rows and columns that allow it to be analysed and searched. For example, Table 7.1 shows some structured data.

Table 7.1 Structured data

First name	Surname	Date of birth	Salary
Jane	Smith	1/6/1981	£22,000
Ashley	Hardy	13/2/1985	£37,200
Joanne	Wright	9/1/1982	£26,950
Jamie	Peacock	10/7/1975	£36,000

Structured data can be quantitative or qualitative.

Unstructured

Unstructured data is not organised. It may be descriptive data and often cannot be put into a structured format; for example an email is unstructured data. Other examples are:

- videos
- images
- sound files

Some data within these formats might have the ability to be structured, but some aspects of them cannot be; for example, the message inside an email cannot be organised as it is descriptive.

KEY TERM

Information – data which is processed, organised and structured into a meaningful context.

KEY TERM

Data analysis – the processes of examining, cleansing, transforming data into a model.

Data and **information** are also described in Unit 2 LO3 (page 60) and LO5 (page 72).

GROUP ACTIVITY

(10 minutes)

As a group, make a list of what data your school or college may collect and store about its students and staff. For each item, decide if it is qualitative or quantitative and whether it is structured or unstructured.

1.2 Stages of data analysis

Data analysis involves a series of steps that transforms the data collected into a model that can be used to support decision making within an organisation. For example, data about customer feedback is stored and examined to find out which areas customers are happy with and what improvements need to be made.

Data analysis and the stages involved in it are also described in Unit 2 LO3.

Investigate information requirements

The first stage in the analysis is to identify what needs to be known, or found out, i.e. what results are required from the data. Several examples are described below, but there are many information requirements that you could come across.

Market share

The market is the total number of a specific product or service sold. The market share is the proportion (usually a percentage) of that market that one company, or product, holds. For example, according to IDC, in the second quarter of 2015 Samsung has a 21.4 per cent market share in smartphone sales worldwide. That means that during that period, 21.4 per cent of all smartphones sold worldwide were Samsung.

The information requirements may be:

- the total number of products (or service) sold by everyone in the market
- the total number of that product (or service) sold by a specific company.

Particulates in the air

Particulate matter refers to the particles, in this case of pollution (often dust). A sensor could be used to detect the number of particles.

The information requirements may be:

- the number of particles in the air at a particular time
- the time the measurements are made.

Testing of new drugs

New drugs need to be tested before being made available for public use. The information requirements may be:

- the drug's performance over time
- the changes that take place on a body or organ as a result of the drug
- any other effects or changes during its use.

Data collection

The method(s) used to collect data can vary considerably, and are dependent on the situation and the type of data to be collected. A number of methods are described below; however, you may need to use other methods for collecting some types of data.

Observations

Observations involve recording what is happening; for example, by making notes about what is taking place. This could involve recording a series of actions: what people are doing, what is happening, or recording changes that take place.

These may be unstructured, for example writing notes or taking photos of what is happening, or structured, for example recording the temperature in a room in degrees Celsius.

For example, the observer of how people use a computer system may make notes on the actions performed and take photos of how the system is used.

Observations must be unbiased, so that the observer does not record their own qualitative findings as opposed to factual events.

Observation is also covered in Unit 6 LO2.1 and Unit 11 LO2.2.

Interviews

An interview can be used to gather information by asking people questions. The different types of question that can be asked are described in Unit 6 LO2.1.

Depending on the questions asked, the data may be a combination of data types identified in LO1.1, for example open questions usually generate unstructured data, while closed questions could be either structured or unstructured depending on what they are asking.

Review of existing data

Existing data can be collected, rather than observed and recorded again. For example, historic figures can be collected if considering marketing trends, or data about the use and performance of a system can be collected ready for analysis.

Other methods of data collection which may be appropriate to your scenario are also described in Unit 6 LO2.1 and Unit 11 LO2.2.

Data organisation

Data can be organised (recorded) in a number of ways. Several examples are described below, but you may need to use other methods.

Digitalisation

This is the conversion of information into a digital format, so it can be stored electronically on a computer. For example, images or paper-based data may be scanned into a computer to create a digital (electronic) version.

Transcription

Transcription involves writing or otherwise recording data that does not come in a written form. For example, the responses from an interview may be recorded as an audio file, but typed (transcribed) into a written document.

Sorting

The data may require sorting into appropriate groupings or in a specific order. For example, data from a collection of interviews may be sorted by question (all responses to one question are put together). Data may be sorted into alphabetical or chronological order.

Data mining

Data mining is the process of searching for, and examining, data held in large databases. These large sets of data are known as **big data**.

For example:

- The sales figures for a piece of software may be mined, retrieving the total sales. This may involve looking through vast quantities of sales data from a range of organisations.
- A large shop may have a loyalty card and use data mining to find about card holders' shopping habits.

Data storage

Once collected and organised, the data needs to be stored in an appropriate place.

In-house

This uses storage methods within the organisation, for example on a hard drive in an office or on a central server. There is more control than using external methods; however, internal IT staff are responsible for the upkeep of the hardware, they need to manage access to ensure only those with correct credentials can access it and they have responsibility for creating data backups in case of loss.

External

Data can be stored externally, for example in the 'cloud' – on another organisation's server that you have to access. There is less control over this method as you do not own the hardware, and you may need to pay for the storage on a monthly basis. However, you may be able to increase the storage capacity (or reduce it) as needed. The organisation that stores the data is responsible for backing it up and this is usually part of the agreement you undertake to reduce the risk of data loss.

Data cleansing

Some methods of cleansing data (amending it to make it more useful) are described below, but there are others.

Errors

Any errors within the data need to be identified and corrected. This can be difficult and time consuming when dealing with large quantities of data. It is best practice to identify errors when they are input by using validation and

KEY TERM

Big data – very large sets of data that are analysed to produce information such as trends.

verification, but these processes are not guaranteed to detect all errors, especially where the data does not confirm to standard restrictions.

Missing elements

Any missing data needs to be identified and updated; for example, through further research and data collection to complete a gap or by carrying out the research again.

Duplicates

Duplicates are not all necessarily surplus to requirements; for example, if you are recording the number of times a customer has purchased an item it is valuable to know about these repeat sales. However, when they are not necessary, they need to be identified and removed. This reduces the quantity of data and therefore the time taken to analyse it.

Data manipulation

The manipulation of data involves turning it into a form that can be used to present results. There are a number of ways that data can manipulated, and these depend on the data being used and the results required. As well as those described below, there may be further methods that you could use.

Arranging

Data can be arranged in a specific order or format. For example, data may be presented in a graph or a table. If specific data needs to be extracted, you can use search criteria or add a filter to a set of data.

The arrangement method and design depends on the type of data collected and its purpose; for example, a graph may be appropriate to show numeric values over time but would not be appropriate to show the information entered into a computer system.

Collating

Collating is the collecting and combining of data into a suitable format. Data may be arranged over a number of different files so, by collating it, the data is combined into a single file to allow further analysis.

Aggregating

Aggregate data combines data from a range of sources and summarises it, usually in a written report format. For example, data about the spending habits of customers may be presented as a summary description of the data.

Interpreting

This involves making sense of the data that has been collected and presenting conclusions or facts about what it shows. For example, data about the spending habits of customers may show that there has been a decrease in the average spend per customer.

Correlation

A correlation is a pattern between two sets of data; for example the colder the weather, the more customers spend – as the temperature decreases, the average spend increases.

Correlations are often shown as a chart. A positive correlation is when values increase and decrease together. Figure 7.1 shows an example of a positive correlation.

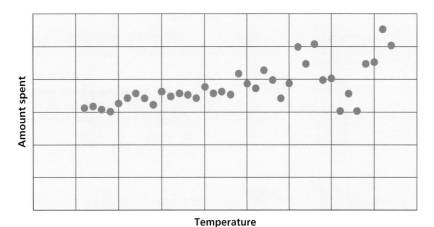

▲ **Figure 7.1** An example of a positive correlation

A negative correlation is when one value increases as the other decreases. Figure 7.2 shows an example of a negative correlation.

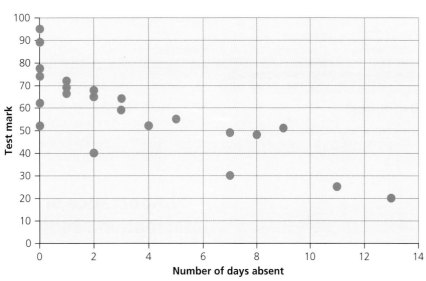

▲ **Figure 7.2** An example of a negative correlation

> Correlations may not be wholly dependent on each other (causality). For example, if a correlation shows that average spend in a clothes shop dropped dramatically in August, this does not mean the drop was caused by the month of August itself – the causes are likely to relate to hot weather or people being on holiday. It is important that this distinction is identified as it may feed into conclusions.

A correlation can also be calculated from the numerical data using Pearson's correlation. This returns a value between -1 and +1. The closer the number is to -1, or +1, the stronger the correlation; for example, 0.8 represents a strong positive correlation, -0.8 represents a strong negative correlation. Some software, such as a spreadsheet, may work this out for you automatically using a function, for example a function called CORREL in Microsoft Excel.

Presentation of findings

When the manipulation of the data is complete, the results need to be presented in an appropriate format, either through a physical presentation or in a written report. Some of these methods are described below; you may need to use others.

Tables

A tabular format uses rows and columns to display data. The top row is often the field names, identifying the data listed below.

Charts and graphs

The terms 'chart' and 'graph' are often interchangeable, and many types can be used. Table 7.2 identifies some common types of graph and chart.

Table 7.2 Common types of graph and chart

Type	Use
Scatter graph	Values are plotted against two variables
Pie chart	Shows percentages of a whole
Bar chart	Shows the quantity of different data items
Line graph	Shows how one value changes compared to a second

Graphs and charts can give a clearer representation of the data without viewers needing to read and interpret figures. For example, a bar chart can clearly show which bar is the highest and lowest, while it takes longer to identify this information in numerical data.

Dashboard

A dashboard collects graphs and tables together on a screen where you can see the range of results, and select particular parts to find out more.

Reports

A report is a written account of the findings. This usually includes the graphs or charts produced, and tables giving the key points from the analysis. The main body of the report does not include detailed copies of data but provides a summary of the findings. An appendix can include further evidence, such as larger tables of data, in case the reader wants to, or needs to, see further detail.

1.3 Importance of accurately defining information requirements

The information requirements for the business need to be carefully considered, researched and defined prior to the collection of data. Example requirements are described in Unit 9 LO2.1. Several reasons why it is important that these are defined are described below; there may be further reasons to explore.

Prevents time wasting

If the information requirements are not clearly and accurately defined then time can be spent collecting unnecessary data, or required data may be missed and time has to be spent collecting it later, potentially requiring redoing the analysis.

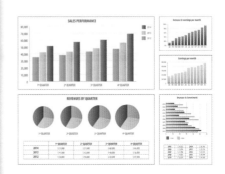

▲ **Figure 7.3** An example of a data dashboard

INDEPENDENT ACTIVITY 👤

(10 minutes)

Produce a presentation to explain to someone the stages of data analysis.

Aids planning

Data capture

If you have accurately and clearly defined information requirements, then the method you use to collect the data can be planned correctly. Errors in the definition of the requirements can lead to time and resources being spent on designing inappropriate data capture methods that need to be changed later in the process.

Data organisation and storage

By accurately defining the information requirements, suitable methods for organising and storing the data can be chosen. This allows for the method of organisation to be prepared before data is collected to ensure that any technology required is available, such as a scanner, sound recorder, etc. The method for storing the data can also be planned and put into place in advance of data collection to ensure it is ready to receive the data. If the requirements have not been defined accurately and further, or different types of, data is required, then the organisation and storage may need to change.

Cleaning and manipulation

If you have accurately defined the information requirements, you may be able to plan in time for cleaning the data as you can identify what you need to remove and plan for appropriate data entry methods. The methods of manipulation depend on what is collected and are specific to different types of data. By ensuring these have been clearly defined, the manipulation can be planned in advance.

Presentation of results

Through planning the information requirements accurately, and using this to design the data manipulation, you can also plan for how you present the results. The tables, graphs and/or summaries needed can be planned and targeted from the start of the process.

PAIRS ACTIVITY

(10 minutes)

Read the article located at tinyurl. com/z47w9cr.

Identify the problems caused by the inaccurate identification of requirements.

KNOW IT

1 Explain the difference between qualitative and quantitative data.
2 Explain the difference between structured and unstructured data.
3 Identify four stages of data analysis.
4 Describe what is meant by 'data mining'.
5 Describe three different methods of manipulating the data.
6 Describe two different methods of presenting the findings.

LO1 Assessment activities

Below are three suggested assessment activities that have been directly linked to the pass and merit criteria in LO1 to help with assignment preparation; they include Top tips on how to achieve the best results

Activity 1 – pass criteria *P1*

Create a four-page A5 leaflet that explains the different data types: quantitative, qualitative, structured and unstructured.

Activity 2 – pass criteria *P2*

Produce a paper-based guide that summarises the stages of data analysis. This could be an addition to the leaflet produced for P1.

Activity 3 – merit criteria *M1*

For each of the data analysis stages you referred to in Activity 2, explain why it is important to accurately define information requirements prior to data collection, using examples to support your explanations.

LO2 Be able to investigate client requirements for data analysis *P3 P4 M2*

GETTING STARTED 👤

(5 minutes)

Imagine that data has been collected about customers and how much they spend each time they visit a shop. How can this data be analysed? What could you do with it? What do you want to know?

2.1 Investigate information requirements

This involves finding out what information you, or the business, needs to know. Information differs from data, as it is the conclusions that have developed from the data analysis. If you are investigating the information requirements, you are finding out what the business needs to know and then you can begin to identify the data that you need to provide this information. Several examples of information requirements are described below; however, you may need to explore others.

Business intelligence

Business intelligence is the combination of tools and software used to analyse the data. For example, a business may have a management information system. This is a large database into which data is input from all aspects of a business, and produces reports summarising the data for managers in different areas of the organisation.

> Different types of business systems are described in Unit 1 LO3.5 and Unit 2 LO3.3.

When investigating business intelligence requirements, you need to examine the required outputs. This is the information produced by the system, for example the reports or graphs that are needed, who needs them and when they are needed. The processes can be designed to turn the data input into the information output for the business.

Scientific research

In scientific research, information requirements are likely to be the results of an investigation or experiment. When investigating these, you need to find out what values or results are needed; for example, a graph could show effects over time. If the research involves measuring changes to the environment, such as the particulates in the air over a period of time, then the information requirements could be the average number of particulates over a 24-hour period.

Medical research

Medical research may involve the testing of medicine or surgical procedures on animals or humans. When investigating the information requirements, you need to find out what results the doctors or researchers need; for example, reports that summarise the impact of a specific medicine on a group of test users, by providing information about the changes in the test user's body chemistry.

Political

Politicians may require information about their constituents, for example which political party they are currently supporting, or their views on specific topics such as education or immigration. The information requirements may include percentages to show how support is split, or more detailed information such as the percentage of support for a party for each social demographic (this could be based on total household income).

GROUP ACTIVITY

(10 minutes)

Consider your school or college. Discuss what business intelligence your school or college may need.

2.2 Techniques

These techniques are methods that you can use to collect the data from a business. Several techniques are described below, but you may need to explore and use others in your scenario.

Holding focus groups

A focus group is where a group of people, for example stakeholders, are brought together and led in a discussion. The discussion may be recorded to be transcribed later, or notes taken during the focus group. Focus groups are also described in Unit 11 LO2.2.

Preparing and distributing questionnaires and surveys to stakeholders

A questionnaire can be given to a range of stakeholders to ask open and/ or closed questions. When the questionnaires are returned they can be digitised or transcribed to produce data. Questionnaires are also described in Unit 11 LO2.

Analysing current documents

Documents can be gathered to record the data that they hold, or to be digitised or transcribed. Analysis of existing documents is also described in Unit 6 LO2.1.

2.3 Qualitative data analysis

When the data has been collected it needs to be analysed. The methods below explain how qualitative data can be analysed.

Typology

Typology is a set of attributes or classification given to specific responses. For example, they may refer to the background or opinion of the person who made a comment. A number that may need consideration are described below, but others may be relevant to the data you have collected. The typology is usually given as a description against the obtained data.

Activities

Classifying by activity would involve identifying the different activities, and summarising the data that was gathered for each activity. For example, following political research, the activities may be the jobs held by individuals within an area, with the qualitative data being their opinions on current political agendas. The data collected is categorised by the activity each person takes part in.

Actions

Classifying by action would involve identifying the event or process that has taken place and the data that relates to the action. For example, in political research, opinions before and after a key speech may be gathered and categorised as pre- or post-speech.

Relationships

Classifying by relationships would involve identifying the different relationships that exist between objects or people, and categorising the data according to those relationships. In this case, a relationship may simply be a connection (physical or otherwise) with another object. For example, in political research, the links between people being interviewed and the political party they last voted for would be a relationship.

Event analysis

An event is an action, process or change that impacts the data. Event analysis identifies the events that have taken place and describes the

PAIRS ACTIVITY

(45 minutes)

Discuss the different techniques described above. Identify the benefits and drawbacks of each method. Identify any other techniques that you could use to collect data.

KEY TERM

Typology – classifications that data can be put into, or organised into.

data associated with it. In qualitative data analysis, it is usually a narrative analysis; this means a description of what took place during or after the event. For example, in political research, news stories about immigration could be identified as events, and the changes in the data collected about personal political views can be described according to the response to these events.

Logical analysis

A logical analysis attempts to identify causation – what caused something to happen. This is often investigated through an interpretation of the qualitative data gathered; for example, transcriptions of how stakeholders use a computer system can be interpreted as a list of steps or actions.

This is often produced in a diagrammatic format, for example as flow charts (which show how elements relate to each other or the stages involved in a process) or flow diagrams (which show the movement of data within a system, identifying its input, storage, processing and output).

2.4 Quantitative data analysis

Quantitative data analysis usually involves calculations to generate results from the numeric data. A number of common actions that can be performed are described below.

Mean

The **mean** value is an average calculated by adding all the numbers together, and dividing the total by the quantity of data.

For example, the mean amount customers have spent needs to be calculated. Table 7.3 shows the amount each customer has spent.

Table 7.3 Amount spent by customers

Customer number	Amount spent (£)
1	102
2	56
3	75
4	41
5	66
6	77

The mean is calculated by adding the amount all the customers spent:

102 + 56 + 75 + 41 + 66 + 77 = 417

This total is divided by how many pieces of data there are, in this case six:

417 ÷ 6 = 69.5

The mean amount spent is £69.50.

Median

The **median** is the middle value when all values are listed in numerical order. This is calculated by adding 1 to the quantity of numbers, dividing this total by 2 and selecting that value. If there is no 'middle' value, as there is an even quantity of numbers, then the number between the two middle values is taken.

PAIRS ACTIVITY

(45 minutes)

Read the document at tinyurl.com/zqpgkbp.

Identify other methods of qualitative data analysis that you could use.

KEY TERM

Mean – the calculated average of a set of numbers.

KEY TERM

Median – the middle number in a set of numbers.

Using the data from Table 7.3, the amount spent is put into numerical order:

41, 56, 66, 75, 77, 102

The two middle values are 66 and 75.

75 + 66 = 141

111 ÷ 2 = 70.5

= £70.50

Standard deviation

The **standard deviation** is how far numbers are spread out. The smaller the standard deviation, the closer to the mean the values are. If the standard deviation is large, then the values are further from the mean. The result is in the same units as the original data.

The mean is calculated (in this case, £69.50) and subtracted from each number in the list to give the difference. This difference is squared. This is shown in Table 7.4.

Table 7.4 Calculations for standard deviation

Customer number	Amount spent (£)	Difference	Difference^2
1	102	102 – 69.50 = 32.5	32.5^2 = 1056.25
2	56	56 – 69.50 = –13.5	–13.5^2 = 182.25
3	75	75 – 69.50 = 5.5	5.5^2 = 30.25
4	41	41 – 69.50 = –28.5	–28.5^2 = 812.25
5	66	66 – 69.50 = –3.5	–3.5^2 = 12.25
6	77	77 – 69.50 = 7.5	7.5^2 = 56.25

The mean of the differences is then calculated:

$$\frac{1056.25 + 182.25 + 30.25 + 812.25 + 12.25 + 56.25}{6} = \frac{2149.50}{6} = 358.25$$

The square root of this value is then calculated:

$\sqrt{358.25}$ = 18.93 (*to 2dp*)

This result shows that the standard deviation is £18.93 away from the mean.

Range

The range is the difference between the highest and lowest numbers; it is a second way of measuring the spread of values. The smallest number is subtracted from the largest, for example using the values in Table 7.3:

102 – 41 = 61

The range of values is 61.

KNOW IT

1 Identify two methods of gathering data.
2 Describe one method of analysing qualitative data.
3 Describe one method of analysing quantitative data.
4 Explain the difference between the mean and median.
5 Describe how to calculate the standard deviation of a set of numbers.

LO2 Assessment activities

Below are three suggested assessment activities that have been directly linked to the pass and merit criteria in LO2 to help with assignment preparation; they include Top tips on how to achieve the best results

For these activities, investigate the data requirements for a specified business need. This could either be a real example from our experience or an appropriate scenario, such as:

Your school (or college) canteen is considering changing the menu and needs to gather students' opinions on the current menu and what they would like to eat in the canteen. Investigate the data requirements for the canteen.

Activity 1 – pass criteria *P3*

Investigate the data analysis and design requirements for the business to be identified.

Identify the qualitative and quantitative data that you need to gather and identify where this data will come from.

Produce a written report that details your investigation.

Activity 2 – pass criteria *P4*

Identify the techniques that you are going to use to gather the qualitative and quantitative data you identified in P3. Add a description of your choices to the report you wrote for Activity 1, making sure you justify your decision.

Use these methods to gather and collate the required data.

Activity 3 – merit criteria *M2*

Analyse the data you have acquired, using both qualitative and quantitative data analysis methods. Add the results to the report you wrote for Activities 1 and 2. Make sure you add the results of calculations, diagrams produced and any narrative outcomes.

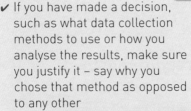

TOP TIPS

✔ If you have made a decision, such as what data collection methods to use or how you analyse the results, make sure you justify it – say why you chose that method as opposed to any other
✔ Check your calculations twice to make sure they are accurate
✔ If transcribing your data, or copying it from one place to another, verify you have done so correctly, as errors can invalidate your results

LO3 Be able to develop data design solutions to meet business requirements *P5 D1*

GETTING STARTED

(5 minutes)

Discuss the terms 'conceptual', 'logical' and 'physical'. What do these terms mean? How do you think they could be applied to data?

3.1 Levels of data model design

A **data model** is used to design the storage and use of data within a business or system. The four levels of data model are described below.

Conceptual: relationship between entities

The **conceptual model** shows the entities within the business and the relationships that exist between them. This is usually represented as an **entity** relationship diagram (ERD). It is not focused on *how* the data is actually stored, but shows the data that is needed. It does not use technical terminology, but is a general overview that all managers and users can understand.

Figure 7.4 shows a conceptual model for an ordering system. It does not show how the data will actually be stored within the system, but it does list the type of data to be stored.

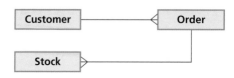

▲ **Figure 7.4** Conceptual model for ordering system

The different relationships within an ERD are described in Unit 6 LO3.1 (page 179) and Unit 11 LO3.1 (page 283).

Enterprise: unique business requirements

An **enterprise model** is a diagrammatic representation of all the data used by a company. While a conceptual model may only address the area the focus is on, an enterprise model incorporates all possible data sources and uses. This is usually shown as a structure diagram; a partially complete enterprise model for a clothes store is shown in Figure 7.5.

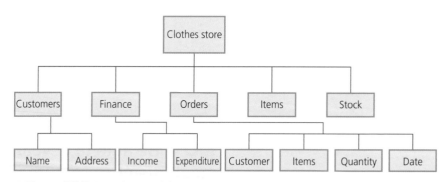

▲ **Figure 7.5** Enterprise model

Logical: specific entities, attributes and relationship in a business function

A **logical data model** gives a detailed view of the data the company stores. At this level the entities, attributes (properties) and relationships for how the data will be stored are identified. This can be expressed using an entity attribute relationship diagram (EARD), and for a database needs to be normalised. Figure 7.6 shows an example EARD for the ordering system.

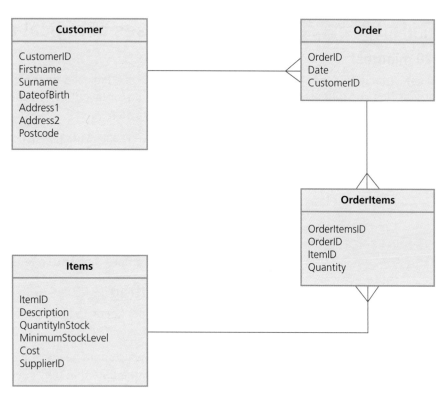

▲ **Figure 7.6** Logical model presented as an EARD

Physical: application and database specific implementation of the logical data model

The **physical model** takes into account the actual implementation of the logical data model, i.e. it looks at how it will be produced. This includes more detail than at the logical level, for example identifying the key data types involved in a database. This is often represented as a physical data dictionary.

The data model may be implemented in other forms, such as a spreadsheet or as a file to import into a computer program. The data dictionary differs according to the method being used. Table 7.5 shows an example data dictionary for part of a database order table.

Table 7.5 Data dictionary for table: order

Table: Order				
Field	**Data type**	**Validation**	**Primary key**	**Foreign key**
OrderID	Text	N/A	Yes	No
CustomerID	Text	N/A	No	Yes
Date	Date/Time	>01/01/2015 AND <=today	No	No

If the data model to be used is a spreadsheet, then the data dictionary can identify the properties, data types and **validation** used. If a file with records is to be used, then the properties each record contains can be identified.

(20 minutes)

Create a table that identifies the similarities and differences between the four data models.

3.2 Phases of logical data modelling

Structure

The structure of a logical data model involves identification of the rules that govern the data, or layout of how the data is going to be stored. This may include identifying:

- Entities: the real world objects that are being represented; for example, customers, stock items.
- Attributes: the individual properties, or pieces of data to be stored; for example, customer name, address, date of birth.
- Relationships: the links between different entities. These could be one to one or one to many.
- Queries: searches performed on the data, usually with specific criteria, e.g. finding all orders that were made on 1 January 2016.

Manipulating

The data model needs to identify how the data will be manipulated. This can include:

- Updating: which data needs to be updated and given new values.
- Retrieving: the data that may need to be accessed and the circumstances that require its retrieval.
- Editing: the data that may need to be changed, whether to amend with up-to-date data, or correct errors.
- Deletion: the data that may need to be deleted and the circumstances requiring its deletion.

There may be additional ways that the data in the system you are investigating needs to be manipulated.

Integrity

The data needs to have integrity – that is, be accurate and consistent. This is usually built into a system through validation. Validation techniques make sure that data is realistic when entered, and that it meets a set of predefined rules. Table 7.6 describes a number of validation techniques.

Table 7.6 Validation techniques

Validation technique	Description
Length check	A restriction on the length of the data, i.e. the number of characters
Range check	A restriction on a numeric field, stating that the data must be between two values
Format check	A restriction on the characters that can be entered, for example an ID may have to be two letters, followed by two numbers
Type check	A restriction on the data type that can be entered, e.g. only numbers, of letters
Presence check	This states that the data must be entered
Lookup check	Restricting the data to a selection of possibilities

In the logical data model, any validation techniques need identifying along with the data they apply to.

The need for integrity of data is also described in Unit 3 LO1 (page 86).

GROUP AND PAIRS ACTIVITY

(60 minutes)

Discuss the data your school or college may use. As a group, develop an enterprise and conceptual model for the data.

In pairs, take an aspect of the conceptual model and develop a logical and physical design. When creating the logical design, consider the phases (structure, manipulation and integrity).

> **KNOW IT**
>
> 1 Identify the four different levels of data model design.
> 2 Describe the difference between the enterprise and conceptual data models.
> 3 Describe the difference between the logical and physical data models.
> 4 Identify two elements that need to be designed as part of the structure phase of a logical data model.
> 5 Identify three elements that need to be designed as part of the manipulation phase of data modelling.
> 6 Describe four different validation techniques.

TOP TIPS

- ✔ Start by looking at the enterprise model to gain an overview for the system, then begin to narrow down the details.
- ✔ If creating a database model, make sure you normalise your data by removing any many to many relationships.
- ✔ Keep referring back to the data you collected as part of the LO2 assessment activities, as you must have evidence of where you developed your data model from.

LO3 Assessment activities

Below are two suggested assessment activities that have been directly linked to the pass and distinction criteria in LO3 to help with assignment preparation; they include Top tips on how to achieve the best results.

For these activities, use the same scenario that you investigated as part of the LO2 assessment activities.

Activity 1 – pass criteria *P5*

Produce a design for each phase of the data design model for your chosen scenario. Create a report that summarises each phase and your design model, including appropriate diagrams and data dictionaries.

Activity 2 – distinction criteria *D1*

Create a logical data model for your chosen scenario. This should include the structure (aided by appropriate diagrams), manipulation of the data and how integrity of the data will be maintained.

LO4 Be able to present data analysis and design solutions to stakeholders *P6 M3 D2*

4.1 Data design documentation

Once the data model designs have been completed, a design needs to be produced for the proposed solution. This can be done in several ways; some are described below but there are others that you may need to investigate.

Data flow diagrams (DFDs)

A flow diagram shows the movement of data within a system, identifying the input, storage, processing and output for data. Flow diagrams are described in more detail in Unit 11 LO3 (page 280) and Unit 2 LO5 (page 74).

Information flow charts

An information flow chart shows how information is used within a system and the processes that are applied to it, along with what is input and output. Flow charts are described in more detail in Unit 6 LO3 (page 176) and Unit 11 LO3 (page 281).

Entity attribute relationship diagram (EARD)

These are in the same format as an Entity Relationship diagram (ERD) but they have the attributes included in each entity. Figure 7.6 is an example of an EARD, where the entity name is above the line in bold, and the attributes associated with it are below.

Hierarchical tree diagram

This diagram shows the structure of the data, starting with the system (or database) name at the top and splitting down into individual sections. Each of these are split further until each one is an individual data item.

Hierarchical tree diagrams are described in more detail in Unit 11 LO3 (page 283).

Events

An event is an action, process or change that will impact the data, for example by updating it, searching it, changing it or manipulating it. The design of these can vary; for example, flow charts can be used to show the inputs, processes and output associated with the event. Flow charts are described in detail in Unit 6 LO3 (page 176).

Entity life history (ELH)

An ELH diagram takes an object and identifies how it is produced, what happens to it, and how it 'dies'. These are described in detail in Unit 11 LO3 (page 284).

4.2 Presentation of solution

Once a solution has been designed, it needs to be presented to the stakeholders. Several points to consider within the presentation of the solution are described below, but there are others that you may need to consider.

Reflects all aspects of design

The presentation must include all aspects of the design, including the different levels of the data model that you have designed and all the requirements you identified.

Can be understood by audience

The stakeholders may not have a detailed understanding of data models or data storage; therefore, the presentation needs to ensure it is simple enough for them to understand, without a lot of technical jargon, yet still cover all the requirements. You need to use your knowledge of the stakeholders and their experience to achieve the right balance. You can always include more detail as appendices, or additional print outs in case they are needed.

Format

The format you choose for the presentation depends on the situation, the stakeholders and yourself. The two most common formats are a report-based presentation or a physical presentation. Whichever is chosen, the solution needs to be presented with the support of the data model developed and the data design diagrams.

If it is to be a presentation, ensure speaker notes accompany the presentation, that the narrative is clear, it explains the recommendations made in the presentation, and justifies the decision.

In a report, the recommendations and justification need to be supported by diagrams and data models.

PAIRS AND GROUP ACTIVITY

(20 minutes)

In pairs, make a list of what makes a good presentation.

Work as a group to produce a group-set of guidelines to follow when giving a presentation.

4.3 Evaluation of design solution

After the design has been produced and presented to the stakeholders, the logical data model needs to be evaluated to assess its success and suitability. A number of points to consider are described below; however, there may be others.

Meets business requirements

At the beginning of the project you will have researched and identified the business requirements. The logical data model needs to be compared to each of these requirements, describing the extent to which they have been met.

This evidence can be produced as a narrative report or a table of the requirements and the evaluative comments put alongside each requirement.

Achievable

Is it possible to produce the solution that has been designed?

This can be evaluated against a variety of points, such as the storage required, the design structure and the events that will take place.

Manageable

How easy is it for the solution to be maintained and used?

For example, an extremely large database that requires a lot of input and changes may be difficult for the company to manage because of the time required to maintain it.

Extendable

Can additional elements can be added to the solution?

For example, is it possible to add data storage to meet additional requirements? A solution should be able to adjust to new requirements as a business evolves, otherwise the life of the solution is limited and the business will need to invest in a new solution in the near future.

 **PAIRS ACTIVITY**

(30 minutes)

Create a mind map or spider diagram for 'Evaluation'. Include the four requirements described in this section, and expand each with additional points, explanations and examples. Add at least **two** additional features that should be included in an evaluation.

KNOW IT

1 Identify four diagrams that you could use within your data design documentation.
2 Explain how to produce a data flow diagram.
3 Describe the contents of an entity attribute relationship diagram.
4 Explain the difference between two different formats you could use to present your solution.
5 Describe three elements that should be discussed in your evaluation.

LO4 Assessment activities

Below are three suggested assessment activities that have been directly linked to the pass, merit and distinction criteria in LO4 to help with assignment preparation; they include Top tips on how to achieve the best results

For these activities, use the same scenario that you investigated as part of the LO2 and LO3 assessment activities.

Activity 1 – pass criteria *P6*

Write a report to detail the data design for the business solution you identified as part of the LO2 and LO3 activities. Use a range of diagrams, including those from the LO3 activities to support your design, and make sure you justify any decisions you have made.

Activity 2 – merit criteria *M3*

Present your report to the stakeholders. Record the feedback they give, and the recommendations they make for changes.

Activity 3 – distinction criteria *D2*

Produce a written evaluation of your data design model.

- Compare the model to the business requirements.
- If you have made any changes from the original requirements, make sure you fully justify them.

Discuss the feedback you received from Activity 2, when you presented your solution to the stakeholders. Identify any changes that you should now make, justifying each one based on the feedback you received. You are not required to make the changes.

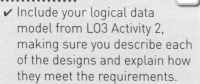

TOP TIPS

✔ Include your logical data model from LO3 Activity 2, making sure you describe each of the designs and explain how they meet the requirements.
✔ Make sure your report has appendices with evidence of where the design came from, e.g. transcripts of interviews, questionnaires and the calculations that produced the decisions.
✔ Plan ahead of the presentation for any questions that the stakeholders may ask, so that you have potential answers ready and the evidence to back up your answers.

Read about it

This website shows the difference between conceptual, logical and physical data model designs:

tinyurl.com/yduomk6

This website has clear descriptions and examples for each type of data model:

tinyurl.com/zmr2rjq

A chapter that describes different methods of qualitative data analysis:

tinyurl.com/zqpgkbp

A chapter that describes different methods of quantitative data analysis:

tinyurl.com/zuq4baa

Unit 08

Project management

ABOUT THIS UNIT

IT projects should be developed and implemented on time, within budget and to the standard of quality required. This needs careful planning and recording of all the activities involved in developing systems.

In this unit you will learn about the different ways in which projects are managed and the stages from initial planning to the evaluation of the completed project. You can use the skills and knowledge that you learn in this unit to manage projects that you may carry out for other units, such as Unit 9.

In order to manage the project, you will need to engage with other project team members, the project sponsor, clients, stakeholders and end users, to ensure that the product not only meets the agreed requirements but also that it is created in a timely and cost effective way.

How will I be assessed?

You will be assessed by producing evidence from set scenarios or from work that you carry out as part of a work placement or employment. The evidence will show that you managed a project in a professional manner, following appropriate actions in the project management cycle and recording the outcomes using recognised techniques and documentation. This evidence will be assessed by your tutor.

LEARNING OUTCOMES

The topics and activities in this unit will help you to:

1 Understand the project lifecycle.
2 Be able to initiate and plan projects.
3 Be able to execute projects.
4 Be able to carry out project evaluations.

How will I be graded?

You will be graded using the following criteria:

Learning outcome	Pass assessment criteria	Merit assessment criteria	Distinction assessment criteria
You will:	To achieve a pass you must demonstrate that you have met all the pass assessment criteria	To achieve a merit you must demonstrate that you have met all the pass and merit assessment criteria	To achieve a distinction you must demonstrate that you have met all the pass, merit and distinction assessment criteria
1 Understand the project lifecycle	**P1** Explain the different phases within an identified project lifecycle		**D1** Evaluate the importance of each phase of the identified project lifecycle
	P2 Describe different project methodologies	**M1** Compare the features and benefits of different project methodologies	
2 Be able to initiate and plan projects	**P3** Complete the documentation for the initiation phase for an identified project		**D2** Create a business case to support an identified project
	P4 Develop a project plan for the identified project	**M2** Carry out and document a phase review of the project plan	
3 Be able to execute projects	**P5** Follow the project plan and conduct a phase review of the identified project		**D3** Prepare a project closure report based on the execution phase review of the identified project
4. Be able to carry out project evaluations	**P6** Evaluate feedback from client and team in relation to the project	**M3** Recommend potential improvements for future projects based on the outcome of the project evaluation	

LO1 Understand the project lifecycle *P1 D1*

GETTING STARTED 👤

(15 minutes)

Why do projects need to be managed? In pairs, discuss reasons, other than timeliness and cost effectiveness, why you think that projects should be managed. Keep the list to help you reflect on what you have learned as the unit progresses.

1.1 Project methodologies

The purpose of project management methodologies is to achieve a defined product, which may be a new network, computer system or software installation. Project management is the means by which individuals and

Structured methodology – clearly defined steps or stages which enable projects to be managed in a logical, controlled way.

Methodology – an agreed set of methods brought together to achieve a goal or set of goals.

PRINCE2 (Projects IN Controlled Environments) – a process-based project methodology.

Standard – a national or internationally agreed group of tools and techniques, used in a specified manner to manage a project.

organisations ensure that the product is achieved within budget, on time and to the agreed quality. **Structured methodologies** follow the same stages as those identified in the waterfall model, discussed in Unit 9 (see page 245). It is also important to recognise a project which needs managing. All projects have:

- a clearly defined goal or objective
- a deadline for completion
- the need for a combination of expertise, experience and skills from different people, groups or organisations.

Clients may specify particular methodologies or you may be free to decide the most appropriate one for the project.

Waterfall model

The waterfall **methodology** was originally used for the development of software. There are different versions with different numbers of stages (see Unit 9 LO1.1, page 245). It will work in the same way whichever version you choose. You move down the stages, rather like water cascading over a waterfall. All stages must be carried out in order and no stage can be omitted.

PRINCE2

The original waterfall methodology merely stated the stages to be undertaken, with little guidance on how each stage should be carried out or monitored. As projects became larger and more complex, more guidance was required on how to manage each stage. This resulted in the development of structured methodologies such as **PRINCE2**, shown in Figure 8.1. These include detailed documentation and clearly defined processes which enable not only the development of the product but also the management of the development process.

PRINCE2 has seven stages and refers to products rather than deliverables:

1 Starting a project: a brief statement of why the project is required and what it will achieve. If approved, a more detailed brief is produced, containing information on actions required, necessary expertise, resources, etc.
2 Directing a project: the project board reviews the detailed brief, considering business need and likely success before deciding whether to appoint a project manager with agreed responsibilities.
3 Initiating a project: the project manager creates the project initiation documentation as described in LO2.1.
4 Controlling a stage: the project manager monitors and controls a particular stage to ensure that it remains on course, e.g. by approving the work to be undertaken, keeping the team informed of progress, noting any changes, reporting the status to the project board and taking any corrective actions if issues arise.
5 Management product delivery: this is the equivalent of the execution phase described in LO3.1. The products or deliverables are allocated across the team and produced to the agreed **standard**. Progress is monitored and the completed products approved.
6 Project closure follows the activities described in LO3.1.
7 Planning: this is the equivalent of the planning phase described in LO2.2 as well as a technique known as 'product based planning' which requires creating:

> PRINCE2 does initiate, plan, execute and evaluate the project but, compared with other project methodologies, it has stronger management and control written into the methodology before the project starts. The directing of the project by the project board and the control of the project is not considered a separate stage by other methodologies.

a A project product description: what exactly is the final product?

b The product breakdown structure: the project outcome is broken down into major projects which are broken down into further outcomes until there is a hierarchical plan of how the project or product is created.

c Product descriptions: each product is described, including its quality criteria.

d Product flow diagram: the sequence that individual products will be developed and how they relate to each other.

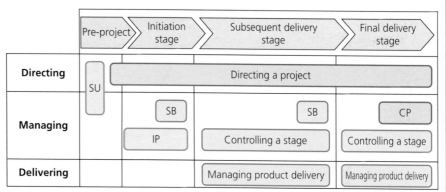

Key
SU = Starting up a project
IP = Initiating a project
SB = Managing a stage boundary
CP = Closing a project

Figure 8.1 PRINCE2 structure

Spiral methodology

This is a prototyping methodology (see Unit 9, LO1.1, page 245), slightly adapted to produce a project management system which emphasises the importance of risk analysis. It has four phases:

1 Planning: the project requirements are gathered and recorded in the form of, for example, a business requirement specification which focuses on what the business needs rather than how to achieve it, and a system requirements specification, which focuses on how the business needs are to be achieved. It will identify, as a minimum, the data and functional requirements of the system that is being developed, including security, safety and quality constraints.

2 Risk analysis: risks to successful development are pinpointed and, if appropriate, alternative solutions identified. At the end of this phase a prototype is produced, which takes account of the risks.

3 Engineering: the product is developed and tested to ensure that it meets at least some of the business needs and take account of the current risk analysis outcomes.

4 Evaluation: the customer evaluates the output and comments on the quality, usefulness and other factors before the project team, taking note of the findings, starts the risk analysis phase again.

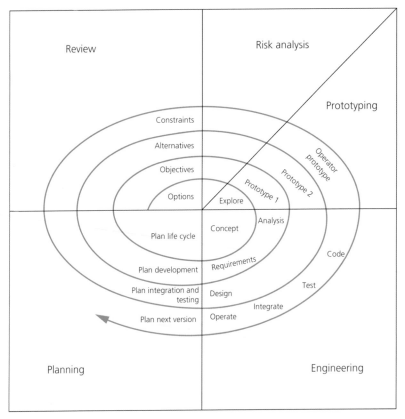

Figure 8.2 The spiral project management model

The spiral methodology is particularly useful when:

- the project risks are high and their evaluation important
- the users are unclear as to their needs
- the speed of completion of the project is essential due to economic constraints
- the project requirements are very complex and difficult to prioritise.

Agile development

The **agile methodology** argues that large projects cannot be planned as the client is likely to change their objectives. No project can be wholly protected against change during development, because of these changing objectives and also due to unforeseen circumstances. This means that it does not make sense to set inflexible project development processes.

Twelve principles of agile development underpin these arguments:

1 The highest priority is to satisfy the customer through early and continuous delivery of software.
2 Welcome changing requirements, even late in development. Agile processes harness change for the customer's competitive advantage.
3 Deliver working software frequently, from a couple of weeks to a couple of months, with a preference to the shorter timescale.
4 Business people and developers must work together daily throughout the project.

5 Build projects around motivated individuals. Give them the environment and support they need, and trust them to get the job done.
6 The most efficient and effective method of conveying information to and within a development team is face-to-face conversation.
7 Working software is the primary measure of progress.
8 Agile processes promote sustainable development. The sponsors, developers and users should be able to maintain a constant pace indefinitely.
9 Continuous attention to technical excellence and good design enhances agility.
10 Simplicity – the art of maximising the amount of work not done – is essential.
11 The best architectures, requirements and designs emerge from self-organising teams.
12 At regular intervals, the team reflects on how to become more effective, then tunes and adjusts its behaviour accordingly.

(Source: www.agilemanifesto.org)

Agile phases are:

1 Envision: the project scope and objectives are explored and the project team appointed. This is similar to the initiation phase in a structured method.
2 Speculate: similar to the planning phase. Risks are identified, and organisational resources and needs recognised. The customer and project team work together to gather and analyse necessary data and information and to estimate expected costs. Additionally, the initial steps of starting the development process are prepared.
3 Explore and adapt: these two phases can be run simultaneously throughout the project lifecycle. They include a range of activities:
   a managing tasks and workload
   b collaboration between the project team and the customer
   c design and redesign of products
   d decision making about next phase, design, redesign, adaptations to enable further improvement, etc.
   e progress monitoring
   f evaluation and reporting.
4 Close: similar to the closure procedures of the structured method (see above).

Modified versions of the agile methodology, such as scrum, are described in Unit 11 page 274. Each stage is reviewed and the results of the review fed back, to decide whether to repeat the stage or move on to another stage. The project manager role is shared between the team members.

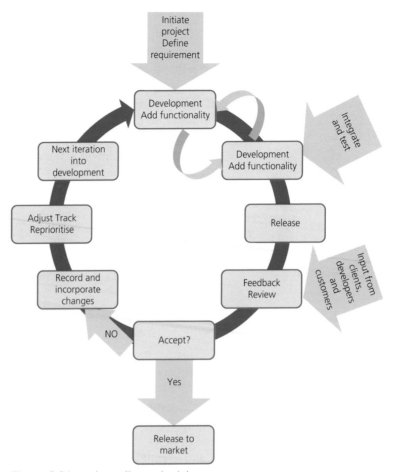

Figure 8.3 Iterative agile methodology

GROUP ACTIVITY

(40 minutes)

In small groups, identify a structured and an iterative project management methodology and compare:

- Industry recognition of each methodology e.g. accreditation, qualifications.
- Tools and techniques.
- The stages of the methodology.
- Risks of using the methodology.

Produce a presentation on your choices and findings to the wider group for discussion.

1.2 The project lifecycle

Development lifecycles have phases where activities take place. The names of these phases can differ, as can their content and scope. However, we shall briefly look at the key stages that all projects require.

Initiation phase

This is the starting point for a project. It requires the project leader and the client or stakeholders to consider:

- Why do we need this project? Is it really necessary?

- Who is it for?
  - Stakeholders (those with an interest in its development and who will be affected by its outcomes)?
  - Clients (those who will ultimately benefit from the project)?
  - Target audience (those who need to communicated with during the life of the project, e.g. stakeholders, clients).
- What do we want to achieve? What is our goal?
- Who is going to carry out the project?
- Who will need to be involved (for example, stakeholders and project and IT specialists)?
- Does it have the necessary support from potential users, senior managers, etc?

Details about the initiation phase are in LO2.1 (page 231).

Planning phase

This phase takes the outline plans identified in the project initiation phase and converts them into a detailed project plan. This will be used as a reference document by the project manager and sponsor throughout the life of the project. It will be used to monitor and control the time, costs and quality of the project.

Details about the development project plan are in LO2.1.

Execution phase

This is the longest and most complex stage of most projects. The deliverables are produced and the project manager and project team use the project plan to identify the steps that need to be taken and monitor and control the pace of development. The achievement of milestones against the projected timings is monitored using tools such as **Gantt charts** (Figure 8.4) and the **critical path method** (CPM) (Figure 8.5). In CPM, all the tasks in the project are identified on the chart to show what must be completed, how long it will take and which activities are dependent upon each other. The critical path shows how long the project will take to complete if everything runs to plan.

🔑 **KEY TERMS**

Gantt chart – a visual method of measuring proposed timings of activities against the actual times.

Critical path method – a process that identifies the activities which must be carried out to the agreed timescales if the project is to be completed on time.

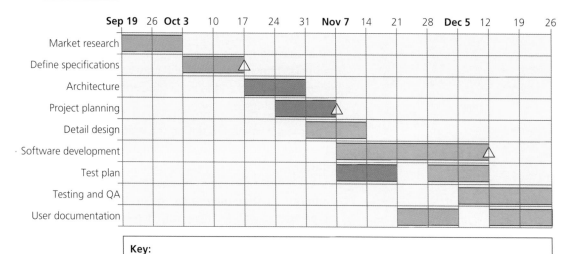

Figure 8.4 An example of a Gantt chart

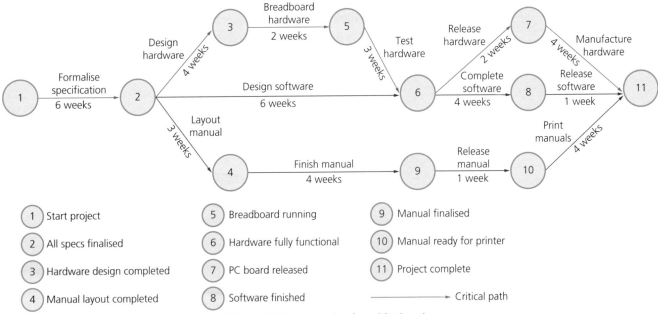

1 → Formalise specification → 6 weeks → 2

2 → Design hardware → 4 weeks → 3

3 → Breadboard hardware → 2 weeks → 5

5 → Test hardware → 3 weeks → 6

2 → Design software → 6 weeks → 6

2 → Layout manual → 3 weeks → 4

6 → Release hardware → 2 weeks → 7

7 → Manufacture hardware → 4 weeks → 11

6 → Complete software → 4 weeks → 8

8 → Release software → 1 week → 11

4 → Finish manual → 4 weeks → 9

9 → Release manual → 1 week → 10

10 → Print manuals → 4 weeks → 11

1 Start project
2 All specs finalised
3 Hardware design completed
4 Manual layout completed
5 Breadboard running
6 Hardware fully functional
7 PC board released
8 Software finished
9 Manual finalised
10 Manual ready for printer
11 Project complete

———→ Critical path

Figure 8.5 An example of a critical path

The project manager will also monitor all elements of the project including costs, quality, risk and communications.

Details about the initiation phase are in LO2.1 (page 231).

Evaluation phase

This phase reviews project in terms of:

- the quality of the deliverables
- the overall success of the project
- team performance
- the application of tools and techniques
- risks and issues and how they were resolved
- lessons learned which can improve future projects.

1.3 Project issues

Communication

Communication is an essential skill for project managers and team members. It involves verbal and non-verbal methods of communication, the ability to listen and to adjust the communication to suit the audience. Examples include:

- The project manager setting the vision for the team – the purpose of the final outcomes and important details which the team need to grasp quickly.
- Team members need to be able to communicate technical information to others, adjusting their language for those with the same knowledge and expertise as well as those with different skill sets.
- The project manager needs to be able to communicate with sponsors, stakeholders and clients. This requires the ability to translate technical terms into language that these non-specialists can understand, so that they make correct decisions.

The types of communication can vary depending upon the requirements but can include:

- Active communication, such as face to face meetings, presentations, webinars, tele- or video-conferencing.
- Passive communication such as reports, emails, podcasts, webcasts, blogs or bulletin boards.

External and internal factors

While the project manager can try to develop a project plan, which protects against disruptions, some factors can cause problems.

External factors are outside the control of the project manager or the sponsor, such as client or supplier bankruptcy or changes to laws or regulations which must be incorporated in the project plan.

Internal factors affect those involved with the project, such as the inability to employ staff with the necessary skills set or lack of accessibility to resources such as equipment or facilities.

Conflicts

Several issues can cause conflict in the project team:

- Scheduling of team meetings. The team may be dispersed over significant distances and have multiple roles, which can make attending meetings difficult. One solution is to set aside one day a week for team meetings from the start of the project.
- Project priorities. The team may be working on other projects or be part-time members of the team. Everyone must understand the priorities and, if necessary, the project manager should adjust workloads to ensure priorities are met.
- Resourcing issues and disagreements. These can include lack of specialist staff.
- Access to specific project assets. Arguments can arise when two or more individuals wish to use to same equipment or software at the same time. The timeline of activities and deliverables could be used to identify the most deserving case.
- Project manager's management style. This must be appropriate for the team and organisation ethos.

There can also be conflicts between the team and stakeholders, for example:

- Stakeholders could all have their own requirements and, where these requirements are very different, disagreements can lead to difficulties in getting the deliverables agreed or signed off.
- Disagreements with suppliers can occur over the quality of the supplied items, the timeliness of the delivery, for example.

The project manager must develop good interpersonal skills, demonstrating active listening and making compromises where this will not damage the project but will keep the team working.

Lack of management/leadership

Lack of management and leadership can cause conflict within the team, lack of progress, failure to resolve issues, poor project control and failure to maintain up-to-date records. It often arises because the project manager has limited experience and/or not enough training.

Poor planning

This can include a limited project plan or even no plan at all. The plan may lack clear timelines and milestones, or the activities required to create the deliverable may not be properly defined. Resources may not be linked to the activities and timeline and are not available when required.

The team need information and guidance to know what exactly they are expected to do and when they have to complete the task.

Legislation and regulation

At the start of the project, the project manager should ensure that legislation such as the Data Protection Act (1998), the Health and Safety at Work Act (1974) and the Equality Act (2010) will be met. The exact legislation and regulations depend upon the project, but the project team will need to comply. Issues can arise when regulations and laws change or new legislation and regulatory requirements are brought into being during the project. This can result in changes to deliverables or team working practices which can require additional resources and changes of focus to comply.

1.4 Documentation

Whatever methodology is used, documentation will be created. Table 8.1 provides an overview of types of document and their purpose.

> ### KEY TERMS
>
> **Project sponsor** – the senior manager or group who sets out the aims and outcomes of the project, agrees that it meets a business need and appoints the project manager and carries overall organisational responsibility for the project.
>
> **Cost/benefit analysis** – the estimation of the costs of carrying out the project and the benefits studied to aid a decision on whether to start or continue the project.

Table 8.1 Project documents and their purposes

Document	Purpose	Why it is important?
Project brief/project mandate (overview of project/scope/objectives)	It lays out the reason for the project and the objectives it must meet (e.g. create an electronic customer order system which can process x orders per hour but will not include the order picking system or link to the accounts system).	It briefly sets out the purpose of the project. All other documentation and activities flow from it.
Project initiation document (PID)/project definitions document	The top level planning document which provides, in a single place, all the information required to start the project.	It identifies all those with an interest in the project, e.g. client, stakeholders. It also sets out clear aims and refined objectives, the required resources and deliverables.
Contract (agreement from **project sponsor**/budget holder to start project)	The agreement by the project sponsor and budget holder (who may also be the project sponsor) that the project should go ahead.	It proves what was agreed, what would happen if the project was to stop early and who is financially liable for any overspends or overall failure.
Business case (project justification, cost versus benefits) or client acceptance form (to obtain agreement from project sponsor/budget holder that project is complete)	It provides a written explanation of why the project should be carried out and provides a **cost/benefit analysis**.	It provides the project manager with a guide to the design and management of the project together with how it can be evaluated. This ensures that the project manager and the sponsor have an agreed view of what is required.

Document	Purpose	Why it is important?
Work breakdown structure	It converts the complex activities identified in the project plan into a set of separate tasks which each have a time limit. As the tasks are clearly defined, they can be assigned resources and funding, which helps to manage the project budget.	It lets project managers plan their work and manage the project budget more efficiently.
Project progress report (status updates while project is in progress)	It enables the project manager to have a clear understanding of the deliverables or tasks that have been completed, those that are in progress and those yet to be started. It may also include how issues are being dealt with.	It provides reassurance to the project manager, the project sponsor and other stakeholders that progress is being made and that everything is moving smoothly and it will be completed on time. It also provides an opportunity for stakeholders to evaluate the project success this far and possibly make recommendations.
Project closure report (indication of outcomes)	It is produced at the completion stage or at an earlier point if the project was stopped following a phase review.	Every task required to close the project must be listed and described so that project closure is smooth and efficient.
Lessons learned report (survey)	It provides details of what went wrong or adjustments which had to be made during the lifetime of the project.	It enables those involved in future projects to learn how to avoid or mitigate similar issues, leading to smoother project development and possible reduction in costs and timescales.

Other types of documentation support the planning and control of the project. Table 8.2 outlines the most common documentation together with its purpose and relevance.

Table 8.2 Planning and control documentation for project management

Documentation	Purpose	Why is it important?
Project planner	A visual representation of the project timelines and all the activities that have to be completed, e.g. as a Gantt chart, PERT chart or critical path chart.	It allows stakeholders to quickly observe where activities are on track, delayed or not yet started. This allows swift action to be taken when timing issues arise.
Risk register	A detailed record of all risks and their significance.	It helps the project manager to monitor and manage risks and also identify record and monitor new ones should they arise.
Issues register	A detailed record of issues and how they are being addressed.	It ensures that the project manager is aware of all issues, and to monitor and manage how they are being addressed and whether the approach is appropriate.
Lessons learned register	A detailed record of how problems were dealt with during the project life and whether attempts to overcome them were successful, partially successful or had to be discarded.	It provides detailed evidence for the 'lessons learned' report created at the end of the project to aid the smooth development of future projects.

KNOW IT

1 What types of project methodology are PRINCE2 and SCRUM?
2 What are the stages of the project lifecycle?
3 Describe three types of project issues, giving an example of each.

LO1 Assessment activities

Below are two suggested assessment activities that have been directly linked to the pass, merit and distinction criteria in LO1 to help with assignment preparation; they include Top tips on how to achieve best results.

Activity 1 – pass criteria *P1*, *P2* and merit criteria *M1*

1 Research three different project management methodologies.
2 Compare the different methodologies, explaining their strengths, weaknesses and appropriateness to different types of project and describing their features and benefits.
3 Draw a diagram of each method and annotate each one with a brief summary of the purpose of each phase.

Activity 2 – distinction criteria *D1*

1 Using your work for Activity 1, assess the importance of each phase in managing the project to a successful conclusion.
2 Identify the similarities and differences between the methodologies and briefly explain how these would influence your choice of methodology for a given project.

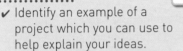

TOP TIPS ✔

✔ Identify an example of a project which you can use to help explain your ideas.
✔ Your diagram can be hand drawn or computer generated but, if you draw it yourself, use a pen and ruler or other guide to ensure that it looks professional.

LO2 Be able to initiate and plan projects *P3 P4 M2 D2*

GETTING STARTED 🧍

(10 minutes)

You have been asked to project manage the development of a new website for the catering outlet at a local college. The manager has told you that it must promote the different food and drinks offered by the outlet and the special offers which are changed weekly. As he is leaving, he tells you that he is sure that the college IT manager will be happy to host the site on the college system.

Produce a list of further information you will need to gather before you can start planning the project.

Project techniques such as schedule compression are also resources. This is used when a deliverable is falling behind schedule or even the whole project is running late. Two techniques are:

- Fast tracking: tasks are performed in parallel rather than sequentially, thus reducing the time required.
- Crashing: where additional resources are brought into the project, which while speeding up the process may also result in a significant financial cost.

2.1 Initiation phase

The project leader or proposed leader will produce a **feasibility study** which answers the questions in LO1.2. It will include:

The stakeholders, clients and target audience

The stakeholders and clients will normally be those who will be affected by the success or failure of the project and its deliverables. The target audience may be different and there may also be more than one; for example, government agencies, European funding agencies or local authorities may have to be kept informed about the progress and outcomes of the project.

Scope

This is the breakdown of the tasks and actions needed to achieve the project goal. It includes the boundaries of the project; it is as important to know what the project will not do as it is to know what it will. Many projects have failed because the team became side-tracked into looking into areas which they thought were interesting rather than necessary for success. When this happens, budgets, resources and timescales almost always collapse.

Project objectives

What do we want to have achieved at the end of the project? For example, a new inventory system which will allow us to monitor the order from our customers and ensure we have the necessary raw materials available, as they are required. Purchasing will receive warnings if the projected quantity of materials falls below the level required for one day's production.

Resources

These are the things needed to complete the project, from specialist human resources, such as designers and testers, to computers, plotters, networks and video-conferencing equipment.

Tools

Tools used by the project manager and team help them to deliver the project to time and to standard. They include software tools such as Gantt charts, which provide a visual plan of the expected timescales against the actual timings.

Alternatively, the precedence diagram method (DPM) provides a visual representation of the activities to be carried out in the project. It helps to identify errors such as missing activities or dependencies, and the critical activities which will have the most impact on the project schedule if they hit problems.

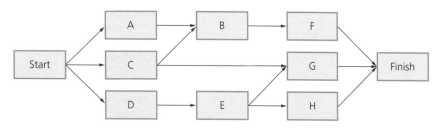

Figure 8.6 An example of the precedence diagram method (DPM)

A variant of this technique is the arrow diagramming method (ADM), which uses arrows to represent the scheduling of the activities, the flight being the start and the arrow point the end of the activity timeline.

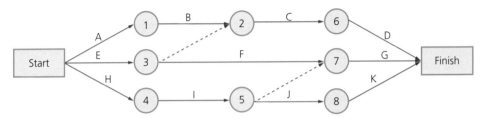

Figure 8.7 An example of the arrow diagramming method (ADM)

Deliverables

These are the tangible and measurable outcomes that must be achieved in order for the project to be successful. A deliverable should always be useful to the client or stakeholder.

Timescales and milestones

How long will the project and its individual deliverables take to complete? At which point should a particular activity or deliverable be started or completed?

Structure

The project manager brings together a team with the required skills set to achieve a successful project outcome. It will include specialist project members but also administrative staff, designers, etc. The project manager will also oversee the internal structure of the team, such as the formation of specialist groups with their own designated leaders.

Business case

This is usually a document, but it can be a spoken presentation. It explains the value of the project to the client and provides options for achieving the required goals, with cost/benefit analyses, risks and potential issues for each option. It should include a final recommendation on the choice of solution, but the project sponsors or owners will make the final decision.

Feasibility study

This document evaluates each option and recommends a specific way forward. The deliverables that the project will produce are identified.

Phase review

At the end of the initiation phase and subsequent phases, the sponsors and project manager discuss the report and its recommendations. The result will be a decision to continue to the planning stage or cancel the project.

Finally, a project charter may be created. This will cover the responsibilities of the team members such as:

● Attendance at staff meetings.
● When to update their part of the work plan.
● To whom you should escalate problems and issues.

- Provide support to other members of the team, especially when project progress is under threat.
- Communicate changes to the project immediate using the appropriate team communication system.

GROUP ACTIVITY

(45 minutes)

Research a template for a feasibility study. One person must act as the catering manager and provide further detail on exactly what the website should look like, what it must deliver, how long the project can take and what funding is available. Using this information as your starting point, complete the initiation phase document.

2.2 Planning phase

Project planning is one of the most important stages of project management. If the plan is inadequate or incorrect then the next stage is not only likely to be problematic but it could also prevent the project from meeting its goals. Attempts to correct it can result in rising costs and missed deadlines.

The plan must:

- State the activities required to complete the project. This can be a single report or a set of reports covering groups of related activities.
- Provide an estimate of the work required to carry out the project, identifying each task and how long it will take to complete.
- Confirm the final project **milestones**. These are the points in the project by which certain deliverables must be completed or started.
- Create a schedule of activities to achieve the milestones in the given timescale.
- Include a resource plan, including human resources like the project team, IT or business specialists, as well as computers, design packages, servers and even paper and paper clips which the project will consume or use during its life.
- Include a detailed financial statement or plan which calculates the costs of the project. This will include salaries, capital and consumable costs, utilities and rental costs, if appropriate.
- Include a statement or plan of the quality objectives; for example, that the project deliverables are complete and correct as stated by the client and how this is to be monitored and controlled.
- Identify project risks and produce the necessary risk plans to reduce or remove the risk. Risks can include resignation of key team members, lack of expertise, poor communications and technical issues.
- State the project tracking procedures, such as Gantt Charts, PERT charts, etc.
- Describe team composition and any training requirements.
- Include an acceptance plan which clearly states the conditions which must be met for the customer to accept the deliverables.
- The schedule of work which should indicate:
  - all the work required to complete the project
  - which resources, including human resources, will be needed to perform the work
  - the timeframes within which each work task must be completed.

- Phase review: at the end of the planning phase, the sponsors and project manager discuss the deliverables that have been produced. They will ask:
  - Is the project on schedule and within the agreed budget?
  - Have the deliverables been produced to the required standard and are the outcomes acceptable?
  - Have any risks been identified and managed appropriately?
  - Have any problems arisen and have these been solved?

They will decide whether to continue to the execution stage or cancel the project.

The schedule of the activities required is created from this information.

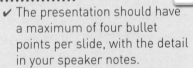

KNOW IT
1 Identify four types of resources which may be required for a project.
2 State the purpose of a phase review.
3 Identify three statements or plans which must form part of the overall project plan.

. . . .

LO2 Assessment activities

Below are three suggested assessment activities that have been directly linked to the pass, merit and distinction criteria in LO2 to help with assignment preparation; they include Top tips on how to achieve best results.

Activity 1 – pass criteria *P3 P4*

Develop a project plan for the website project, based on your initial findings and any further information which may have become available, through discussions with the IT manager (one member of the group should act as the IT manager).

Activity 2 – merit criteria *M2*

With another group acting as the sponsors, carry out a phase review and make a presentation, with speaker notes, to the 'Sponsors'.

Activity 3 – distinction criteria *D2*

Create an outline business case for the catering website, assuming that the aim is to increase sales by 25 per cent and to introduce a new special events package for business meetings.

TOP TIPS
- ✔ The presentation should have a maximum of four bullet points per slide, with the detail in your speaker notes.
- ✔ Do not read your notes – you should practise the presentation so that you only need to refer to them occasionally. You will look more confident and professional, which is important when facing clients.
- ✔ Research templates for business cases and select one which meets your requirements. It is not necessary to invent one for yourself.

LO3 Be able to execute projects *P5 D1*

(10 minutes)

Discuss issues which might arise as the website project is being carried out. As a wider group, make a list of your ideas.

3.1 Execution phase

In this phase, the deliverables are created and the project manager will monitor and control the phase through carrying out a range of management activities as described below.

Time

Each activity will have been allocated a start and finish date. This will be compared to the actual timing of the activity. If the activity is taking longer than expected, the project manager will need to consider:

- Is the activity on the critical pathway? Is failing to meet the deadlines likely to result in delaying completion of the project?
- How can it be brought back on track?
- Is there a case to spend additional resources to bring the activity to a timely completion or at least to reduce the delay?

The project manager should adjust the time plan if necessary.

Cost

Each activity has been costed for the resources, including time, which it will require to be completed. The project manager will:

- Compare the actual cost of each activity with proposed costs in the plan.
- Record the costs on the finance plan.

If the activity costs are higher than those in the plan, the project manager will have to consider whether to use savings elsewhere in the plan to offset the additional costs. Alternatively, they can request an increase in the budget.

Quality

The project manager needs to monitor the quality of the processes being carried out by the team:

- Are they in line with the procedures laid down?
- Are they ensuring that the deliverables are being created in a timely manner to the required standard?
- Are the deliverables of the standard demanded by the client and sponsor?

A quality management plan identifies and manages these quality standards. Quality audits throughout the project review the quality standards and the assumptions made at the start of the plan to ensure that the standards are being maintained, including under budget and to the time agreed. Quality control is also part of the plan, ensuring that the deliverables meet the standard agreed at the start of the programme.

Change

The project manager needs to consider any proposed changes to the project, the reasons for the requests and the effect that change will have on the timeliness and costs contained in the plan. The project plan should be updated and the changes approved with the project sponsor.

 **PAIRS ACTIVITY**

(30 minutes)

Investigate projects in the public and/or private sector and identify changes which were made to the project during the execution stage. List the types of changes made.

Risk

The risks identified in the plan need to be monitored. As the project develops, some risks may no longer be relevant and this is recorded on the plan. Other risks may arise, such as changes or additions to the deliverables being requested by the sponsor or the departure of a team member with specialist knowledge. Changes to the level of risk arising from these events must be recorded, together with any steps taken to reduce the risk to a manageable level.

Issues

Issues are not the same as risks. Risk can be anticipated; for example, the risk of not finding staff with a particular skill set. Issues arise unexpectedly; for example, a supplier suddenly going bankrupt or a natural event such as a flood or earthquake disrupting the project. The project manager must ensure that:

● Issues are recorded and prioritised so that the most serious are dealt with first.
● A team member or group is made responsible for resolving it.
● The method of resolving the issue is recorded for use in future projects.

Communication

Communication will take place between project team members, between the project manager and the team and with stakeholders such as end users and clients. Individual project team members may need to communicate with end users to clarify the requirements of the project. It is essential that the message goes to the intended recipients in a format and language that they can understand.

Table 8.3 identifies the principal communication requirements and the communication methods which would be appropriate.

Table 8.3 Communication methods

Information to be communicated	Appropriate communication method(s)	Presenter(s)	Receiver(s)
Project budget status (under, over or on target)	Verbal presentation and/or report, webinar	Project team Project manager	Project manager Stakeholders, project sponsor, clients, team members
Project on track against agreed schedule	Verbal presentation and/or report	Project manager	Stakeholders, project sponsor, clients Project team
Deliverables completed and accepted	Verbal presentation and sign-off document	Project manager	Project sponsor
Acceptance report	Verbal presentation and report for signature	Project manager	Project sponsor, clients
Issue resolution	Verbal discussion and record of outcomes, emails	Project manager Team members	Project team, end users, clients Team members and project manager
Risk control and mitigation	Verbal confirmation and written records of actions, emails	Project manager Project team	Team members, project sponsor Project manager
Phase review	Presentation and written report	Project manager	Project sponsor
Agreement of project to continue	Written confirmation	Project sponsor	Project manager
Project closure report	Written documentation	Project team Project manager	Project manager Project sponsor
Project summary	Written document	Project manager	Project sponsor
Project performance	Written document and presentation	Project team Project manager	Project manager Project sponsor, clients, stakeholders, project team

> ## CLASSROOM DISCUSSION
>
> ### (20 minutes)
>
> Discuss the different approaches to communication which would be required when dealing with technical and non-technical receivers. Identify specific examples for each of the receivers identified in the table.

Acceptance

The client or sponsor should formally accept that all of the project deliverables are complete and confirm whether the project achieved its overall goal or goals. This avoids any later disagreements and possibly expensive court cases as to what had been agreed. The acceptance document will include a range of information such as:

- project title
- project sponsor/client
- project manager and their contact details
- project team members
- project start date
- project end date
- each deliverable with its name, data of complete and who approved it
- project goal: measured against the success criteria has the goal been fully, partially or not met at all?

- a statement of who will complete the closure process including the post project review and lessons learned
- sponsor or client acceptance confirmed by dated signature together with the sponsor name and title.

Phase review

At the completion of each stage, as you will have seen from LO1 and 2, there must be a phase review to consider whether to continue with the project or, in the case of the execution phase, to confirm that the project is ended. Phase reviews can be carried out by the project manager, but an independent external reviewer can also take the role to offer a fresh look by someone who is not too close to the project and may be able to see the progress more clearly. Whoever carries out the review, a number of areas must be addressed:

- Have the agreed deliverables been produced?
- Have the deliverables produced been approved?
- What issues have arisen and have they been resolved?
- Have the risks been managed and have any others been identified?
- Is the project on course?

At the end of the review the sponsor will have to agree the report and make a decision as to whether to proceed with the project or cancel it at that point.

Project closure

Hopefully, at the agreed end point of the project with all deliverables delivered on time and to the standard agreed, the project will close. A project closure report is produced so that the formal closure of the project can be agreed. Project closure documents will include:

- A project summary: a brief statement outlining the:
  - project aim
  - outline of the planning stage
  - outline of the execution stage
  - outline of any issues and changes which occurred
  - outline of the final outcomes.
- The reason for closure. This will be because:
  - The project has been completed successfully with all deliverables achieved on time and to budget.
  - The project has been completed successfully but has taken longer than intended or proved costlier than anticipated.
  - The project has been stopped before completion, e.g. run out of budget, run out of time, lack of technical knowledge.
- Assessment of project performance requires the actual outcomes to be measured against the projected outcomes which were laid out in the business plan.
  - Were all the project objectives, outputs and activities met in full? In other words, did the project plan and execution result in a successful project or not?
  - Did the project meet its planned timescales? These should be easily discovered by a review of the Gantt charts, for example.
  - Were the resources sufficient? Did additional resources have to be provided?
  - Were the costs of the project kept with the agreed budget?

If any of these elements are not the same as those agreed, then reasons for the differences must be explained. Even if fewer resources, less time or costs are incurred, it is still important to know why.

- Lessons learned: at the start of the project, it was assumed that certain benefits would be gained from the project, such as reduced costs, better customer services, faster response times. Have they been achieved? If not, why not? Were they too optimistic? Was the technology not sufficiently developed? Was the expertise required not available? All of these provide useful lessons for future projects.
- Celebrating success: what were the greatest successes for the project? These can include timely delivery, satisfied stakeholders, added value, meeting the project goals and objectives, underspending the budget.

Next steps: projects do not normally come to a sudden end. Projects have outcomes and these will need to be managed in the future. These may include:

- Staff performance evaluations and reports completed, signed and dated.
- Termination of project staff contracts, as not all staff will be retained.
- Termination of supplier contracts. Formal contract closures are important to ensure that all parties agree that all liabilities, e.g. outstanding payments or goods are resolved.
- Sign-off of outstanding expenditure and checking of financial records.
- Closure of site operations such as computer networks: some operations will have been put in place simply to aid the smooth running of the project so, once the project is finished, these need to be closed to avoid unnecessary further charges.
- Disposal of equipment and materials. Some of these may be recycled, sold or destroyed for security or safety reasons.
- Secure destruction of sensitive data and information in line with organisational and statutory requirements.
- Completion and storage of project files for future reference.
- Formal announcements of completion, internally and externally.
- Handover of maintenance and support to responsible parties.
- Any ongoing risks identified and communicated to responsible parties.
- Recognition of ongoing dependencies, such as the outcome from this project will be fed into another project, or the lessons learned from this project are required for another project. These must be passed on to the responsible individual or group.

> It is important for the project team, the project sponsor and stakeholders that successes are identified and appreciated. As well as this information contributing to successful future projects, everyone likes to be thanked for a job well done.

KNOW IT

1 What sort of information would be best communicated verbally?
2 What information should be included in a project acceptance document?
3 How would you assess project performance at the end of a project?
4 Why is it important to identify lessons learnt during the project?

- ✔ If you have carried out a project in class, use this experience to help you explain how you would carry out the website development.
- ✔ All the documentation must look professional, so you must check your spelling and grammar, use page numbering and correct document titles.
- ✔ Each section within the document must have a title that clearly identifies its purpose.

LO3 Assessment activities

Below are two suggested assessment activities that have been directly linked to the pass and distinction criteria in LO3 to help with assignment preparation; they include Top tips on how to achieve best results.

Activity 1 – pass criteria *P5*

Using the example of the website development, explain how you would carry out the plan and the types of risks, changes and issues which might have arisen and ways in which they could be overcome.

Activity 2 – distinction criteria *D3*

Using the information developed from Activity 1, prepare a project closure report. If you don't have enough information to complete any of the elements of the report, explain what type of information you would include in these sections.

LO4 Be able to carry out project evaluations
P6 M3

GETTING STARTED

(10 minutes)

In pairs, discuss the last time you received feedback. How did it make you feel? Did you make a change as a result? How could it have been more helpful?

4.1 Evaluation phase

Evaluation is a fundamental requirement of any project. Although there is a formal evaluation phase, successful project management comes from continuous assessment of progress throughout the project. Therefore, some of the areas we will cover here can be used throughout the project. The evaluation is not restricted to the views of the project manager or even the project team – it includes the views of the project sponsor, clients, stakeholders and end users, even the views of a **critical friend** or external specialist who has observed some or all of the project but was not actively involved in it.

Obtain feedback

This seems straightforward but it does require detailed thought and planning. First, consider the different groups from which you might want to receive feedback. Table 8.4 describes some of those who may provide feedback for a project and possible ways of gathering this information.

Table 8.4 Type of feedback during the evaluation phase

Group	Role	Method of gaining feedback	Feedback required
Client	The direct recipient of the result of the project, which may be products or services.	Hard-copy satisfaction survey, telephone survey, web-based survey, focus group.	Has the client's experience improved since the completion of the project? How has it improved? Are there any issues which have arisen or not been addressed?
Stakeholder	Anyone who will gain or lose as a direct consequence of the project.	Group meetings, face to face interviews, presentations, walkthroughs.	Have the business benefits, laid out in the business case, been achieved? Have additional benefits that were not identified in the business case been achieved? Which benefits have not been achieved?
End user	Those who will work with deliverables from the project.	Testing the product for their work purposes. User feedback sessions.	Has the project improved efficiency, effectiveness or satisfaction? What do they like? What issues remain?
Project team	Those who have worked to deliver the product in line with the business case and the **terms of reference** (TOR).	Review meetings. Surveys. Workshops. Presentations. Review of project documentation. Outcomes from feedback from clients, users and stakeholders.	Have business benefits been achieved? Were TORs met? Was resource usage in line with the resource plan? Did the project scope change? Was the quality plan met? Were the deliverables produced on schedule? Was the budget, defined in the financial plan met? Was the management of the execution of the project as agreed? How did the selected tools and techniques used influence the outcome of the project? What were the major achievements? What positive effects did the project have on the client's business? What failures (if any) occurred? How did the failures affect the client's business? What lessons have we learned from this project process? How can we improve our approach to similar future projects, as a result of what we did and what we have found?

All of the feedback, together with reports on the stages of the project, issues identified and how they were resolved, will be reviewed, and from this a final evaluation report produced.

The report will include:

- The name of the owner of the report (normally the client or sponsor) who is responsible for the storage and dissemination of the contents.
- The name of the individual who led the evaluation, which may be the project manager, the sponsor or an external facilitator.
- The individuals or groups who participated in the evaluation process, such as project team, clients, stakeholders and end users.
- Project successes, including whether the overall project met its objectives or which elements were successful; for example, what met the resource requirements, achieved the deliverables or was kept within budget. These are important learning points for future similar projects.
- Project failures – again these may include the overall failure of the project or specific areas.
- Lessons learned and actions which should be taken to ensure that they are built into future projects.
- An action plan to solve any outstanding problems, identifying who will be responsible for ensuring that the plan is carried out.
- Appendices, including relevant project documentation, results and analysis of feedback, copies of all presentations, questionnaires, meeting minutes and other information.

KNOW IT

1 What is the role of the critical friend in project evaluation?
2 Identify five groups that may contribute to the project evaluation phase.
3 Who could lead the evaluation phase?
4 Give three examples of project success.
5 What is the purpose of the 'lessons learned' section of an evaluation report?

LO4 Assessment activities

Below are two suggested assessment activities that have been directly linked to the pass and merit criteria in LO4 to help with assignment preparation; they include Top tips on how to achieve best results.

Activity 1 – pass criteria *P6*

1 Identify the individuals and groups from whom you would seek feedback for the website project and the type of feedback you would request.
2 Design a draft questionnaire for the end users and questions for a focus group, explaining your reasons.
3 Explain how you would evaluate the feedback from the client and from your project team.

Activity 2 – merit criteria *M3*

Design an action plan for potential improvements that will benefit future websites, based on the outcome of the project evaluation. This may be an animation or interactive element.

Unit 09

Product development

Developing a product is a fundamental process that you will undertake during this course. In this unit you will learn about the stages involved in this process, and develop skills relating to developing a product.

You will also learn about the product development lifecycle, including methodologies and activities that need to be carried out. You will learn the importance of testing and of the product meeting the client's requirements.

You can apply the skills and knowledge that you gain in this unit when you design or develop a prototype or the full product in another unit. During this process you will need to engage with your client to create a product that meets their requirements. You will be required to compare development methodologies and produce documentation for your development of a prototype including a requirements analysis, design documentation and plans for testing.

LEARNING OUTCOMES

The topics and activities in this unit will help you to:

1 Understand the product development lifecycle.
2 Be able to design products that meet identified client requirements.
3 Be able to implement and test products.
4 Be able to carry out acceptance testing with clients.

How will I be assessed?

You will be assessed by producing evidence from set scenarios or from work that you carry out as part of a work placement or employment. This evidence will be assessed by your tutor.

How will I be graded?

You will be graded using the following criteria:

Learning outcome	Pass assessment criteria	Merit assessment criteria	Distinction assessment criteria
You will:	To achieve a pass you must demonstrate that you have met all the pass assessment criteria	To achieve a merit you must demonstrate that you have met all the pass and merit assessment criteria	To achieve a distinction you must demonstrate that you have met all the pass, merit and distinction assessment criteria
1 Understand the product development lifecycle	**P1** Outline the phases of the product development lifecycle	**M1** Compare and contrast different product development methodologies	**D1** Assess the potential impact of constraints upon product development
2 Be able to design products that meet identified client requirements	**P2** Develop a product requirements specification to meet an identified client's requirements		
	P3 Present an outline of the design solutions to the identified client and obtain feedback	**M2** Agree the inclusion of features that extend or enhance the functionality of the chosen design solution with the identified client	
3 Be able to implement and test products	**P4** Develop the product in line with the agreed design solution		
	P5 Conduct product testing	**M3** Analyse the results of testing and recommend improvements and enhancements to the design solution	
4 Be able to carry out acceptance testing with clients	**P6** Carry out acceptance testing for users in line with the agreed design solution		**D2** Discuss with the identified client potential enhancements, upgrades and maintenance of the final product

LO1 Understand the product development lifecycle *P1 M1 D1*

GETTING STARTED 👤

(5 minutes)

What is product development? In pairs, discuss and identify the different steps and stages that you think are involved in the development of a product.

1.1 Product development methodologies

There is a range of product development methodologies. Each one has general benefits and drawbacks and may be more appropriate for some scenarios or products. A few of these are described below.

Waterfall methodology

This methodology allows you to follow the stages of development in order. However, you can go back a stage (go up the waterfall) to revisit the previous stage if you encounter a problem or need to change your plan. You can go back again, through each stage as needed, but you must go back down in order, without missing out any stages. Figure 9.1 gives a visual representation of how you can move down and back up the waterfall methodology.

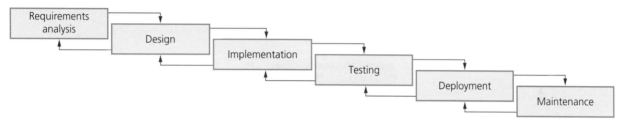

▲ **Figure 9.1** The waterfall methodology

Incremental methodology

This allows you to split a project into smaller tasks, each of which is developed using the lifecycle until the whole system is complete. For example, a program may be split into 20 modules. In the first iteration one module may be designed, built and tested. In the second iteration one or more additional modules are designed, built, tested and added to the product. This allows a product to be built piece by piece, or incrementally. Figure 9.2 shows the individual development of two modules that are added to the system.

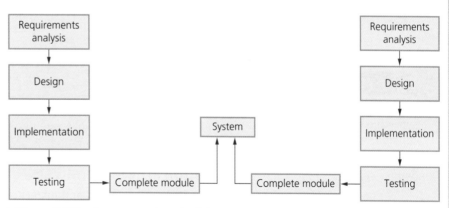

▲ **Figure 9.2** The incremental methodology

The spiral methodology

This makes use of **prototypes** that are worked on and refined as the lifecycle repeats. The first time through, a prototype is developed which is evaluated. This leads to further design and adaptation of the prototype, which is tested and evaluated, leading to further design changes and so on. This continues

KEY TERM

Prototype – a preliminary model of the product that may not be functional or only partly functional and is used to give an indication of how the final product will look and/or work.

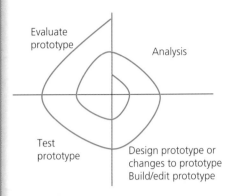

Evaluate prototype

Analysis

Test prototype

Design prototype or changes to prototype
Build/edit prototype

▲ **Figure 9.3** Spiral methodology

until the developer and client are satisfied with the product. Figure 9.3 shows the cycle of analysis, design and creation or editing of a prototype, testing and evaluation leading back to further analysis.

Agile development

In agile development, a product is worked on, changed and improved iteratively. This may start with a small part of the product meeting some of the requirements, then the next version may have additional features added to meet further requirements. This process repeats until a final product is developed. A variety of other methodologies may also be applied, for example extreme programming, where multiple programmers collaborate to produce a high quality product through each iteration.

There are similarities and differences between each of these methodologies; for example, agile, spiral and incremental all involve repeating the cycle and producing prototypes or modules, whereas in the waterfall methodology an entire stage needs to be revisited each time through.

GROUP ACTIVITY

(40 minutes)

Split into small groups. Divide the methodologies between the groups so each one has spiral, waterfall, agile development or incremental.

Research the benefits and drawbacks of your group's methodology. Begin by considering:

● speed of creation
● cost
● best interests of client
● type of system.

Present your findings to the other groups.

Then create a document summarising each of the methodologies and the similarities and differences between them.

1.2 Phases of the product development lifecycle

Development lifecycles follow set phases during which particular activities take place. The names of these phases can differ, as can the content and **scope** of them. The main phases are outlined below.

Requirements analysis

This phase takes place at the start of a project while the requirements for the development of a product are investigated. This may involve talking to the client to discover their needs, investigating existing solutions or competing products and analysing any limitations that may restrict the scope of the product. The developers may develop a prototype (like one you may have produced in another unit).

During this phase the developers will produce a requirements specification that introduces the product and states what it needs to do. Requirements may be expressed as a list of functional and non-functional requirements. The requirements specification will identify any constraints; for example, the timescale for when the product is required.

You will look at the requirements analysis in more detail in LO2 where you develop a requirements analysis for a product (see page 252).

Design

In the design phase, solutions are outlined and presented to the client. As with the requirements analysis this can include both functional and non-functional details, for example **interface** designs, processes, inputs and security. These designs are refined until the client and developer agree they are suitable, at which phase the final design is created. This should include a time plan for the implementation, and the designs and test plans. You will look at the design phase in more detail in LO2 when you design a product to meet client requirements (see page 255).

Implementation

The main component of the implementation phase is the creation of the product. This includes implementing testing strategies during the creation process, the results of which are used to correct or refine the product. This may be interlinked with the testing phase as you will need to be testing your product during its creation. You will look at the implementation phase in more detail in LO3 where you create a product for a client (see page 261).

Testing

Many testing strategies can be implemented during and after the creation of the product. These can involve the developer testing units or modules within the product, as well as final product testing and acceptance testing, where the client or users are involved in testing to ensure that the product meets the original requirements. You will look at testing strategies in more detail in LO3 and LO4 where you create and test a product for a client (see page 261).

Deployment

After the acceptance testing is complete, the client will decide whether the product is accepted (it meets all the criteria and is ready to use), the product is not accepted (it does not meet the criteria and is not fit for purpose), or the product will be accepted after modifications have been made (the system is altered and re-tested). You will look at deployment in more detail in LO4 (see page 265).

Maintenance

After the product has been successfully deployed, there is a need for it to be maintained. Maintenance can involve adapting the system to meet new requirements, provide upgrades or to correct bugs. You will look at maintenance in more detail in LO4 (see page 265).

1.3 Constraints

When developing a product there may be a number of **constraints** that need to be considered before, or during the development lifecycle.

> ## 🔑 KEY TERM
>
> **Interface** – the point at which two elements interact, e.g. the interface between the user and a computer is the operating system.

> ## 🔑 KEY TERM
>
> **Constraint** – a limitation or restriction; for example a time constraint may be that a product is needed within seven days.

Time

A time constraint could be when the product needs to be ready, or a timescale within which it needs to be produced; for example, a client may need a website developing, deployed and ready to use in seven days. In this case the developer would need to assess the product requirement and determine if they are able to complete the stages of development within that time.

For example, a secondary school teacher would like a bespoke online network to be created in order for their students to interact. They would like this to be implemented within the next two months. The developer would need to look at the two-month timescale and decide if they can produce this product in the time available.

Time constraints may alter the system development methodology chosen; for example, a system that is needed very quickly would lend itself to agile development where the creation of the product has a greater emphasis than following a structured process.

Financial

A financial constraint is a limit on the money available in relation to the likely cost of developing the product. If the client has a limited budget, the developer would need to assess if the product can be developed within that budget.

A minimum viable product has all the features necessary for the lowest cost to be incurred. This does not involve creating the smallest product, but producing one that is desired and fits the most important needs of the client and market within the financial constraints.

For example, the secondary school teacher who would like an online network has only £500 to spend. The developer needs to determine how much it will cost to produce the basic functionality of this product and whether any elements need to be left out or delayed until later to ensure that the initial development meets the available budget. This will involve agreeing what the 'minimum viable product' will look like – outlining the basic required functionality that would deliver a good enough development that could be revisited and added to later.

Financial constraints will impact on the final product, and the emphasis placed on different stages of the lifecycle; for example, a costly analysis into the development of a complex product may be impractical where the funding is available to only create a very basic version of the product.

Social

Products are likely to have target markets that they need to be tailored for, such as a specific gender, age and/or language. This could influence the language used in the interface of the product, as well as the support documentation and help tutorials. For example, a translation may be required if users are unlikely to have English as their first language. If the market is young children then the language must be for an appropriate reading age.

For example, the secondary school teacher's system is to be used by Year 12 and 13 students within the United Kingdom. The developer will need to consider the complexity of language used in the user interface and support documentation to make sure it can be understood by users.

Regulation

Developers need to follow a number of regulations and ensure their products adhere to them. These could be internal regulations, such as a company code of practice, or external regulations, such as national and international laws.

For example, the teacher's product will require personal information about the students to be stored. The developer will need to make sure the product is designed to collect and store the students' data in line with the Data Protection Act (1998).

Regulations may impact the final product in numerous ways, such as its functionality, end use or restrictions for use or access in other countries. This will need to be considered from an early stage to avoid late modifications. For more about regulations, see Unit 2 – Global Information (page 70).

Standards

Certain standards need to be considered when designing, producing and maintaining a product. Standards apply to a range of product development features, such as the design of the system itself (e.g. the layout and tools within an interface).

For example:

- USB is a hardware standard. New devices created by different companies will use USB as a method of connection because it is widespread. Many different devices have USB ports and therefore they are helping their product's compatibility.
- HTML is a software standard. Websites use HTML as a base language for the design, to ensure compatibility between different web browsers. If a developer created a website in a new language that was not supported by accepted web standards and browsers, people may not be able to view it.

When developing a product, these standards will impact decisions about the design and possible functionality of the product. This may involve allowing for additional costs to ensure the standards are followed, and will need to be considered and assessed throughout the development lifecycle.

Standards also relate to the level of quality the end product should attain. For example, in an e-commerce system, personal data must be kept secure and payments made securely and reliably. The reliability of a system will be assessed, to ensure it conforms to an agreed standard of quality.

Standards organisations

There are organisations that publish standards for companies or developers to follow. Standards are endorsed and published by organisations such as the International Organization for Standardization (ISO). A standard can be set by a government, which is required to be followed by law.

Some standards organisations allow developers to become members by signing up to their codes of conduct. By advertising yourself as a member of one of these organisations you are informing clients that you will follow these guidelines and this can improve your chances of being appointed to develop products.

PAIRS ACTIVITY

(10 minutes)

Research a standards organisation; for example, the IEEE (Institute of Electrical and Electronics Engineers) or ISO (International Organization for Standardization). Find out how they are run, who adopts their standards and what standards they produce or endorse.

The need for compromise

When assessing the constraints during the development, it may not be possible to create the system the client has asked for. There may need to be a compromise between what is expected or achieved. Some areas of development may not be worth the additional cost, i.e. the cost is more than the benefit it brings, and therefore an alternative, which costs less but differs from the original plan, may be considered. This is sometimes known as a 'minimum viable product'.

Another compromise may relate to the complexity of a product. The more complex a solution, the greater the chance of an error being introduced and the longer the time required for development. Depending on the situation and the seriousness of the potential error, a compromise may be needed to reduce the complexity but ensure the product is fully error free and delivered on time.

PAIRS ACTIVITY

(30 minutes)

A client has an idea for a new games app that they would like you to build. Customers would download the app and pay for items that they can use to progress through the game. In pairs, discuss the possible constraints for this product.

Create a presentation (with speaker notes) to show the impact these constraints may have on the development of the app.

> **KNOW IT**
> 1 What is the difference between the waterfall methodology and the spiral methodology?
> 2 Describe two benefits of agile development.
> 3 Explain two social constraints on product development.
> 4 What is a minimum viable product?
> 5 Give an example of how regulation can be a constraint.

LO1 Assessment activities

Below are three suggested assessment activities that have been directly linked to the pass, merit and distinction criteria in LO1 to help with assignment preparation; they include Top tips on how to achieve the best results.

Activity 1 – pass criteria *P1*

Create a presentation that describes each phase of the product development lifecycle. Make sure you include a description of the processes that take place, and what documentation is produced at each stage. Include speaker notes to expand on your presentation points and remember you must include the main characteristics of each phase.

Activity 2 – merit criteria *M1*

Add to your presentation a description of at least three different product development methodologies. Include a diagram of each one and explain the processes involved. Compare the different methodologies, giving the benefits and drawbacks of each, and give examples of scenarios where each one would be best used. Include speaker notes to expand on your presentation points.

Activity 3 – distinction criteria *D1*

For each phase of the product development lifecycle, consider the constraints that may occur and the impact these will have on the development together with the possible knock-on effects to subsequent phases.

Add these points to the speaker notes for each slide of your presentation.

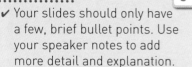

TOP TIPS
- ✔ Your slides should only have a few, brief bullet points. Use your speaker notes to add more detail and explanation.
- ✔ Include images to enhance your information, as pictures are easier to understand than text.

LO2 Be able to design products that meet identified client requirements *P2 P3 M2*

GETTING STARTED 👤

(5 minutes)

Your school or college has requested a bespoke virtual learning environment (VLE), to allow staff to upload work and activities for students. The students will also be required to upload their work to the VLE where it will be marked with feedback and made available to the student.

What further information would you need to know before starting to create this product?

2.1 Requirements analysis phase

The requirements analysis phase involves investigating the scenario and determining the requirements of the end user. This results in the production of a requirements specification that presents the results of this investigation.

You will need to conduct a requirements analysis for your product, including the development of a requirements specification, following some or all of the points covered in this section.

Market analysis

The investigation needs to find out what the client and end user needs from the product and what they want it to do. These may differ as the end user may want more functionality of features than the basic requirements. The client and end user are often different people, or groups of people; both need to be investigated as the client may not use the product and therefore may not always be aware of the end user's requirements. This is where the 'minimum viable product' discussed in the previous section can be determined.

The method of investigation will differ according to the situation. Methods may involve any of:

- interview
- observation
- meeting
- questionnaire or survey.

GROUP AND INDEPENDENT ACTIVITY

(20 minutes)

Each method of investigation listed here has its benefits and drawbacks. Discuss the benefits and drawbacks of each and when you may, or may not, use each.

Consider the product you will be developing, either from the previous activity or another product. You will consider this product in the remaining activities in this unit. Which method(s) should you use? What information will it provide you with?

The market may already have competing products. These need to be explored to determine their strengths and weaknesses to ensure the product being created incorporates the best features and minimises the weaknesses.

Limitations

During the investigation, limitations found within the organisation need to be identified as they can impact on the product to be designed. These can include:

- Target platform: what hardware or software are currently in use? This will impact on the hardware and software you use in your development as you must ensure compatibility.
- Bandwidth: a product that requires internet use or large amounts of data transfer (internally or externally) needs the bandwidth in place to support it. This can impact on the functionality you build into your product.

- Development resources: these can range from humans to hardware and software. If pre-existing hardware, software, etc. is to be used, this can limit the product that you produce to ensure it will work with the resources available.
- Human resources: these include all people who use the product, or are reliant on it within the organisation. The skills, knowledge and number of these people can influence how the product is produced. For example, if only one employee is going to use the product, the solution will be limited to that one person's needs.

PAIRS ACTIVITY

(10 minutes)

For the VLE scenario in the Getting Started task, discuss the limitations within your school or college that would impact on this product.

GROUP ACTIVITY

(10 minutes)

Several limitations have been given. Discuss what other limitations may impact on the development of a product and how they will impact the development (for example, costs).

Prototyping

A prototype is a small aspect of a product, that is not (or only partly) functional. It can be used to demonstrate features or ideas to the client, and to gather feedback to amend and/or improve the design solution.

In the requirements stage, a prototype can be developed to clarify aspects of the design with the client and ensure the requirements specification includes all requirements.

Product requirements specification

This is the document that is created at the end of the requirements analysis. This will start with an introduction to the product and situation (the environment where the product is being produced for the organisation). This is followed by a more in-depth description of the purpose of the product that explains the context of the product, including the tasks that it needs to perform, where it will be used, who will be using it, and what they will be using it for.

Any assumptions being made will need identifying. Some of these may be developed from your limitations, for example identifying the hardware and software specifications that the client will be using, or the technical skills and experience of the staff in using the technology.

The specification should also describe any constraints that have been identified.

Finally, the requirements specification would identify the functional and non-functional requirements of the product.

Functional and non-functional requirements

The requirements summarise the needs of the client and the product. The requirements provide an outline to the system designers of what the product has to do and how it must function. At the end of the system lifecycle, the product's success will be assessed according to these requirements.

> Not all types of requirements will be required for all products, e.g. a piece of software may not have the safety requirements that a piece of hardware has.

Table 9.1 Functional requirements identify what the product has to do

Content	Description
Main functional requirements	A list of every action the product has to perform. These need to be precise and complete, covering all aspects in sufficient detail and unambiguous. These should be given a priority to make it clear which requirements are the most important and necessary.
Target user profiles	For each type of end user, end user needs, knowledge and experience should be identified, along with the client's goals for the product.

Table 9.2 Non-functional requirements identify aspects of the product other than its core functionality

Content	Description
Usability	Usability may be difficult to measure as it is subjective. This may cover: • The ease of use: this can include how easy it is to learn, how user friendly it is, if there are shortcuts for more experienced users. • Clear operating procedures, e.g. each task has a clear set of steps to follow that make sense and are logical.
Performance	• The capacity, e.g. the quantity of data can be stored or processed. • The speed of transmission of data between components or within the product. • The response times, e.g. how long it takes to perform a task the user has requested. • Environmental issues, e.g. disposal of hardware, electrical usage, physical environment where the product is to be used.
Safety	• Appropriate safety features need identifying to ensure the users are not exposed to any danger, e.g. automatic shutdown system on hardware. • There may be specific regulations for the product that need to be adhered to. • The product needs to be secure against system failure to make sure data is not lost by a sudden shut down, hardware or software failure.
Security	The product must comply with current legislation and regulations and ensure that it is secure both in terms of privacy of data, and resistance to external attacks such as viruses (e.g. Trojans), hacking, etc.
Maintainability	A product will need to be maintained, for example: • The system may be required to adapt to new requirements in the future. • There may be a need to build a method for updates to be installed, e.g. to correct errors or bugs. • The system may need to recover from errors that could occur. • The ability to adjust to updated software that the product interacts with, or works on.
Interfaces	• Hardware, e.g. if data is to be input, what hardware will be used to do this? Does it need a keyboard to type words? Or a joystick to manoeuvre other components? • Hardware can also cover outputs, e.g. will the product respond on screen, in audio, with an actuator or as LED lights? • Software and user: If a solution requires a software interface, e.g. is a **GUI** (Graphical User Interface) required? Or will there be a **command line interface**? It could be software that is integrated into new technology such as a smartwatch. • Communications, for example, will the system need to transmit data? Is this internal (within the system), or external (to another system)? How will this be transmitted?

(30 minutes)

Individually identify some of the functional and non-functional requirements that may be included for the VLE scenario. Make a list of these.

As a group, combine the requirements into one set.

Appendices

An **appendix** will contain additional items that could be referred to in the requirements specification, or add to the content.

A glossary of terms can clarify any terms that are unique to the organisation, or technical terms for the client. Although the design of the processes is a priority in the design stage, it may be necessary (and helpful) to include diagrammatic representations of some processes, especially if these are complex and do not translate well into words.

The timescales may be identified in the non-functional requirements, but these may be shown in more detail in the appendix, with a plan for the development of components with deadlines.

A list of TBD (to be determined) items may be included, covering areas that have not yet been decided, or that may change during the development. These are important as they may not appear in the actual requirements at this stage, but the client needs to know that they are included and will be addressed.

2.2 Design phase

The design phase starts when the requirements specification is complete and the client has agreed to any decisions made.

Outline solutions

The outline should build on the requirements specification.

Hardware and software

The hardware and software from the requirements should be reviewed and adjusted, if needed, before being restated with any amendments. Both of these may be presented as minimum specifications.

Functional and non-functional details

These, again, should be taken from the requirements (refer back to Tables 9.1 and 9.2) but may be amended or added to. For example, as the product is designed, more detail may be added to the processes or they may need editing to take into account unforeseen elements.

Data that is to be input into the product needs to be identified, along with its type and size (e.g. is it numeric or text based?). The input design may also involve a design of the interface, what it will look like and how it will work; for example, for a software product the graphical user interface may be designed to show how data will be entered.

Outputs will be designed in terms of hardware and software; the components that will be used as well as the design of any on-screen, or physical (e.g. reports) outputs.

KEY TERM

Appendix – a section at the end of a document with additional material that should be referred to within the document.

PAIRS ACTIVITY

(10 minutes)

Use the internet to find two examples of requirements specifications, one for software development and one for a computer system development. Compare the documents with each other, and the sections in this chapter. What are the similarities and differences?

PAIRS ACTIVITY

(5 minutes)

If you were the client requesting the VLE from the Getting started task to be created by a product developer, what would you like the designers to show you before they start developing it?

The input and output designs may be presented to the client as a prototype, with or without functionality, to allow them to see the designs as they will appear in the end product and provide feedback.

The processes are the steps that the product performs (and will usually include the functional and non-functional requirements), for example how the output is produced from the input. This can include a range of diagrams to show how they work.

A flow chart shows the steps involved in the processes, and can work with data and programming algorithms. Figure 9.4 shows a simple example of a flow chart checking a valid date of birth has been entered.

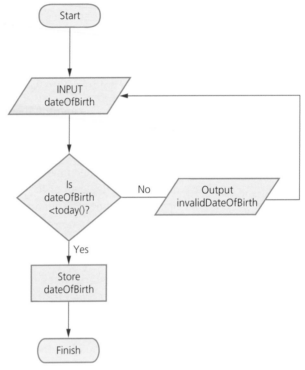

▲ **Figure 9.4** Example flow chart

A structure diagram may be used to show how the product will be split into modules and what each module is made up of. Figure 9.5 shows an example of a structure chart checking a username and password.

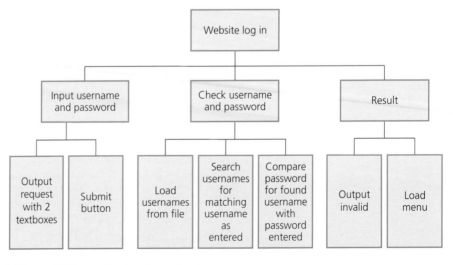

▲ **Figure 9.5** Example structure chart

A data flow diagram may be used to show how data moves through the system, from the inputs to the outputs. It can also be used to show the people involved in the system and how they interact with it. Data flow diagrams can be drawn at multiple levels, for example from an overview of the entire system, to one aspect. Figure 9.6 shows an example data flow diagram at a low level, checking the username and password.

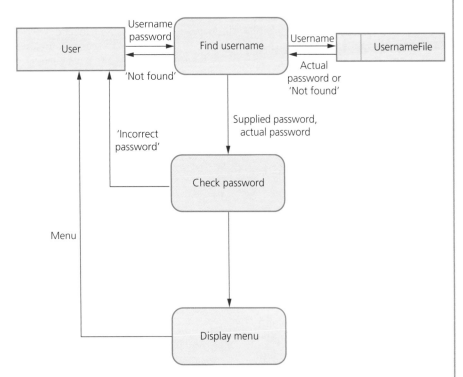

▲ **Figure 9.6** Example data flow diagram

Prototypes may be developed, or those created for the requirements specification may be built upon, depending on the lifecycle followed.

A test plan is part of the design process and will be produced to identify how the product will be tested during its creation and after. This will need to include the inputs, processes and outputs. There are a range of test strategies that will need to be considered for implementation, as well as the client's involvement. A test plan will identify what is being input, or what action is being performed, and identify what the expected outcome is. This test plan needs to cover all functional, and non-functional requirements, and test normal use, extreme or boundaries, and erroneous or invalid.

Table 9.3 shows an example test plan. A few example tests have been completed, for testing a 'log in' feature in a system.

Table 9.3 An example test plan

Test no	Feature tested	Input	Test type	Expected output	Actual output	Resolution	Re-test no
1	Logging on with correct username and password	Username: frank1 Password: he982Jhd	Normal	Main menu loads	Main menu loaded	N/A	N/A
2	Logging on with incorrect username	Username: jane Password: lkoip	Erroneous/Invalid	Error message: 'Invalid username or password, please try again'	Main menu loaded	Check validation rules to prevent incorrect username being entered	6
3	Logging on with correct username, but incorrect password	Username: frank1 Password: hh982Jhd	Erroneous/Invalid	Error message: 'Invalid username or password, please try again'	Main menu loaded	Check validation rules for password to ensure that case sensitivity is required	7

PAIRS ACTIVITY

(15 minutes)

Discuss the differences between the requirements specification and outline solution in the design stage. Consider what changes may need to be made to the outline solution to meet the requirements specification. Why might these be needed and when might they be identified?

Presentation of outline solutions to the client

The outline solutions need to be presented to the client before the final design is determined. This can be done through a physical or virtual meeting. The method of presentation will depend on the type of meeting and the product. It may be a formal presentation, or the documentation may be provided and discussed, or it could be a practical demonstration using prototypes. This meeting will give the client the opportunity to assess the completeness of the design, and highlight any amendments or additions needed.

This presentation to the client may take place multiple times; for example, if they highlight areas that are missing and other issues that have not been previously identified. The product developer can adapt the design before presenting the new design. This can be an iterative process until the client is satisfied.

CLASSROOM DISCUSSION

(30 minutes)

Consider how you will present your design ideas for the product you are creating. Will you use a face-to-face meeting, a virtual meeting, or another method? Will you use a combination?

How will you present your designs? Think carefully about the context of both your product, and the meeting you are going to use.

Present your ideas and ask for feedback. Do others have other ideas that can help you?

Any points made by the clients, and decisions that are made, need to be recorded to ensure that there is a record kept, and any actions that are needed (e.g. to redesign an element) are recorded with deadlines for their completion.

The client may need to make decisions about the functionality (both additions and removals) and the minimum viable product. For example, the cost to create all functions may be too large, and therefore the client may agree to remove some of the requirements. The product developer should have produced several different designs for the client to choose between. The client might request extended features of functionality from the product that were not included in the original requirements specification.

CLASSROOM DISCUSSION AND INDIVIDUAL ACTIVITY

(15 minutes)

Discuss how you will record the changes the client may want.

Then individually produce a document that includes the key elements and questions that you have all decided should be included. Set it out as a document that can be completed and used when you are presenting your design to your client.

Final design solution

When the product developer has completed the list of actions, and the client has agreed that they are happy with the design, the final design solution is produced. The precise elements included will differ according to the product.

The implementation plan will provide a list of the steps or actions that will take place during the creation of the system and the deadlines for each section. This may be produced as a Gantt chart (see Figure 8.4 on page xxx) or a PERT chart.

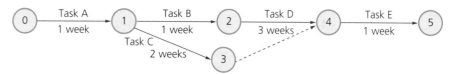

▲ **Figure 9.7** Example PERT chart

The PERT chart in Figure 9.7 shows the same tasks as in the Gantt Chart. The PERT chart shows the movement between each task to key points (numbered 0 to 5). The dashed line is a dummy task, i.e. Task E cannot start until point 3 has also been reached.

From these diagrams, the critical path can be obtained. This is the key sequence of tasks which provides the total estimated length of the time the development will take. In the case of Figure 9.7, it will be Task A, Task B, Task D and Task E – giving a total of six weeks. Task C is not included as it can be carried out alongside Tasks B and D, so it should not impact the total length.

Other items to be identified or produced include:

- Hardware and software minimum specifications, along with any adaptations needed to current models or additional equipment required, e.g. upgrades to existing software to ensure compatibility.
- Additional resources, which may be hardware or software, but also human resources (e.g. employees to run, maintain, or manage the new system).
- Adapted functional requirements and non-functional details based on those developed in the requirements analysis need to be listed, ensuring they cover all elements of the system and the proposed enhancements from the client.
- The design documentation that the client has agreed, including all input, process and output designs, e.g. algorithmic diagrams and interface designs.
- Different user profiles, listing all types of user and their requirements.
- A proposed acceptance test plan identifying how the functional and non-functional requirements will be tested by the client and end-user(s) at the end of the project. The plan can take a variety of forms, e.g. a table or list, but it needs to cover all agreed requirements. This is a separate test plan to those produced previously.

Table 9.4 shows an example of the content of this test plan, with the requirement on the left-hand side, and an area for the client and/or end user(s) to add comments and to identify areas for improvement. This is a different test plan from the one you create when you test the functionality of the system yourself.

Table 9.4 An example of part of an acceptance test plan

Test	Passed (Y/N)	Comments
Allow a user to set up a new account		
Let a user log in with a valid username and password		

LO2 Assessment activities

Below are two suggested assessment activities that have been directly linked to the pass and merit criteria in LO2 to help with assignment preparation; they include Top tips on how to achieve best results.

Computer Sales is a small independent electronics retailer with three shops and a large online business, selling a range of computers and electrical equipment. They would like to expand their online sales by producing an app for customers to browse products, make purchases and track their orders.

Activity 1 – pass criteria *P2*

Produce a product requirements specification for Computer Sales' app. Work in pairs or small groups to practise interviewing each other, with one person acting as the company's manager, the other the interviewer.

Activity 2 – pass criteria *P3* and merit criteria *M2*

Produce your design documentation for your outline solutions and present it to the person you interviewed. Produce a client feedback form and complete record your 'client's' comments and feedback on it.

Based on the feedback, identify and agree the features you could add to extend or enhance the functionality of your design.

LO3 Be able to implement and test products
P4 P5 M3

GETTING STARTED

(5 minutes)

As a large group, discuss why it is important to test a product. What could happen if the product is not thoroughly tested before being given to, or installed for, the client?

3.1 Implementation

The implementation involves the actual creation of the product.

Unit testing

Unit testing needs to be carried out during the implementation. Although you will tend to test each function as you develop the product, you need to record these tests as part of your log. For example, if you are building a web page, you may test how it functions after you have added some JavaScript code. This is a unit test. The evidence can come from a screenshot, photo or video, depending on your product. A completed test table contains the tests and evidence.

Integration testing

Once several sections of your product have passed unit testing, you need to combine them into one sub-system. For example, if you are building a website with multiple pages, they will need joining together before carrying out **integration** testing. This tests that, once joined, the units are still working correctly. Again, this needs evidencing in your log. Figure 9.8 shows how these units can be combined into sub-systems, and the sub-systems are combined into the system.

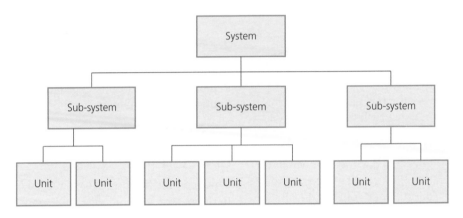

▲ **Figure 9.8** Testing structure

Product testing

Once the final solution has been developed, it will need thorough testing to ensure that the sub-systems have been joined together successfully, and that it covers all of the original requirements. Although these tests may have been planned in the design stage, they will need revisiting and revising to cover any changes made during the implementation.

Table 9.5 is one example of a completed test table, where the first test did not work as planned, but the second did. The evidence, in this case, is linked too – this could be in any appropriate form (screenshot, photo, video etc).

Table 9.5 An example of a completed test table

Test number	Test data/action	Expected result	Result	Evidence/ evidence location
1a	Entering valid username and password	Menu is displayed	Error message appears	1.1
1b	Entering invalid username and password	Error message appears	Error message appears	1.2

The developer finally needs to test the product against the functional and non-functional requirements to ensure that it meets the original requirements.

Using results of unit testing and integration testing to improve or enhance the product during implementation

While creating and testing your solution, you are likely to come across problems or errors. This is to be expected. Errors are recorded in the implementation log, and as you correct them and re-test, the results showing the corrections need adding. This demonstrates that you are improving the solution during the development.

Upon completion of testing (i.e. when the product is working), the results need to be analysed. This involves a discussion of the testing, identifying the positive areas you found, for example one element of the product may perform better than expected, or you may have succeeded in meeting a set of the requirements. Areas of weakness need to be identified, along with any improvements that could be made and any **enhancements**.

An improvement involves building upon what you have already produced, e.g. you could make a product more user friendly, or more efficient, or a process could be made shorter for the user.

An enhancement involves adding something extra to the product. This is something that you may not have identified in the design specification, but would be beneficial to add.

Both the improvements and enhancements need to be described in the context of the product, and justified to show how they would improve or enhance the product, explaining what benefit this would be to the client.

Implementation log

While building the solution, you will need to produce an implementation log to record the steps you took when creating the product. It can be completed as a table, an annotated copy of the implementation plan, a diary, or any method that is appropriate for your product, for example it might involve taking photos and videos of the activities.

GROUP AND INDEPENDENT ACTIVITY

(30 minutes)

As a group, discuss different approaches to the implementation log. What needs to be included and how can this be presented?

Individually, create your own implementation log ready for producing your solution.

Revisit the implementation plan

The final design solution required you to create an implementation plan which could be presented as a Gantt or PERT chart. This should be revisited and updated during the implementation stage to include any changes that need to be or have been made. This is especially important with respect to deadlines for completion, as any delay can have an effect on any of the other deadlines.

> ### KEY TERM
> **Enhancement** – a change or addition that improves the product.

When developing your product, you do not need to make improvements or enhancements unless you are sure they meet the client's requirements; for example, tests that stop the product working will need correcting as part of the implementation process to ensure you have a working product. You do, however, have to consider these improvements and enhancements and present your ideas to the client.

KNOW IT

1 Identify two types of testing that need to be carried out.
2 Explain the difference between an improvement and an enhancement.
3 What needs to be filled in and completed throughout the development of your product?
4 Why would you need to produce an implementation log?
5 Explain the purpose and need for Gantt and PERT charts.

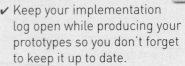
LO3 Assessment activities

Below are two suggested assessment activities that have been directly linked to the pass and merit criteria in LO3 to help with assignment preparation; they include Top Tips on how to achieve best results.

Activity 1 – pass criteria *P4*

Produce a prototype for Computer Sales' App. You will need to keep evidence of your implementation log that includes the unit and integration testing you perform during the development.

Activity 2 – pass criteria *P5* and merit criteria *M3*

Create a test table for your product, including a range of tests which will confirm that the final product meets the design specification. Complete this by testing your completed product against it, producing evidence of the outcomes. Produce a written document, summarising your testing results, discuss any problems that arose and describe some improvements or enhancements that you think could be made to this completed product.

GETTING STARTED

(5 minutes)

Discuss in pairs the difference between testing by the product developer, and testing by the end users and client. Why is it important to have both?

LO4 Be able to carry out acceptance testing with clients *P6 D2*

Acceptance testing is completed against the functional and non-functional requirements listed in the design specification, and the testing by the client and/or the end user.

4.1 Acceptance testing with target users

Acceptance testing against the agreed design specification

The acceptance test plan in the final design solution will need to be revisited before the testing is undertaken, in case of changes that occurred during the development. This must include the functional and non-functional requirements as individual tests.

Acceptance testing with target users

In the design stage the different user profiles will have been identified. A target user from each of these profiles will need to carry out the testing, to ensure it meets all of the different users' requirements. A minimum of three users must take part in the acceptance testing.

The plan should offer the users the opportunity to feedback comments, positive and negative, within their testing. An example of part of a completed acceptance test table is shown in Table 9.6.

Table 9.6 An example of a completed acceptance test table

Test	Passed (Y/N)	Comments
Allow a user to set up a new account	Y	New account set up easily. Suitable data saved for the account.
Let a user log in with a valid username and password	N	I tried to log in with the account I just made, but it told me I had an invalid username.

Deployment decision by client

When acceptance testing is complete, the client will be required to make a decision regarding the deployment of the product. They could decide on:

- Acceptance. The product meets all, or the majority of, the important requirements, and the client agrees to its deployment.
- Non-acceptance. The product does not meet some, or all, of the requirements and the client decides that it cannot be deployed. The project stops at this point.
- Acceptance after modifications and re-test. The product does not meet some, or all, of the requirements. The client, however, is happy for the product to undergo further work to correct the problems. The product developer will need to amend the product, and re-test it, before presenting it for acceptance testing again.

The decision needs to be confirmed in writing and agreed by the client. If the decision is for deployment, then the product manager and client need to complete and sign a handover document. This will state the date and location of deployment, and give a description of the product agreed on, and how it is being delivered (e.g. it will be delivered the following working day, or it was provided on a memory stick at the meeting).

GROUP AND INDEPENDENT ACTIVITY

(30 minutes)

In groups, find examples of handover documents for the types of projects described in this unit and compare their contents and structure. Discuss your group's findings with the other groups and identify common features.

Individually create a handover document for use with your product, using the features the groups identified.

4.2 Maintenance phase

After the implementation of a product, maintenance is required.

Routine maintenance

Routine maintenance involves the general upkeep of the product (e.g. backing up and archiving files, cleaning and aligning components, etc.) on a regular basis. This could, for example, take place weekly, monthly, quarterly or annually, depending on the situation and agreement by the client.

These activities will need to be identified at the point of deployment, and agreed to by the client.

Enhancements to product features and functions

Enhancement maintenance activities are changes to the features and functions in the product. These may arise from the discovery of an error, or bug, in the product by the client that requires correction. It may have been discovered, through the use of the system, that some changes are needed to how the product works; for example, the data to be input.

Product upgrades

An upgrade will provide additional functionality to the product. The client's organisation may have changed slightly, and the system requires adaptation to incorporate the new requirements.

You will need to identify and discuss required maintenance for the product: routine maintenance, enhancements and product upgrades.

After discussing it with the client, the decision will need to be recorded, along with justification for each decision. This could be made during the handover meeting, or through a separate face-to-face meeting, online meeting, or email discussion.

You will need to provide evidence of agreeing the maintenance with the client, but you are not required to implement these changes.

 RESEARCH ACTIVITY

Failed products and projects of all types are often reported in the news and online. Find and read some of these stories. Look at the reasons given for their failure and consider what part or parts of the development process were probably not followed.

Read the 1993 IEEE standard for software maintenance:

tinyurl.com/jptzb7x

Don't create more work for yourself. The possible enhancements should come through your discussions with your client, not your own ideas. Make use of their knowledge of the organisation and requirements of the product.

KNOW IT

1 Describe how acceptance testing differs from unit and sub-system testing.
2 Who carries out the acceptance testing?
3 Explain the importance of acceptance testing.
4 Identify the three types of maintenance.
5 Explain why maintenance requires planning.

LO4 Assessment activities

Below are two suggested assessment activities that have been directly linked to the pass and distinction criteria in LO4 to help with assignment preparation; they include Top tips on how to achieve best results.

Activity 1 – pass criteria *P6*

Produce an acceptance plan test that covers all of the functional and non-functional requirements.

Ask the person who acted as your client for LO2 to test the product and complete the acceptance test plan.

Activity 2 – distinction criteria *D2*

Produce a product handover document.

Discuss the potential enhancements you identified after testing, the results of their acceptance testing and the possibility of upgrades and maintenance with the person acting as your client.

Complete the product handover document with your 'client'.

TOP TIPS

✔ Make sure your acceptance test plan covers all of the requirements your client gave you.
✔ Discuss the product with the client whilst they are testing it – do not leave them to test it alone in case they raise points or ask questions that you need to answer.
✔ Complete your product handover document on the computer to ensure there is sufficient space for their points, then print it and sign it by hand.

Unit **11**

Systems analysis and design

ABOUT THIS UNIT

Information systems are used in all types of business and organisation; for example, a shop will use an information system to allow orders to take place, to report on sales, check stock levels, etc. These systems need to provide useful, reliable and validated data through a combination of hardware, software and humans that work together in processes that help the organisation to meets its internal goals and external obligations. In this unit you will learn about the analysis and design stages involved in the development of an information system, and develop the skills to analyse the requirements of, and design, an information system.

You will learn about the different types of lifecycle that can be followed, as well as the components that make up these lifecycles. You will investigate the requirements of a business, determining which investigative techniques are most appropriate for the scenario. Using the three view approach you will design a model for the business system and use UML diagrams to produce designs for the objects and processes. Finally, you will produce a logical and physical design for the information system, before presenting this to a range of stakeholders involved in the system. This will allow you to analyse their feedback and adjust the designs to meet their requirements.

How will I be assessed?

You will be assessed by producing evidence from set scenarios or from work that you carry out as part of a work placement of employment, as well as through assignments and tasks set and marked by your tutor.

LEARNING OUTCOMES

The topics, activities and suggested reading in this unit will help you to:

1 Understand the role of the systems analysis and design in relation to the systems development lifecycle.
2 Be able to use investigative techniques to establish requirements for business systems.
3 Be able to develop and document models for business systems.
4 Be able to create logical and physical designs for specified business systems.

How will I be graded?

You will be graded using the following criteria:

Learning outcome	Pass assessment criteria	Merit assessment criteria	Distinction assessment criteria
You will:	To achieve a pass you must demonstrate that you have met all the pass assessment criteria	To achieve a merit you must demonstrate that you have met all the pass and merit assessment criteria	To achieve a distinction you must demonstrate that you have met all the pass, merit and distinction assessment criteria
1 Understand the role of systems analysis and design in relation to the systems development lifecycle	**P1** Summarise the main components of the systems development lifecycle	**M1** Compare and contrast a range of systems development lifecycles	
2 Be able to use investigative techniques to establish requirements for business systems	**P2** Explore the business requirements for an identified business system		
	P3 Use different techniques to support the analysis of the identified business system		
3 Be able to develop and document models for business systems	**P4** Use the three view approach to document the design model for the identified business system	**M2** Develop a set of Unified Modelling Language (UML) diagrams for the identified business system	**D1** Evaluate the design model for the identified business system against original business requirements
4 Be able to create logical and physical designs for specific business systems	**P5** Create a logical design for the identified business system	**M3** Present the logical and physical designs for the identified business system to relevant stakeholders	**D2** Refine the logical and physical designs for the identified business system incorporating any stakeholder feedback
	P6 Create a physical design for the identified business system		

LO1 Understand the role of systems analysis and design in relation to the systems development lifecycle *P1 M2*

GETTING STARTED

(5 minutes)

Discuss what is meant by a lifecycle. Discuss different applications of the terms, such as in biology or geology. Discuss what it specifically means in systems development.

1.1 The components of the systems development lifecycle

A range of different systems development lifecycles can be used to create an information system. Within each are a number of phases that may be used formally and/or informally. These phases are also described in Unit 6 LO1 and Unit 9 LO1.

Feasibility study

The feasibility study determines if it is possible to create a system. The feasibility study is also covered in depth in Unit 8 LO2 (page 231).

Financial aspects

The analysis needs to assess if it is financially possible to produce the information system, especially as the client is likely to have a limit on what they can spend. This may involve carrying out a cost/benefit analysis, where the strengths and benefits of producing the system are compared to the costs, to determine whether or not the benefits make the financial cost worthwhile.

Business aspects

The potential positive and negative impact on the business needs to be analysed. This could include looking at the operational impact; for example, on the environment and the people who will be affected and whether the information system can work within the organisation.

This may also require an assessment of the resources within the organisation, human and technological. Will the information system require new staff, new equipment, or new structures and, if so, are these possible to implement successfully?

Technical aspects

The technological requirements of the new information systems need to be assessed and compared with what currently exists both within the business and externally to produce the new system. It may be that the business will need to upgrade, or change their systems; if so, consider if this is possible within the financial constraints.

Outcomes

The client's constraints are the restrictions imposed by the client, environment or externally. Constraints are covered in more detail in Unit 6 (see LO1.2) and 9 (see LO2.2). It needs to be determined whether the information system can be developed successfully within these constraints.

Requirements engineering (i.e. business and user)

When an information system has been determined to be feasible, the requirements need to be gathered and agreed by the business and potential end users. Requirements analysis is also covered in LO2 of this unit, Unit 6 (see LO2) and Unit 9 (see LO2.1).

Requirements gathering

The business needs investigating to identify how the information and processes are currently gathered and performed, and what the client and end users require of the new system. This investigation will need to find from the users what is needed, as well as any concerns that they have about how the new system will work, or how it will impact them and their work. Unit 6 LO2 has further detail on methods of collecting this information.

The functional and non-functional requirements need to be identified and agreed with the client. These are covered in more detail in Units 6 (see LO2.2, page 171) and 9 (see LO2.1, page 252). They determine if the system can be developed, and if it is possible to meet the requirements of the client. This may include identifying the essential elements of a minimal viable product, and some of the requirements are put aside as not feasible within the constraints.

Requirements analysis

When the relevant information about the requirements has been gathered, it needs to be analysed. This process will assess the information and determine the final requirements that will be presented to the end user. The requirements may not cover all elements that were investigated as they may not be achievable within constraints such as time, or financial costs.

The final set of functional, and non-functional requirements need to be:

- Sensible: appropriate to the situation and manageable.
- Achievable: feasible, valid and able to be met within any identified constraints.
- Affordable: their completion must be possible within the financial constraints.

The requirements should identify those that are essential, and those that are requested but may not be possible. There should also be a minimum viable product, which identifies what can be done within the constraints, but also identifies what has been left out and why. This often provides the client with the opportunity to add features or to compromise on a final set of agreed requirements.

See also Unit 9 (see LO2.1, page 252).

Requirements sign off

The requirements are usually presented to the client as part of the requirements analysis documentation. This is likely to be a presentation or a discussion of the findings from the investigation, and the list of functional and non-functional requirements. There may be changes needed based on the discussions with the client. Once any changes have been agreed, and both the analyst and the client are satisfied, the requirements are signed by both parties as an agreement of what will be produced.

Requirements monitoring

A plan, or structure, should be in place to monitor the agreed requirements throughout the development lifecycle of the information system. Many people may be involved in designing, developing and implementing the system, and the requirements, or perceived requirements, can change if requirements are not monitored.

System design including virtualisation

Once the requirements analysis has been agreed with the client, the information system can be designed. The design is also covered in LO3 and LO4 of this unit, as well as Units 6 LO3 and 9 LO2.

In the design phase, the processes, inputs, outputs and data will be identified and designed. These can include a range of diagrammatic designs such as data flow diagrams.

When designing an information system, it is beneficial to virtualise the solution. This involves considering the data, processes and functions of the solution and determining what data it will need to handle, and how it will handle this. Through virtualisation, consideration can be given to:

- The capacity: how much data will the system need to store?

- The performance: how fast will the system need to respond? When does the system need to be operating? Is it 24 hours a day or just between 9 am and 5 pm?
- The throughput: How many transactions will it need to deal with per second? Minute? Day? How many inputs, or consecutive inputs, will it need to handle?

CLASSROOM DISCUSSION

(10 minutes)

A business uses e-commerce to sell clothing. Their information system needs to store customers, orders, stock, etc. and generate reports on sales.

Discuss the capacity, performance and throughput that this information system may require.

The completed design is presented to the client and any changes are discussed before the information system can begin development.

Software development

When the client has agreed to the design, the solution can be created. The agreed design and the functional and non-functional requirements are followed during the development. Software development is also covered in Unit 9 LO3.

Testing of the software

During the development of the software, and when the software is complete, testing takes place. This can use a variety of methods, such as unit testing, integration testing, etc. (see Unit 9 LO3.1).

Testing ensures that all elements of the software function correctly in a range of circumstances, such as with normal, borderline and invalid data.

Systems testing

When software has passed its testing, it is tested against the functional and non-functional requirements set out in the requirements analysis to ensure it meets these agreed requirements. System testing is described in Unit 9 LO3 and 4.

Next, it is tested with, or by, the target users as part of the acceptance testing. The client can suggest amendments or accept the software for implementation. This process is described in Unit 9 LO4.1 (page 264).

Implementation

Upon completion of testing, and acceptance by the client, the product can be implemented or installed in the business environment. The method of implementation will vary depending on the environment but could include:

- Pilot: the system is implemented in one element, section or part of the business, for example sales. It is thoroughly tested here and any problems corrected, before it is implemented in a second area.
- Phased: part of the system is implemented throughout the business, for example the storage of data may be implemented first. When this is

PAIRS ACTIVITY

(20 minutes)

Investigate the four different methods of implementation. Find and list the benefits and drawbacks of each method.

successful and problems have been corrected, a second part of the system is implanted.

- Direct: the whole system is implemented in every part of the business at the same time.
- Parallel: the new system is implemented alongside the old one until any problems have been removed.

These methods can be combined; for example, a phased implementation can use parallel implementation.

INDEPENDENT ACTIVITY

(10 minutes)

Create an A5 booklet to explain the different components of the systems development lifecycle.

1.2 Lifecycles

The components of the system's development lifecycle can be followed in a variety of different lifecycles; where they may be combined, some may not be explicitly followed or followed in different order. These are grouped into three different types: linear, evolutionary and agile. Lifecycles are described in detail in Unit 9 LO1.1 (page 244).

Linear

> **KEY TERM**
>
> **Linear development** – developers follow a series of stages to create a system, moving through the stages one at a time, in a set order.

A **linear development** lifecycle follows stages in a series of steps, moving through the stages one at a step, in a set order. Examples are described below but you may want to research alternatives.

Waterfall model

In the waterfall model, the stages are followed in order, but there is an allowance to move back to the previous stage if needed. This can be repeated, back through as many stages as required. Once the developer is ready to continue, the phases are followed in order again. The waterfall model is described in more detail in Unit 9 LO1.1 (page 245).

V model

The V model separates the stages of the system development lifecycle into verification and validation phases (see Figure 11.1).

The testing strategies (validation phases) on the right hand are aligned with the verification phases on the left. This model identifies when each part of the lifecycle is tested, e.g. the detailed designs are tested as part of the unit testing and the overview of the design is tested in the integration testing.

Incremental

The incremental lifecycle is an iterative process, where the project is split into smaller sections. The lifecycle phases are used in the development of one of these modules. This is followed for additional modules which are combined. The incremental lifecycle is described in more detail in Unit 9 LO1.1 (page 245).

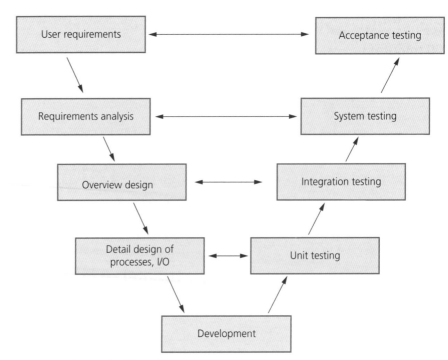

▲ **Figure 11.1** V model lifecycle

Evolutionary

Evolutionary development builds upon what has been created previously. It is an iterative process (it repeats) until a final solution is developed. A number of evolutionary lifecycles are described below; there are other alternatives that you may want to research.

Iterative

One part of the system is worked on, following the lifecycle stages. The stages are repeated with additional elements added in each repeated cycle. The iterative lifecycle is described in more detail in Unit 6 LO1.2 (page 167).

Spiral

Prototypes are worked on through each cycle of the stages. The spiral model is described in more detail in Unit 9 LO1.1 (page 245).

Agile

Business systems are worked on, changed and improved in an iterative process that does not follow designated lifecycle stages, but adapts to the situation. A number of agile lifecycles are described below; you may want to research others.

Scrum

Required actions or features are listed by priority and grouped into sections to be implemented with milestones identified. This list is known as the product backlog.

The development of each phase is called a sprint, taking a maximum of one month each.

During the sprint there is a daily meeting (the scrum) that allows developers to discuss what was achieved the previous day, what is to be done next and any changes that are needed.

KEY TERM

Evolutionary development – developing a system by building upon and expanding it, such as through the use of prototypes.

At the end of a sprint is an evaluation and either a new sprint begins, or software is developed for external testing.

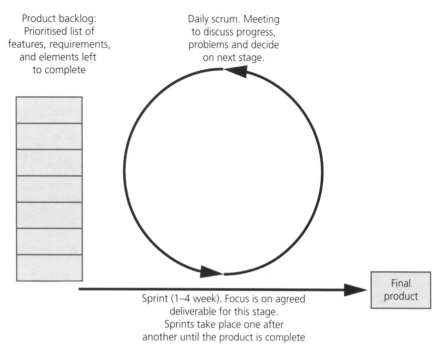

▲ **Figure 11.2** Scrum model

Agile unified process

This agile lifecycle uses modelling and test-driven development to produce the system. It follows four phases:

- Inception – this equates to the requirements analysis phase but extends to look at an initial design for the system.
- Elaboration – developers work on producing the foundations of the system.
- Construction – developers work on developing the software.
- Transition – the system is tested and implemented in the environment.

The software is developed as models – smaller versions that build upon the previous ones and that are implemented in stages. The whole system may take months to produce, but elements will be implemented throughout the process.

INDEPENDENT AND GROUP ACTIVITY

(30 minutes)

Independently, create a table, such as Table 11.1, and add each of the different lifecycles, completing the table to identify the benefits, drawbacks and scenarios where each one would be most beneficial.

Table 11.1 Lifecycles

Type of lifecycle	Lifecycle name	Description	Advantages	Disadvantages	Scenarios
Linear	Waterfall				
Linear	V model				

Work as a group, share your tables and add content to your own that you find you are missing.

1 Identify three different stages of the systems development lifecycle.
2 Describe what is involved in the system design stage of the lifecycle.
3 Explain the difference between systems testing and acceptance testing.
4 Identify two different linear lifecycles.
5 Compare the linear and evolutionary type of lifecycle.

LO1 Assessment activities

Below are two suggested assessment activities that have been directly linked to the pass and merit criteria in LO1 to help with assignment preparation; they include Top tips on how to achieve the best results

Activity 1 – pass criteria *P1*

Create a presentation that identifies and describes the main elements of the systems development lifecycle. Describe how the different elements are linked, i.e. how the information gathered and produced in one stage feeds into the next. Add speaker notes to explain the points in your presentation.

Activity 2 – merit criteria *M1*

Add to your presentation a description of a range of system development lifecycles. This must include at least **three** different lifecycles, one from each type (linear, evolutionary and agile).

Compare and contrast the lifecycles in a table and identify a situation where each could be used. Attach this as a link to your presentation. Add speaker notes to explain the points in your presentation.

TOP TIPS ✔

✔ Keep the number of bullet points in your presentation minimal; use speaker notes to add the detail.
✔ Make sure you have chosen a lifecycle from each of the three different types.
✔ Compare and contrast means identifying the similarities as well as the differences.
✔ Use images, diagrams and tables in your presentation to help explain your points.

LO2 Be able to use investigative techniques to establish requirements for business systems *P2 P3*

GETTING STARTED 👤

(5 minutes)

Have you ever been interviewed? Or filled in a questionnaire?

Discuss what this experience was like. What sort of questions were asked? Was the questionnaire easy to use? Did you have to give single word answers or give detailed responses?

2.1 Business requirements

When investigating a business in preparation for developing an information system, you need to explore a number of key areas.

Business systems

All businesses use a range of systems that may be entirely independent (they act on their own), may feed into other systems (data is transferred between systems) or may be combined (different areas use what looks like their own system but these elements are all parts of one central system). For example, a human resources system stores details of staff, and another system is used for finance. The details about the staff, such as their hours and wages, may be exported from the human resources system to the finance system.

Businesses have their own solutions, and they may be very different in both need and expectation. All systems that the business you are investigating use need exploring to determine how the system you are producing will interact with them.

Business analysis processes and models

A business will have a series of models, and/or processes in place that already perform tasks. They should include the following.

- The people involved in the processes.
- The data to be input (where this comes from, and by what means).
- The actions that are performed.
- The output (the format, content, where this goes).

By gathering the information, and/or investigating the systems currently used, the business tasks performed can be identified and described.

Identify business requirements

Functional and non-functional requirements need to be gathered, by analysing the results of the investigations. These should identify what the system needs to do to meet these requirements. Requirements are covered in detail in Unit 9 LO2.1 (page 252) and Unit 6 LO2.2 (page 171).

Deliverables from business analysis

The **deliverable** from business analysis for an information system should be a description of the system to be developed that has arisen from the investigation and the requirements identified.

KEY WORDS

Deliverable: the agreed product, products or features that are to be developed for the client.

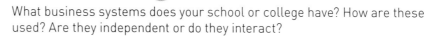

GROUP ACTIVITY

What business systems does your school or college have? How are these used? Are they independent or do they interact?

Investigate the different systems by talking to the people who use them (you may not be allowed to view them due to confidentiality).

2.2 Techniques

A range of methods can be used to investigate the business and its systems. Several of these are also described in Unit 6 LO2.1 (page 169).

Interviewing stakeholders

In this case, a stakeholder is any person with an interest in the business system being investigated, or a representative of an organisation. This will be all types of end user – all of the people, or roles, who interact with or depend on the system.

An interview is usually face to face or by telephone, often on a one-to-one basis. This allows the interviewer (the investigator) to ask specific, planned questions to gather the information they need. Interviews and different types of questioning techniques are described in more detail in Unit 6 LO2.1 (page 169).

Conducting workshops

A workshop is an environment where a group of people, perhaps from different roles within the business, work together to perform actions and develop ideas. The selection of these people needs to be carefully considered, so a range of stakeholders with different needs work together.

It may, for example, be used to develop ideas for what they would like from a system. A facilitator provides the tasks and leads the group.

When conducting a workshop, the goals (or objectives) need to be clearly defined, identifying what the participants are there to achieve or develop. The activities need to be planned to allow the participants to work towards this goal.

Observing worker activities

To see how a business works, and how people and systems interact, you can observe specific actions or activities by workers. You will be able to make notes, take photos and collect documentation to explain how the activities are performed. For example, the worker(s) who produce the payroll for an organisation may be observed while performing this task, so when it is implemented in the new system, the process will be complete and any problems observed can be minimised or resolved.

The observation of activities is also discussed in Unit 6 LO2.1 (page 170).

Shadowing workers

Shadowing specific workers will allow you to gain an insight into who and which systems they interact with and what these interactions involve. This differs from observing the activities, as it may involve shadowing them over a several hours or days, recording all activities that they take part in, rather than focusing on one activity. For example, a worker within the finance department may be shadowed for a day, looking at what and who they interact with, what systems they use, the data they enter, what happens to this, etc.

Preparing and distributing questionnaires and surveys to stakeholders

A questionnaire can be conducted on paper or via a computer. You may use this alongside other methods where there are a large number of stakeholders and/or end users and the results collected and compared. For example, it would not be feasible to engage all employees of a large business in interviews, workshops or to shadow them. Instead, a small number are gathered to take part in these methods of collection, but the remainder can still be consulted through a questionnaire. However, a questionnaire offers little interaction with the stakeholders, so answers cannot be necessarily expanded or clarification gathered.

Analysing current documents

The information system, whether computer or paper based, will already have documentation in place. This documentation needs to be collected and analysed to determine its purpose, the data that the documentation collects, records or uses. This can be combined with shadowing workers, as documentation can be gathered and combined with the information about where and how they are used, but it is unlikely that all documentation can be collected this way.

The analysis of documents is also discussed in Unit 6 LO2.1 (page 170).

Identifying deliverables

Through combinations of these techniques, the investigators can identify what product(s) and features are required.

INDEPENDENT ACTIVITY

Create your own version of Table 11.2. Add all the different techniques in the first column, then fill in a description for each one. Research the benefits and drawbacks of each method and add these to the table. Consider in what type of scenario each technique would be most appropriate, e.g. questionnaires are suitable when there are a large number of stakeholders. Add these to the table.

Table 11.2 Investigation techniques

Technique	Description	Benefits	Drawbacks	Scenarios
Interview				
Workshop				

KNOW IT

1 Identify three different business systems that may exist within a business.
2 Explain the importance of developing business requirements.
3 Identify four different methods of gathering information.
4 Explain the difference between a workshop and a focus group.
5 Explain why it is important to analyse the business's current documents.

LO2 Assessment activity

Below is a suggested assessment activity that has been directly linked to the pass criteria in LO2 to help with assignment preparation; it includes Top tips on how to achieve the best results.

For this activity, you need to have access to a system that is to be developed. This could be as part of an additional unit; for example, a system you are going to build or a prototype you may be developing. You need to be able to explore this system and the client's business, so make sure you have suitable authority and agreement to do so before beginning.

Activity – pass criteria *P2 P3*

Plan and carry out a study of the business requirements for the system you are investigating. Consider what techniques you are going to use, such as interview, questionnaire, collection of business documents. Make sure you use at least three of the techniques identified in LO2.2.

Carry out your investigation; make sure you have a record of it, for example recordings of interviews, transcripts of discussions, the documentation you have collected, etc.

Write a report to present the findings of your investigation, and include the records you made as an appendix to the report.

TOP TIPS

✔ Plan your interviews, questionnaires etc. carefully. Test them out on someone else before you use them to ensure they make sense and cover everything you need.
✔ Documentation you gather can be annotated to explain its purpose, and what different elements of it are for.
✔ Do not go overboard on your investigation. You need to balance investigating thoroughly with producing so much evidence that you cannot analyse it.
✔ Make sure you identify a range of stakeholders, i.e. all the people who use the system(s) in different ways.

LO3 Be able to develop and document models for business systems *P4 M2 D1*

GETTING STARTED 👤 ....

(5 minutes)

Discuss what is meant by the word 'model', and the action of modelling. How does this relate to business?

3.1 The three view approach

This identifies three areas that need to be considered, and designs produced for, when developing a model for a business system. The views are functionality, static data and events.

Functionality

Functionality identifies the different operations, processes and actions that take place in a system. These need to be planned within the model to demonstrate how the system would perform these actions. Three graphical ways to show this are described below.

Data flow diagrams (DFDs)

A data flow diagram shows how data moves through a system – where it comes from, what is input, what happens to this data, what is output or how it is output and where it is stored within the system.

Figure 11.3 shows the three main symbols used in a data flow diagram. Entities are the external people, or systems, where data is input from or output to. Processes describe the actions to be performed, and the data store is the data storage within the system; for example, a database table, a text file, .csv file, etc. The data flows are shown with arrows moving from one element to another. A DFD is unlikely to explain how the processes take place, how calculations are performed etc.

There are many industry-standard DFD symbols – all are acceptable.

There are different levels of DFD. A level 0 DFD shows the external entities and the system as a process. For example, Figure 11.4 shows an example level 0 diagram for a system being produced to pay wages.

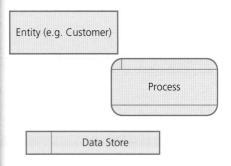

▲ **Figure 11.3** Common data flow diagram symbols

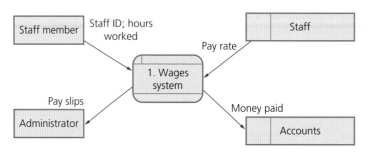

▲ **Figure 11.4** Level 0 DFD

The system is represented by a single process: the wages system. The data stores are shown, along with the external entities (staff member and administrator). Each data flow (arrow) identifies what is being sent through the system at that point.

When producing DFDs it can help to write a list of what happens in a system; for example, in the wages system:

- the employee enters the hours they have worked that week
- the system gets their hourly rate from the staff database
- the system works out how much they should be paid
- the system sends this amount to the accounts database
- the system produces a pay slip
- the pay slip is sent to an administrator
- the administrator sends the pay slip to the correct employee.

The system is not involved in the final action, so this is excluded from the DFD. When you have a complete list, the process in a level 0 DFD is expanded to produce a level 1 DFD (Figure 11.5).

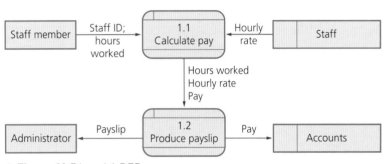

▲ **Figure 11.5** Level 1 DFD

The level 1 DFD has expanded the wages system from the level 0 diagram, and shows more detail about how data moves through the system.

This can be expanded into a level 2 DFD if needed but, in this case, the level 1 diagram clearly shows how all data moves through the system.

Flow charts

A flow chart shows the sequence of actions that take place to perform a process. In this case a flow chart could be used to design the different processes, showing the calculations that are performed and the logic behind the actions. Unit 6, Figure 6.3 (page 176) shows the common symbols that are used to produce flow charts.

The processes can be as specific or unspecific as required, and if needed you can have multiple flow charts at different levels. This all depends on the system you are designing.

Figure 11.6 shows an example flow chart to model how the pay is calculated. This differs from a DFD as it describes how the actions are performed to complete the task.

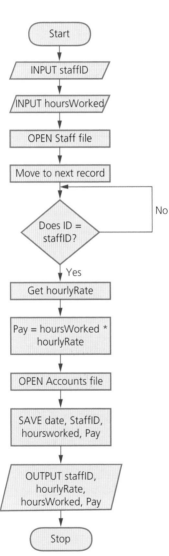

▲ **Figure 11.6** Flow chart for calculating pay

Subroutine – an independent function, or procedure, which performs a singular task. It can be called from the main program, or from another subroutine. It can take values as its input (parameters).

Jackson Structure Chart (JSC)

A Jackson Structure Chart (JSC) shows the different components of a system that allows a structured program to be developed. A structured program is one that is made up of **subroutines** as opposed to a long series of sequential code. A JSC is used to design the structure of the program in terms of subroutines.

Figure 11.10 shows an example four-layer JSC for the wages system. The top box indicates the process that is being shown – the wages system. On the next row down, the wages system can be split into individual processes.

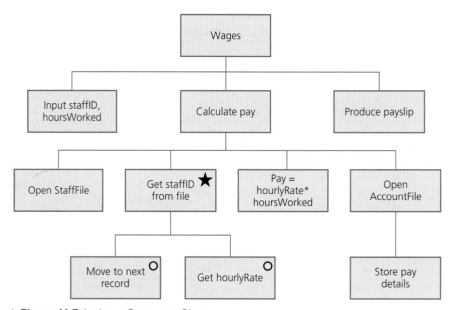

▲ **Figure 11.7** Jackson Structure Chart

The top level is split into Input, Calculate pay and Produce payslip. The first and last, in this case, do not need further detail as they can be written as individual subroutines, but these could also be expanded.

Calculate pay is then expanded. The third level shows the four steps, in sequence, that will be performed in order from left to right. Two of these have also been expanded further.

Get staffID from file has a star in the corner of its box to indicate iteration (repeating the process). This is because the staffID may be accessed many times until the correct one is found.

Below this, are two boxes each with a circle in the corner. The circle indicates selection: one of these will be chosen, but not both. Therefore, when the staffID is retrieved from the file, the program either moves to the next record (and will repeat, get the next staffID and decide what to do) or it will get the hourly rate.

JSCs can go into varying levels of detail depending on what is required; for example, a 2–3 layer JSC is normal.

Static data

Static data identifies the data that is to be stored in the system and how, or where, this is stored. This could refer to tables in databases, text files or any method by which data is stored.

One to one ERD

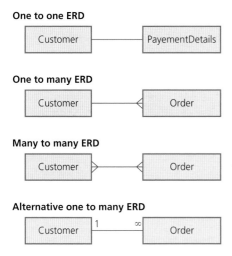

One to many ERD

Many to many ERD

Alternative one to many ERD

▲ **Figure 11.8** Types of ERD

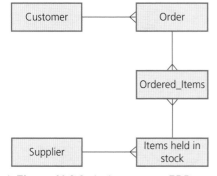

▲ **Figure 11.9** Ordering system ERD

Entity Relationship Diagram (ERD)

An ERD is used to illustrate the relationships between tables in a database. Before creating the diagram, the relationships between the tables need to be identified, for example:

- One to one: each record in both tables refers to one and only record in the other table. For example, a database that stores customers' personal information and their payment details may have two tables to keep the payment details secure: customers, payment. One customer can only have one payment detail, and one payment detail can only be for one customer.
- One to many: one record in Table A can refer to many in Table B, but each record in Table B only refers to one record in Table A. For example, an ordering database may have a table for customers and another for the details of their order. One customer can make many orders, but each order can only relate to one customer.
- Many to many: one record in a table can refer to many in the second table, and one record in the second table can refer to many records in the first table. For example, an ordering database may have a table storing customers and another storing items. One customer can order many items, and one item can be ordered by many people. This relationship is rare because it is removed by normalising a database, but it may be identified at the start of this process before being removed.

When producing an ERD, the tables are each given a rectangle, with lines showing the relationships.

The three types of relationship are shown in Figure 11.8. The '1' side of the relationship is shown as a single line, and the 'many' side of the relationship is shown with two additional lines. There is an alternative way of representing these relationships, as shown in the final example, where a '1' and '∞' are written on the end of the relationship line.

An ERD shows the relationships between multiple tables, in most cases all the tables within a database. An example is shown in Figure 11.9 for an ordering system.

It shows that:

- one customer can have many order details (e.g. the time and date of the order)
- one order details record can have lots of ordered items
- one type of item held in stock can be ordered many times (in the Ordered_Items table)
- one supplier can supply many items.

Hierarchical tree diagram

This diagram shows the system at the top of the diagram, and splits it into the separate data stores (which can be split further if needed).

Figure 11.10 shows a hierarchical tree diagram for the ordering system described earlier.

The ordering system is split into individual tables. In this case, Orders is taken and split further, but these tables could equally be positioned on the first level.

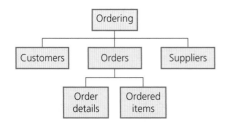

▲ **Figure 11.10** Hierarchical tree ordering system

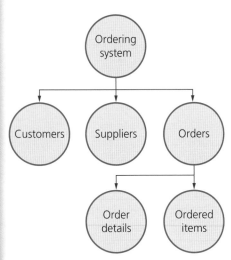

▲ **Figure 11.11** Bubble diagram

Bubble diagram

A bubble diagram is a third way of representing the data and is similar to a mind map.

Figure 11.11 shows an example bubble diagram for the ordering system. The system is identified in the central circle, with the different types of data storage coming from it (in this case the database tables). As with the hierarchical tree, Orders has been separated, but these could be shown on the higher level if appropriate.

Events

Event modelling shows the different stages that a process or object goes through in a system.

Entity Life History

An Entity Life History (ELH) diagram takes an object (e.g. an Order) and identifies how it is produced (an order is made), what can happen to it (an order can be amended) and how it 'dies' (the order is fulfilled and archived).

Figure 11.12 shows an example Entity Life History Diagram for the ordering system.

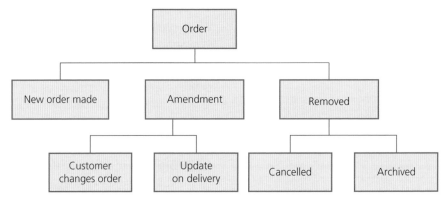

▲ **Figure 11.12** Entity Life History diagram

The object, 'Order', is in the first layer. The second layer is split into life ('New order'), what happens during its life ('Amendment') and how it dies ('Removed'). These are split further to identify how they can happen; for example, an amendment can be either the customer changing the order, or an update on delivery. 'Removed' is expanded as the order can either be 'Cancelled' or 'Archived'.

3.2 Unified Modelling Language (UML)

UML provides a series of standard diagrams to represent a system. Each type of diagram shows a different aspect of the system model and has its own purpose. Several are described below.

Use case diagram

This identifies the external entities (usually people or other systems) that access a system, and what actions they perform within the system.

PAIRS ACTIVITY

(60 minutes)

Choose an information system that is used by your school or college.

In pairs, decide which diagram or diagrams would be most appropriate: DFD, flow chart, Jackson Structure Chart, ERD, Hierarchical tree diagram, bubble diagram or ELH.

In pairs draw your chosen diagram(s) for the system.

For example, in an ordering system (which can be accessed online by customers, or by staff), the external entities are the customer and staff, and their actions are shown inside the system, as shown in Figure 11.13.

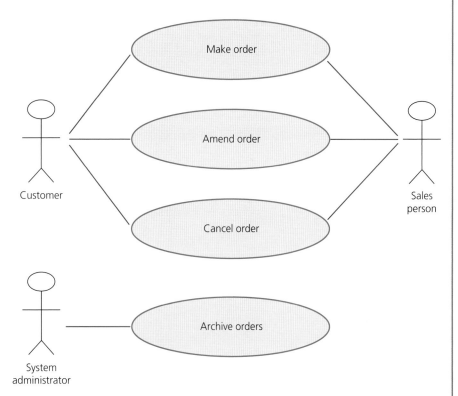

▲ **Figure 11.13** Use case diagram

It shows that both the customer and sales person are able to make an order, amend or cancel it, but only the system administrator is able to archive the orders.

This is only part of a use case diagram for a complete system; there may be additional actions that the entities can carry out in other parts of the system, e.g. adding new stock etc.

See also Unit 6 LO3.1.

Activity diagram

An activity diagram is used to illustrate the logic carried out within a use case scenario. It is started with a filled in black circle and identifies all the activities within that part of the system. These activities are drawn in rounded corner rectangles. Arrows show the movement through the activities and it ends with a black circle with an additional circle around it. If there is a decision to be made it is shown using a diamond (similar to within a flow chart) with the options coming from it. Figure 11.14 shows an example activity diagram for an ordering system.

The system starts by taking the order details. There is then a decision, such as whether the order is invalid or the items are out of stock, and a new order is

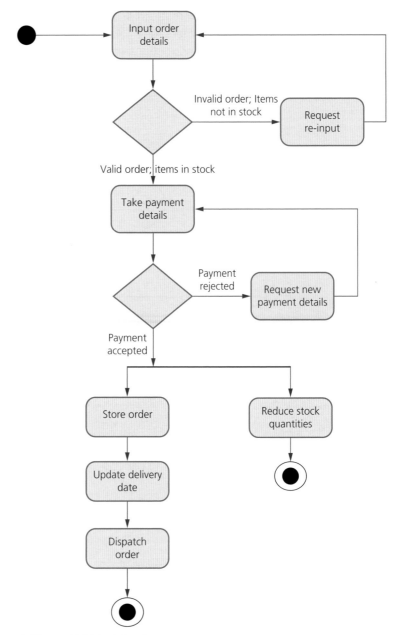

▲ **Figure 11.14** Activity diagram

requested. Otherwise payment details are requested. Again there is a decision over whether they are accepted or rejected; if rejected they are asked for again, otherwise the order is stored and the number of items in stock is reduced (the black line here indicates that two actions result from the decision). The system allows for an update of the delivery date and the order is dispatched.

Interaction diagram

Interaction diagrams show how different elements of a model interact with each other. Examples are described below.

Sequence diagram

This identifies all the objects involved in a process. For the ordering system this would be the customer and the order (in this case the sales assistant will be left out as they are repeating the customer's actions).

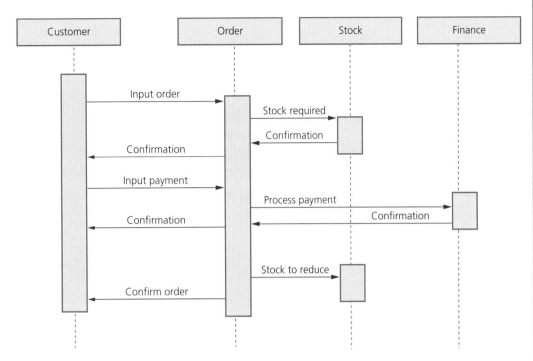

▲ **Figure 11.15** Sequence diagram

Figure 11.15 shows a sequence diagram for part of an ordering system. The objects involved in this process are shown in boxes at the top, each one having a lifeline (dashed line).

The diagram shows the sequence of actions between the objects, running from top to bottom. The box on the lifeline of the objects shows when that object is in use. For example, the 'Customer' inputs the order which goes to the 'Order', which checks the stock in the 'Stock' table, which returns a confirmation, which is sent back to the customer.

The customer can input their payment details, which are dealt with by the object 'Finance'. If these are accepted a confirmation is returned to the order, and the customer. When this confirmation has been received, 'Order' reduces the number of items in 'Stock' and confirms the order with the customer.

Communication diagram

A communication diagram shows how messages move between different objects in object-oriented programming. The classes, objects and methods are identified and used to show where and when each method is used. Figure 11.16 shows an example communication diagram for an ordering system.

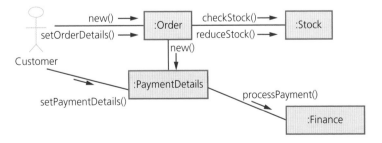

▲ **Figure 11.16** Communication diagram

The objects in the program are shown in the rectangles, with the lines showing the connections between each object. The methods are described above or below the arrows, showing the direction of communication and the method being used. For example, the 'Order' object calls the 'checkStock()' method within the 'Stock' object.

Timing diagram

This shows the actions that objects perform during a set period of time, which is given in the diagram. The first step is to list all the events numerically, with options being written as A and B. For example, in the ordering system:

1 Customer enters order details

2 Stock is checked

2A Out of stock

2B In stock

3 Payment details are entered

4 Payment details are processed

4A Payment accepted

4B Payment rejected

5 Stock updated

6 Order saved

Figure 11.17 shows this list of events in a timing diagram.

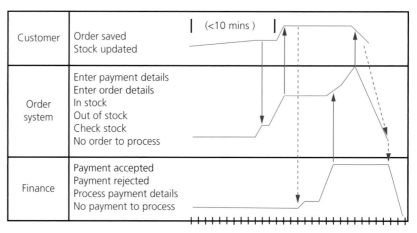

▲ **Figure 11.17** Timing diagram

The three objects are identified on the left-hand side (customer, order system and finance). The events are listed in order from bottom to top within each object. Each object has a lifeline that moves between the events. Arrows between objects show where one event cannot start until another object's process has finished; for example, the stock cannot be checked until the order details have been entered. The timing diagram finishes with the destruction (the lifeline for all three objects returning to no order, or payment).

Interaction overview diagram

This diagram is structured in a similar way to an activity diagram but it also includes frames that can host other types of interaction diagram, such as a sequence diagram, to show where some of the processes take place.

Figure 11.18 shows part of an interaction overview diagram for the ordering system. It uses the same symbols as an activity diagram, but in this case has incorporated a sequence diagram to show how it checks if the items are in stock. This allows for more detail as to how the actual processes take place and how the objects interact.

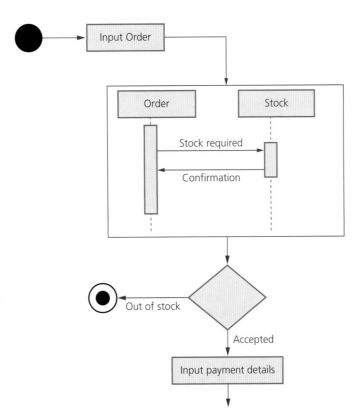

PAIRS ACTIVITY 👥 ············

(30 minutes)

Work in the same pairs as the previous task. Using the same system, choose one type of UML diagram. Draw the UML diagram for the chosen system.

▲ **Figure 11.18** Part of an interaction overview diagram

KNOW IT 💡

1. Identify the three different parts of the three view approach.
2. Describe the purpose of a Jackson Structure Chart.
3. Explain the difference between a hierarchical tree diagram and an entity life history diagram.
4. Explain the purpose of UML diagrams.
5. Identify three different UML diagrams.
6. Describe the purpose of an activity diagram.

L03 Assessment activities

Below are three suggested assessment activities that have been directly linked to the pass, merit and distinction criteria in LO3 to help with assignment preparation; they include Top tips on how to achieve the best results.

For the activities below, use the same system that you identified in the LO2 assessment activities.

Activity 1 – pass criteria *P4*

Produce a design model for the requirements you identified in LO2. Use the three view approach and **at least one** diagram from each of the three views (functionality, static data and events).

Activity 2 – merit criteria *M2*

Using the diagrams you created for Activity 1, produce a set of UML diagrams for the system. You must use at least **one** use case diagram, **one** activity diagram and **two** interaction diagrams.

Activity 3 – distinction criteria *D1*

Produce a report to evaluate the design model you have produced against the original business requirements that you identified from the activities in P2 and P3. This must include the diagrams you produced as part of Activities 1 and 2.

This report will need to be communicated (or given) to one internal stakeholder (someone who works within the business and will make use of the system) and one external stakeholder (someone who is not part of the business but who will use, or interact with, the system). This means the detail will need to be appropriate for the stakeholders, ensuring there are explanations and detailed annotation to explain the design model.

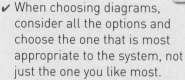

TOP TIPS

✔ When choosing diagrams, consider all the options and choose the one that is most appropriate to the system, not just the one you like most.

✔ Before starting to design the business model, make sure you have clarified all the requirements and you have all the information you need. Do not try and guess what should happen – go back and investigate further if needed.

L04 Be able to create logical and physical designs for specified business systems *P5 P6 M3 D2*

GETTING STARTED

(5 minutes)

Discuss the terms 'logical' and 'physical'. What do these terms mean in general? What do they mean in terms of a computer system?

4.1 Logical design

A logical design looks at how a system is structured; for example, its entities and the relationships between those entities. It can identify the inputs, outputs and processes that are part of the system and how they are to be stored.

Platform independent

Logical design does not require the **platform** to be identified. When analysing and producing the inputs, outputs, entities, etc. it does not matter what platform the system is to be produced on. The actions will be the same; the platform only affects the physical design and how the system will actually be built.

Inputs

The inputs to the system need to be identified and listed. For example, in a wages system the inputs may include:

- staff ID
- hours worked.

When identifying the inputs, the type of data and any validation rules that are needed can also be listed. Table 11.3 shows an example of how this could be illustrated for the wages system.

Table 11.3 Identifying inputs for wages system

Data	Data type	Validation
Staff ID	String	Existence – must already exist within the system
Hours worked	Decimal numbers (Real)	Must be between 0.5 and 200

The logical design of the inputs does not identify how these are input, or what the method of input looks like, it is only concerned with what is being input.

Outputs

The outputs of the system need to be identified, as well as their format and contents. In the logical stage, the actual layout and appearance is not considered, as with the inputs.

For example, wages system's output is the payslip. The logical design for this would identify the elements that appear on this output, for example:

Output: payslip

Contents: StaffID, firstName, surName, address, NI_Number, hoursWorked, payPerHour, GrossPay, TaxDeduction, NI_Deduction, NET Pay.

Data

In a logical design, the processes need to be identified but also designed to show how they will work. This can be done using the diagrams described in LO3 (page 280).

Any data to be stored within, or by, the system needs to be identified. For example, in the wages system, the tables within the database could be identified as Staff, PayRecord. Then the data in each of these could be listed, as shown in Table 11.4.

Table 11.4 Example data listing

Data	Data type
Staff ID	String
FirstName	String
Surname	String
NI_Number	String
HourlyRate	Currency
DateOfBirth	Date
Etc.	Etc.

This format can be used for database tables and other types of file where data is to be stored.

4.2 Physical design

The physical design is how the actual system will look and function.

Platform dependent

The physical design of a system is dependent on the platform; depending on the system this could include both the hardware and software as described in the following sections.

Hardware

The hardware to be used needs to be identified before the design is produced, to ensure the design is compatible. For example, two computers created by different manufacturers may be unable to use the same peripherals unless they are compatible. Very specific systems may also have bespoke hardware that needs consideration.

Software and implementation environment

A wider range of software possibilities needs to be considered.

- The operating system (OS). It may be that the OS is limited and the designer has no choice about what is being used. For example a business that uses primarily Apple computers is likely to want a design that is compatible with Mac OS.
- The software to be used to develop the system. The business may have specific software that it uses already, and would like the new system to use the same software. Alternatively, there could be restrictions on the programming language as the business must have the relevant software to run it. For example, if Java is to be used, the business will need a Java runtime environment.
- The implementation environment is the hardware and software that the software will be run on. This may need to consider:
  - the operating system
  - the make and model of hardware used
  - the network set up and infrastructure
  - the web browser.

The identification of the software will impact the physical design to ensure the design can be implemented.

4.3 Refining designs based on stakeholder feedback

Once the logical and physical designs have been produced, they need to be presented to the stakeholders to gather feedback. A description of how this can be done and the areas that need to be addressed is described in Unit 6 LO4.5 and 4.6.

Analyse the feedback

The feedback from the stakeholders will need analysing to assess the comments and to identify the types of problem that have been raised. A description of this process and identifying required changes is in Unit 6 (page 192). If several stakeholders are involved, the analysis needs to compare the feedback from each stakeholder and to check for consistency; for example, one stakeholder may raise an issue that is not raised by the others.

Decision on whether the refinements are viable

The analysis of feedback should lead to the identification of changes needed to the design. The feasibility of these changes needs to be assessed. For example, the stakeholders may request a significant change that will increase the time needed to produce the system and the cost. Each change needs to be assessed and justification provided for any that are not implemented.

Make changes to design in line with feedback and viability considerations

Once an assessment has been made of the requested changes, those considered possible need to be implemented. This may result in changes to both the logical and physical designs. Any changes need to be justified in terms of the feedback, and explained in the designs produced.

INDEPENDENT AND GROUP ACTIVITY

Individually take one of your designs from the previous activity. Present your design to another member of the group and ask for feedback. Consider the changes that they would like to have made to the design and decide if these changes are viable. Justify your decision.

KNOW IT

1 Describe the difference between logical and physical design.
2 Identify two elements that need to be designed as part of the logical design.
3 Identify two elements that need to be considered in the physical design.
4 Explain why the designs should be shared with the stakeholders.
5 Explain why changes need to be checked to find out if they are viable.

LO4 Assessment activities

Below are four suggested assessment activities that have been directly linked to the pass, merit and distinction criteria in LO4 to help with assignment preparation; they include Top tips on how to achieve the best results

For the activities below, use the same system that you identified in the LO2 and LO3 assessment activities.

Activity 1 – pass criteria *P5*

1 Create a logical design for the system. Use a range of diagrams, at least **one** diagram or description for each of the areas: inputs, outputs, processes and data. Make sure this is a complete design that covers all aspects of the system.
2 Produce a report, including all elements of the logical design and annotated diagrams, to explain their purpose and how they fit in the system.

Activity 2 – pass criteria *P6*

1 Create a physical design for the system. Make sure you consider the physical requirements and that it is a complete design that covers all aspects of the system.
2 Add the physical designs to the report you produced in Activity 1.
3 Make sure all designs are fully annotated to explain their purpose and how they fit in the system.

Activity 3 – merit criteria *M3*

1 Present your report to a range of stakeholders (at least three).
2 Discuss the designs with them and gather their feedback; this could be done through a recording, interview or questionnaire.

Activity 4 – merit criteria *D2*

1 Analyse the feedback you received in Activity 3. Identify the changes that the stakeholders have requested and consider if each one is viable.
2 Refine the designs by making viable changes.
3 Justify the reasons behind any changes you have made, and those you have decided not to make.
4 Produce a new design report, incorporating the edited designs, analysis of feedback and justification of changes.

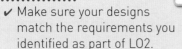

TOP TIPS
✔ Make sure your designs match the requirements you identified as part of LO2.
✔ Make use of the diagrams you created as part of the business model in LO3. These should have identified the inputs, outputs and processes required.
✔ Plan how you are going to gather the feedback from the stakeholders carefully. This will depend on the number of stakeholders, and whether they are evaluating the designs individually or as a group.

Read about it

For detailed descriptions of the different types of UML diagram along with examples of their implementation, read:

www.agilemodeling.com.

Other websites that can help with UML diagrams are:

● www.uml-diagrams.org
● www.tutorialspoint.com/uml/index.htm

For a free online tool that allows you to draw UML diagrams, visit:

www.gliffy.com/uses/uml-software/

Unit **12**
Mobile technology

LEARNING OUTCOMES

The topics and activities in this unit will help you to:

1 Understand mobile technologies.
2 Be able to investigate how businesses use mobile technologies.
3 Be able to determine solutions for the use of mobile technologies.
4 Be able to present solutions for the use of mobile technologies.

How will I be assessed?

You will be assessed by producing evidence from set scenarios or from work that you carry out as part of a work placement or employment. These tasks will be assessed by your tutor.

You will be graded using the following criteria.

Learning outcome	Pass assessment criteria	Merit assessment criteria	Distinction assessment criteria
You will:	To achieve a **pass** you must demonstrate that you have met all the **pass** assessment criteria	To achieve a **merit** you must demonstrate that you have met all the **pass and merit** assessment criteria	To achieve a **distinction** you must demonstrate that you have met all the **pass, merit and distinction** assessment criteria
1 Understand mobile technologies	**P1** Describe different methods of mobile device connectivity	**M1** Compare and contrast different operating systems used in mobile technology	**D1** Evaluate the suitability of mobile technologies for different situations
2 Be able to investigate how businesses use mobile technologies	**P2** Carry out research on the impact of mobile technologies on businesses (*Synoptic assessment from Unit 1 Fundamentals of IT, Unit 2 Global information and Unit 3 Cyber security)	**M2** Examine the ethical implications of the use of mobile technologies	
3 Be able to determine solutions for the use of mobile technologies	**P3** Investigate the mobile technological requirements for an identified business need **P4** Plan a mobile technological solution for an identified business need	**M3** Prepare a technology business plan to support the implementation of the mobile technological solution for the business	
4 Be able to present solutions for the use of mobile technologies	**P5** Promote the mobile technological solution to relevant stakeholders **P6** Improve the proposed mobile technological solution based on stakeholder feedback		**D2** Predict the effectiveness of the mobile technological solution for the identified business need

LO1 Understand mobile technologies *P1 M1 D1*

GETTING STARTED

(10 minutes)

Compare the mobile devices available to the members of your group (including your tutor). Do different people have different devices and, if so, is there any pattern to these?

1.1 Devices

Sizes

Mobile devices come in many different sizes. Mobile phones have become a lot smaller since they were first available, and now have more functionality than just phone calls. In fact, most mobile phones could be considered to be small computers that can also make phone calls or send texts.

Phablets are larger phones that are smaller than tablets. The driving factor in the size of these devices is the need to have a screen that is large enough for the user to use and interact with.

Tablets are effectively mobile computers. Typically, they have touch screens. Some tablets have physical keyboards, whilst others have an on-screen keyboard.

Sat-navs use satellite signals sent from satellites to pinpoint their position. In the simplest devices, the output is the location's longitude and latitude. In more complex systems, the position is shown on a map or a visual display of the area through which the sat-nav is moving.

A smartwatch is a computerised watch, with extra facilities, other than keeping the time. Recent examples may be considered to be computers in their own right.

Active devices require a separate power source to run, while passive devices do not. Therefore, a passive device can be plugged into a computer and it will run (e.g. a wired mouse), while a set of speakers may be either passive (if they do not include batteries) or active (if they do).

Embedded

Embedded devices are fully functional devices embedded within larger devices. For example, a car may have embedded devices that monitor speed and braking strength. This system could be used by insurance companies to assess how safe a driver is.

Input

Input devices are part of the interface between humans and machines and take the user's actions and input them into the system. With mobile technology, input devices can include mini keyboards and touchscreens, as well as voice input.

Output

Mobile devices also include output alerts; for example, audio output via a speaker, or vibrations from mini motors built into the devices.

Some devices also include the ability to print, although many still require separate printers for high-quality work.

1.2 Connectivity

Wired vs wireless

Connectivity between devices is their ability to connect and transfer data. Wired devices have a physical cable along which data can flow, while wireless devices use radio waves to transmit the data.

Wireless and wired connectivity offer many differing characteristics. For example, the range of a wireless signal is affected by the system you have. A wireless system based on 802.11g technology has a range of up to 100 metres indoors but it is unlikely that you would achieve this at home.

For wired technology, Cat 5 and Cat 6 cables also have a range of about 100 metres but are reliable at that distance, while wireless is not.

Wired methods provide a faster rate of data transmission than wireless methods, although the speed of data transfer in wireless networks has improved over recent years.

Security can also be an issue. Wired signals can only be accessed by a device that is connected to the wired network. Wireless, however, is a broadcast system that sends out the information to any machine capable of receiving it. Wireless connectivity can be protected by passwords, but this extra layer of security is not required for wired systems.

One advantage of wireless technology is that it allows for flexibility and mobility. Unlike wired technology, users are able to move around and take their own device with them. This means that office designs have changed, as has the likelihood of delegates bringing their own phones and tablets to meetings and conferences.

Cellular technologies

Mobile phones use separate technology to handle their signals. For example, CDMA is a group of technologies used for sending voice and data around mobile phone networks. GSM allows mobile phone signals to move through the network of base stations.

Routing

This is a process of sending messages, broken down into packets of data, through a network so that the message sent from one computer is either received in the target computer, or the original sending computer is informed that the message has not been sent. The process also selects and uses the fastest route through which data may be sent.

IP address

An IP address is a unique set of numbers assigned to every item on a network. No two devices on that network should have the same IP address.

IPv4 and IPv6

There are currently two methods of creating IP addresses. The first, IPv4, is based on four groups of figures, each ranging from 0 to 255. For example, 93.225.67.21 is an IP address in IPv4 format. This is a 32-bit number (see Unit 1, page 16) and so offers few number combinations. The IPv6 system is based on 128-bit technology and is written in hexadecimal, rather than binary; 128-bit technology allows for far more numbers and connections than IPv4 technology. It also has a built in auto-configuration, so that any device can generate its own IPv6 address as soon as it is switched on.

DHCP vs static IP

The DHCP protocol allocates IP addresses whenever a request is made by a computer or other networked device. This means that devices joining a network can be allocated a different IP address whenever they are switched on.

A static IP is an IP address that is applied to a device and which that device retains.

GROUP ACTIVITY

(30 minutes)

Research CDMA, TDMA, GSM and CDS cellular technologies.

Create a presentation that compares these four technologies and identifies their relative advantages and disadvantages.

The benefit of a DHCP is that there is no need for a network manager to allocate IP addresses and the IP addresses are automatically unique.

Default gateway

The default gateway is the one location on a network that is able to pass packets of data between the network and other networks. In practical terms, the default gateway is the router.

Subnet mask

A subnet mask divides an IP address into the two parts of the network address and host address (see Unit 1, LO2.9, page 25 and Unit 4, LO1.7, page 116).

MAC address

A MAC address is used to identify the network interface card or wi-fi card on a network. These addresses are usually set by the manufacturer of the card. As with IP addresses, each MAC address on a network has to be unique, so that the card may be identified as a distinct point on that network.

Network characteristics

Networks can have different characteristics.

- Bandwidth: the rate at which data is able to transfer around the network. The higher the bandwidth, the more data can be transferred per fixed period of time.
- Latency: the extent of delays in a network. A network with high latency has lots of delays, while one with low latency does not have many delays.
- Jitter: when a message is split into packets, each will be sent at a fixed rate, for example one every 10 milliseconds. If every packet is received at the same rate, the network has no jitter. A difference indicates jitter. Because jitter results in individual packets taking longer to arrive, packets could arrive in a different order to that in which they are sent.
- Reliability: the result of many factors ranging from the quality and age of the equipment, to the environment in which the network operates. Different networks may have different levels of reliability and, due to the impact of geographical features and distance to access points, for example, two devices on the same network may have different levels of reliability if they are in different locations.

Standards

There is a range of different standards for connectivity on mobile devices.

- GPS (Global Positioning System) is a worldwide positioning system that uses time signals sent from military satellites to identify the longitude and latitude of the device receiving the system. Many different devices use this system, ranging from smartwatches and phones up to specialist trekking equipment and tracking devices in lorries.
- 3G, 4G and 5G are three generations (hence the 'G' part of the name) of data connections used in mobile devices such as smartphones and tablets; 5G is the most recent development and offers speeds beyond that available on 4G, which itself was faster than 3G.
- Wi-fi is another cross-platform communication platform that allows devices from different manufacturers to communicate via a wireless

PAIRS ACTIVITY 👥 ··········

(15 minutes)

Research the impact of jitter on a network. Is jitter more or less important if the network is used to send VOIP messages?

Present your answer as a written report.

network, which require a wireless network access point to which all wi-fi-enabled devices connect.

● Bluetooth technology is based on UHF radio waves and is useful for transferring data over a small distance.

● USB was defined in the 1990s as a standard for wired communication as part of a bus configuration (see Unit 1, LO1.2, page 9). The standard allows for a data and power transfer between any devices that have a USB connection.

Limitations, ranges and uses of different standards

The standards discussed above have different features which make them either more or less suitable for use in certain circumstances.

The standard should deliver suitable signal strength for its purpose and in the locations needed. Different standards are impacted by the distance between devices and any intervening objects. GPS, for example, uses a broadcast signal sent from satellites. These signals are generally accessible anywhere in the world, although are not as effective indoors. Bluetooth uses a wireless technology and so is able to work well through walls. However, the presence of metal, such as piping or wiring in walls, interferes with the system.

The IEEE 802.11 specifications (see Unit 4, LO1.5, page 112) apply to wi-fi network settings and define the common specifications for wi-fi communication. As the technology has developed, so the standards have extended to take in the improvements made. The current standard can achieve speeds of up to 6912 mbit/s, compared to 2 mbit/s for the 802.11 a and b systems.

Radio frequency covers electromagnetic communication from 3 Hz to 300 GHz. This range is split into different bands. Industrial, scientific and medical bands have defined roles. The 2.4 GHz and 5 GHz bands are within this group and are reserved for fixed satellite, radio location and mobile use. The 5 GHz band offers higher maximum data transfer rates than 2.4 GHz.

Each wi-fi band is also split into channels and most wi-fi devices allow the user to switch between different channels so that interference caused by other devices using the same channel may be reduced.

Radio frequency (RF) is how often the radio wave occurs. This wave can be modulated, either by changing its amplitude (AM waves) or its frequency (FM waves). FM signals have a lower signal-to-noise ratio than AM signals so are considered to be a higher quality signal.

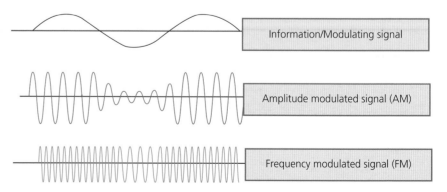

Figure 12.1 AM and FM modulated signals

INDEPENDENT ACTIVITY

(15 minutes)

Access the management module of your home wi-fi system. Which channels are available? Investigate the potential benefit to be gained from switching from your current channel to a different one.

As radio signals are sent as a wave, they can also have differing bandwidth. This refers to the gaps between the waves and can be a significant factor in allowing different signals to be delivered over a close geographical distance without interference.

Antennas convert electronic power into radio waves and vice versa. Therefore, radio waves need to be accessed and sent by antennas. The most frequent type is the omnidirectional antenna, which is part of a system that receives or sends signals in any horizontal direction. Semi-directional antennas send and receive signals from a narrow direction, while bi-directional antennas only receive signals when pointed directly at the sending antenna.

1.3 Mobile device operating systems

Mobile devices, like any other form of electronic device, have an operating system that controls their basic functions and input/output interface. As with other devices, there is a range of different operating systems with advantages and disadvantages.

Android

Android provides the user with a touch control system intended to mirror real gestures, such as swipes and taps, and also includes an on-screen keyboard that can be used for data entry. It also uses features of the device on which it is installed to provide the user with further methods of input, such as an accelerometer, which can be used during game play, and built in haptic devices which provide outputs such as shaking, linked to an event in a game.

Windows

The Windows mobile operating system is closely associated with the standard Windows operating system on desktop and laptop computers. The functionality of the mobile system is matched to the desktop version, to the extent that the same apps may be used on mobile devices as on desktop computers.

Decisions made on a mobile device running Windows are applied to all devices that the user accesses with the same logon. For example, if a notification is dismissed on a Windows tablet device, that notification will not appear on any other device. This reflects the extent to which it is intended to be seen as a subset of an operating system that applies across many types of device.

iOS

iOS is the operating system used across all Apple mobile devices ranging from phones to tablets (iPads). Using the iOS interface has been described as a more tactile experience than using Windows, as it supports input through direct manipulation. The system responds to various user gestures, such as pinching, tapping and swiping.

Linux based

Linux open source systems are also available for mobile devices, the Sailfish OS and the Ubuntu Touch being examples. The Android OS is based on Linux.

PAIRS ACTIVITY

(40 minutes)

Research the Android, Windows, iOS and Linux mobile operating systems. Compare the features, advantages and disadvantages of each system.

Your results could be presented in the form of a table or report.

The Internet of Things is all devices that are connected and exchange data – computers, sensors and controls for heating systems and remote controls that can open a car door via an internet connection, for example.

See Unit 17 for more details about using mobile devices for the Internet of Everything.

Future operating systems

Not only are operating systems taking on more of what used to be covered by other programs (such as having inbuilt printer drivers), but future operating systems may support the work of devices that currently do not have an operating system. Irons, for example, could be controlled by an operating system, with inbuilt sensors reducing the chances of clothing being damaged by irons that are too hot.

Future developments in operating systems could place the mobile device at the centre of everything we do. It is already possible for apps on phones to be used to control Smart TVs, heating systems and sound systems, but it is likely that mobile devices will become even more central to our lives.

1.4 Current and potential future uses

There are many current and potential future uses to mobile technology. In this section, we will discuss how some of these are currently used and speculate on how their use may develop.

Smart city

A smart city is basically a geographical version of the Internet of Things. All its resources are linked so that they may be managed and used efficiently. For example, sensors, such as GPS trackers on buses, provide travellers with real-time information about when a bus is due, which may also control other parts of the transport network, so if a bus is delayed, connecting services will wait for it, for example.

INDEPENDENT ACTIVITY

(60 minutes)

Research how public services are linked in your nearest city or town. Can you identify or think of improvements that could be made using mobile technology and the impacts these would have?

Create a presentation for an audience of local councillors, highlighting how the town or city could become more smart by using mobile technology and how this would benefit all of those who live and work there.

Tagging endangered species

Tagging endangered species allows them to be tracked so that their movement can be monitored and dangers identified, such as whether a particular animal is approaching an area of land clearance which may result in the animal's death, for example. Generations of the animal can be tracked, providing useful information about their breeding and behaviour.

Robotic devices

The iRobot vacuum cleaner can be scheduled via a mobile app and uses sensors to clean floors and avoid obstacles, such as furniture, so that it does not need to be operated manually. This is an example of the potential of robotics to have a beneficial impact on our lives.

Remote robotic devices can also be used for purposes as diverse as remote business or medical communications to unmanned military surveillance.

▲ **Figure 12.2** The iRobot vacuum cleaner

Sat-nav

Satellite navigation combines the GPS system, wi-fi connectivity and a visual presentation so that the user is presented with a visual representation of the roads they need to follow.

Future developments could be a far more representative experience, by combining the street view available from Google maps, for example.

Health monitors

Health monitors could be considered to be an extension of the Internet of Things. Pacemakers are fitted inside the patient to monitor and regulate heart rate patterns. They store this data for analysis by doctors, to provide a picture of the patient's recent heart health.

Heartrate monitors worn by those exercising can link to mobile devices via Bluetooth connections and transmit heart rate, so that exercise regimes can be assessed and altered if necessary. Wearable devices such as Fitbit activity trackers can also link into exercise and fitness apps on devices so that calories burnt and even body fat are also tracked, providing the user with information to help plan their food intake and fitness regimes.

As technology improves, health monitors will become more important. At present, a lot of the functionality of these devices is to react to events, but in the future they could use data to provide support by suggesting courses of action that could be followed to avoid health problems.

CCTV

Examples of CCTV use are when cameras are placed in shops to watch for criminal activity; on bridges and the side of roads to check that vehicles have the necessary paper work to allow them to be on the road; or in travel hubs, such as railway stations, to monitor the number of people using the station.

At present, CCTV devices are not necessarily connected, so that private CCTV is not part of any wider surveillance system. However, in the future, all CCTV cameras may one day be connected.

Drones

Drone is the popular name for an unmanned aerial vehicle – a remotely controlled flying object.

Drones can provide airborne CCTV or deliver packages to homes, for example. They also provide remote access to dangerous conditions, hence their use in a military context. Drones can be flown into inspect hard-to-get-to areas, such as the top of chimneys, reducing the need for a person to risk the climb.

Drones are now becoming available to the public, which makes their use harder to control and regulate. They may be used for entertainment but can also be used to spy in a neighbour's garden, or to watch a game of football at the local stadium without paying.

Stock control and theft reduction with RFID

Small RFID (radio frequency identification) tags in devices allow them to be located via the radio signal they transmit.

Stock checking is verifying what is on the shelves of a warehouse or shop. It used to be a long and tedious process of checking shelves, writing down box numbers, collating results and comparing numbers to those expected. With RFID, items can be located via a centralised system that excludes the need for physical counting. This lowers staff costs and increases efficiency, especially as stock checks were traditionally done after hours, or over weekends, when staff would need to be paid a premium rate to compensate them for working beyond their contracted hours.

RFID also provides a powerful form of theft reduction, as the signals can be checked at doors, setting off an alarm. Thieves could also be tracked beyond the store.

Car trackers

Car trackers are fitted to vehicles and allow them to be followed and found. The security impacts of being able to track a stolen car or lorry are clear. They are also useful to insurance companies, which can track speed and driving habits and set premiums accordingly. Also, an employer may be interested to know where an employee is driving their company car, or how many breaks they are taking on their journey.

More sophisticated tracking devices can also link into the vehicle's management system, so that the vehicle can be disabled, or doors locked, if necessary.

KNOW IT

1 Identify one similarity between a smartphone and a phablet.
2 Describe two differences between a smartphone and a phablet.
3 Explain how a MAC address may be used within a network.
4 Describe the difference between an omni-directional and bi-directional antennas.
5 Describe one limitation of each of the following types of connectivity standard:
   a 3G
   b 4G
   c Bluetooth.

TOP TIPS ✔

✔ Think about different types of mobile device connectivity and how these may suit different situations; for example, Bluetooth connectivity is used to transfer files over small distances.
✔ The features of different mobile device operating systems are those services and other tasks included with the operating system.
✔ When evaluating, consider situations which allow some technologies a clear advantage over others.

LO1 Assessment activity

Below is a suggested assessment activity that has been directly linked to the pass, merit and distinction criteria in LO1 to help with assignment preparation; it includes Top tips on how to achieve best results.

Activity 1 – pass criteria *P1* merit criteria *M1* and distinction criteria *D1*

You work for an IT blog and have been asked to write a review of the impact that mobile devices have had on society. You have decided to focus on:

● a description of the methods of mobile device connectivity
● comparing and contrasting the features of different mobile device operating systems and explaining how these may benefit users
● an evaluation of how different mobile technologies may be used in different situations.

LO2 Be able to investigate how businesses use mobile technologies *P2 M2*

GETTING STARTED 👤

(10 minutes)

A linked CCTV system may be viewed from a mobile device, which provides various commercial benefits to the owner of the system.

As a group, compare the moral and ethical considerations of using such a system with the commercial benefits to be gained. Do they outweigh the commercial benefits?

If the use of mobile technology improves the welfare of citizens of a country, do you agree that everyone benefits and therefore the cost to one person is outweighed by the benefit to all?

2.1 Uses of mobile technologies

Mobile technologies can be used in many ways to aid business. In this section, we will look at some of these areas.

Access to information from remote locations

Within the news-gathering industry, not only can mobile technology provide information from remote areas that would previously have taken weeks to arrive, such as halfway up Mount Everest, but we can also see it on our screens in real time.

Remote research operations searching for gas or oil deposits are able to feed back results for analysis at laboratories many thousands of miles away, removing the need for an onsite laboratory and avoiding a great deal of cost.

Maintain contact between staff

There are many benefits to being able to maintain communication between staff. Not only can staff collaborate on projects (see below), but they can swap ideas and interact with others. This interaction may be via face-to-face communications using mobile devices, or via email between devices, but the positive impacts enable teams to build and relationships to grow.

Mobile devices also enable lone workers to keep in touch, for example estate agents meeting clients alone in a house, or a construction worker carrying out potentially dangerous work at the far end of a site. They can be checked regularly or used to contact colleagues in an emergency.

Collaborative working

Collaboration is when people work together towards a common goal. Mobile technology enables people to work, virtually, side by side. For example, a 24-hour processing system enables staff from around the world to follow a process in shifts, taking over from colleagues to the east as their working day ends and passing it on to colleagues to the west as their day ends. If a problem is focused on for 24 hours, rather than just an 8-hour working day, logic suggests it can be solved in a third of the time.

Collaborative working can also allow staff to share ideas, perhaps via Skype on their phones or tablets. Documents may be worked on in one location and passed on or screen-shared for checking. Email can be sent via mobile devices if the sender is away from their computer, speeding up work processes and communications.

Within the workplace, there are many possible benefits of sharing a calendar. For example, managers can share their calendars with secretarial staff who can book and check appointments. Sharing task lists enables colleagues to complete tasks that allow the group as a whole to progress towards a common goal more quickly.

Using cloud-based solutions to reduce up-front technology costs

The cloud offers worldwide connectivity at a fraction of the cost of setting up such a system oneself. The ability to store data and information on the cloud means that organisations do not need separate data storage facilities of their own, which saves on technology costs.

Anyone with access permissions can access internet data. To some extent, this removes the need for specialist IT managers, as there is less equipment to maintain within an organisation as virtual storage replaces physical storage. Cloud storage also removes the need for any form of infrastructure, as the infrastructure is provided as part of the cloud. Therefore, organisations do not need to set up, test and train staff; they just need to access the internet. However, those organisations that provide the storage still need to have these key staff in order to maintain their hardware and software.

Files and photos from mobile devices can be automatically synchronised with cloud storage sites such as Dropbox, to be shared with named users.

Increase productivity and profitability

Productivity is the amount of output achieved per person, while profitability is the level of profit achieved relative to the investment. Both are means by which the success of an organisation may be measured.

The ability to have data and information more quickly via mobile technology, for example, will mean that organisations are able to react quicker to events and changes to their market, which may lead to a competitive advantage and, by association, higher profitability.

Increases in productivity may be achieved through the use of mobile technology. Mobile technology means that users don't need to be at their desks to respond to a work issue. The ability to video-conference with colleagues, rather than travel, means that the time away from the desk is minimised. Even when the meeting is only a few miles away, the time gained by not having to drive across a busy city centre will impact on productivity.

Using social media for digital marketing

See also Unit 13.

2.2 Ethical

Ethics may be described as what we do to other people, while morals may be what we do to ourselves. There are clear ethical considerations when it comes to the use of mobile technologies by businesses.

Child tracking

Rather like the car tracking device, child tracking devices allow parents to track the location of their children. These tend to be in the form of watches, jewellery or phone apps, using GPS, GSM or Bluetooth. Some enable children to send a message in an emergency. On one level, the ability to know where a child is may be useful, but is it ethical? Even when used by a parent, there is an argument that says that any individual deserves some privacy.

Personal data

Personal data presents an ethical dilemma for organisations (see Unit 2 LO1.8, page 54). This data may be used when provided willingly, such as belonging to a loyalty card system that tracks purchases and delivers personalised advertising to analyse purchasing patterns. However, when collected via mobile devices, the case is less clear.

Exercise apps can use GPS to track journeys and provide feedback to the user on how many calories they have burned, for example, but it may present that journey on a map. While some of this information may also have been collected by CCTV, such as when the user ran down a busy street, the end and start points of the journey may be private data.

Such location details may be used to provide footfall patterns, which show how many people walked past a particular shop, or can produce maps that show the location of owners of the most up-to-date mobile devices. This information would be invaluable to marketing departments who may want to target particular individuals, but the information has not been given willingly or even knowingly and, ethically, its use is problematic.

Employees always contactable

Mobile devices have eroded the difference between work place and home. Mobile devices now make employees contactable at all hours, even when on holiday. From a business point of view, that employee may be the only person who knows the answer to a question that really must be answered. However, this may be their first family holiday abroad in six years. Do the needs of the business outweigh the needs of the individual? Whether or not the organisation should contact the employee is clearly an ethical consideration that needs to be considered before the phone call is made, or the email sent.

Haves and have-nots

The final ethical consideration is that of those who do and those who do not have access to technology. Imagine that an organisation has developed a product that will revolutionise lives. Is it ethical that their chosen method of advertising that product excludes anyone who does not have access to mobile technology?

The impact of not having access to mobile technology can be huge. To some extent this impact can be reduced by using a desktop computer, but this can only be done from home or other fixed location. The ability to access data and information, communicate with others and to be in electronic contact with the world while also mobile affords a huge advantage to those who have it, if only because of the speed with which they can react to information they would otherwise have to wait to receive.

KNOW IT

1 List two advantages to an organisation of allowing staff to use mobile technology to communicate.
2 Describe how being able to access information from a mining project in a remote location may lead to a manufacturing organisation having a competitive advantage over a similar organisation that does not have this information.
3 How can using mobile technology increase an organisation's productivity?
4 Explain one ethical consideration when using a customer's private information.
5 Compare the benefits of being able to contact employees via mobile technology with the potential costs to the individual. Which consideration is more important?

LO2 Assessment activity

Below is a suggested assessment activity that has been directly linked to the pass and merit criteria in LO2 to help with assignment preparation; it includes Top tips on how to achieve best results.

Activity 1 – pass criteria *P2* and merit criteria *M2*

The report you wrote for P1, M1 and D1 has been positively received by the editors of the blog. You have now been asked to expand your research by investigating the impact of mobile technologies on business and the ethical implications of using mobile technologies in a number of different situations.

Write a post entitled 'What did mobile technology ever do for us, and should we have listened?'

TOP TIPS ✔

✔ Try to get as much real information as you can. Talk to an organisation that makes extensive use of mobile technology if you can.
✔ The ethical considerations may be linked to the direct use of technology by organisations or the creation of apps and other features by organisations.

LO3 Be able to determine solutions for the use of mobile technologies *P3 P4 M3*

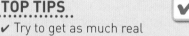

(10 minutes)

How much do you rely on your mobile devices?

As a group, consider how your life would be affected if one of your mobile devices was unavailable. List as many uses of mobile devices as possible and describe how your life would be affected if these were not available.

Solutions for the use of mobile technologies could be about the implementation of mobile technology. While developing an app may be part of this, it should be considered as part of an overall solution. For example, a business could consider using tablets or smartphones to allow more flexible working with employees or to support their sales people while out in the field.

3.1 Investigating business requirements

Business requirements will differ. For example, organisations needing a product for internal use only may be prepared to accept a less professional looking solution than one that is for use by external customers. Other organisations may require a particular piece of hardware, while others may have different time constraints and time frames.

An ability to identify and assess the importance of these requirements is key to identifying the correct solution.

Client needs and wants

The client is, effectively, the employer for the duration of the project. Client needs and wants are the basic requirements of any project. Wants are what the client would like from the project, while needs are what they must have.

End user needs and wants

The end user is the person for whom the project is being run. Their needs and wants may not be the same as those of the client.

Limitations

The client may specify the target platform(s) they want the solution to run on. This platform could be a specific operating system or a type of device.

The client may wish to reach the largest possible market by having a cross-platform solution that runs on Android, iOS, Windows and Linux. However, each OS has a different set of interfaces which won't necessarily work on other platforms, and each is developed using different programming languages (e.g. Java for Android). Cross-platform toolkits enable apps to be adapted but they still need to be tested on each platform and updated as necessary.

Other considerations include bandwidth. For example, it could be slow and expensive for users to download a large app onto their phone if they are not on wi-fi. If the solution is made available on the developer's website rather than an app store, the server needs sufficient bandwidth to cope with simultaneous requests to download the app. If the solution is web-based, available bandwidth and server space should accommodate a large number of simultaneous users.

Development resources are the raw materials for completing the project e.g. hardware and software. These can be a serious limitation, especially if the resources are insufficient or of the wrong type. Similarly, human resources can be a restriction, as these are the people you have available to you to carry out the tasks. Human resources are the skills available or lacking within the team, e.g. the ability to program using Java for Android platforms.

Prototyping

Prototyping is the process of making samples of the completed project, so that they can be checked. A prototype should be close to the intended final product or, if it is not, it should be clear how many of the required final functions the prototype can demonstrate.

The prototype will be the focus of much testing. If the prototype functions as intended, the team can develop the prototype further. Clearly, however, if the prototype exposes shortcomings, these can be worked on.

Interfaces

Your proposed mobile solution will require an interface to allow the user to use it. This is a software solution hosted on a hardware platform and will be restricted by the functionality of the hardware for which you are planning the interface, as well as the software itself.

For example, if you are planning an interface for a mobile device that does not include a separate, physical, keyboard, you need to plan to either use some form of onscreen keyboard or buttons which do not require data entry.

3.2 Planning

Cost

Your planning should take account of the cost of purchase and maintenance for your own equipment, and the cost to users. The initial cost of ownership (the cost of purchase, plus any ongoing costs, such as access to data or insurance), will be a barrier for some. If your design requires an expensive product, such as a top-of-the-range virtual reality headset, which few can afford, fewer users will access your solution.

A further cost is that of upgrading. Technology needs to carry on improving to remain cutting edge. Where improvements are achievable (e.g. upgraded software can still be run on existing devices), there is usually no cost. However, there comes a time when the device will not run the improved software, or on new hardware. The constant drive to maintain the cutting edge position requires new machines with the associated cost of purchase and maintenance. This needs to be factored into planning, as this cost needs to be borne by the project if the technological solution is to make the best use of the most up-to-date technology.

If you are planning to create a solution that may be used across different mobile devices, you need to test it on these devices, with differing operating systems and different sized screens. For example, the size of the screen will dictate the size of the interface. By testing on different sized screens, you will be able to tell whether the user is able to see all the buttons or instructions. However, financial and time costs are associated with this testing process.

You can also test for incompatibility, which is the inability of a product or device to work on a range of different devices.

Risks

Your plan needs to consider the potential risks, of which data security is the most important. If your planned solution uses any form of personal data, risks could arise from accidentally sharing the data, possibly on screen, or via data transfer.

See also Units 2 and 3 for more information on the possible implications of data security breaches.

Constraints

Legal

When planning your solution, you must take account of any possible legal implications. If, for example, you plan to create a mobile app that tracks the location of a lorry, you are also tracking the driver of that lorry. Different countries have different laws about the legality of tracking employees.

Another legal constraint could be any project involving personal data, for which you need to be aware of the Data Protection Act.

Technological

We have already discussed the implications of using cutting edge technology and this should also be considered a constraint. Technology becomes outdated, limiting the life of your solution, so you should consider whether it is more cost effective to use cheaper, older technologies or more expensive technology that will stay current for longer.

Signal coverage areas impose a clear restriction on the use of any mobile device. There may be little you can do, but you could explore the possibility of combining offline content with online content, so that the solution can be used when a signal is not available, such as the ability to download Google maps.

Power requirements

Even passive mobile devices require an electrical power supply. However, an active device will have a greater need for, and drain on, electricity. A solution that will quickly drain a battery (e.g. a GPS tracker) is a significant constraint that needs to be considered.

 **PAIRS ACTIVITY**

(25 minutes)

You have been asked to contribute towards a feasibility study of a project to create an app that checks whether essays submitted by students have been copied from the internet.

The app will take key quotes from the essays and check them against a database of essays. If there is significant correlation, the app will point this out.

Your contribution to the feasibility study is a report into the possible constraints on the project.

You may present your work as a written report.

Staff training

When planning a project, staff training should be seen as a vital contributing factor to its success. Your proposed solution should not be any different.

Training could cover the basics of how to use the device, through to more complex training on how to set the solution up. Give some thought to the content and method of delivery of that training. For example, you may decide that word-processed notes, downloadable from a website, would be a suitable solution. This is a perfectly feasible method but it does pass the responsibility for training onto the person who needs to be trained, as they would need to follow the training program themselves.

Other methods of training are available which offer different advantages to the trainer and the trainee.

INDEPENDENT ACTIVITY

(15 minutes)

Research the advantages and disadvantages of each of the following methods of training:

- face-to-face training (internal)
- online real-time training
- downloadable training videos
- training delivered in chunks supported by face-to-face tutorials.

Your results could be presented as a table or a presentation.

3.3 Technology business plan

A technology business plan may be used to support a presentation about a technological solution. In this section, we will explore how one is constructed.

Current and future use

Your technology business plan will need to highlight how technology is currently used within the targeted area of the business and show how the proposed solution will fit with this use when it has been implemented.

Your plan should show the gaps in the current technological provision and how the proposed solution will fill that gap.

Your plan should also show how the plan will impact in the future. You could, for example, model the impact of your plan on the skill levels of employees in the future.

Identifying appropriate technology

Your plan should identify appropriate technology that may be used in the future and how this would integrate with current systems to achieve the solution. Your focus on technology could consider how your project would address changing and future hardware and software needs, and yet continue to achieve the desired outcome.

You should also consider how your app will integrate with other technology and other systems. This may be a discussion of how your app could work in conjunction with GPS technology, or an app that models the stress patterns within an architectural design, for example.

Allow for advances in technology

The final part of your technology business plan should consider possible advances in technology. Clearly, developments that are set to come on stream within the near future will be easier to predict and integrate, while others, which are still some years off being implemented, will be harder to integrate.

Your plan needs to reflect the differing nature of these advances. Where changes are imminent, clear conclusions about their possible impact may be gauged quite easily and reliably. Your report should make this reliability clear. However, with those advances which are further off, and which are therefore vague in their implication, your report should make it clear that the allowances you are making are based on predictions that are less supportable.

KNOW IT

1 Compare end user wants and end user needs. Which of these may be more important to the measurable success of a technological project?
2 Explain how each of the following factors limits the scope of a mobile technology solution
  a target platform
  b bandwidth
  c human resources.
3 Why should you be aware of legal and technological constraints when planning a mobile technology solution?
4 What impact might staff training have on the success of a project?
5 How can a technology business plan support the implementation of a mobile technology solution?

LO3 Assessment activity

Below is a suggested assessment activity that has been directly linked to the pass and merit criteria in LO3 to help with assignment preparation; it includes Top tips on how to achieve best results.

Activity 1 – pass criteria *P3* *P4* and merit criteria *M3*

You have been approached by Alright Photos. The manager wants a mobile solution to a problem – they are unable to link photographs taken on location with the photographer who took the photograph so they cannot identify which photographer should receive royalty payments for that photo. The current system records photographs taken and their geographical location. The system also records the bookings for each photographer, but does not combine this data together.

1 Research the problem and identify the mobile technological requirements to meet the business need.
2 Plan a mobile solution for this need.
3 Support your proposal with a technology business plan.

TOP TIPS

✔ Consider what technology is currently available to you and which may be used as part of your solution
✔ Create a plan that shows how your suggested solution will combine features that are already found on mobile devices.

LO4 Be able to present solutions for the use of mobile technologies *P5 P6 D2*

(10 minutes)

When presenting to an audience, it is important to project a sense of confidence.

Think of two presenters. These may be tutors at your school or college, or elsewhere. One should be an effective presenter, while one should be less effective.

Compare each person's method and style. How do their confidence levels impact on the how well their message is received by those listening?

4.1 Promoting the mobile technological solution

Summarising technical details to a non-technical audience

Often one of the harder tasks for a technically minded person to perform is to present information in a way that is technically correct, but which is also simple enough for a non-technical audience to understand.

The fear with presenting to a non-technical audience is that one does not really know how much they already know and, secondly, that one will present information in a patronising manner.

It is a good idea to have as clear an idea of the level of understanding of the audience as possible and be able to change the content and level at which you are presenting if you sense that the information is too detailed or specialised.

It helps to think of the content from the audience's point of view. For example, what might they want to find out? Can you explain how your solution meets their needs?

Verbal versus written communication

Verbal communication is the process of using words to pass information (either spoken or written), while non-verbal communication is the messages we pass by the way we stand, the faces we make and other physical gestures, either deliberately or accidentally.

Verbal communication is a far more controllable means of passing information. Any spoken or written confusion is generally insignificant when compared to the possible confusion that can arise from communication based on a shrug of a shoulder or even a smile. Be aware of any physical habits you might have, such as tapping a foot or twisting a ring. Adopting a neutral posture will be less distracting for the audience.

Making a convincing case

Make sure that your argument is sound by covering all aspects of the problem and showing, through examples and statistics if available, why your solution is the best.

In planning your presentation in support of your case, you should make sure that you have covered all possible questions and can counter any arguments. If at any stage of the presentation you appear to be unsure of your facts, or appear to have ignored important restrictions or possible problems, you will have failed to have made a convincing case and will, in all likelihood, have failed to have gained support for your project.

Projecting confidence

When presenting information, use positive language and a positive mindset. A powerful speaker who is clearly enthusiastic about their topic will draw listeners in and tend to get them to agree. Presenters can sometimes overcome gaps in their knowledge simply by the power of their personality and overall confidence.

A timid speaker, whose non-verbal communication suggests that they are not interested in their topic, will dissuade listeners, who might stop listening.

4.2 Improvements to mobile technological solution

It is sometimes necessary to make improvements to proposals. The following section examines methods you could use to do this.

Obtain feedback from stakeholders

Stakeholders are those who are affected by the project. These could be potential users of the product, as well as the client, members of the creative team, or those who would be manufacturing the product. Other areas of expertise could include those who sell the product and so have knowledge of customers' needs.

Before you start gathering any feedback from stakeholders, it is good practice to create a stakeholder diagram. This shows those who are affected and identifies those who are part of the organisation (internal stakeholders), and those who are affected but who are not part of the organisation (external stakeholders).

When deciding on the source of feedback, do not exclude any particular group without first thinking about what they have to offer. For example, the sales team will have a working relationship with the customer and may be aware of issues with similar products. They may be able to identify necessary changes before any other stakeholder looks at the solution. Not only does this save time but it also shows you are able to prioritise information sources.

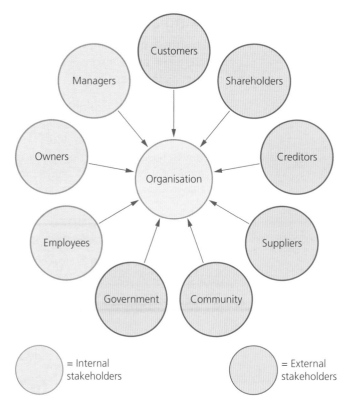

Figure 12.3 A stakeholder diagram

Feedback could be collected by questionnaire or face-to-face interview, for example. A questionnaire would allow you to ask more questions of more people, but a face-to-face interview enables you to explore the answers in more depth. You could use a questionnaire to gather initial, generic, feedback and explore any issues raised in more depth by using face-to-face questioning.

Any questionnaire should have a combination of tick box answers and longer written answers. The advantage of using tick box answers is that they can be completed and collated quickly. The answers are quantitative and so should be easier to analyse.

An example of a tick box type question resulting in quantitative data could be:

The proposed mobile technological solution would fully meet the client's needs.

Fully agree

Mostly agree

Not sure

Mostly disagree

Fully disagree.

Longer, open-ended, questions allow for more in-depth qualitative answers, but can be difficult to collate. For example, the person completing the questionnaire may not answer clearly (which may include having poor handwriting) or may give an answer where they say a lot, but their opinion is not clear.

User testing is another source of feedback. However, as you are designing a plan, rather than an actual product, you would not be asking users to test the product, but rather to feed back on whether they feel the product as planned would be suitable. While this information would be based on impression, rather than actual experience, this feedback could still be useful.

Analyse feedback

Feedback can be analysed in many ways. If using a questionnaire, answers can simply be counted and the balance of different responses to a question weighed up.

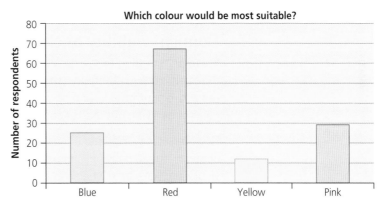

Figure 12.4 Responses to the question 'Which of the following colours do you think would be most suitable?'

In Figure 12.4, it would seem obvious that red should be chosen. However, this assumes that those who completed the survey were representative of end users. If not, this answer could be further explored by a face-to-face interview.

In the example in the section on obtaining feedback from stakeholders (above), we considered the statement 'The proposed mobile technological solution would fully meet the client's needs'. The questionnaire included five possible responses. One method of analysing the answers would be to count the responses, and see which one was most popular. However, how would we react if there was a tie between B (Mostly agree) and D (Mostly disagree)? Would we settle for C (Not sure) as a 'best fit' answer? There is some support for this. However, a more scientific method would be to allocate scores for each answer – so that A would score 1, B would score 2 and so on. By adding these scores up and dividing by the number of responses, the final figure takes account of all responses. Therefore, while B and D got equal votes, the significant vote for A is taken into account and we therefore have an overall more positive view of the effectiveness of our proposed solution.

Do not forget to take account of the qualitative open-ended answers. These can be difficult to analyse, especially as two people may express the same thought in different ways, but if analysed properly, these answers can give you a sense of the meaning behind the tick box answers.

INDEPENDENT ACTIVITY

(30 minutes)

Construct a questionnaire that will gather feedback on the use of mobile devices in a range of settings, such as cinemas, restaurants and on the bus. Focus on how respondents feel about the suitability of using devices in such locations, as well as any other issues that you decide are relevant.

Create a system for collating the answers you collect.

Test the questionnaire on five respondents of different ages. Reflect on any problems that became obvious with your questionnaire (such as a question that did not work, or an option that was not available) and amend it accordingly.

Confirm viability of changes

It can be tempting to research the viability of a project, obtain feedback and make all changes that have been suggested. After all, if you do not trust the results of your questionnaire and act upon what you have found, what is the point of carrying out the research?

However, it is worth spending some time making sure that the suggested changes are actually possible. But where do you draw the line between what is viable and not viable when the changes suggested are not obviously wrong?

One method of confirming whether the suggested changes are viable is to go back to your internal stakeholders. Your client, for example, may have an idea about the change based on its financial implications, or sales staff may have an idea about how well your suggested changes would meet the needs of customers they are already in contact with.

Implement improvements to solution based on viability of feedback

Your research results will be reliable if your planning has been carried out properly and you have taken action to avoid the person asking the questions influencing the answers. Now you just need to find out whether the project can actually be created. For example, even if your research shows that everyone would prefer wireless data transfer speeds of terabytes of data per second, the technology to do this does not exist.

You may consider that your respondents were not sufficiently representative of your target audience. In such a case, any decisions based on the feedback may be unreliable as they do not necessarily reflect the views of the target audience (there is always the chance that the views of your research population align with the views of the target audience, but this would be a coincidence and should not be relied upon).

You may also think that the interviewer has affected the views of those being interviewed. For example, they could have given guidance on how answers should be completed and so affected how the question has been answered, or could have caused offence and influenced those completing the questionnaire to give more negative feedback than they would usually.

Before taking any action, consider how comfortable you are with the feedback and whether any factors may have affected the views that were expressed. If so, you have to make a decision about whether or not to use the answers. If you run the research again, you will delay the project and incur more cost. However, the benefit of rerunning the research is the extent to which the new data is more accurate and the quality of the decisions is more reliable.

4.3 Predicting consequences of change

The final consideration is to try to predict the impact of any changes.

Future actions or events which are measurable

Increased profits

Profit is calculated by subtracting total costs of production from total revenue (the income received from selling the product). Therefore, profits may rise because costs fall, or revenue rises, or a combination of both.

To predict whether profits would rise, you would need to have an idea about how the changes will impact. If the changes are likely to make more people buy the product, this is likely to increase sales, which should increase profit.

If the change means that the same quantity of the mobile technological solution will be sold, but they will be developed or distributed more efficiently, profits will rise as the cost of manufacturing each unit decreases.

Customer satisfaction

Customer satisfaction can be hard to measure, but is sometimes simply a case of 'do people like the product?' This could be measured by sales, or by using panels of representative customers who vote on how much they like the product. Greater satisfaction could be achieved by creating a product with better features, or greater aesthetic appeal, possibly by changing its design.

Other changes that could make customers have a more positive view of the product range from improved packaging to making the proposed solution more eco-friendly.

Maintaining contact with customers and keeping track of market trends will help to predict potential changes in customer attitude, preferences and satisfaction.

Response time

This is a measure of the time it takes the manufacturer to respond to changes in market conditions. For example, if there was huge shift in customer tastes from green to yellow, the response time would measure how long it would take the manufacturer to change their product from green to yellow, or to produce yellow products as an option.

A number of factors can influence response time. For example, if the proposed solution includes raw materials sourced from elsewhere, the lead time – the time it takes the raw materials to arrive once they have been ordered – will affect the response time. Any change in the design of the solution that reduced the reliance on raw materials from elsewhere, or allowed a shift to a supplier with a shorter lead time, would improve the response time.

The degree of complication within the manufacturing process would also affect the response time. If the production process involved skilled workers, any change in the product would require staff to be trained. This would delay the response time. Similarly, any specialist machinery required for the production process would need to be replaced or recalibrated following a change in market conditions.

Therefore, any change which made the production process less complicated or require less specialist machinery would improve the response time.

> **KNOW IT**
>
> 1 Describe two differences between verbal and non-verbal communication.
> 2 What are three characteristics of a confident presenter?
> 3 Why is it important to adopt a confident manner when delivering a project proposal?
> 4 Why should both internal and external stakeholders be consulted when evaluating the effectiveness of a proposed solution?
> 5 What are two possible issues when analysing qualitative feedback?

TOP TIPS

✔ Make sure that you are prepared for your meeting or presentation. Be confident in your solution and present your ideas clearly and with passion.
✔ Gather feedback from a range of relevant sources.
✔ In Activity 1, any prediction of the solution's effectiveness may be based on a number of factors, including your own perception and the views of others, as well as research future technological and market trends.
✔ Your predictions should include measures that can be used to provide evidence to demonstrate the success of the project.

LO4 Assessment activities

Below are two suggested assessment activities that have been directly linked to the pass and distinction criteria in LO4 to help with assignment preparation; they include Top tips on how to achieve best results.

Activity 1 – pass criteria *P5 P6*

Promote your proposed solution to an audience of relevant stakeholders, gather feedback and improve your suggested solution based on that feedback.

Activity 2 – distinction criteria *D2*

Write a report predicting how effective your solution would be as an answer to the initial problem.

Unit **13**

Social media and digital marketing

ABOUT THIS UNIT

Social media is a huge growth area across the world. As users of social media post ideas, thoughts and stories, they create a huge bank of searchable material that can be used for marketing purposes. Also, as they are using social media, users are exposed to direct and indirect advertising, which is likely to be targeted to them because of their online behaviour, such as comments they have made or groups to which they belong.

This unit focuses on the collection and use of data that is generated by social media, as well as how social media can be used to deliver marketing messages to potential and existing customers.

LEARNING OUTCOMES

The topics and activities in this unit will help you to:

1 Understand digital marketing.
2 Understand the use of social media in business.
3 Be able to plan content and propose appropriate social media channels for digital marketing campaigns.
4 Be able to develop social media digital marketing campaigns.

How will I be assessed?

You will be assessed by producing evidence from set scenarios or from work that you carry out as part of a work placement or employment. This evidence will include a review of digital marketing and how it applies to business. You will also plan and create a digital marketing campaign. This evidence will be assessed by your tutor.

321

How will I be graded?

You will be graded using the following criteria:

Learning outcome	Pass assessment criteria	Merit assessment criteria	Distinction assessment criteria
You will:	To achieve a pass you must demonstrate that you have met all the pass assessment criteria	To achieve a merit you must demonstrate that you have met all the pass and merit assessment criteria	To achieve a distinction you must demonstrate that you have met all the pass, merit and distinction assessment criteria
1 Understand digital marketing	**P1** Outline the tools available for digital marketing		
	P2 Explain the stages of the digital marketing lifecycle		**D1** Assess the impact of digital marketing on an identified product
2 Understand the use of social media in business	**P3** Describe how social media may be used to gather data	**M1** Explain how data is used as part of social media digital marketing campaigns	
	P4* Describe the legal and ethical restrictions on the use of social media as part of digital marketing campaigns		
3 Be able to plan content and propose appropriate social media channels for digital marketing campaigns	**P5** Outline social media channels to be used in a digital marketing campaign	**M2** Plan the social media content of the digital marketing campaign to meet identified business objectives	**D2** Justify the use of identified social media channels in the digital marketing campaign
	P6 Describe the target audience for the identified social media channels		
4 Be able to develop social media digital marketing campaigns	**P7** Propose a digital marketing campaign across different social media channels to meet identified business objectives	**M3** Recommend adaptations to current business processes to support social media activities	

LO1 Understand digital marketing *P1 P2 D1*

GETTING STARTED

(10 minutes)

Individually, think about when you have been contacted by email as part of a marketing campaign, or have been tempted to find out more about a product for which you have seen a tweet or a post.

As a group, discuss the ways in which you have been contacted. Do you feel that some methods are better than others? Are you more tempted by one method than by another, or do you think that digital marketing does not work on you?

1.1 The role of marketing within business

Marketing is the process of selling a product. This process involves many different stages. The section below will explore some of these.

Market research

The 'market' is the potential buyers for a product. You will be drawn to some products in your local supermarket, and others you ignore. You do not consider every product because different people have different tastes and interests. Market research finds out about these patterns of interest.

For example, market research could find out whether a certain group would be likely to buy a new product, and how their buying patterns would be affected by changes in price. This information could be gathered in many ways, of which simply asking people is a key method. Unfortunately, gathering data in this way can be expensive. As we shall see, digital media can be used as a cheap method for collecting data.

Raising awareness and affecting perception of need via promotion and advertising

Our opinion of what we must have is, to a large degree, based on what we are told we need. As time goes on, the messages we receive change and so our opinions change. Sometimes we keep buying outdated products, but most people change their purchasing to fit with the messages they receive. This is an outcome of marketing.

Marketing in this area has two key tasks. The first is to make people aware of new products. The second task is based on the assumption that our perception of worth can be influenced.

Marketing to affect a perception of need is based on those who receive the message becoming convinced that they need the product. Need, in this case, translates into people deciding to buy the product.

Selling

Having researched the market for a product and advertised it to that market, the final stage is actually selling the product. Selling can be complex, as it is the process of making products available to people who want to buy them. If you are unable to buy a product because it is sold out or out of stock, this is a failure of this aspect of marketing.

Therefore, for selling to be successful, a number of different functions need to work together, including transport, product placement and manufacturing.

1.2 Digital marketing as a business tool

In this section, we will explore the impact that digital marketing may have on a business as a whole.

Business establishment

Any new business will need publicity if is to grow. Without publicity, very few people would know about the business and so sales would be minimal.

KEY TERM

Digital marketing: the use of digital technologies to communicate with potential and existing customers.

KEY TERMS

Market share: the percentage of the overall market made up by one product or brand or company.

Brand loyalty: the extent to which someone buys one product or brand repeatedly, rather than others.

Marketing mix: the interaction of price, product, placement and promotion as part of the marketing process.

Digital marketing can not only let people know that the business exists, but also provide ways in which the business can be easily contacted and their products researched.

Business growth

Some businesses are happy to establish themselves and stay quite small. Others wish to grow. The size of this growth can be established by a range of different measures, but possibly the most suitable is **market share**.

Market share can be affected by digital marketing, as digital methods, such as social networking, can used to communicate key messages. As we shall see, social networking provides a huge amount of information that can be used by marketing teams to target specific groups of people who may have an interest in purchasing the product or service being advertised.

Business continuity

Business continuity is the attempts of a business to stay in existence. There are many threats to business continuity, including threats to data security. Digital marketing has a particular impact of creating **brand loyalty**, which results in an increased chance of the business surviving.

Regular email newsletters, tweets and Instagram photographs can convert the occasional buyer into a loyal and committed customer who will not only repeatedly buy the original product, but also buy other products. The extent to which this happens is the extent to which the business may guarantee its ability to stay in business.

1.3 The tools of digital marketing

These are ways in which digital technology may be used as part of the **marketing mix**.

Social media types

Social media sites allow members to keep in contact and, in doing so, share details of their lives. There are many types of social media and many ways in which these can be described. The following are suggested descriptions.

- *Publishing*: not only can blogging sites and wikis publish the written word, they can also be used to publish artwork, photography and music. For example, fan fiction allows fans of popular films or books to write their own stories for their favourite characters and get feedback from others. As sources of ready-made communities of likeminded people, these sites provide marketing managers a clear opportunity to contact possible customers.
- *Sharing*: music, video and image files, for example, may be transferred from one person to another, while other sites allow the sharing of ideas. Sites that allow for discussion differ from blogging sites in that they allow two-way conversation between contributors acting at the same level, whilst in a blog, one person 'owns' the site and may control what is published.
- *Networking*: these sites enable members to make contact with each other. For example, on LinkedIn, members can share CVs and other information about their work skills.

Email

Emails are electronic messages delivered to electronic devices ranging from computers to smartphones. The basic message may be in text form, but other digital items, such as images, may be included with the email. Links to the company website, Twitter account or Facebook page may also be included in the body of the email.

When used as part of a digital marketing campaign, emails can be used in many ways, both internally and externally. Within the business, sales sheets may be sent to members of the team, while externally, customers can be sent links to online brochures.

Landing page optimisation

The landing page is the first web page that you land on from an external link

There are five main techniques of landing page optimisation. Three are based on targeting the audience using data, usually supplied either directly or indirectly by the visitor to the site, to change the content of the page to draw the visitor in.

- *Associative content targeting*: the content is influenced by data associated with the general profile of the visitor. For example, geographical data about the visitor can be used to provide information about special offers that are limited to the geographical area where the visitor is based.
- *Predictive content targeting*: this method is based on information that is already held about the visitor, usually from previous sales. This information may be held as cookies on the user's own machine, or as a profile that has been uploaded once the user logged on. Information held about the customer, such as previous purchases, can be a very powerful tool. However, one drawback is that for websites that sell a range of general products, the range of data held may result in a wide range of suggestions.
- *Consumer directed targeting*: content is based on general data, such as reviews from customers and others. Where reviews suggest that an element is not effective, it will be removed from the site. If that item was performing a key task, a new element will be added, hopefully carrying out the task more effectively.

The other two methods are based on experimentation and use a constantly changing set of elements to measure users' opinions.

- *Closed end experimentation*: users are given a range of options from which they can choose their favourite. Eventually, a final structure is arrived at, based on the views of many users. For example, different versions of the landing page could be used and the one with the highest success rate (measured by sign ups or sales, for example), could be chosen as the final version.
- *Open ended experimentation*: in this method, a final version is not settled on. The advantage of never ending the process is that the landing page continues to develop, and so changes as the needs and interests of the users change. There are different versions of the landing page but no assessment is made of which one will be the final version.

Banners and popups/unders

Web banners are advertisements on web pages. The owner of the web page will usually be paid a small fee for each person that clicks on that web banner.

The content of the web banner will be targeted at getting viewers to click on it and will use traditional methods of advertising, including coercion, persuasion and appealing to the viewer's basic needs. As with landing page optimisation, the content of a web banner may change to suit the information held about the person who has logged on to the web page.

Popups and popunders are also intended to attract attention. They are new windows that open on the user's machine, either on top of the main page (popups) or under it (popunders), with the trigger usually being JavaScript code that is embedded on the site.

Popups can often be a source of irritation for visitors to web pages, as they interrupt the viewer's experience of the site. This can have a detrimental effect on the amount of traffic that the original site attracted. As a result, popunders are becoming more frequently used, as they are not immediately apparent and so the user does not know which site included the trigger.

SEO (search engine optimisation)

Search engines are specialist websites that allow the user to find websites based on criteria that the user enters. The list that is returned is called 'natural' or 'organic'. It is possible for a website to pay to be included at the top of the list, but we will consider this later. Results that are paid for are not considered 'natural'. This method is dealt with in the section on Channels (below).

Research suggests that users will only look at no more than the first three pages of any list returned by a search engine. A website that is not on those first pages will be very unlikely to attract any visitors via search engines.

Search engines also show activity on social media sites, such as Twitter and LinkedIn.

Search engine optimisation (SEO) is the process of trying to get the website or another listable web element on which you are working as near to the top of the results as possible. There are two main areas of focus. The first is using data on how people search for items on the web. The second is to do with how search engines rank websites, and so a lot of SEO work requires a technical understanding of how different search engines work. For example, some search engines will rank sites based on how many other sites link to it, and so a lot of work will be done on maximising the number of links to a site.

Channels

Digital marketing channels are the tools used to get the message from the advertiser to the customer.

One channel is to use paid advertisements on search engines. This is where a website will appear at the top of the natural listing returned by a search engine. This is subtler than a banner heading, and is also 'hidden' among the sites returned naturally. Some people are not aware that the site has been artificially placed at the top of the list, and so they will assume it is the most relevant site for their search and click on the link. The site may not be the most relevant and may lead them to make a purchase they would otherwise not have made. However, this is the fundamental aim of advertising!

Other forms of digital channels include Facebook, where brands and businesses encourage as many people as possible to 'like' their page and share their posts. When an item is shared by a Facebook user, this item appears on the homepage of their Facebook friends. Users who receive this shared post are able to 'like' it, which is tracked by Facebook so that users receive similar posts on their home page. The business may use the number of likes and shares as a measure of the post's success.

Facebook also tracks how you follow adverts and apps from your Facebook page, to show targeted adverts on your home page.

'Liking' and 'sharing' makes users suddenly aware of a product or service. Clearly, this provides a huge opportunity to marketing departments for little cost.

Twitter and Instagram allow promoted messages. Even with 140 characters or less, the message has the chance of being seen. Again, such direct marketing offers huge potential.

1.4 Digital marketing

The process of digital marketing combines all these tools to achieve identified aims.

Strategies towards identified marketing goals

Identifying potential customers and markets

Every time that you state on social media that you have eaten at cafe A, been to theme park B, or shopped at shop C, you are creating data about your spending patterns and this data can be used to build up a profile not only of you, but also your friends.

Social media is therefore a huge source of valuable data about our everyday lives. In the past, this data would only have been available to businesses that employed market researchers to stop people in the street and ask questions. Nowadays, not only is this data more freely available, it is also shared between friends and so is more likely to be reliable.

Setting short-term and long-term goals

A digital marketing campaign can have many goals. Some are short-term goals, intended to be achieved over a few months, while others take longer to achieve.

For example, a short-term goal of digital marketing may be to raise awareness of a product or service, for example during a product launch.

A longer term target may be to increase sales. This technique may use contact lists of customers, gathered over time, to identify those who are likely to be tempted back into buying the product. These contacts are sent special offers or other enticements to renew their interest in the product.

Creating a marketing and sales funnel

A marketing and sales funnel describes the route from an initial contact by a member of the public through to the stage at which they give their email address, or buy the product.

Figure 13.1 Example of a marketing and sales funnel

Therefore, a marketing funnel combines together many of the elements we have discussed into one coordinated process.

There are three distinct stages to the funnel.

1 Awareness is simply the process of making sure that the product's name is known.
2 The interest of the potential customer could be measured by social media. For example, the number of clicks on a web banner or the number of likes for a product's Facebook page.
3 The action stage is when the customer does what you want, whether giving an email address or buying a product.

Developing a call to action

A call to action is the particular trigger that makes a person act.

Imagine that your prospective buyer has read your marketing information, has clicked on images and infographics to find out how good your product is, and is at the stage where they will act. If the content you have provided is good enough, a high percentage of people who are asked will follow your suggested action. If this happens often, the call to action has done its job.

Gathering data

This has been dealt with in the section on identifying new customers and markets, but it can also include gathering data that may have a wider impact.

For example, customers and contacts may be asked to complete online forms or questionnaires. These gather data which will be used to inform future decisions. In some cases, questionnaires are structured to hide the true nature of the product to which they are linked. The respondent starts to receive emails or other forms of digital correspondence from a business they have not actively contacted. This information has clearly come from the questionnaire.

Not only is such a practice unethical, it may also contravene the Data Protection Act as the data may be used for a purpose other than for which it was collected. Many websites that gather data with the intention of using it for contact purposes include an 'opt out' button (rather than the more ethical 'opt in' button) as a way of protecting themselves when gathering data for later use.

There is a positive side to using data gathered in this way. Because the data is used to target specific people with specific information, it can cut down on the number of unwanted emails.

Creating traffic

Traffic is the term given to the number of people accessing your digital resource. Traditionally, this referred to people visiting a particular website and was a useful measure when websites were used as the primary means of selling online. However, as digital marketing has developed, the range of selling points has increased, so that sales are not only completed via traditional websites but by other digital means, such as Twitter and Facebook. Consequently, there has been a shift towards 'traffic' being the rate of customer flow across all digital marketing and sales methods.

1.5 Digital marketing lifecycles

The digital marketing lifecycle attempts to describe the process of a digital marketing campaign's development. It can provide the managers of a marketing campaign with a clear timeframe for success, so that they understand that the jump from initial launch to full on massive sales will not happen overnight. Unlike other cyclical concepts you may have studied (such as the product lifecycle), this process is not cyclical, because the final stage does not naturally lead back to the first. In this sense it is a growth model more than a lifecycle.

Stages of the digital marketing lifecycle

The following are the stages that are usually included in a digital marketing lifecycle.

> The information on the digital marketing lifecycle includes typical timescales. Not all products will follow these timescales – some will be much shorter – although they will generally follow the pattern.

Setup (up to 3 months)	
Any action to start acquiring customers e.g. getting potential customers to follow you on social media e.g. including a form to capture email addresses on a website.	• Emails • Social media profiles • Website • Mobile marketing

Traction (up to 6 months from Setup)	
Initial contracts with potential customers become tangible via engagement e.g. the product appears search listings, or calls to action via special offer emails get results.	• Emails • Regular social media posts and responses • Website development • Audience data segmentation • Mobile marketing

Positioning (10 to 15 months from Setup)	
The product or service starts to have a status within the market and is impacting on other competing products. This stage is typified by an increase in sales, moving up search engine rankings and the beginning of brand loyalty (retaining customers).	• Targeted emails • Monitoring social media • Blogs • Games and apps • Videos • Website consolidation • Audience data segmentation • Mobile marketing

Expansion (16 months+ from Setup)	
The product matures to be a major player in the market, with a constant market revenue and a stable position in the search engine rankings.	• Targeted emails • Monitoring social media • Games and apps • Website consolidation • Videos • Audience data segmentation • Content management • Mobile marketing

Viral growth	
The product and all the aspects of digital media associated with it, dominate. In terms of exposure, it is everywhere and is what everyone is talking about.	• Targeted emails • Monitoring social media • Games and apps • Website consolidation • Videos • Audience data segmentation • Content management • Mobile marketing

Figure 13.2 Stages of the digital marketing lifecycle

(40 minutes)

Identify one product that is at each of three of the stages of the digital marketing lifecycle.

Create a document (e.g. presentation, table) summarising each of the stages and how a product progresses through them. Present your findings to the group.

> **KNOW IT**
>
> 1 What is meant by each of the following terms?
>   a market share
>   b brand loyalty
>   c marketing mix.
> 2 Describe the role that marketing plays in the success of a business.
> 3 Explain the importance of market research to a business.
> 4 Describe what is meant by the term 'business continuity'. How can business continuity be affected by digital marketing?
> 5 Describe one method of search engine optimisation.

LO1 Assessment activity

Below is a suggested assessment activity that has been directly linked to the pass and distinction criteria in LO1 to help with assignment preparation; it include Top tips on how to achieve best results.

Activity 1 – pass criteria *P1*, *P2* and distinction criteria *D1*

You work for a small company that creates materials to be used in schools. You have been asked to create a piece about the impact of digital marketing to present to a client.

Your piece should include:

● The tools that are available.
● The stages of the digital marketing lifecycle.
● An assessment of the impact of a digital marketing campaign on an identified product.

TOP TIPS ✔
- ✔ Make sure you clearly identify the product or service you are covering.
- ✔ Your completed work could be presented as a video, sound file or a word processed report.

LO2 Understand the use of social media in a business *P3 P4 M1*

As we saw LO1, social media may be used to support the process of digital marketing. In this section, we will explore this further with particular focus on data, as well as considering the legal and ethical restrictions on doing so.

2.1 Research

Research is the process of finding data. This data is processed and becomes information. There are many ways in which data can be gathered, but the most useful grouping is to consider who collected the data in the first place.

Primary data

Primary data is the data that you, your colleagues or your organisation collects. The advantage of primary data is that the data gathering process has been planned by you and so the data has been gathered to answer your specific question. However, the process of collecting primary data can be expensive and time consuming.

Figure 13.3 What are the advantages and disadvantages of collecting primary data?

(90 minutes)

In pairs or small groups, decide on one of the following research topics.

Each research topic is aimed at students aged between 16 and 18. Each group should find out the answer to the question, as well as research factors that explain the respondent's answer.

- favourite genre of film
- favourite holiday destination
- favourite sporting activity.

Design and create a questionnaire to find the required information.

Test the questionnaire on a sample of suitable students.

Review the answers and amend the questionnaire as necessary.

Review the success of your initial questionnaire and explain any amendments you had to make to improve it.

Secondary data

This is data that is gathered by somebody else and may answer a different question than you are asking. For more general projects, this may not be important. For example, if you needed to know the population of Doncaster, you would refer to data gathered by someone else rather than counting it yourself.

If it is freely available online, the data may be quick and relatively cheap to obtain. However, the more specialist the data you require, the less likely it is that the data collected by someone else is going to match your needs. Also, specialist data is usually bought, so there is a cost implication of using secondary data. It may also be less reliable than your own data. Therefore, the decision to use secondary data should only be made after careful consideration.

CLASSROOM DISCUSSION

(40 minutes)

You have been asked to find information for a number of research projects.

- The number of female students in your school or college who eat in the canteen on a Friday.
- The number of people who live in your street.
- The number of people who shop in the largest retail park in the area, per year.
- The age of the oldest serving member of parliament.
- The number of servings in a jar of peanut butter.

For each project, decide whether you should use *primary* or *secondary* data to provide the information. Be prepared to justify each of your decisions.

Discuss each of the research projects and decide which of the following factors is the most important for each decision:

- cost
- speed of obtaining data
- accuracy of the data achieved.

2.2 Data as a resource

Data management

DAMA, the professional organisation for those involved in the data management industry, describes data management as being 'the development and execution of architectures, policies, practices and procedures that properly manage the full data lifecycle needs of an enterprise'. (Source: damauk.org/)

This means that data management is to do with structures to store data, policies to control and collect data and practices and procedures to manage how data is used.

The structure of a data management team, as well as the way in which an individual organisation may store and use data, will differ. However, any organisation that wants to use data efficiently will have a data management system in place.

Sources of data

The information that is put on social media sites can be used in different ways, e.g. relationship status notifications, information about life history (place of birth and school for example) and announcements about new babies. Other data may be gathered by using web cookies.

INDEPENDENT ACTIVITY

(30 minutes)

List the posts you have added to social media over the past 10 days. What information could be gathered from this and who would use it?

Present your information as a table.

> Generation F (or Generation Z) is the generation that has grown up making use of social media. This generation can be defined as those who see no real difference between online and real world friends and who therefore blur the separation between 'contacts' and 'friends' as they may have been defined by older people.

As Generation F (those who have grown up with social media) becomes older, so their importance as a source of data has grown as they now have opinions, spend money and vote in elections. As they are so used to social media, their interaction with the differing formats, and the extent to which they will freely share information, means that they represent a ready source of data. This data, clearly, becomes more of a meaningful asset as Generation F becomes more dominant in society.

Collection of data

The process of data collecting will depend on your relationship with the social media site from which you want to gather the data. The process will require data entry. This can simply be a case of recording how many times your product was mentioned on Twitter, or how many commented on your new car design, and using this as an indication of interest and success. Some social media platforms, such as Hootsuite, Twitter and Facebook, create reports about individual social media sites that can be downloaded for analysis, thereby making the process easier.

Analysis of data

Data mining is the (usually automated) process of working through the plethora of data that is added daily to social media sites. These posts, tweets and other communication collectively make up a data set, from which patterns, trends, anomalies and relationships may be identified.

The difference between a pattern and a trend in these terms is that the pattern will describe the layout of responses, while the trend will describe how this layout has changed over time. This layout need not be geographical and may show sales of a product across different age ranges, for example, or the level of interest in a particular product on social media in different months.

Many factors might affect the effectiveness of this identification of patterns and trends. The reliability of the original data, as well as the quality of the analysis, can both affect the quality of the conclusions.

(20 minutes)

Divide the methods of gathering and the methods of analysing data between you and research your allotted method.

Create a presentation and handout explaining your method of gathering or analysis to the group as a whole.

Sale of data

As we have seen, data is an asset. It should not be a surprise, therefore, that data, like any other asset, may be sold for financial gain.

The sheer amount of data that is gathered by social media sites means that data is not just gathered for an identified project, but simply as part of the process of running a social media site. This could be data that members add via comments and posts, or may be data that is gathered at the time of registration. The extent to which an organisation may gather data is limited by the Data Protection Act in the UK.

2.3 Use of data

There are four clear areas in which data can be used.

Identification of gaps in markets

A gap in the market is where a product does not currently exist to fulfil a need that does exist.

There will always be a few people who want to buy two left hand gloves, or a kettle with polka dots, and the fact that they are probably unable to do so means that there is a gap in the market. However, the size of the market would be insufficient to generate enough revenue and profit.

If, however, the gap in the market is sizeable enough to suggest that a large revenue will be made, organisations may enter into the market to attempt to close that gap.

Tweets on Twitter or comments on Facebook could be used to identify such a gap. Imagine that someone commented that it would be great if you could buy orange and white washing powder, and this comment was repeated, liked or tagged by thousands. This would indicate that there is a gap in the market for this product.

Identification of changes in customer habits and tastes

As comments are made about what is hot and what is not, or the popularity of individual Twitter accounts changes, so this generates data that can be used to identify trends in the market. The honesty with which individuals will comment on social media sites means that the data collected about current perceptions of product popularity is likely to be more accurate and up to date than data collected in any other way.

Targeted marketing

Those who use social media give information about their likes and dislikes and even contact information. These contact details can be used to send personalised, targeted direct communications to individuals.

Planning campaigns

Marketing campaigns cover the range of activities that will make up the overall attempt to launch, establish and grow a product. As we have seen, data can be at the centre of every aspect of that campaign. For example, if a gap in the market has been identified, and that gap is linked with a specific target audience, then the choice of message and the method by which the message may be sent can be influenced by the data that has been gathered.

2.4 Communications

Between staff

From email to Twitter, the ability to communicate with colleagues quickly, easily and privately is vital. Sensitive information, such as sales targets or issues with suppliers, needs to be sent to those who need to know, but kept away from competitors. Email, for example, provides such a private and secure method.

However, not all communication needs to be totally private and so social media can be used to send less sensitive messages between colleagues. Facebook, for example, can be used to announce that an office is closed because of snow or heating problems. Some job vacancies are advertised on Facebook. However, many people prefer to keep work and Facebook separate.

With customers

Some messages go one way – broadcasts – and other messages are two way – conversations. Most forms of social media can be used as part of a one-way or a two-way conversation.

Twitter, for example, can be used to simply announce an event or it can be used to cover other functions. For example, Twitter can be used to make complaints about a brand, product or service. Because Tweets can be monitored for key words, even posts that only mention the brand rather than being addressed to a business often reach their intended targets.

Similarly, posts on Facebook can lead to direct contact from the business. Some organisations will direct complaints made on Facebook to a complaints form on their website.

2.5 Legislation and business policy and practice

So far, we have looked at how social media and data can be used within an organisation. However, we now need to consider how the use of these may be restricted by legal and ethical considerations.

Legislation

See also Units 1, 2 and 3 (pages 42, 67 and 95).

Legislation

The UK's Data Protection Act 1998 sets out how data may be gathered, processed and stored. For example, it states that data may only be kept for the length of time needed to complete the task for which it was gathered. So, when a business asks a person for their email address, they may only keep that email address for as long as the purpose for which it was supplied exists. Clearly, therefore, the wording on any data collection form has to be carefully constructed so that such data may be kept for as long as possible.

One further impact of the Data Protection Act is that even when data has been collected and stored correctly, the person who the data relates to can place further restrictions on how that data may be used; for example, they can request that the data may not be used for direct marketing purposes. Another example is that it must be easy to unsubscribe from emails.

In some cases, the use of data may be based on the job that individuals do. For example, teachers do not have access to all the data that is held about a student, as this is considered to be beyond the level of information they need to complete their job. By contrast, where the data is processed for national security, for example to gather information about terrorist suspects, the Data Protection Act does not apply.

In both cases, the restriction or relaxation of the Data Protection Act applies to cases that are outside of the general use of data and social media.

Business policy and practice

Each business will have its own internal policies. These define how staff must operate to meet the legal restrictions on the use of data, as well as other special restrictions and controls that the organisation wants to apply. Here are some examples.

Acceptable use policy (AUP)

This describes how individuals should use the internet when doing their jobs. The policy will list ways of working which are acceptable, and starts with an assumption that legal restrictions are already being observed. Therefore, an AUP is a business-specific extension to any legal restrictions.

An example of a restriction is whether an individual is allowed to use personal webmail within their day-to-day working life, or whether they are restricted to using the 'official' business email account provided by the employer. Further items included in an AUP could be whether the employee is able to access online sales sites.

Social media policy

A social media policy will include clear instructions on the acceptable use of social media by all staff, as part of their work. Clearly, this differs from the use of social media by market analysts and others employed to actually gather the data that will be used for marketing purposes.

A social media policy covers two key areas. The first is avoiding risks to the business, such as from malware, while the second is dealing with the erosion of the difference between work life and private life which access to social media provides.

PAIRS ACTIVITY

(40 minutes)

Research the eight principles of the Data Protection Act 1998.

Create a presentation describing in your own words each of the principles.

The fifth principle is to keep data for only as long as it is needed. Explain how each of the seven remaining principles may influence an organisation collecting and using data captured via social media.

INDEPENDENT ACTIVITY

(40 minutes)

Research the AUP for your school or college.

Describe FOUR ways that this AUP impacts on the day-to-day working practice of your tutors or lecturers.

INDEPENDENT ACTIVITY

(40 minutes)

Write a social media policy for one of the following:

- a school
- a hospital
- an office.

Recruitment policy

This final restriction not only really relates to the use of data, but also defines the business's own rules on how they will recruit staff. This policy is generally linked to anti-discrimination policy and the Equality Act of 2010, but may also include sections on how to deal with recruitment to specialist roles. In some cases, organisations will use social media to reduce the list of possible candidates, but it can also be used to check for positive attributes. Comments made, images posted and organisations linked to are all types of data on which such research will focus. Recruitment policy will place restrictions on how far such research will go, how data is interpreted and what weighting is given to individual items. For example, racist comments would be treated far more seriously than photographs of a party.

2.6 Ethical and moral issues

Some restrictions the business imposes on itself. A cynic may feel that these decisions are based on how the individual business wants to present itself to prospective customers, but many businesses have taken excellent ethical positions that have influenced working practices throughout the world. Examples of such positive impacts would include the ethical and sustainable stance taken by the Cooperative Bank.

Bias

Bias is how data is interpreted. When working with data, organisations need to be aware that personal opinions may influence how data is interpreted and need to take action to make sure that facts play a stronger part than opinion. For example, if one believes that Wales is a superior part of the United Kingdom with a better education system than the rest of the country, one could take the views of people in Wales as being more in-depth and relevant than those given by others.

However, such an interpretation would be based on a clear bias and should be avoided.

Bias may also occur in areas where sponsorship, for example, may impact. Any data that is influenced by sponsorship, or payment for opinions, should be avoided. It is also useful for any organisations involved in data gathering and analysis to ask staff and others to declare any other interests they may have which could affect how they interpret data.

Integrity

Each business needs to consider how it will use the data it gathers. A lot of opinion on social media sites will be negative towards products. If a competitor finds this information, they will need to decide how they are going to use it. Do they, for example, use that negative opinion to make their own product appear better?

Competitions are another way in which integrity can be considered. For example, a competition could be held that asks customers to design a new logo for a café. The prize would be the exposure that the winning artist receives. In return, the café gets hundreds of pounds of design work competed for free. While some people may think that this is an excellent opportunity for a local artist, others would feel that the prize does not match the work involved and so is unacceptable. As the opinion of at least some of the target audience may be negative, it is best to avoid such practices.

KNOW IT

1 What is meant by each of the following terms?
   a bias
   b acceptable use policy
   c data mining.
2 Describe the restrictions that the Data Protection Act 1998 places on a business that uses personal data.
3 Compare primary and secondary data.
4 Describe the content of a social media policy.
5 With examples, explain how data may be used to identify a gap in the market.

LO2 Assessment activity

Below is a suggested assessment activity that has been directly linked to the pass and merit criteria in LO2 to help with assignment preparation; it includes Top tips on how to achieve best results.

Activity 1 – pass criteria *P3* *P4* and merit criteria *M1*

You work as part of a marketing team. Your team has been asked to explore the use of social media as a source of data.

Write a proposal to your manager that supports the use of social media as a means by which data may be gathered. Your proposal should include:

● A description of how social media may be used to gather data.
● An explanation of how the data that is gathered may be used as part of a digital marketing campaign.

Your proposal should also include a section that explains the legal and ethical restrictions which need be taken into account when using social media in this way.

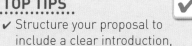
TOP TIPS
✔ Structure your proposal to include a clear introduction, explanation and conclusion.
✔ Make sure you include the section on the legal and ethical restrictions.

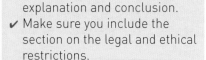
GETTING STARTED
(10 minutes)

Working individually, create a mind map of all of the possible social media channels that you could use to launch a new film aimed at people between the age of 16 and 23.

Develop your mind map further to show how each channel could be used.

LO3 Be able to plan content and propose appropriate social media channels for digital marketing campaigns *P5 P6 M2 D2*

In this section, you will plan the content for a digital marketing campaign. When working on any project, it is a really good idea to keep in close contact with your client.

3.1 Social media channels

We discussed social media channels in LO1.3. In your work for this section, you will need to suggest channels that are appropriate to the digital marketing campaign you have been asked to propose. Clearly, the requirement for the channel to be appropriate will place some restriction on the channels you propose.

As well as the channels included in LO1.3, you could also consider Myspace, Snapchat and Wikipedia.

3.2 Potential outcomes

We have considered some of the range of potential outcomes of a digital marketing campaign. The impacts were all positive. In order for you to complete your work for this area, we need to consider a few more positive outcomes, as well as the range of possible negative impacts.

> Planning techniques will include meetings with the client to set success criteria, mind maps, flow charts and time planning techniques, such as Gantt and CPA charts.

Positive outcomes

Customer services

One possible outcome of an effective digital marketing campaign could be an improvement in customer service. As the campaign runs, so more data on customers could be gathered. If this is used to improve the targeting of customers, this would mean a reduction in emails to those who do not want or need the product, and more effective emails to those who do.

Effect on product lifecycle

The product lifecycle is a model of the life of a product from its initial inception and design, through its launch, growth into a product that is established in the marketplace and eventual decline as market tastes and consumer needs change.

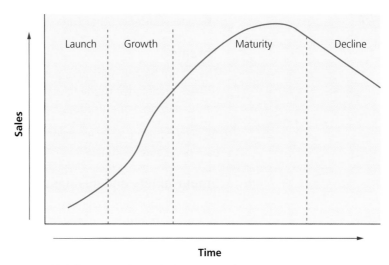

Figure 13.4 Progress through the stages of the product lifecycle

An effective digital marketing campaign will have a positive effect on the product lifecycle. However, because there are many different possible outcomes of a digital marketing campaign, each will affect the product lifecycle in a different way. For example, a digital marketing campaign that supports the launch of a product should reduce the time taken for customers to become familiar with it. Alternatively, a campaign intended to slow the rate of decline of a product should extend the decline stage, so that the product will have a longer life.

Financial impacts

A digital marketing campaign could affect business finance in several ways. If, for example, the campaign reduces the time it takes to introduce the product, then the product will enter the growth stage more quickly so the period when sales and therefore revenue are high is reached more quickly.

Similarly, if the campaign slows the rate of decline, then the period over which the product will be sold will increase, which would increase the total sales and the revenue.

Negative outcomes

Work rate

Social media is available anywhere with access to the internet and can be extremely distracting. Therefore, unless access is controlled, the work rate of an individual can be negatively affected, as they spend more time on social media than they do on their jobs.

Bullying

Cyber-bullying is a real threat in all areas of society and the work place is no exception. Whatever the source of bullying, the impacts of bullying via social media have a proven detrimental effect on employees and any digital marketing campaign should take account of the possibility of bullying in the design of the campaign itself, as well as in any plans about how the data gathered by the campaign is to be used. For example, it is better if emails are sent from a special 'No-reply' account than a personal account as, otherwise, negative responses would be sent to an individual, with possibly offensive content rather than general comments.

Threats

This could be considered an extension to bullying, as threats could be direct threats of violence made to staff or to the organisation itself. However, it could also be digital threats, such as malware or denial of service attacks.

As with bullying, any campaign needs to at least have considered this issue as a possibility and have included some provision should it occur.

Employability and business image

Employability is the ability of an individual to work in the future, while business image is the way in which the business itself is viewed. These could both be negatively affected by any digital marketing campaign that fails to achieve its set targets. For example, a campaign that misuses data would have a negative effect on the business image, especially where this misuse leads to action being taken under the Data Protection Act. This would impact on any staff who were involved in the project, as they could be seen as being inefficient by association with a failed project.

If the content of a campaign was seen as racist, homophobic or otherwise disrespectful, this would have a negative impact on a business or organisation, as rather than increase sales, or extend the life of a product, sales would fall as people chose to boycott the product.

3.3 Potential restrictions

Any plan should include a consideration of possible restrictions or constraints, and these should be addressed in your plan.

Legislation

We considered this in section 2.5. When planning your content and the media channel(s) to use, you will need to show that you have taken account of relevant legislation.

Technological constraints

These are the restrictions that are placed on the plan by technology. This restriction may be based on the absence of the required technology on a wider scale or within the organisation.

Any plan that deals with technological constraints should include some discussion of the financial restriction placed on the ability to remedy a technological constraint where the technology exists in society but not within the organisation.

Skills constraints

Does the organisation have sufficiently skilled staff? Are there experts in SEO (search engine optimisation) available or could this be completed by someone with only limited skills in the subject? When planning, you need to be clear about what can be done with the staff that are currently available, or who could be employed quickly and cheaply.

As with all constraints, a lack of sufficiently skilled staff can be overcome, given the time and the use of finances, and so a report that was dealing with skills constraints should include some discussion of how these constraints may be remedied via the use of training of internal staff, or the recruitment of suitably skilled staff from other organisations.

3.4 Target audience

Your content and choice of channel(s) should be based on the target audience. You will need to have a clear understanding of what generally appeals to this target audience. 'Generally appeals' is a key term here, as you will need to target your product at the average likes of the target audience, rather than the interests of a small minority within the target audience.

There are many ways that you can describe your target audience. Typically, the target audience is broken down into four key areas. You may find that not all of these factors are relevant when you complete your design. However, you should at least be aware of them, as you may be surprised at how important each is.

Figure 13.5 Who is your target audience?

The four key definitions of a target audience are:

- age
- gender
- income
- educational background.

Age would usually be expressed as an age range rather than an exact age.

Gender should also be clear.

Income may be another factor to be aware of, depending on the initial brief. Income usually influences the target audience because as an individual person's income increases, so their demand for certain products diminishes, while their demand for others increases. Typically, luxury goods, such as expensive clothing, are linked to high incomes, while cheaper products are linked to lower incomes.

Educational background can have an impact on the sort of language that you use in your campaign. At its most basic, this could be using shorter words and images for explanation in a project aimed at one group, while using longer words and more detailed questioning for another.

Target audience can be a useful way to help you design a campaign and it will help if you have a clear direction from the brief. If, for example, the campaign needs to be aimed at men aged between 21 and 30 and you know that this age group really likes cute kittens, you can include that in your design. However, there are times when the target audience is so wide that it is impossible to define. This is usually because the product itself is extremely general and is not readily identified with one only group.

> **KNOW IT**
>
> 1 What is meant by each of the following terms?
>   **a** skills constraint　　　　　　**b** target audience.
> 2 Describe two possible positive outcomes of a digital marketing campaign.
> 3 Identify two possible negative outcomes of a digital marketing campaign. For each possible negative outcome, describe how this threat may be avoided.
> 4 Describe the stages of the product lifecycle. For each stage, explain how this may be affected by a successful digital marketing campaign.
> 5 Compare the effectiveness and suitability of three digital marketing channels of your choice as part of a campaign to launch a new model of family saloon car.

LO3 Assessment activity

Below is a suggested assessment activity that has been directly linked to the pass, merit and distinction criteria in LO3 to help with assignment preparation; it includes Top tips on how to achieve best results.

Activity 1 – pass criteria *P5 P6* merit criteria *M2* and distinction criteria *D2*

You have been asked to plan and propose suitable social media channels for a digital marketing campaign to launch a new model of family saloon car.

Plan the content and provide justification for your choices.

LO4 Be able to develop social media digital marketing campaigns *P7 M3*

GETTING STARTED

(10 minutes)

How would you propose a project to a group of friends? Would you simply tell them all of the reasons why they should take part and ignore the possible negative effects?

Think of a project with which you have been involved. What were the positives of that project and what were the negatives?

Did you know about both sides of the project before you started?

In this final section, you will develop a social media digital marketing campaign. This section will bring together all that you have learnt about the use of social media channels, as well as how they may be used to gather data and present messages to prospective and existing customers. Throughout this section, keep in mind that your client is an important point of reference.

4.1 Features of a social media marketing campaign

Appropriate staffing mix

The staffing mix is the structure of the team working on a project. A successful team will include a mixture of creative, technical and managerial staff who will work together towards a successful outcome. For any project, there is an optimum staffing mix and the closer the actual team structure is to that theoretical structure, the more likely is the project to succeed.

Clear objectives and shared targets

Even when working individually, a clear set of objectives is vital to prevent a project losing its focus. Clear objectives give a clear outcome against which the success of the project can be measured and so give a clear focus for all involved, whether they are an individual or many. These objectives need to be communicated to the whole team.

Any plan should have clear objectives and a clear method by which these are to be shared and, if necessary, any amendments to these plans passed on. This communications plan should be included in the structure of the social media marketing campaign.

Core message

This is the key impact that the campaign is trying to achieve and may be summed up as a simple statement – such as 'Our shoes are best' or 'Parents who know best buy our apples'. The core message is that good parents should buy this product.

The core message is the key point around which the whole campaign is written and should be the foundation of the whole campaign. When planning the campaign, care should be taken to make sure that other aspects of the plan do not get in the way of this core message.

Unique selling point (USP)

The USP is a key concept in marketing, as it is the feature that allows you to differentiate your product from all of the others. In some cases, the USP is clear, possibly because your product is clearly the only one of its type, while in other cases the USP may be a relatively small feature that you accentuate through advertising, such as the fact that your product comes in red, white and blue, while competitors' products only come in white or blue. The fact that the product comes in red does not affect the quality of the product, but through skilful advertising it could be made to appear hugely significant.

When you develop your campaign, you will need to identify one feature of your product that will be the key focus.

Company image

This is the image that the company portrays to the outside world and may be something on which the company has spent many years working. It is extremely unlikely, therefore, that any campaign would be at odds with this image, as the change in company image could have an overall negative effect. For example, a brand associated with healthy food would not benefit from a message implying its products are a high calorie treat.

When implementing a social media marketing campaign, the company image needs to be considered unless a clear decision has been made that it should not be, or if one of the intended outcomes of the campaign is to change the company image.

Social media channels

These have already been discussed and should also have been part of your work for LO3.

Timescales and review dates

Your campaign will need to have clear and realistic dates by which key elements should have been achieved. The section on the digital marketing lifecycle in LO1.5 gives an indication of what may be achievable within certain timescales.

Your plan should also include review dates – when you will sit down and check that you have achieved what you want to achieve. It would be a good idea to arrange for at least one of these reviews to be carried out with your client (who could be your tutor), so that you can check that you are progressing towards an outcome that matches what the client wants.

Social marketing funnel

This campaign feature was discussed in LO1.

Social media tools

Three examples of key tools are as follows.

Social media measurement

This is the process of gathering data from social media sources. As your campaign is fundamentally based on social media to gather data, this aspect must be covered in your plan.

Social network aggregation

This is the process of combining data gathered from different social media channels into one overall package of data. This section of your plan could end up being extremely complicated, as the process involved in the industry includes the use of specialist software and service providers. For example, Hootsuite is a social media management tool that works with a number of different forms of social media.

However, at its simplest level, the process is one of counting. If, for example, a project wanted to affect customer awareness, this could be assessed by measuring how often a particular product has been mentioned at the start of the project and again at the end. For some types of social media, gathering the source data for this is a relatively simple process, especially where the channel automatically provides such data (such as the number of hits, likes or re-messaging).

Social media mining

This is the final stage of data gathering and is where patterns in any data are identified so that action can be taken. This process involves representing the data, possibly in diagram form; analysing the data from the representation (so that if the data has been presented as a diagram such as a graph, trends would be identified) and extracting patterns from which action points can be created.

4.2 Campaign considerations

Any social media digital marketing campaign must take account of various considerations. Some of these are concepts we have already discussed.

Business objectives

You will have considered business objectives as part of your work for LO3.2.

Alignment with wider organisational marketing programme

There are many reasons why any marketing plan should take account of marketing programmes that already exist within the organisation, not least because the skills used within the wider marketing programme may be relevant to the specific campaign that is being planned. Alongside this, if the specific campaign is to contribute to the overall public image and opinion of the organisation as a whole, the marketing campaign should be seen as part of this whole. Where the marketing campaign does not agree with the overall programme within the wider organisation, it runs the risk of undermining the effectiveness, possibly by damaging the image of the organisation.

Format and restrictions on content

The content is what you choose to include in your digital marketing campaign. The format is the type of content and how it is to be presented. For example, a campaign could decide that it wants to feature children strongly. The format would be the manner in which those children appear in the campaign. Examples could be as video, images or simply as voices. There could, for example, also be a discussion of whether the children could be presented as cartoons or real life characters.

There should also be a consideration of any restrictions on content. These could be age based restrictions, such as imagery and content that would not be appropriate for a specific target audience, such as children under 10. The intended target audience is a good starting point for this area of consideration.

Channels

We have discussed channels above and this should have also been considered in your planning work above.

Frequency

This is the consideration of how often a particular message needs to be sent. For example, a digital media campaign that uses Twitter as its main form of contact with customers needs to have a clear view on how often new tweets should be sent. If too many tweets are sent, the audience may become bored with the message, but if too few are sent, the audience may forget about the product.

Image

This is the feel of the overall campaign and should closely match the intended outcome for the project. If, for example, the overall image does not appeal to the target audience, then the outcome of the campaign could be adversely affected.

Bias

The successful campaign will need to show an awareness of bias and, simply because the campaign is suggesting that the product is better than any other, how it can be used.

Benefits and disadvantages

With any campaign, there is the potential for negative effects, as well as positive. The section on positive and negative impacts of a social media campaign, in section LO3, should be used as a source of possible issues. The benefits should, hopefully, match the intended outcomes, while the disadvantages should be kept to a minimum.

4.3 Effectiveness of digital marketing

There are many ways in which the success of a digital marketing campaign can be measured.

Comparison to original targets

This comparison is made simply by looking at what the campaign intended to achieve and what it actually achieved. The more the original targets have been broken down, the greater the detail that can be used at this stage.

Feedback from the client or other suitable source

Unfortunately, many people fail to appreciate when their work is not up to standard. Therefore, any project should be assessed via the view of others, as this will bring a fresh eye to the process. The client is clearly a key person to call on as they are the person for whom the product has ultimately been created.

When gathering feedback from a client, it can be useful to remind them of the success criteria that were negotiated at the start of the process, as these have been the targets to which the project has worked and so become the standard against which the project should be assessed. See also Unit 6 (page 191).

Assessment against measurable outcomes

The previous two methods of checking are based on opinion and so can be influenced by discussion. Measurable outcomes differ in that they are based on statistical evidence.

Effect on sales and income

How has the campaign affected sales and income? This is easily measured. Positive impacts would include:

- Maintained: the current levels have not changed.
- Increased: there has been an improvement.
- Decline slowed: this would be where the campaign was on behalf of a product that may have peaked already and so was part of a remedial action. To analyse this, the rate of decline prior to the campaign would be compared with the rate of decline after the campaign.

Effects on customer loyalty

This could be measured in many ways. For example, this could be a case of measuring repeat sales, or the frequency of sales.

Effects on customer service

This is a quantifiable area, but due to the way in which it is gathered is based on opinion. The key focus here is on customers' opinions of how well they are being treated. Data for this can be gathered by questionnaire or responses to popups.

4.4 Recommend improvements to business processes to support digital marketing campaigns

There are three key areas for consideration.

Analyse assessment of measurable outcomes

The analysis of the measurable outcomes provides clear evidence that is based on numerical data and not on opinion. Therefore it is seen as a pure form of information about the effectiveness of any project.

Review business processes in order to identify source(s) of failure or shortcoming

A business process may fail for one or many reasons. A single ill-thought-out social media post or hashtag could have a huge effect, as could a combination of smaller mistakes. Once you have the evidence from the analysis of measurable outcomes, you need to go through the business processes to identify areas where blame for any of the issues identified lies.

A starting point for this process will be the nature of the shortcoming. If there has not been any positive effect on sales, for example, then an analysis of the marketing function within the business would be a starting point.

Make recommendations to identified business processes in order to improve effectiveness of digital marketing campaigns

This is a relatively straightforward task and is the final report that reflects on all the research you have conducted as part of this final analysis. Any suggestions made should be presented with supporting evidence as well as a rationale for why the changes should be made. This should link the recommendation to the shortfall and explain how the change would remedy the problem.

> **KNOW IT**
>
> 1 What is meant by each of the following terms?
>   a unique selling point (USP)
>   b staffing mix
>   c company image.
> 2 What is your USP? Explain how and why you would use your USP to market yourself.
> 3 a What is meant by the 'core message' of a campaign?
>   b Explain why the core message should match the already existing image of a business.
>   c When might the core image not match and yet still be successful?
> 4 Explain the importance of having a clear timescale and review dates for a digital marketing campaign.

• •

LO4 Assessment activity

Below is a suggested assessment activity that has been directly linked to the pass and merit criteria in LO4 to help with assignment preparation; it includes Top tips on how to achieve best results.

TOP TIPS
....
✔ Use the proposal you developed for LO3.
✔ Consider how existing business processes may need to change to carry out the campaign. Consider the functions and skills within a typical business.

Activity 1 – pass criteria *P7* and merit criteria *M3*

Your proposal for the digital marketing campaign to launch a new family saloon car has been accepted.

● Develop, review and adopt your campaign.
● Recommend adaptations to current business processes to support the social media activities you have proposed.

Unit 17

Internet of Everything

ABOUT THIS UNIT

'The Internet of Everything' (IoE) is also known as the 'Internet of Things'. Whichever term you use, it is about interconnectivity and being able to link people, data and devices using a range of networks and communication channels to provide new ways of working, thinking, entertaining, co-operating and learning. Whether networks are local or global, the electronic world provides both opportunities and risks.

This unit will enable you to understand the current Internet of Everything, to see new opportunities for using technology across a range of areas and to present your ideas to those who can make it happen.

How will I be assessed?

You will be assessed by producing evidence from scenarios provided by your tutor, or from activities that you carry out as part of a work placement or employment. This evidence will be assessed by your tutor.

LEARNING OUTCOMES

1 Understand what is meant by the Internet of Everything (IoE).
2 Be able to repurpose technologies to extend the scope of the IoE.
3 Be able to present concept ideas for repurposed developments.

You will be graded using the following criteria:

Learning outcome	Pass assessment criteria	Merit assessment criteria	Distinction assessment criteria
You will:	To achieve a pass you must demonstrate that you have met all the pass assessment criteria	To achieve a merit you must demonstrate that you have met all the pass and merit assessment criteria	To achieve a distinction you must demonstrate that you have met all the pass, merit and distinction assessment criteria
1 Understand what is meant by the Internet of Everything (IoE)	**P1** Explain the concept of the IoE	**M1** Analyse the global impacts of the IoE on society and the environment	
	P2* Explain the four pillars of the IoE and how its innovations can transform businesses (*Synoptic assessment from Unit 1 Fundamentals of IT, Unit 2 Global information and Unit 3 Cyber security)		**D1** Evaluate the potential negative impacts of these innovations on businesses
2 Be able to repurpose technologies to extend the scope of the IoE	**P3** Outline potential development projects that could extend the scope of the IoE	**M2** Conduct a feasibility study on one of these development projects	
3 Be able to present concept ideas for repurposed developments	**P4** Prepare a business proposal for the chosen development project		
	P5 Deliver a business proposal pitch to potential stakeholders on the chosen development project	**M3** Revise business proposal for the chosen development project incorporating stakeholder feedback	**D2** Evaluate the success criteria that would be used to judge the sustainability of the chosen development project

LO1 Understand what is meant by the Internet of Everything (IoE) *P1 P2 M1 D1*

GETTING STARTED

(10 minutes)

List five devices that you use which:

● connect you to other devices or machines
● provide you with assistance
● help you to interact with your community.

How do you use them to do these things?

1.1 Things and 1.2 Where the IoE is used

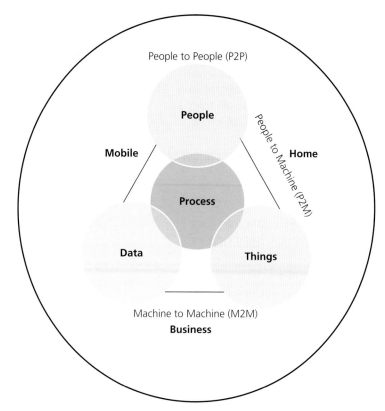

People to People (P2P)

People

Mobile

Home

People to Machine (P2M)

Process

Data

Things

Machine to Machine (M2M)

Business

Figure 17.1 The Internet of Everything

> **KEY TERM**
>
> **Internet of Everything (IoE)** – the bringing together of people, process, data and things to make networked connections more relevant and valuable by turning information into actions that create new capabilities, richer experiences and economic opportunity for business, individuals and countries.

When we speak of the internet or network we tend to think of hardware and software. The **Internet of Everything** (or Internet of Things) includes much more – the connection of devices, large and small (each with their own internet protocol (IP) address) to other devices across the internet. This includes computers, printer and routers, and allows humans to interact, but it also includes:

- Physical objects such as:
  - drones
  - smart TVs
  - smart fridges
  - microchips tracking pets and farm animals.
- Experiential interactions such as:
  - using virtual reality to experience extreme sports, visit locations, etc.
- Aids to people such as:
  - medical devices, e.g. heart monitoring implants
  - hearing aids which automatically adjust noise level and pitch
  - fitness trackers.

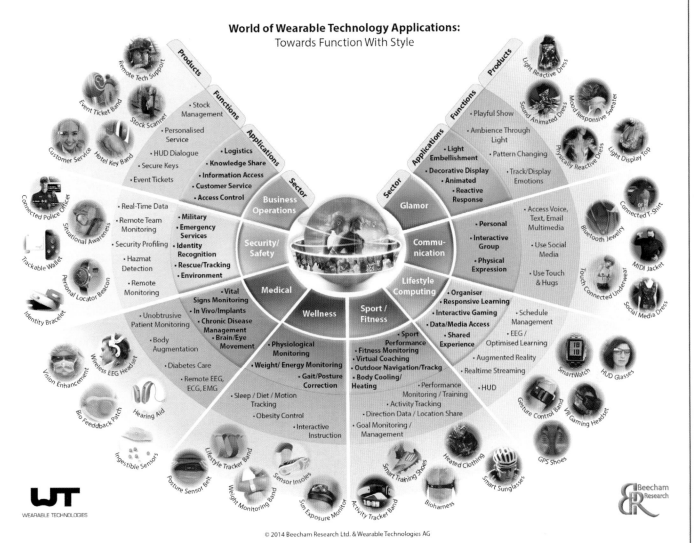

World of Wearable Technology Applications:
Towards Function With Style

© 2014 Beecham Research Ltd. & Wearable Technologies AG

Figure 17.2 The range of wearable technology applications which form part of the Internet of Things

● Aids to society/community such as:
  • drones delivering supplies to remote settlements
  • sharing experiences and information with friends and family
  • using public transport, leading to improved services.
● Machines: in previous units, we have concentrated on machines as a means to transfer, manipulated or store data and information. However, Figure 17.3 shows a range of devices which contribute to a range of applications.

From these examples, it is clear that the IoE already affects many areas of our lives and this range of areas will increase.

 **PAIRS ACTIVITY** ································

(30 minutes)

Research three examples, not already identified, where the IoE is used. Present your findings to the wider group.

1.3 Applications of the use of the IoE

We will take a brief look at five of the main current areas of IoE development.

Body/health applications

The King's Fund, a major health charity, suggests that eight technologies will change health and care by applying the IoT concepts (Source: www.kingsfund.org.uk). We shall outline two examples here; others are in Figure 17.3.

- *Apps:* various applications monitor a range of medical conditions. One example is Ginger.io, which lets people suffering from depression track their mood. By linking this information with data from other apps such as telephone usage, social media, etc and sharing it with clinical and support workers, triggers can be identified and, if appropriate, support can be put in place. This allows faster and more focused use of resources.
- *Home or portable diagnostic tools*: this is not new – doctors and nurses have visited people in their home and used diagnostic tools (e.g. the stethoscope, eyes, noses, touch) since ancient times. Now blood tests, blood pressure and heart rate monitoring, for example, can all take place in the home through the use of wireless sensors, with the results being sent to the surgery or hospital via smart devices.

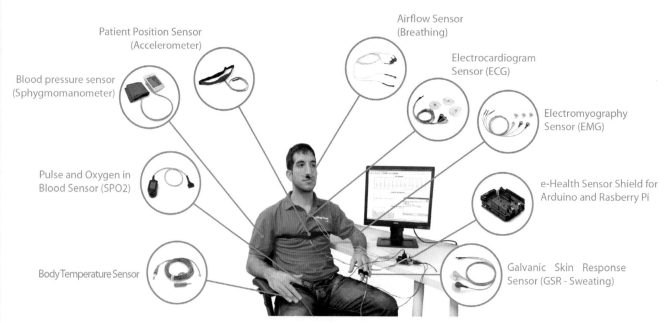

Patient Position Sensor
(Accelerometer)

Airflow Sensor
(Breathing)

Electrocardiogram
Sensor (ECG)

Blood pressure sensor
(Sphygmomanometer)

Electromyography
Sensor (EMG)

Pulse and Oxygen in
Blood Sensor (SPO2)

e-Health Sensor Shield for
Arduino and Rasberry Pi

Body Temperature Sensor

Galvanic Skin Response
Sensor (GSR - Sweating)

Figure 17.3 Examples of diagnostic tools used check the health of patients

Home/garden applications

The ability to control home appliances has grown; using webcam devices to ensure that babies are sleeping and not in distress, to check that a young person at home on their own is doing their homework or being able to switch on the central heating remotely are just a few examples. Others include:

- Controlling lighting via your smartphone so that, when you leave home, the lights go out and external doors lock through a smart locking device. This allows the sensor for the security system to note that the lights are off and doors are locked and immediately set the system, which has a direct link to the local police, if the alarm is triggered.

- While you are on a Christmas break, frost is forecast and you realise that your prize fuchsias, wintering in the greenhouse, are at risk. Using your smartphone, you can send a signal to switch on your greenhouse heater and even programme it to come on automatically, day or night, if the temperature drops below 2 degrees Celsius.

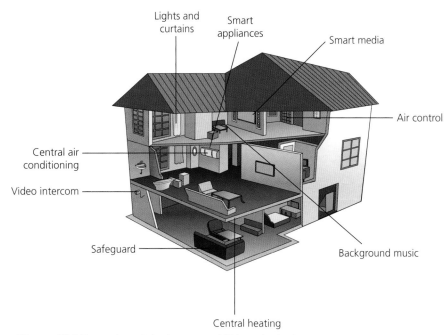

Figure 17.4 Examples of the Internet of Things in the home

City and neighbourhood applications

The range of services required by towns and neighbourhoods are diverse, but they too can make use of IoE to improve and personalise services. Examples are:

- Council buildings can have their heating and lighting monitored and controlled centrally by sensors that identify whether rooms, floors or buildings are occupied; if not, lighting can be switched off and heating reduced. Movement sensors used to control lighting in some buildings can also trigger security systems if the building is known to be closed and locked.
- Street lighting is expensive and, by using sensors which monitor activity, the lighting can be adjusted up or down, depending on whether pedestrians or vehicles are using the streets. How would the lighting system know? The satnav in your car or the smartphone in your pocket will send a signal!

Industry applications

The case for industry to join the IoE is predominantly because of claims by firms such as IBM that up to one trillion devices (Source: www.ibm.com) will be connected to the internet within ten years. This could significantly increase a country's gross domestic product (GDP: the monetary value of all the finished goods and services a country produces) if they participate in this growth, for example, for the USA this could be between 2–5 per cent. (Source: www.slideshare.net). Where there is growth, there is profit.

- Smarter office management includes electronic diaries and calendars linked to bookings for meetings rooms or other facilities. The meeting host or organiser will tell the tablet or smartphone that a meeting is required at a particular location, time and place and who is to attend. The meeting host's device will communicate with the devices of the attendees, the room booking system and the meeting room resource facility to ensure that the digital white board is available and book the meeting. If there is a problem, the device automatically collects availability data, reschedules for a time when everyone is free and updates the meeting host.

● An organisation's technical support attaches monitoring devices to all its products and systems to continuously monitor the state of each and identify issues and failures as they occur. If there is an issue, the device raises a job card stating what the problem is, and passes it to the engineer's device, which checks availability and books an appointment. If the issue is mission-critical and the engineer is not available, the monitoring device will find an engineer who is free or reschedule the engineer to allow them to attend to the issue.

Environmental applications

● Smart home systems are also relevant to the workplace; for example, setting the correct temperature and lighting levels.

● Sensors on shredder bins monitor when they are full so that they can be emptied, ensuring that they are available for use and avoiding unnecessary visits from the waste disposal firm.

● Sensors can monitor water quality in lakes, rivers, reservoirs and canals. These notify the monitoring and control centre which can automatically dispatch specialist clean-up services to polluted areas. If the sensors can accurately analyse the contaminant, specialist services, equipment or chemicals can be ordered simultaneously to arrive with the clear-up team.

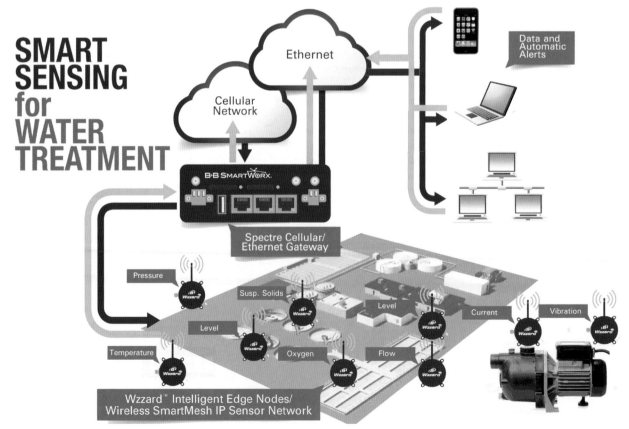

Figure 17.5 Example of how the Internet of Everything can allow smart water treatment

(20 minutes)

Identify at least one application from each of the areas identified above and briefly outline how they utilise the Internet of Everything.

1.4 Global impacts

It could be argued that, even without the Internet of Everything, the world wide web has already improved global communication, business collaboration and social and personal interactions.

Examples of positive impacts

The universal availability of high-speed, low-cost networks connected across the globe enhances the experience of individuals and communities through delivering services such as education, medical advice and support at a reduced cost, especially in remote regions.

Also in remote areas, the opportunity to sell skills, build businesses including travel and tourism, and create call centres can produce new sources of income.

Examples of negative impacts

Currently, there is a lack of standards. Manufacturers and vendors (e.g. Cisco, IBM, Google, Microsoft and Samsung) are independently developing machine to machine (M2M) and smart systems in the hope that their approach will become the standard. One IoE protocol is AllJoyn, an open source project. Intel, Google and others are also seeking to lead in this area.

Why does this matter? If you have studied Unit 4 Computer Networks or Unit 1 Fundamentals of IT, you will know that agreement on protocols is essential for individual devices to communicate with each other. Without it, the concept of billions of devices across the globe talking to each other is in danger, compromising development of the IoE.

Other potential negative impacts are loss of privacy and poor security, which we will discuss in LO1.6 and 1.7 (page 358).

1.5 The four pillars of the IoE

People

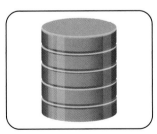

Data

Process

Things

Figure 17.6 The four pillars of IoE

These are four pillars or major components of IoE. These are:

1 People: those who engage with the devices and system which make up the IoE. They can be creators, users or passive receivers of the technology. We shall discuss this further in LO1.6 and 1.7.
2 Data: the raw material of the IoE. The technology enables enormous amounts of data to be collected, manipulated, stored, shared and disseminated. We will discuss this further in sections LO1.8, 1.9 and 1.10.
3 Process: being able to generate and manipulate vast amounts of data is pointless unless it can provide accurate, useful and timely information to people or other devices. So the processes which ensure that the right information reaches the right person or device at the right time form one of the main pillars.
4 Things: any physical object or device sharing connections with the internet and each other to support rational decision making and deliver services. This is why it is often referred to as the Internet of Things (IoT).

1.6 and 1.7 People and how they connect

We will consider how groups of people do, or may one day, interact with the IoE.

Students

No one will know more about how students interact with technology than they do, and no one knows more about the difficulties and triumphs of working with students than their tutor or assessor. So we will start with an activity.

CLASSROOM DISCUSSION

(40 minutes)

Consider how you interact with the internet for learning and social activities. Build a list of 'what we use now'.

Discuss how the IoE could provide additional or replacement opportunities to develop new skills, knowledge and understanding of a range of subjects and interests. How can IoE aid tutors in delivering knowledge and developing student interpersonal skills? The discussion could cover:

● devices which are or could be used to deliver IoE to learners. We have looked at a number already in this unit and other units, such as Unit 1, Unit 4, Unit 5 and Unit 12
● social networks
● wearables, e.g. smart wristbands that could aid the tracking of student progress, attendance, etc.

Members of society and connecting people in relevant ways

For our purposes, this is the widest description of the interactions of human beings locally, nationally and internationally.

The cement which holds the four pillars of the IoE together is data sharing. There are approximately 7,500,000,000 people and approximately

1,000,000,000,000 devices – if all of these 'components' are linked together, data protection and privacy become major issues. Organisations, governments and even individuals being able to monitor the activities of groups in society has implications for social change which we may not yet fully understand. The BCS, in a report on social impact (Source: www.bcs.org), has provided a useful example which helps us to understand the potential issues.

A country decides to roll out smart energy meters to every household to encourage users to be more aware of the cost of leaving their appliances switched on. However, the output from the meter can also identify when the occupants are not at home, because they show a reduction in energy usage. This information could be used to provide evidence to a court or, of course, to a local burglar who has hacked into the system, to plan the next robbery.

Bearing this in mind, we shall now consider some of the devices that could be used by society. Already tablets, smartphones, smartwatches and apps on computers (see Units 17 and 12) allow individuals to control their lives and connect with each other. Some examples are:

- smart medical monitors (Figure 17.4)
- **RFID**, e.g. tracking event attendees through their badges or the use of library system kiosks when RFIDs in books enable readers to self-check books in and out.
- fitness trackers
- Bluetooth jewellery.

So how can these tools, linked together in the IoE, help society? Smartphone, tablets and Bluetooth jewellery, for example, allow us to link to friends, colleagues, family – in fact, all of our social groups, however wide the geographical distances. They can also allow people to link together in times of crisis, such as earthquakes or terrorist attacks, by following social media to check on the safety of friends and colleagues and to quickly raise funds to support the injured and bereaved through online giving (crowdsourcing).

Individuals with particular concerns or interests can come together, using social media to raise political issues (crowd sensing).

Smart medical monitors sending back information on blood pressure, blood sugar, heart rate and pulse may seem to be an individual rather than a social issue, but doctors and researchers can pool this information from millions of patients and use it to develop better treatments.

Patients, rather than attending a surgery or hospital, may soon be able to take a pill containing a miniaturised diagnostic laboratory which automatically sends data about narrowed arteries, damaged heart valves or underactive glands. The results could be verified and treatment started, possibly by another internet-linked device. Instead of having electrodes stuck on the skin, linked by wires to heart monitors, where a wire might disconnect or an electrode fall off, smart clothes, Bluetooth jewellery and smartwatches could automatically collect the heart data and send it to the doctor.

Solo sailors and mountaineers could swallow a RFID before their trip, knowing that they are being monitored through GPS for their position and by their medical team.

KEY TERM

Radio frequency identification (RFID) – small electronic chips with an antenna that can each hold up to 2,000 bits of information including identification data. Used in the same way as a barcode.

Mobile crowd sensing (MCS) uses mobile technology, such as cameras, GPS and microphones, with the weight of evidence from a crowd of users to collect data. This data can range from local issues such as the number of potholes in a road in a local area to personal views about events.

The data can be collated and interrogated to identify trends or issues which, because of the number of users involved, can result in a demand for action or change. However, there are issues around privacy and the ownership and security of personal information.

CLASSROOM DISCUSSION

(20 minutes)

Identify existing and potential ways in which IoE can support society and its groups and individuals, and how they could be connected to enable these activities.

Write up the outcomes and use them as learning material for the rest of the unit.

1.8 Converting data into information to allow people to make decisions and 1.9 Data

Data, information and how they are related are described in Unit 2 LO3, Unit 3, LO2 and Unit 7 LO1.

The IoE will enable connected things to pool their data rather than each type of device only sharing data with similar devices in a recognised group. For example, to help manage road usage and traffic congestion, motion data from buildings in a town can be merged with data about traffic levels at different times of the day, and GPS data from vehicles owned by businesses and their employees. This could result in better road management as routing guidance is provided automatically to the vehicles, adapted to take account of the time of day and the likelihood of hold ups, and provide alternative routing.

For this to become a reality will require developments in areas such as artificial intelligence (AI); the concept of machines being able to think like humans. Currently they do not but they can be trained to do some things faster and better than a human. With greater amounts of data being collected from more and more 'things', it must be sorted, analysed, aggregated and passed quickly and accurately and AI is an important tool for this.

Linked to existing programming techniques for analysing data and performing particular action, fuzzy logic is a set of human language rules converted into mathematical equivalents. These can handle incomplete data sets – even the Internet of Everything may not be able to provide every piece of the data jigsaw. It uses 'if-then' rules. For example, *if* the temperature is 75° *then* turn on the air conditioning. This type of logic statement was always used in computing. However, if we change it to: '*if* it feels hot *then* turn on the air conditioning', it becomes 'fuzzy': what does 'hot' mean? To you it may be a temperature over 80°C but to me it may be 70°C. This is where fuzzy logic is required.

Another tool is 'what if', also known as 'if-then-else'. Taking our previous example, *if* the temperature is 75°C *then* turn on the air-conditioning *else* switch on the central heating. In this case, if the statement is true, that is to say the temperature is 75°C, then one option is taken (turn on the air-conditioning). If it is false, then take the second option (turn on the central heating). This method is used where the values are exact, e.g. 75°C.

These tools and techniques will help provide the analysis, decision making and results for the machine or people who need the information to make decisions of their own.

1.10 Information gathering devices

These have been discussed throughout this unit and in Unit 12 LO1 (page 302).

(30 minutes)

Research the following types of device for information gathering:

● sensors ● tracking devices ● resource management.

Select two examples of each, not already identified in this unit, where the IoE is used. Present your findings to the wider group.

1.11 Process

This is the means by which the other three pillars of the IoE work together to bring value to the decision-making processes, the decisions made as a result of connecting things and collecting their data. Processes are normally focused on reaching a single goal or position, but in the IoE the data is used in new ways, such as using RFID technology to track activities on a production line or to move raw materials to the production point. Data analysis can reveal poor performance or issues. For example, moving large components to the next stage of production is often assumed to be along a straight line from point A to point B.

Figure 17.7 How can warehouse distribution be made more efficient?

However, the forklift driver knows that it cannot fit down the aisle which runs from A to B because the component overhangs the side of the forklift. Instead, the driver has to take a longer route: A to C to D to B. The data tracking reveals this longer route, which comes as a surprise to management but explains why production slows at this point. By analysing this data, an adjustment to spacing at one point on the route means that the driver can now go from A to B, saving time and thus money.

CLASSROOM DISCUSSION

(15 minutes)

Discuss how using data collected in the IoE, in areas such as medicine, traffic and offices, may identify and improve processes.

1.12 Processing capabilities

The IoE requires increasing data processing facilities. High-speed data gathering is one thing, but doing something useful with the data is quite different. What is needed is real-time **analytics**. The requirements are:

- Very large storage capacity on servers, locally or in the cloud.
- Making additional analytics available to work with the incoming data as it arrives, for example:
  - Senior management information (strategic level information).
  - Status (of the system at a given moment).
  - User preferences (how the user needs the data to be presented to make it useful).
  - Configuration policies describe the default setup for a particular component of the system, such as the user profile, software or hardware. These policies remain in place, even if updated, for the life of the component.

This would ensure that data enrichment (the use of various processes to improve or filter raw data) is already underway. Examples are:

- Real-time intelligent decisions mean using big data analytics to drive data enrichment forward providing notification and alerts as events happen.
- Dashboard systems which automatically display real-time data so that what is happening now can be monitored and, if necessary, actions taken.
- Store the outcomes from these activities for future, historical analysis.
- Ensure that the results of historical analytics are available to be considered alongside the real time data to improve decision making.

GROUP ACTIVITY

(30 minutes)

Research one example of big data technology and one example of cloud services which support data processing in IoE. Present your findings to the wider group.

1.13 Connectivity and 1.14 Networked connection

The principles and application of connections and networking have been discussed in Unit 4, Unit 2 LO1 (page 50) and Unit 12 LO1 (page 297).

In IoE, three types of connection are particularly referred to; they make use of connectivity and networks in the following ways:

- P2P: person to person (the most widespread type)
- P2M: person to machine
- M2M: machine to machine.

All of these connections are designed to enable individuals to have:

- improved quality of life
- the information to make better decisions
- the information to be more productive.

With IoE, a further way of interpreting connectivity and networks is the 'network effect', attributed to the founder of 3Com, Robert Metcalfe. It states that 'the value of a network increases proportionally to the number of users' (source //www.cs.umd.edu). He was talking about devices, but it can be applied, with care, to the IoE. The value of a network, whether it is formed through talking to groups of friends, work colleagues, those with similar needs using computer networks to link with organisation or to promote and provide business and services, is measured by the individual or group who pays for or owns the network. The measure is: 'Does it help me to achieve my goals?' Dave Evans, the Chief Futurist and Chief Technology Officer of Cisco said, 'When the history of IoE is written, its success or failure will be determined by answering one question: How did IoE benefit humanity? In the end, nothing else matters' (source: www.memoori.com).

GROUP ACTIVITY

(30 minutes)

Identify two potential or current uses for IoE and discuss how you would measure their connectivity in terms of the value service or support that they provide. Justify your choices.

1.15 Security issues

These issues have been widely discussed in Unit 1: LO1, Unit 4: all LOs, Unit 3: all LOs, Unit 12, LOs 1 and 3 and are as relevant to the IoE as they are to organisations, individuals and traditional networks.

CLASSROOM DISCUSSION

(60 minutes)

Consider the range of security issues identified in Units 1, 3 and 4 and discuss which ones pose the main threats to the Internet of Everything. As a group, agree:

- The main threats.
- A brief summary of the nature of each threat.
- The steps which could be taken to try and remove or reduce the risk of each threat.

KNOW IT

1 Name three physical objects which form part of the IoE.
2 Identify four types of application enabled by the IoE.
3 Briefly outline two positive and two negative global impacts of the IoE.

LO1 Assessment activities

Below are three suggested assessment activities that have been directly linked to the pass, merit and distinction criteria in LO1 to help with assignment preparation; they include Top tips on how to achieve best results.

Activity 1 – pass criteria *P1*

Produce a poster explaining the concept of the Internet of Everything.

Activity 2 – pass criteria *P2*

You work for the chief technical officer of a large manufacturing organisation which sources its components from around the world. She has asked you to prepare a presentation for senior managers explaining the structure of the IoE. Produce the presentation, including the four pillars and how they combine to provide innovative ways of transforming businesses.

Activity 3 – merit criteria *M1* and distinction criteria *D1*

The chief technical officer tells you that senior management is getting carried away with the idea of the IoE. She asks you to make a further presentation on the global impact of IoE, looking at the positives and negatives by identifying two examples of each from a social and environmental perspective. She suggests that it would be helpful if you also provided an evaluation of any possible negative impacts that IoE could have on business.

> **TOP TIPS** ✔
> - ✔ Identify a specific type of manufacturing organisation you are familiar with, or for which you can obtain sufficient information, to identify potential uses for IoE.
> - ✔ Consider linking Activity 2 to your assessment activities in Unit 2 and Unit 3.

> **🔑 KEY TERMS**
>
> **Miniaturisation** – the process of making objects smaller by using modern technology.
>
> **Grid-based data collection** – data collected, analysed and stored by a large numbers of dispersed computers connected to solve a complex problem.

> **INDEPENDENT ACTIVITY**
>
> Table 17.1 shows repurposed technologies. Investigate an example of each and explain it briefly. One example for each area is completed for you.

LO2 Be able to repurpose technologies to extend the scope of the IoE *P3 M2*

> **GETTING STARTED**
>
> **(10 minutes)**
>
> 1 Identify three technologies which are used in different ways in the IoE.
> 2 Outline three different ways in which Bluetooth is used in IoE.
> 3 What are the stages of a feasibility study?

2.1 Developments

The growth in connectivity and the **miniaturisation** of sensors and wireless antennae, in particular, provides opportunities to repurpose a range of technologies to further expand the range of the IoE applications. To aid this development, we will consider examples from five different areas which are either available or being developed.

Table 17.1 Repurposed technology for IoE

Development area	Technology	Example
Body/Health	Sensors	• You swallow an ingestible sensor as a pill alongside prescribed medicines. • Your body's stomach fluids fuel the sensor and act as antennae, sending a unique identifier. • A patch on your body (like a plaster) has a receiver which reads the body's reaction to the medicine as well as other useful information such as heart rate, whether you are active or resting. • The patch sends a message to your mobile device. • This device can then send the data to a secure location for you and medical staff to review.
	Social safety wearables	
	Bluetooth stethoscope	
	Bluetooth weather sensor	
Home/garden	Bluetooth tape measure	• The tape measure case contains a small Bluetooth device which allows you to capture height, width and depth or the distance between two points. It also calculates the centre of a distance, changes the units from imperial to decimal, stores and recalls previous measurements. • Bluetooth links the tape measure to an app on a mobile device which records the measurements. This is useful, as a pen and paper is rarely to hand when you decide to measure a room or space between two objects and it is not always convenient or possible to enter the readings into a mobile device either.
	Smart locks	
	Bluetooth flower pots	
	Solar powered window blinds	
City/neighbourhood	Smart signage	• Delivers traffic signs straight into the vehicle via a radio signal which is received from a transmitter at the site of the signs. • It can appear on a LCD screen or directly on the windscreen, allowing the driver to concentrate on driving rather than trying to read signs which are not ideally located.
	Intelligent street lights	
	Wearable air quality sensor	
	Connected car safety devices	
Industry	Industrial smart helmet	• A display on the visor of the helmet mixes safety information, real-time and augmented information, company policies and maintenance and repair information, as required by the wearer. • It uses process, sensors, computer navigation, 360° degree sensor arrays, video and thermal sensors to enable the user to carry out maintenance tasks, find tools and identify possible issues.
	Wireless pest monitoring	
	Smart noise sensors	
	Real-time remote excavation	
The environment	Environmental monitoring	Geographical information systems using **grid-based data collections** monitor the environment to identify and monitor the progress of pollutants, e.g. chemical spills or toxins that have been accidentally released into the atmosphere.
	Wildlife tracking	
	Flood detection network	
	Landslide detection systems	

2.2 Feasibility study

Feasibility studies were discussed in Unit 8 LO2.1 (page 231). A feasibility study for presenting a case to support the investigation of new opportunities for the IoE is no different, but below are some of the questions which need to be addressed within it.

Identify new opportunities through investigative process

Just as the project team must identify new or better working practices to see if the project is worth pursuing, so you must be able to justify your ideas for new applications for the IoE. You must carry out careful research to see if:

- Anyone else has already identified this opportunity
- If so, whether they have a product already and if it is successful. If it is not successful or the idea was dropped, why was this? Can you learn anything from this example or can you build a better version?

Evaluation and analysis of the proposed concept proposal

If no one has thought of this already, why is this? You can get an idea about whether it is innovative or plain silly by asking yourself and others:

- What would the benefits be to:
  - the business
  - your industry or market as a whole
  - individuals?
- Do the 'things' required to make this a reality exist or will they need to be developed?
- What are the likely timescales and costs?

Evaluation of alternative proposals

It is helpful to have a range of proposals so that their validity can be compared. Considerations will include:

- The costs.
- Technical skills of the workforce (e.g. will specialist knowledge or skills need to be learned or bought in)?
- What are the benefits and drawbacks of the proposals?
- How likely are they to meet the needs of the user? Will it improve efficiency, productivity, safety, etc. (depending upon the nature of the concept)?

Market assessment

Some market research must be carried out to see if the perceived customers are interested in the product. Revisit the discussion on market research in Unit 13, LO1 (page 323).

Results and conclusions

A set of recommendations must be presented, the first of which is whether to proceed to development of the ideas or not. If yes, then the choice of approach will also be presented.

Research is the methods by which we find things out. In this unit, you will be looking for ideas to develop new applications for the IoE by asking questions of yourself and others. How do you do this?

- READ: find articles and ideas from the internet, newspapers, journals, etc.
- THINK: what would you like to be able to do, using your mobile or tablet, that you cannot at the moment? Have you seen other people struggling because they cannot find or use the information they need?
- OBSERVE: Look at the world and people around you and observe what they are doing and how they do it.
- LISTEN: hear what people around you are saying. Are there things they hate, or want to change?
- QUESTION: ask your friends, your employer, local business, customers (if you have access to them).
- RECORD: make notes of what you have found out.
- THINK/ANALYSE: think about all you have discovered and then analyse it to understand whether there is a problem to be solved, what a possible solution could be and if you could find a possible way of achieving the solution.
- MAKE A DECISION: whether to go ahead with your idea or to abandon it.

This section should summarise your findings from the work carried out earlier and clearly state why you have made the recommendation.

> **KNOW IT**
> 1 Identify three technologies repurposed for use in home or garden.
> 2 Identify three repurposed technologies used in managing the environment.
> 3 Outline the steps of a feasibility study for an IoE development opportunity.

LO2 Assessment activities

Below are two suggested assessment activities that have been directly linked to the pass and merit criteria in LO2 to help with assignment preparation; they include Top tips on how to achieve best results.

Activity 1 – pass criteria *P3*

You have been asked to identify possible development projects that would be useful extensions to the IoE. Outline three examples, each one from a different category from the list in LO2 of the unit. From this, select one possible development to carry forward.

Activity 2 – merit criteria *M2*

You mention to your chief technical officer that you have an idea for an IoE project which you would like to develop. She suggests that you produce a feasibility study which she will review to see if your idea is realistic. Prepare the feasibility study and present it to her.

> **TOP TIPS** ✔
> ✔ Identify a specific type of manufacturing organisation with which you are familiar or for which you can obtain sufficient information to identify potential uses for IoE
> ✔ Try to identify possible projects from different areas of the business before deciding which one to take forward.

LO3 Be able to present concept ideas for repurposed developments *P4 P5 M3 D2*

This process is similar to the planning phase described in Unit 8, LO2.2 (page 233), so you should re-read that section now. If your feasibility study is accepted, you need to present your plan to those who can support the development – the stakeholders. Who they are will depend upon the context: are you producing this for your own manager or senior managers or is it for an external client? You will have to present your ideas using language and examples appropriate to the type of stakeholder. To do that you will need a proposal.

> **GETTING STARTED** 👤
>
> **(10 minutes)**
> ● Who should receive a copy of a business plan?
> ● What is a stakeholder?
> ● What does the term 'pitch' mean when someone says that they are 'making a pitch for a new project'?

3.1 Business proposal

This document should have:

- A title page: including your name, your organisation's name, the name of the individual or group you are preparing this (your target audience) for and the date.
- Table of contents: gives the reader an idea of how long the proposal is and where to find the bits they are interested in.
- An executive summary: an overview of the content, but most importantly focuses on why the proposal is a good idea.
- Statement of the concept you are trying to sell: show that you understand what the clients need and know how to produce it.
- Methodology: demonstrate that you can fulfil the requirement to develop the concept by going through the steps needed to achieve it. Do not get too technical but do give enough information for stakeholders to believe that you could complete the development to time and in a cost effective manner. It should include the:
  - processing needed to provide the information expected from the application (see LO1, especially sections 1.5 (page 357) and 1.11, page 361)
  - data that will be gathered, shared or exchanged between the components
  - 'things' that are involved; remember our fourth pillar – the devices and objects which will be linked to enable the concept to become a reality – are they existing, new or repurposed things?
  - networking requirements, e.g. sensors, routers, Wi-fi access points, Bluetooth, internet; these may use existing networks or build new ones using the available communication channels
  - devices which will be used; remember these are anything with their own IP address and may include computers, sensors, data stores, tablets, mobile phones, etc.
  - security required to protect individuals (e.g. maintain privacy), organisations (e.g. protect them from theft, loss of confidentiality and loss of reputation), the networks and things (e.g. from viruses, hacking, denial of service).
- Benefits of creating the application.

3.2 Pitch

This is where you speak directly to your client, to convince them that your ideas and plans are essential to their success. You can present your pitch in a number of ways, for example:

- Sending your business plan in a format agreed with the potential client, making sure that your executive summary and personal skills in terms of delivering the project really stand out.
- Making a presentation in person:
  - Use slides with only one or two bullet points.
  - Do not waffle, keep to the most important facts.
  - Do not use jargon or abbreviations which only an expert would understand.

- Talk about your skills and experience to demonstrate your commitment and abilities.
- Practise, so that you can make your pitch without reading from your notes or, worse, reading the slides.
- Creating a webcast multimedia presentation.
  - The same issues as for presentations apply here – remember you still need to practise for a webcast.

PAIRS ACTIVITY  ···

(15 minutes)

Keeping your project in mind, discuss the pros and cons of webcasting your pitch to the client.

3.3 Feedback

At the end of your pitch, you should ask for feedback to improve the final plan. Feedback can come from:

- Stakeholders, when you made your pitch:
  - What questions did they ask?
  - What did they seem to feel most positive about?
  - What seemed to cause them particular concern?
  - Did they follow up with any written comments via email, letter or annotations to the report?
- Developers. When reading through your plan, they may ask questions in person or send you comments. Study these carefully to see if their issues arise because you have not been clear in your ideas or whether they are demonstrating that your plan to be successful will need some adjustment.

> Once the feedback is given, use it! Some of it may not be relevant but do not be dismissive; you must demonstrate that you are willing to listen and if necessary, make adjustments.

3.4 Stakeholder considerations

The main question that stakeholders may ask is:

- Who benefits from this application?

Will it be companies in a particular business sector or several sectors? Will it be society as a whole, through improving living conditions or health and safety?

This question matters because the stakeholders, who may be clients, managers or investing money in the project, will need to feel that their expenditure of time and money will provide a return on investment in some way. This may not always be recouping costs but it may be reputation or a wish to do something for the greater good of society.

Another likely question is:

- Who is going to develop the application?

Is it just you? Is it your own company staff or contractors?

This question makes clear the cost implications in terms of staffing. If you need to hire staff or charge for your colleagues, the costs will increase. Also, if you need to employ contractors, you will need to advertise the posts and interview potential employees, which will increase the timescales for development.

3.5 Revision of proposal

Following on from the pitch and the feedback from stakeholders and other interested parties, you must review your plan and revise it if necessary.

Analyse feedback

You should analyse all of the feedback and ask:

- What does it mean?
- Did several stakeholders make similar comments about the same point? If so, it is probably worth tackling this issue first.
- If stakeholders contradicted each other with their comments, why was this? Which comments should you take into account?
- Did they identify any points which you had overlooked or had not previously thought were significant?
- Is anything important missing?

Decision on whether the proposal is still viable

Does your analysis of the feedback mean that:

- The proposal should continue to completion as it is?
- It should be amended and completed?
- It should not be taken forward?

Your decision must link back clearly to the feedback you have received.

Make changes to proposal in line with feedback and viability considerations

If changes are to be made, make them now and document them in an updated plan which will again be presented to the stakeholders for their final sign off.

3.6 Possible success criteria

How will you and your sponsors or stakeholders, know that the application has been successful? The criteria you choose must be measurable, for example:

- It will improve efficiency by 50 per cent over three years.
- Profits will increase by 25 per cent in the first year
- Productivity will increase by 48 per cent in two years.
- Downtime of machinery reduced from 4 hours a week to 1 hour.
- Overheads will be reduced by 25 per cent per quarter.

KNOW IT

1 List the sections of a business proposal.
2 Identify two different types of formats that could be used to provide feedback on a business proposal
3 State four stakeholder concerns when they review a business proposal.

LO3 Assessment activities

Below are four suggested assessment activities that have been directly linked to the pass, merit and distinction criteria in LO3 to help with assignment preparation; they include Top tips on how to achieve best results.

Activity 1 – pass criteria *P4*

Your idea for a development project has been accepted for further consideration by the chief technical officer. Prepare a business plan to submit to senior managers. It should be a formal document, carefully checked for spelling, grammar and punctuation as well as for the accuracy of technical content.

Activity 2 – pass criteria *P5*

Your business plan has been accepted for further consideration and you have been asked to make a presentation or pitch to the senior managers. Prepare your presentation, which may be face-to-face or a webinar, and make a pitch of no more than 15 minutes to people role-playing the senior managers.

Activity 3 – merit criteria *M3*

You receive feedback from the senior management team and realise that your plan could be improved. Revise your plan to include the feedback from senior managers ready for sign off.

Activity 4 – distinction criteria *D2*

Use your project identified in Activity 3 and create a set of measureable criteria which will enable the stakeholder to recognise the success or failure of the project. Evaluate how you will know if your development project is sustainable and workable and how your stakeholders will know whether it is worthwhile. Include detailed speaker notes listing the criteria, why you have chosen them and what the measurement is e.g. a reduction in response times of 45 per cent within two years.

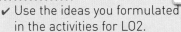

TOP TIPS
- ✔ Use the ideas you formulated in the activities for LO2.
- ✔ You will need role play for the pitch and it would be useful if the stakeholders were played by business studies students or staff as well as IT students and staff.

Glossary

Agile methodology: an iterative approach which develops prototypes and uses customer feedback to develop the next version.

Algorithm: the series of steps used to solve a problem, in application design it may involve a flow chart or pseudocode to design a solution.

Analytics: the logical analysis of data using computers.

Appendix: a section at the end of a document with additional material that should be referred to within the document.

Application development model: a method of producing an application that divides the process of development into distinct phases.

Asset: anything of value owned by an individual or organisation.

Augmented reality: the process of manipulating reality as seen by a user.

Automation: the use of computers and electronic equipment to carry out tasks that were previously done manually.

Big data: very large sets of data that are analysed to produce information such as trends.

Biometrics: the measurement and statistical analysis of people's physical and behavioural characteristics. As each biometric is unique, this is a highly effective method of identifying individuals.

Brand loyalty: the extent to which someone buys one product or brand repeatedly, rather than others.

Carbon footprint: the impact of organisations and individuals on the environment.

Central processing unit (CPU): the unit that controls the actions of the computer system and manipulates the data required for particular tasks.

Cloud storage: online storage capacity.

Code: groups of symbols, characters, words, letters or figures used to represent messages or instructions.

Code of practice: a set of rules which explains how people working in certain professions are required to behave.

Command line interface: an interface that uses text commands, not graphic icons.

Computer components: items which together form a computer system.

Conceptual model: an overview of the entities and relationships that exist within the business.

Connectivity: The ability to connect with another computer or information system.

Constraint: a limitation or restriction; for example a time constraint may be that a product is needed within seven days.

Cookie: a small text file sent from a web server that is stored on the user's computer to track and store information about the user's activities.

Cost/benefit analysis: the estimation of the costs of carrying out the project and the benefits studied to aid a decision on whether to start or continue the project.

Critical friend: a trusted individual who is able to ask challenging questions and offer unbiased, knowledgeable insight into a situation or issue.

Critical path method: a process that identifies the activities which must be carried out to the agreed timescales if the project is to be completed on time.

Cyber dependent crime: crimes that can only be carried out using computer networks or systems. These include: spreading malware, hacking and denial of service attacks.

Cyber enabled crime: committing crimes such as fraud, theft and bullying via IT.

Data: raw, unorganised facts that need to be processed.

Datagram: a discrete independent message, sent over a network, which has its source and destination information attached to enable accurate routing.

Data analysis: the processes of examining, cleansing, transforming data into a model.

Data mining: the use of sophisticated tools, such as artificial intelligence techniques, neural networks and statistical tools to identify trends and patterns in large data stores.

Data model: a way of showing how pieces of data relate to each other, usually in a diagrammatic format.

Data packet: data is not sent as a single stream across the internet but instead it is parcelled into one or more packets, each of which has a header with additional information such as the IP address of the sender and the receiver.

Data redundancy: data that is repeated or excessive, i.e. not required.

Data set: a group of related data.

Deliverable: the agreed product, products or features that are to be developed for the client.

Deployment: the implementation of a product.

Design specification: a document that describes the type and nature of the product to be created and gives enough information for the success criteria to be identified.

Digital divide: the difference in access to digital resources in different areas of the world.

Digital footprint: any traceable action you or others take on the internet.

Digital marketing: the use of digital technologies to communicate with potential and existing customers.

Enhancement: a change or addition that improves the product.

Enterprise model: a business-level view of data.

Entity: a type of real world object that has data stored about it, e.g. student, group. Entities can have relationships between other entities.

Ethics: the accepted behaviours and beliefs of society or groups within it which influence how people react to situations.

Evolutionary development: developing a system by building upon and expanding it, such as through the use of prototypes.

Feasibility study: a document that provides judgements on a range of potential solutions to a business need including the technical feasibility (whether the project can be carried out) and the economic feasibility (whether the potential gain is worth the risk of the cost in money and reputation).

Firewall: a form of network security that monitors data traffic into and out of a network. The traffic is assessed against set rules and only allowed through the firewall if it fits those rules.

Gantt chart: a visual method of measuring proposed timings of activities against the actual times.

Graphical user interface (GUI): an interface that uses graphic icons to replace words, e.g. buttons, symbols, icons, menus and pointers.

Grid-based data collection – data collected, analysed and stored by a large numbers of dispersed computers connected to solve a complex problem.

Haptic devices: devices that simulate touch.

Icon: a symbol or image on a computer screen of a program, option or selection.

Information: data which is processed, organised and structured into a meaningful context.

Input devices: devices that allow the user, which may be another computer or a measuring device, to give instruction or provide data to the computer system.

Integration: combining multiple items into one item.

Interface: the point at which two elements interact, e.g. the interface between the user and a computer is the operating system.

Internet of Everything (IoE): the bringing together of people, process, data and things to make networked connections more relevant and valuable by turning information into actions that create new capabilities, richer experiences and economic opportunity for business, individuals and countries.

IP: Internet Protocol short for TCP/IP which is the Transmission Control Protocol/Internet Protocol which sets the rules by which computers communicate.

IP Address: the way in which devices communicate via the internet. It consists of four numbers, each with a value of between 0 and 255, separated by a full stop or dot, rather like a post code and house number.

Iteration/iterative: repeating a process or processes.

Linear development: developers follow a series of stages to create a system, moving through the stages one at a time, in a set order.

Logical data model: describes all of the data to be included, without identifying or looking at how it will be constructed.

Malware: short for 'malicious software', it includes viruses, worms, Trojan horses, ransomware, adware, spyware and any other piece of software which can harm the system, the computer or the individual who uses it.

Market share: the percentage of the overall market made up by one product or brand or company.

Marketing mix: the interaction of price, product, placement and promotion as part of the marketing process.

Mean: the calculated average of a set of numbers,

Measureable process: an action (e.g. calculation) that a user (or tester) can identify has happened correctly or not. For example, a measureable process is that a submit button stores data in a database: this either happens, or does not.

Median: the middle number in a set of numbers.

Methodology: an agreed set of methods brought together to achieve a goal or set of goals.

Milestone: a point in time when a particular objective is expected to be met.

Miniaturisation – the process of making objects smaller by using modern technology.

Module: a small part of the whole, e.g. one independent part of a program.

Money laundering: the process by which criminals hide the origin of the proceeds of their crime by transferring the money through different bank accounts and countries to make it look as if it comes from a legal source.

Network benchmarking tools: software which carries out one or more tests to compare current performance against an agreed standard.

Network ID: the part of the TCIP/IP address which identifies devices on a LAN or internet. It is vital to the tracking and management of hardware, data and devices required by users and also helps to maintain security of the network.

Network interface: the hardware or software which connects two or more devices to each other.

Network map: a graphical representation of the computers and devices on the network that shows how they are connected.

Node: a connection, redistribution or end point on a network; anything with an IP address.

Output devices: devices that enable the computer system to provide information, data or instructions to another user, which may be computer or human.

Person hours: one person hour is the work one person can do in one hour. A job that requires five person hours can be done by five people in one hour, by one person in five hours, or somewhere between the two.

Physical model: a representation of how the data will be structured and stored.

Pitch: the delivery of a business plan, usually performed verbally, e.g. through a presentation.

Platform: the hardware and/or software that a system runs on, e.g. each make of computer has its own machine language, so a program made for one computer may not run on a different one.

PRINCE2 (Projects IN Controlled Environments): a process-based project methodology.

Project sponsor: the senior manager or group who sets out the aims and outcomes of the project, agrees that it meets a business need and appoints the project manager and carries overall organisational responsibility for the project.

Protocol: a set of rules, standards and principles which allow network devices to exchange data.

Prototype: a preliminary model of the product that may be not be functional or only partly functional and is used to give an indication of how the final product will look and/or work.

Qualitative: information which includes descriptions, opinions, attitudes and views.

Quantitative: factual, often numerical, information.

Repurposing: taking something that is made for one purpose and using it for a totally different one.

RFID (radio frequency identification): tiny computer chips which hold information that is transmitted when it passes close to a scanning antenna.

Scope: the potential to include something, taking into consideration any limitations.

Source code: code, written by programmers in a high or low level programming language, which is converted into a list of instructions for the computer to provide various functions and actions.

Standard: a national or internationally agreed group of tools and techniques, used in a specified manner to manage a project.

Standard deviation: a measure that shows how spread out a set of numbers are from the mean.

Structured data: data that has been organised, e.g. in a table.

Structured methodology: clearly defined steps or stages which enable projects to be managed in a logical, controlled way.

Subroutine: an independent function, or procedure, which performs a singular task. It can be called from the main program, or from another subroutine. It can take values as its input (parameters).

Success criteria: a list of things that must be achieved by a project if it is to be considered a success.

Terms of reference: a brief summary of the background and purpose of the proposed project and a list of objectives it will achieve.

Throughput: the speed with which a given amount of data can be processed or passed between nodes.

Trigger image: visual elements such as photos or icons which, when touched or scanned, activate further functionality.

Troubleshoot: the ability to analyse and solve issues with information systems.

Typology: classifications that data can be put into, or organised into.

Unstructured data: data that is not organised.

Validation: a check to make sure data is reasonable and meets a set of rules.

Virtual reality: the process of creating a virtual world into which the user or experiencer is thrown.

Whistle blowing: making a disclosure that is of public interest.

WYSIWYG (What you see is what you get): a visual method of creating a product by adding elements so that the position of the elements and how they react is determined visually and not by direct coding.

Index